ALEXANDER

Guy MacLean Rogers

A L E X

ANDER

The Ambiguity of Greatness

RANDOM HOUSE NEW YORK

LIBRARY OF CONGRESS CATALOGING-IN-PUBLICATION DATA
Rogers, Guy MacLean.
Alexander: the ambiguity of greatness / Guy MacLean Rogers.
p. cm.
Includes bibliographical references and index.
ISBN 1-4000-6261-6
1. Alexander, the Great, 356–323 B.C. 2. Greece—History—Macedonian Expansion,
359–323 B.C. 3. Generals—Greece—Biography. 4. Greece—Kings and rulers—Biography.
I. Title.
DF234.R73 2004   938'.07'092—dc22   2004046813
[B]

Preface

I have written this book to provide readers with a clear and balanced account of the life and legacies of Alexander the Great. The narrative is fundamentally rooted in the ancient sources for Alexander's deeds. For a critical review of those sources readers should consult the appendix at the end of the book, Sources: Flacks, Hacks, and Historians.

Almost all historians have judged Alexander III of Macedon to be a military genius. Somewhat curiously, however, few scholars have explained why this is the case, at least in any detail. In this work I do. In fact, I hope to show why Alexander should be considered the greatest warrior in history.

In an ideal, peaceful world, Alexander's military tactics, logistics, and strategic vision would be largely of antiquarian interest. But we do not live in such a world. Alexander never lost a battle and conquered the ancient world's greatest empire in less than a decade. His unparalleled record of military success is more, not less, relevant today.

I also will argue that Alexander was a kind of unacknowledged proto-feminist, limited multi-culturalist, and religious visionary who planned to establish a world empire of the "best." His idea of establishing such an empire was based upon his belief that while all men were the sons of Zeus, the ruler of Mount Olympus had a particular fondness for the "best" among mankind. While Alexander's attempt to institute a global empire of the best was not successful, I will show how Alexander nevertheless laid down the foundations of Western civilization and continues to influence the religious beliefs of countless people today in unexpected ways. We may see Alexander primarily as a great conqueror. But it arguably was the son of Macedon's greatest "Prince," and not the carpenter's son from Nazareth, who made it possible for the "greatest story ever told" to become our world's dominant myth.

Although this biography of Alexander has been written primarily for a general audience, it certainly does address many detailed and controversial scholarly questions about Alexander's life and historical effects. In doing so, this work either implicitly or explicitly refers to the arguments of many other scholars. It is a pleasure to acknowledge my deep debt to those scholars who have influenced my own understanding and presentation of Alexander, especially: E. Badian, E. Borza, A. Bosworth, P. Briant, A. Devine, D. Engels, P. Fraser, P. Green, W. Heckel, F. Holt, A. Kuhrt, R. Lane Fox, and W. Tarn. It is particularly important to express my deepest admiration for the inspiring scholarship of these great historians in light of the fact that I fear that I have differed so often here from their interpretations of Alexander's actions. I would encourage readers who become captivated by Alexander, as I have been since I was six years old, to consult the works of the historians and scholars listed in the Select Modern Bibliography.

In Greece, Dimitros Grammenos, the director of the Archaeological Museum of Thessaloniki, kindly granted permission for me to reproduce pictures of the ivory portrait heads of Alexander and Philip from the excavation of the royal tombs of Vergina. I thank my gracious Wellesley colleague Anastasia Karakasidou for helping to make that possible.

While I was writing this book, my companions Harry Cladouhos, Constantine "Gus" Kaloidis, and Piero Antinori provided me with invaluable feedback, nourishment, and inspiration. I would like to thank, at Wellesley College, my personal bodyguard: Thomas Cushman, Barbara Geller, Jonathan Imber, Fran Malino, and Rod Morrison. Only they know how often they have saved me from today's Mallians.

This book grew out of the Internet course on Alexander the Great that I created several years ago with Alexander Parker and Jeff Kunken of the Global Education Network in New York. For those who would like the opportunity to take a version of the course I have taught at Wellesley College for the past twenty years, you can log on to Gen.com.

This project never would have seen the light of day without the encouragement and help of Catharine Sprinkel, Lynn Chu, and Glen Hartley of Writer's Representatives in New York. From the submission of the original book proposal to the completion of the project, Lynn and Glen have listened to my ideas and helped me to clarify them. I am sure that I have learned more from them than they have from me. When the going has gotten a bit tough they also have been there in my corner, providing wisdom and good old-fashioned common sense.

At Random House, it is a pleasure to record my gratitude to my editor, Will Murphy, for taking this book on in the first place and for his willingness to spend many hours attempting to quiet the choppy waves of my prose; it is rare (bordering on impossible) today to find such an enthusiastic, constructive critic of writing about antiquity, particularly one with such a wonderful sense of humor. To Will's assistant, Evelyn O'Hara, I would like to give thanks for her unfailing courtesy and for help with all matters logistical, despite my incomprehensible handwriting and Delphic e-mails. Everything that is beautiful about the presentation of this book is due to the talents of Dana Blanchette. Finally, only Dennis Ambrose knows how much I owe him for actually seeing this book through to its final production; by a country mile he is the best production editor I have ever been blessed to know and work with on any project.

As always, my brothers and sister (Mark, Christopher, and Sara) have shown great interest in another one of my books, and have pushed me to keep in mind the all-important question of why any of this matters to anyone, apart from a few odd classical scholars. Long live the veterans of Bear Hill.

Perhaps the decisive influence upon the completion of this book, however, has been my partner, Dr. Nancy Thompson of The Metropolitan Museum of Art. Descendant of a long line of distinguished editors from the great state of Iowa, Dr. Thompson improved this book at every stage of its writing and production. Everyone knows that she is both the brains and the beauty behind the operation.

This book is dedicated to the memory of my father, Orris Arleigh "Buck" Rogers, who passed away from Alzheimer's disease in March

1996. As now noted in several accounts of life in Litchfield County, Connecticut during the 1960s, Buck Rogers was simply too good-looking, too talented, and too charming for his own or anyone else's good. Alzheimer's robbed Buck of his looks and his creative talents—but not of his humor or sense of style.

Shortly before he died, I visited Buck in the nursing home where he lived during the last few years of his life. Since he was no longer able to speak clearly, but obviously still enjoyed listening to music, I brought along a CD of Glenn Miller's greatest hits to listen to together. Among his numerous artistic talents, Buck was an excellent drummer and loved big band music of the 1940s in particular. As the first notes of "In the Mood" came floating out of my portable CD player, Buck suddenly jumped right out of his wheelchair and began to dance to the rhythm.

"Hey, Buck," I said, "you've got it!"

To which he replied, "I always did."

Guy MacLean Rogers
Toll Court
September 28, 2004

Contents

PART ONE
"Alexander, Son of Philip, and the Greeks"

List of Maps

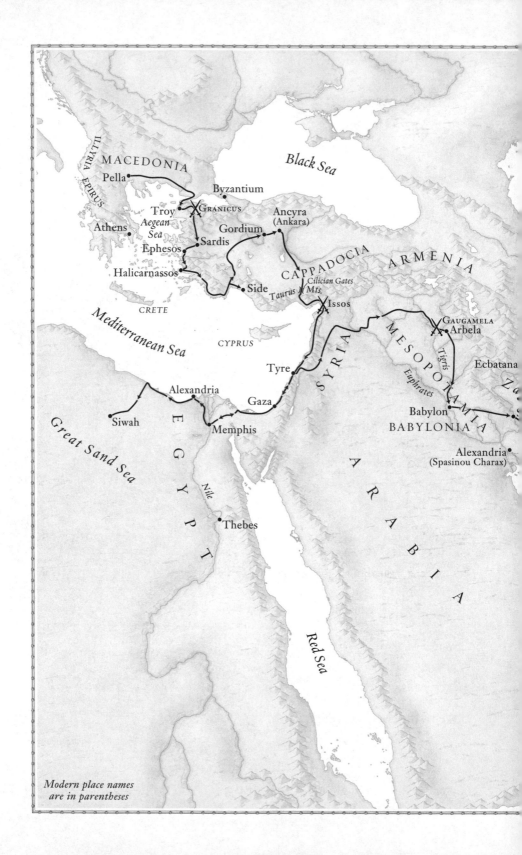

MACEDONIA

ILLYRIA

EPIRUS

Pella

Black Sea

Byzantium

Troy

GRANICUS

Ancyra
(Ankara)

Athens

*Aegean
Sea*

Gordium

Sardis

Ephesos

CAPPADOCIA

ARMENIA

Halicarnassos

Side

Taurus Mts.

Cilician Gates
Mts.

Issos

GAUGAMELA
Arbela

Tigris

CRETE

Mediterranean Sea

CYPRUS

Tyre

SYRIA

MESOPOTAMIA

Euphrates

Ecbatana

Za

Alexandria

Gaza

Babylon

Siwah

Memphis

BABYLONIA

Great Sand Sea

E
G
Y
P
T

A
R
A
B
I
A

Alexandria
(Spasinou Charax)

Nile

Thebes

Red Sea

*Modern place names
are in parentheses*

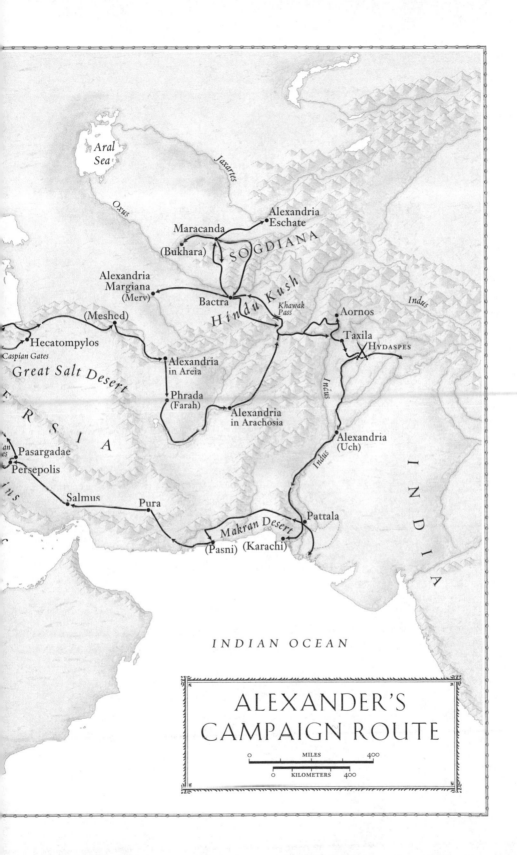

Aral
Sea

Jaxartes

Oxus

Maracanda
Alexandria
Eschate

(Bukhara) SOGDIANA

Alexandria
Margiana
(Merv) Bactra *Hindu Kush* *Khawak Pass* Aornos *Indus*

(Meshed) Taxila HYDASPES

Hecatompylos
Caspian Gates Alexandria
in Areia

Great Salt Desert

Phrada
(Farah) Alexandria
in Arachosia *Indus*

Alexandria
(Uch)

PERSIA

an es Pasargadae

Persepolis I N D I A

ius Salmus Pura Pattala

Makran Desert

(Pasni) (Karachi)

INDIAN OCEAN

ALEXANDER'S CAMPAIGN ROUTE

0 MILES 400

0 KILOMETERS 400

Introduction

The Real Alexander

Throughout most of history Alexander III of Macedon has been seen as a hero, or even more than a hero. Indeed, during the first half of the twentieth century, one scholar argued that he was a kind of Platonic philosopher-king or even a messianic figure like Jesus, sent on a "mission from the deity to harmonize men generally and to be the reconciler of the world."

More recently, however, a far less flattering portrait of Alexander has been drawn. Some have portrayed Alexander as an unstable alcoholic, prone to wine-fueled rages and violence. Others have implied that he was a megalomaniac precursor of the political terrorist Stalin or the genocidal mass murderer Hitler. Historians also have denied that Alexander had any lasting effects upon the ancient world. Or they have compared his effects to the ones that Hernán Cortés and the conquistadors had upon the Aztecs of Mexico between 1519 and 1522.

Although the popular view of Alexander perhaps remains a largely favorable one, a new scholarly orthodoxy about Alexander has emerged over the last half century, as the eminent scholar Frank Holt has argued. Alexander should be rechristened Alexander "the Terrible," or Alexander "the Insignificant." Called to account before the prosecuting historians more than 2,300 years after his death, Alexander has been retroactively stripped of his reputation and his epithet.

This new image of Alexander has resulted (in part) from the adoption of a more critical and skeptical attitude toward the ancient Greek and Roman sources for his life. As scholars have analyzed the methods of the ancient writers and compared various accounts, they have reconstructed a far less heroic picture of what Alexander did and therefore who he was.

Most of the proponents of the new orthodoxy also have written in the long, dark shadows cast by various modern tyrants over the last century. Looking out over the wreckage wrought by figures such as Hitler, Mussolini, Stalin, and Milosevic, many historians have brought to the subject of Alexander an explicitly negative attitude toward nationalism, conquest, and empire.

Of course, we should read all historical sources critically. Moreover, modern historians should neither be cheerleaders for history's victors nor advocates for the vanquished. Nevertheless, the new orthodoxy itself is based upon a somewhat selective use of the ancient sources, and the overall historical framework that Alexander operated within has never been properly represented.

In this book it will be shown that Alexander's actions must be understood first of all within the context of a long, historical struggle between Persia and Greece, which both sides saw in religious terms. The "real" Alexander is then inferred from an accurate and balanced chronological account of his deeds, based upon analysis of all the main ancient sources. Located historically within such a context, Alexander "the Inferred" will emerge here, first, as a creative artist of warfare, perhaps the greatest warrior in world history. But Alexander, it will be argued, also was a pious religious traditionalist, whose quest to establish a global empire of the best was sanctioned by the gods whom he honored throughout his life. Although he failed to do so because of his early death, it has never been properly appreciated how Alexander set in place the fundamental political, cultural, and religious framework from which Western civilization eventually was born.

WHAT DIFFERENCE DOES IT MAKE?

In less than a decade Alexander conquered the Persian empire, the largest and most successful empire in the history of the ancient Near East. At the time of its greatest extension, the Persian empire today would subsume all or part of the modern nation-states of Turkey, Syria, Lebanon, Israel, Egypt, Iraq, Iran, Afghanistan, Pakistan, Turkmenistan, Uzbekistan, Tajikistan, and India. How Alexander managed to conquer and then govern a territory of such immense size and ethnic diversity in such a short period of time should be of interest not only to professional historians of warfare and imperialism; the tale is important to anyone who wishes to understand clearly the deep historical roots of the deadly conflicts that currently plague the lands he once ruled, and that threaten to enflame the entire world.

Within his empire Alexander implanted the fundamental physical, political, and social organization of Greek civilization, the *polis*, or city-state, at strategic points all over the map of the Near East, from modern Egypt to Tajikistan. In Alexander's city foundations, military settlements, and refoundations of cities, Greek became the dominant public language of administration, commerce, law, literature, and religious expression.

It was in the Greek language that Alexander brought with him from Macedon that some of history's most influential ideas were formulated and spread all the way to India. In turn, within the city-states founded by Alexander and his successors, ideas and religious works of peoples from outside of Greek civilization were translated into Greek and then disseminated throughout the Mediterranean. This cross-fertilization continued even after the Romans conquered the successor kingdoms of Alexander's empire in Greece, Macedon, and the East.

In the East the Roman conquests of Alexander's successor kingdoms led to the creation of an amalgam Greco-Roman civilization. That amalgam civilization persisted into the seventh century c.e. It was either within or on the borders of that civilization that the three great religions of the book, Rabbinic Judaism, Christianity, and early Islam, either evolved or were created. These religious traditions developed in relation to, and frequently in opposition to, Greco-Roman civilization.

Although Alexander himself envisioned a very different kind of world empire, he ended up laying down some of the foundations for what was to become Western civilization as it grew out of Greco-Roman antiquity. To the political, cultural, and religious heirs of the civilization Alexander helped to found, it matters quite a bit who Alexander III of Macedon was.

Alexander still matters now because he was one of the decisive founders of Western civilization: he is who we are, in some sense, or rather who we wish to be—or fear we are. It is perhaps for that reason that scholars have been led to create such contradictory historical portraits of Alexander. At stake is a part of the self-image of the West. We construct "Alexanders" in the image of the civilization to which we aspire or from which we recoil.

Alexander, however, cannot be resolved into an individual who was either gay or straight (as some have claimed), an ultranationalist or someone who went native, a mass murderer or a messiah. Rather, Alexander was an ambiguous genius who defeats our polarized and polarizing modern categories. Like the Persian king Darius, we fight hard, but, as the Delphic oracle prophesied, Alexander is *aniketos*—invincible. He cannot and never will be defeated by simplification.

But while Alexander's ambiguity cannot be unraveled without distorting the historical record of what he did, that fact should not undermine our appreciation of his "Greatness." Throughout history the great have often been possessed of godlike abilities, and all-too-mortal flaws and weaknesses. Indeed, it is the flaws and mistakes of the great that allow us to appreciate their gifts, and it is by their missteps and failures that the great are ultimately redeemed as human beings. Great as he was, in the end Alexander turned out to be a mortal, just like the rest of us, if only in that one inescapable way. If we can accept that fact, as Alexander himself was finally forced to, perhaps we can forgive him for the ambiguity of his greatness.

The Main Characters

ABREAS: Macedonian soldier on double pay for military service; died protecting Alexander inside the walls of the Mallian town.

ACUPHIS: chief of Nysa, city in Bajaur named after Dionysos' nurse.

ADA: Hecatomnid princess; surrendered key city of Alinda to Alexander; reinstated as governor of Caria by Alexander in 334 B.C.E.; adopted Alexander as her son.

AGIS III: king of Sparta; raised a revolt against Macedon in the summer of 331 B.C.E.; crushed by Alexander's regent in Macedon, Antipater.

ALCIMACHUS, SON OF AGATHOCLES: brother of Alexander's bodyguard Lysimachus; in the summer of 334 B.C.E. sent on a mission to the Aeolian and the Ionian cities still subject to the Persians, dispossessing the ruling factions and establishing popular (democratic) governments in their place.

ALEXANDER OF EPIRUS: king of Molossia in Epirus, 342–330/29 B.C.E. Brother of Olympias; married Philip's daughter Kleopatra in 336 B.C.E.

ALEXANDER, THE SON OF AEROPUS, OF LYNCESTIS: accompanied Alexander into the palace after the assassination of Philip II, armed like his master; his brothers Heromenes and Arrabaeus were executed for their part in the conspiracy to assassinate Philip; executed in the wake of Philotas' treason.

ANAXARCHUS OF ABDERA: philosopher who consoled Alexander after his murder of Cleitus; supported Alexander's introduction of *proskynesis* (prostration) in front of him.

ANDRONICUS, SON OF AGERROS: sent to suppress rebellion of Satibarzanes; husband of Lanice, Alexander's childhood nurse; may have been killed at the battle of the river Polytimetus.

ANTIPATER, SON OF ASCLEPIODORUS: father was satrap of Syria; joined conspiracy of the pages to assassinate Alexander because of punishment of Hermolaus or because of his father's demotion; executed.

ANTIPATER, SON OF IOLAOS OF PALIOURA: sided with Alexander after the death of Philip II; served as Alexander's viceroy in Europe when Alexander departed for the east; involved in frequent disputes with Olympias; in 324 B.C.E. Craterus was sent back to Macedon to replace him.

ARISTANDER OF TELMESSUS: Alexander's seer; predicted Alexander would take Tyre, but with the labor characteristic of his kinsman, Herakles; that Alexandria in Egypt would be the nurse of men of every nation; and that the Macedonians would achieve victory at the battle of Gaugamela based upon an eclipse of the moon on September 20, 331 B.C.E.

ARISTOBULUS OF CASSANDREIA: minor officer in Alexander's army, wrote a history of Alexander's reign sometime after 301 B.C.E.

ARISTOTLE OF STAGIRA: born c. 384, died in 322 B.C.E. Brought to the Macedonian capital of Pella to serve as Alexander's educational tutor. Annotated special copy of the *Iliad* for Alexander. His kinsman Callisthenes served as Alexander's official historian. Greatest philosopher in Western history.

ARTABAZUS, SON OF PHARNABAZUS: lived at Pella; surrendered to Alexander after the death of Darius; became satrap of Bactria.

ATHENAEUS OF NAUCRATIS (EGYPT): wrote *Deipnosophistae*, or "Learned Banqueteers," completed in the years immediately following the death of the Roman emperor Commodus (c. 192 C.E.), a report on discussions among guests about philosophy, literature, law, medicine, and many other topics at a banquet over a number of days, during which events and incidents related to Alexander's life were discussed.

ATTALUS: born c. 390; his niece Kleopatra married Philip II in 337 B.C.E. At the wedding feast, Attalus prayed for a legitimate heir to the Macedonian throne; appointed as one of the commanders of the expeditionary force to Asia in 336 B.C.E. After Philip's assassination executed with the complicity of Parmenio.

BAGOAS: handsome young Persian eunuch brought to Alexander by Nabarzanes in Hyrcania as a kind of gift; Alexander kissed him in a theater in Salmus in Carmania; Alexander and Bagoas perhaps had an intimate relationship.

BALACRUS: Macedonian officer, commanded javelin throwers at Gaugamela; responsible for effectively eliminating Persian scythed chariots.

BARSAENTES: satrap of Arachotia and Drangiana; murdered Darius; later executed by Alexander.

BARSINE: daughter of Persian nobleman Artabazus; ex-wife of Memnon of Rhodes; she became Alexander's mistress; the relationship produced a son, Herakles.

BARSINE (STATEIRA): Darius' eldest daughter; Alexander married her according to the Persian custom in Susa in 324 B.C.E.

BATIS: eunuch, ruler of Gaza on behalf of the Persians; commanded a force of mercenary Arabs who resisted three Macedonian assaults upon their city; captured and dragged around the city by his ankles at the rear of a chariot, as

Achilles had dragged Hektor's corpse around the walls of Troy, probably in retaliation for the assassination attempt on Alexander.

BESSUS: the satrap of Bactria; assumed power after murder of Darius; captured in the summer of 329 B.C.E.; later executed.

BOLON: lesser Macedonian officer, who had risen from the ranks; made damaging speech against Philotas at his trial in Phrada in October 330 B.C.E.

BRANCHIDAE: descendants of the priests and caretakers of the oracular shrine of Apollo near the Greek city of Miletos in Asia Minor; handed over treasury of shrine to Xerxes in 479 B.C.E. Resettled on other side of Oxus River; wiped out by Alexander.

BUCEPHALAS: Alexander's favorite horse. Big, black horse brought to Philip by Philoneicus of Thessaly; won by young Alexander in a wager with his father that he could tame the wild horse; Alexander rode Bucephalas to India, where Bucephalas died of old age and exhaustion at the age of thirty; Alexander named a city after Bucephalas.

CALANUS: Indian ascetic philosopher who tried to teach Alexander doctrine of good government; accompanied Alexander back westward; committed suicide in Persis.

CALLINES: Macedonian officer in the Companion cavalry; during the mutiny at Opis begged Alexander on behalf of the soldiers to be able to kiss Alexander and be called his kinsman.

CALLISTHENES OF OLYNTHOS: official (contemporary) historian of Alexander's campaigns, wrote the *Deeds of Alexander*; helped to scuttle Alexander's plans to introduce the custom of *proskynesis* into his court; charged along with a group of the royal pages with conspiring to murder Alexander; died in one of five ways.

CAMBYSES (reigned 530–522 B.C.E.): Persian king, son of Cyrus the Great; conquered Egypt and brought it under Persian rule, with the help of local elites.

CEBALINUS: brother of Nicomachus; revealed Dimnus conspiracy to Alexander in Phrada in October 330 B.C.E.

CHARES OF MYTILENE: Alexander's usher or court chamberlain, wrote *Histories of Alexander.*

CLEANDER, SON OF POLEMOKRATES: commander of mercenaries at Ecbatana and Coenus' brother; played key role in assassination of Parmenio in the fall of 330 B.C.E. Executed in Carmania in 324 B.C.E. for maladministration and crimes against natives.

CLEITARCHUS OF ALEXANDRIA: wrote a history of Alexander's reign in at least twelve books that may be dated as early as 310 B.C.E.

CLEITUS, THE "BLACK," SON OF DROPIDAS: brother of Alexander's nurse Lanice; commanded the Royal Squadron of the Companion cavalry; saved Alexander's life at the battle of the Granicus River; killed by Alexander in a drunken brawl centering on Alexander's orientalizing and claims of divine parentage in 328 B.C.E.

COENUS, SON OF POLEMOKRATES: commander of infantry from Elimiotis in Upper Macedon; fought in all of Alexander's major battles; wounded at Gaugamela; spoke out against Philotas at his trial in Phrada in 330 B.C.E.; at the Hyphasis River advised Alexander to stop; died of natural causes in 326 B.C.E.

CRATERUS, SON OF ALEXANDER (NOT ALEXANDER III, KING OF MACEDON): from Orestis in Upper Macedon; commanded left of phalanx at Issus and Gaugamela; hostile to Philotas; perhaps Alexander's most reliable general during campaigns in Sogdiana and India; in 324 B.C.E. appointed Alexander's viceroy in Europe to replace Antipater; "lover of the king."

QUINTUS CURTIUS RUFUS: wrote ten-book history of Alexander (*Historiae Alexandri Magni*), probably during the reign of the Roman emperor Claudius (41–54 C.E.).

CYRUS THE GREAT (reigned 557–530 B.C.E.): founder of the Persian empire; built royal residence of Pasargadae, where he was later buried; had crossed the deserts of Gedrosia where his army supposedly was nearly wiped out.

DANDAMIS: Indian philosopher who asked Alexander why he had come to India.

DARIUS I (reigned 522–486 B.C.E.): usurped Persian throne; created royal residences in Susa and Persepolis; crushed the Ionian revolt (499–494); his general Datis was defeated at Marathon (490) by the Athenians.

DARIUS III (reigned 336–330 B.C.E.): Persian king; Alexander's rival; usually depicted in the Greek and Roman sources as cowardly and indecisive; a more sophisticated reading of the sources reveals that Darius was a competent and flexible leader.

DEMETRIUS: bodyguard of Alexander; part of Dimnus' conspiracy against Alexander; exposed in Phrada in October 330 B.C.E. Executed by the Macedonian army; replaced as bodyguard by Ptolemy.

DIMNUS: plotted against Alexander in Phrada in October 330 B.C.E.; committed suicide or killed by guards while being arrested; Philotas and Parmenio executed in wake of the conspiracy.

DIODORUS SICULUS (FROM SICILY): books 17 and through 18.9 of his *Bibliotheke*, or *Library* (completed around 30 B.C.E.), treat the reign of Alexander from his accession to his death in Babylon.

EPAMINONDAS: Theban general; defeated Spartan army twice, at Leuctra (371 B.C.E.) and Mantinea (362), at which he died; innovative tactician of hoplite warfare, from whose tactics (esp. oblique lines of attack) Philip II probably learned.

ERYGIUS OF MYTILENE: born c. 380 B.C.E.; among friends of Alexander banished in the spring of 336 B.C.E. in the wake of the Pixodarus affair; later commanded allied cavalry forces; killed rebel Satibarzanes in hand-to-hand combat.

EUMENES OF CARDIA: Alexander's royal secretary; with Diodotus of Erythrae, kept the *Royal Diaries*.

LUCIUS FLAVIUS ARRIANUS (ARRIAN): lived c. 86–160 c.e. His *Anabasis* ("Journey Up-country") of Alexander, in seven books, begins with Alexander's accession and ends with his death in Babylon in 323 b.c.e.; shorter companion work, the *Indike*, recounts Nearchus' voyage from the mouth of the Indus River to Susa.

GLAUCIAS: Hephaestion's physician; crucified after he failed to save Hephaestion's life in Ecbatana in October 324 b.c.e.

GLYCERA: "Honey"; Athenian courtesan; second mistress/girlfriend of Harpalus in Babylon; kept in exceeding luxury, provided with a way of life that was fantastically expensive.

HARPALUS, SON OF MACHATAS: one of Alexander's boyhood friends; banished by Philip in the wake of the Pixodarus affair; later served as Alexander's treasurer; fled from Alexander twice; was killed on Crete in 324 b.c.e.

HEGELOCHUS, SON OF HIPPOSTRATUS: cavalry commander; great nephew of Attalus; perhaps plotted against Alexander in Egypt with Parmenio; opposed Alexander's claims to divine parentage; died at the Battle of Gaugamela.

HEPHAESTION, SON OF AMYNTOR: from Pella in Macedon; Alexander's dearest friend; possibly his lover; wounded at Gaugamela, where he commanded the *agema* of the *hypaspistai*; after death of Philotas shared command of the Companion cavalry with Cleitus the Black; died at Ecbatana in October 324 b.c.e.

HERACON: Macedonian officer; summoned to Alexander in Carmania in 324 b.c.e.; put on trial; originally acquitted; later indicted by natives of Susa; tried again and executed.

HERMOLAUS, THE SON OF SOPOLIS: student of Callisthenes; slew boar before Alexander; initiated plot to kill Alexander in revenge for punishment or because of the demotion of his father; executed by stoning.

HIERONYMOS OF CARDIA: history for which he is best known began at the death of Alexander in 323 B.C.E. and continued to at least the death of King Pyrrhus of Epirus (272 B.C.E.).

ISOCRATES OF ATHENS: Athenian orator, composed the *Panegyricus* (380 B.C.E.) and a *Letter to Philip* (346/5), urging Philip II of Macedon to begin a military campaign against Persia.

MARCUS IUNIANUS IUSTINUS (JUSTIN): third or fourth century C.E. author of a Latin *epitome* (abridgment or summary) of the otherwise lost "Philippic Histories" (*Historiae Philippicae*) of Pompeius Trogus, a late-first-century B.C.E. Vocontian from Gallia Narbonensis (Vasio or Vaison-la-Romaine) who covered Macedon in books 7–12 of his histories.

KLEOPATRA: niece of a Macedonian nobleman, Attalus; married to Philip II in 337 B.C.E.; Attalus' toast at her wedding feast to a legitimate heir to the Macedonian throne caused a brawl between Alexander and Philip, which led to Olympias' withdrawal to Epirus, and Alexander's to Illyria.

LAOMEDON, SON OF LARICHOS, OF MYTILENE: younger brother of Erygios; also exiled for his part in the Pixodarus affair; knew Persian; one of the *trierarchs* (essentially, ship commanders) of Alexander's fleet.

LEONIDAS: relative of Olympias, put in charge of the nurses, pedagogues, and teachers who were expected to educate Alexander; known as a strict disciplinarian.

LEONNATUS: related to mother of Philip II; in 332/1 B.C.E. became one of Alexander's seven personal bodyguards; probably was one of the soldiers who fought to protect Alexander inside the walls of the Mallian city; defeated the Oreitai; awarded a gold crown in Susa.

LYSIMACHUS OF ACARNANIA: Alexander's pedagogue; ingratiated himself to Alexander by calling Philip "Peleus," nicknaming Alexander "Achilles," and styling himself "Phoenix," Achilles' old tutor. Later, rescued by Alexander during a raid against the Arabians who lived in the area of Mount Antilibanus.

LYSIPPUS OF SICYON: active c. 370–315 B.C.E.; Alexander's favorite sculptor; created much-copied bronze prototypes of Alexander as crown prince and heroic, leonine warrior.

MAZAEUS: sent forward to forestall Alexander's crossing of the Euphrates; commander of lowland and Mesopotamian Syrians at Gaugamela.

MEDIUS OF LARISSA: host at the drinking party that Alexander attended on the night he either came down with the fever that led to his death, or was poisoned.

MEMNON OF RHODES: military commander in the service of the Persian kings; recommended scorched-earth policy before battle of the river Granicus; his advice was rejected by the Persian satraps and military commanders; organized defense of Halicarnassus in 334 B.C.E. His death at the siege of Mytilene in the summer of 333 led to the collapse of the Persian naval strategy.

MENIDAS: Macedonian officer; commanded mercenary cavalry at Gaugamela; left at Ecbatana with Parmenio in 330 B.C.E.; perhaps involved in Parmenio's assassination; in Babylon when Alexander died.

MUSICANUS: ruler of the richest realm in the Indus Valley; surrendered to Alexander, giving lavish gifts; confirmed as a vassal king; later revolted; executed.

NABARZANES: Persian cavalry commander; instigated murder of Darius; later surrendered to Alexander; his friendly reception was helped by the presence of the eunuch Bagoas.

NEARCHUS OF CRETE: commander of Alexander's fleet when it sailed down the Indus River and from the mouth of the Indus River along the seacoast, eventually to the mouth of the Euphrates; wrote memoirs of the campaign.

NICANOR, SON OF PARMENIO: younger brother of Philotas; commanded Guards (hypaspists) at Granicus, Issos, and Gaugamela; died of an illness of some kind in Areia, where his brother Philotas was left to conduct funeral rites.

NICOMACHUS: boyfriend of Dimnus, to whom Dimnus' conspiracy against the life of Alexander was revealed in Phrada in October 330 B.C.E.

OLYMPIAS OF MOLOSSIA: daughter of King Neoptolemus of Molossia; married Philip II of Macedon c. 357 B.C.E.; gave birth to Alexander III of Macedon in July 356 B.C.E. Devotee of Dionysiac cults.

ONESICRITUS OF ASTYPALAEA: helmsman of Alexander's royal galley; later wrote a work called *The Education of Alexander*, a history of Alexander.

ORXINES: Persian nobleman; traced his descent from the great Persian King Cyrus; wealth was partly inherited and also had been amassed during the long period when he had served as a satrap; indicted and convicted of robbing royal temples and of illegally putting many Persians to death; executed by Alexander's command.

OXYARTES: Bactrian nobleman; captured by Alexander at the Rock of Sogdiana; his daughter Roxane married Alexander in the spring of 327 B.C.E.

PARMENIO: Philip's best general; led expeditionary force to Asia in 336 B.C.E. Commanded the left wing of the army at Granicus, Issos, and Gaugamela; assassinated in 330 B.C.E. by Alexander's command after his son Philotas was found guilty of committing treason.

PARYSATIS: the youngest daughter of the Persian king Artaxerxes III Ochus (359–338 B.C.E.); Alexander married her in Susa in 324 B.C.E.

PAUSANIAS, SON OF KERASTOS: from Orestis in Macedon; assassin of Philip II, in revenge for his gang rape by the muleteers of Attalus.

PERDICCAS, SON OF ORONTES: from Orestis in Macedon, commander of a brigade in the infantry; became one of Alexander's bodyguards by 330 B.C.E. After the death of Hephaestion became cavalry commander of the first *hipparchy* of the Companion cavalry; received Alexander's signet ring from Alexander at his death.

PEUCESTAS, SON OF ALEXANDER (NOT ALEXANDER III): from Mieza in Macedon; wounded protecting Alexander after Alexander himself was wounded fighting inside the Mallian town; became Alexander's bodyguard; later satrap of Persis.

PHILIP OF ACARNANIA: Alexander's doctor; cured Alexander when he became ill after swimming in the freezing-cold waters of the Cydnus River.

PHILIP II OF MACEDON: born c. 382 B.C.E.; became regent for Amyntas IV in 359; architect of Macedon's first-rate army; father of Alexander III (the Great); defeated Greeks at Chaeronea in 338; declared leader of war of revenge against Persia at Corinth in the summer of 337; assassinated in the autumn of 336 B.C.E.

PHILOTAS: son of Parmenio, commanded Companion cavalry during the early years of Alexander's campaigns in Asia; executed in 330 B.C.E. after failing to report a plot against Alexander's life.

PIXODARUS: Persian governor of Caria, 341–336 B.C.E.; offered his eldest daughter to wed Philip Arrhidaeus, son of Philip II and Philinna of Larissa. Marriage undermined by intervention of Alexander, who offered himself as the groom instead.

L. MESTRIUS PLUTARCHOS (PLUTARCH): born probably before 50 C.E. and died after 120; wrote twenty-three parallel lives of famous Greeks and Romans, pairing life of Alexander with that of Julius Caesar.

POLYDAMAS: Parmenio's dispatch rider at the battle of Gaugamela; later played a crucial role in the assassination of Parmenio.

POLYPERCHON, SON OF SIMMIAS, TYMPHAIAN: born c. 390 or 380 B.C.E.; infantry commander; made fun of one of the Persians who performed prostration in front of Alexander.

PORUS: towering Indian king; Alexander's opponent at the battle of the Hydaspes in May or June 326 B.C.E. After defeat became an important ally of Alexander's.

PROTEAS: nephew of Cleitus the Black; heavy drinker; probably was present at Alexander's final, fatal dinner party.

PROTESILAUS: Greek hero who led the Thessalian contingent to Troy. In book 2 of the *Iliad* Homer tells us that Protesilaus had been brought down first by a Dardan spear. Alexander sacrificed at his tomb in Elaeus.

PSAMMON: philosopher in Memphis with whom Alexander may have had a philosophical exchange about Zeus being the father of all mankind and his preference (according to Alexander) for the best.

PTOLEMY I OF EORDAIA (IN MACEDON): Alexander's bodyguard, later satrap, founder of Ptolemaic dynasty in Egypt; much later wrote history of Alexander's reign.

PYTHONICE: Athenian courtesan; most dazzling courtesan of her day; mistress of Harpalus; lived with Harpalus in Babylon; when she died, she was given a magnificent funeral and a costly monument of the Attic type.

ROXANE: "Little Star"; daughter of Bactrian nobleman Oxyartes; Alexander's first wife, married in the spring of 327 B.C.E. Her child with Alexander (Alexander IV) was born after Alexander's death.

SATIBARZANES: made satrap of Areians by Alexander; later revolted; killed by Erigyius in the spring of 329 B.C.E.

SEMIRAMIS: legendary Assyrian queen with whom Alexander had a rivalry; she too had crossed the deserts of Gedrosia coming back from her conquests of India.

SISYGAMBIS: mother of Darius III; taken captive after the battle of Issos; treated with great respect by Alexander; Alexander later gave to her the title of his "mother," and gave her lessons in Greek.

SITALCES, SON OF KERSOBLEPTES: prince of royal house of Odrysia; commander of Thracian javelin men; played key role in execution of Parmenio in autumn of 330 B.C.E.; in 324 B.C.E. executed for maladministration and crimes against natives.

SPITAMENES: Sogdian warlord; handed over Bessus to Alexander but then rose in rebellion; defeated Andromachus, Menedemus, Caranus, and Pharnuches at the river Polytimetus; killed by his own wife or his own allies, the Massagetae.

STRABO OF AMASEIA: born c. 64 B.C.E., survived until after 21 C.E.; book 15 of Strabo's *Geographia* supplies valuable geographical and ethnographic information about Alexander's campaigns, especially in India; based upon Nearchus, Megasthenes, and Onesicritus.

TAXILES/MOPHIS: ruler of Taxila who entertained Alexander, giving Alexander many gifts, for which he received in turn 1,000 talents from the booty Alexander was carrying, plus large quantities of gold and silver dinnerware, Persian clothing, and thirty horses from his own stable, together with their trappings.

THAIS: Athenian courtesan; allegedly inspired Alexander to burn the palace complex of the Persian kings; later mistress of Ptolemy.

THALESTRIS (OR MINYTHYIA), THE QUEEN OF THE AMAZONS: traveled thirty-five days to conceive a child with Alexander.

XERXES (reigned 486–465 B.C.E.): Persian king, built palaces in Persepolis; directed the capture and sacking of Athens in 480 B.C.E., including the destruction of the temples on the Athenian acropolis; driven from Greece after defeat of his navy at the battle of Salamis.

Rulers of Persia and Macedon

Kings of Persia from the seventh century until the death of Darius III (all dates are B.C.E.). Based on the splendid work of A. Kuhrt, *The Ancient Near East c. 3000–330 BC*, volumes 1 and 2 (London, 1995).

Teispes	650–620
Cyrus I	620–590
Cambyses I	590–559
Cyrus II (the Great)	559–530
Cambyses II	530–522
Bardiya	522
Darius I	522–486
Xerxes	486–465
Artaxerxes I	465–423
Darius II	423–405
Artaxerxes II	405–359
Artaxerxes III	359–338
Artaxerxes IV	338–336
Darius III	336–330

The Argead kings of the Macedonians from the early fifth century B.C.E. through the reign of Alexander III (the Great). Based on the exemplary work of E. Borza, *In the Shadow of Olympus* (Princeton, 1990), p. xviii.

Amyntas I	498/7
Alexander I	498/7–454
Perdiccas II	454–413
Archelaus	413–399
Orestes	399–398/7
Aeropus II	399–395/4
Amyntas II	395/4
Pausanias	394/3
Amyntas III	393–370/69
Alexander II	370/69–367
Ptolemy	367–365
Perdiccas III	365–360/59
Philip II	360/59–336
Alexander III	336–323

Chronology

1187 D.O.D.		Capture of Troy
559–530		Reign of Cyrus II, the Great
499–494		Revolt of Ionian Greeks
490	*September*	Persian defeat at Marathon
480	*September*	Destruction of the temples on the acropolis of Athens; Persian defeat at Salamis
479		Persian defeat at Plataea
450		Peace of Kallias
431–404		Peloponnesian War
387/6		"King's Peace"
382		Birth of Philip II
380		*Panegyricus* of Isocrates
371	*July*	Battle of Leuctra
369–367		Philip II hostage in Thebes
362		Battle of Mantinea
360/59		Death of Perdiccas III (brother of Philip II)
356	*20 July*	Birth of Alexander
346		Isocrates' letter *To Philip*
338	*August*	Battle of Chaeronea

336	*spring*	Macedonian Expeditionary force crosses Hellespont
336	*October*	Assassination of Philip II
334	*late spring*	Battle of the Granicus River
334	*early summer*	Alexander in Ephesos
334	*summer*	Capture of Miletos
334	*summer*	Siege of Halicarnassus
334/3	*winter*	Alexander's campaigns in Caria, Lycia, Pamphylia, Phrygia
333	*spring*	Memnon's naval offensive
333	*spring/summer*	Alexander in Gordium, campaigns in area
333	*late summer*	Alexander into Cilicia
333	*end of summer*	Alexander in Tarsus
333	*September*	Darius in the Amik Plain
333	*November*	Battle of Issos
332	*January–July*	Siege of Tyre
332	*Sept.–November*	Siege of Gaza
331	*late winter*	Alexander's visit to Siwah
331	*April 7*	Inauguration of Alexandria
331	*spring*	Alexander in Memphis
331	*April*	Alexander leaves Memphis
331	*9 P.M., Sept. 20*	Eclipse of moon after Alexander crosses Tigris
331	*October 1*	Battle of Gaugamela
331	*end of Nov.*	Alexander leaves Babylon
331	*end of Dec.*	Alexander leaves Susa
330	*Jan.–May*	Alexander in Persepolis
330	*July*	Death of Darius
330	*August*	Alexander in Zadracarta
330	*October*	Dimnus conspiracy
330	*autumn*	Deaths of Philotas and Parmenio
329	*March*	Alexander in Helmand Valley (Afghanistan)
329	*spring*	Death of Satibarzanes
329	*spring*	Alexander crosses Hindu Kush
329	*summer*	Capture of Bessus

329	*autumn*	Revolts of Sogdians, Bactrians
329	*winter*	Alexander in Bactra
328	*spring–summer*	Campaigns in Sogdia, Bactria
328	*summer*	Capture of Rock of Sogdiana
328	*autumn*	Death of Cleitus in Maracanda
328/7	*winter*	Army rests in Nautaca (Karshi)
327	*spring*	End of Sogdian revolt
327	*spring*	Alexander marries Roxane
327	*late spring*	Alexander introduces *proskynesis*
327	*late spring*	The conspiracy of the pages
327	*spring/summer*	Macedonians across Hindu Kush
327/6	*winter*	Hephaestion to Indus; campaigns in Swat
326	*late winter*	Capture of Aornus
326	*spring*	Army reassembles at Indus
326	*May/June*	Battle of the Hydaspes
326	*summer solstice*	Alexander at Chenab
326	*summer*	Mutiny at the Hyphasis
326	*late summer*	Alexander back at Hydaspes
326	*August*	Death of Coenus
326	*early November*	Alexander begins journey down Hydaspes
326/5	*winter*	Alexander wounded in Mallian town
325	*July*	Alexander in Pattala
325	*late August*	Alexander leaves Pattala
325	*early October*	Alexander leaves Oreitai
325	*early November*	Nearchus sets sail along south coast
325	*December*	Nearchus arrives in Salmus
325	*late December*	Alexander leaves Carmania
324	*March*	Alexander back in Susa; mass marriage ceremony; paying off of debts; arrival of Successors
324	*midsummer*	Alexander at Opis
324	*summer*	Mutiny and banquet at Opis

324	*August 4*	Decree about exiles announced at Olympia
324	*October*	Death of Hephaestion in Ecbatana
323	*early in year*	Alexander leaves Ecbatana
323	*spring*	Alexander back in Babylon
323	*late May*	Alexander falls ill
323	*June 10*	Death of Alexander

PART ONE

"Alexander, Son of Philip,
and the Greeks"

CHAPTER 1

The Blood of Heroes

PREDICTIVE PRECOCITY

When Ludwig van Beethoven was eleven years old, he composed some piano pieces too difficult to play with his small hands. His music teacher was said to have remarked, "Why, you can't play that, Ludwig." To which the boy replied, "I will when I am bigger."

History is full of the notable quotes and feats of precocious geniuses. The common thread of such stories is that they foreshadow the great deeds to come. Of course young Beethoven knew that someday he would be able to play the most difficult works for piano; after all, he was Beethoven!

Many such stories were told about Alexander the Great. Most can be found in the first ten chapters of Plutarch's biography. Plutarch relays them to suggest Alexander's future invincibility; his vehement nature (barely controlled by his self-discipline); his self-possession; his confidence; and his wit. The adult Alexander was famous for all of these. It would be a mistake, however, to forget some salient facts about his background and upbringing as we read through Plutarch's delightful litany of youthful triumphs.

Alexander was a prince, with the blood of some of Greece's greatest heroes (real and mythical) flowing through his veins from both sides of his family tree. Moreover, this young prince did not grow up among "barbarians," as some ancient writers have intimated, but at a wealthy, sophisticated royal court filled with great painters, writers, diplomats, and soldiers. He also received the finest education possible. Unless we keep these facts in mind we can never understand how Alexander, the Macedonian prince, eventually became the king of Asia and a god.

THE BLOOD OF HEROES

Alexander's mother, Olympias, was a princess of the royal house of Molossia in Epirus (northwestern Greece). Molossos, after whom the royal house was named, was supposedly the son of Andromache and Neoptolemus. It was Neoptolemus who had slain King Priam at the altar of Zeus Herkeios ("of the Household") during the sack of Troy. He also happened to be the son of Achilles. On his mother's side, Alexander was thus a blood descendant of the flawed hero of the *Iliad* and his savage son. To Alexander, the significance of his descent from the heroes of Greece's epic past was not a matter of passive identification with ancient history; the past was alive, and Alexander was part of a living epic cycle.

Alexander's father, Philip II of Macedon, had fallen in love with Olympias when both were initiated into the mysteries of the Kabeiri (earth gods) on the island of Samothrace. Later on, Olympias was known to be devoted to ectastic Dionysian cults. During their ceremonies she entered into states of possession, and to the festival processions in honor of the god she introduced large, hand-tamed snakes that terrified the male spectators.

Strong-willed, intelligent, and ruthlessly committed to Alexander's interests as she saw them, Olympias apparently never read the chapter in the textbook of Greek culture that forbade women to meddle in politics. She also passed along to Alexander her unshakable belief in his special connection to the gods and his unique destiny. Alexander may have been the only man in Macedon who was not afraid of his formidable, some have said terrible, mother.

Olympias probably married Philip in 357. We are told that before Alexander's birth she dreamed that she had heard a crash of thunder and that her womb had been struck by a thunderbolt. There followed a blinding flash of light. A great sheet of flame blazed up from it, spreading far and wide before it disappeared.

Philip, too, had a prophetic dream. He saw himself sealing up his wife's womb; on the seal was engraved the figure of a lion. Interpreting this dream, Aristander of Telmessus, who later served as Alexander's seer during his campaigns, declared that Olympias must be pregnant, since men did not seal up what was empty, and that she would bear a son whose nature would be bold and lion-like.

That bold and lion-like son probably was born on July 20, 356, the very day when the great Temple of Artemis at Ephesos, one of the seven wonders of the ancient world, burned to the ground. Hegesias of Magnesia claimed that the conflagration was no wonder: Artemis was away from her shrine attending the birth of Alexander.

Philip received the news of his son's birth just after he had captured the important city of Potidaea. In fact, three happy messages were brought to Philip that day: that his one and only general, Parmenio, had defeated the Illyrians in a great battle; that his racehorse had been victorious at the Olympic games; and that Alexander had been born. Philip's soothsayers predicted that a son whose birth coincided with three victories would be invincible.

The soothsayers were right; but of course, they also knew that the blood of some nearly invincible heroes flowed through the infant's veins. Olympias did nothing to discourage Alexander's belief in his descent from heroes and divinities. When she sent Alexander off to lead his great expedition, we are told that she disclosed to him the secret of his conception and exhorted him to show himself worthy of his parentage. (Unfortunately, Alexander never revealed what his mother had told him.)

Even as a young boy, according to Plutarch, Alexander revealed his ambitious nature. He was a fine runner, and when friends asked him whether he would be willing to compete at Olympia, he replied that he would—"if I have kings to run against me." He also astonished some visiting Persian ambassadors by questioning them about the distances they had traveled, the nature of the journey into the interior of Persia, the king's character and experience in war, and the nation's military strength. His close interrogation of these ambassadors was later seen as particularly significant.

Indeed, even before he reached puberty, Alexander had already planned his career. Whenever he heard that his father had captured some famous city or won an overwhelming victory, he was annoyed and complained to his friends, "Boys, my father will forestall me in everything. There will be nothing great or spectacular for you and me to show the world."

THE TAMING OF BUCEPHALAS

Alexander's precocity and ambition are perhaps best illustrated by the delightful story of the horse named Bucephalas—"Oxhead," for the shape of the mark on his forehead. The big black horse had been brought to Philip by Philoneicus the Thessalian, who had offered to sell him for the huge sum of thirteen talents. When Philip and his friends went down to watch Bucephalas being put through his paces, however, they found him quite wild and unmanageable. He allowed no one to mount him; nor would the horse endure the shouts of Philip's grooms. He reared up against anyone who approached him. Angry at having been offered a vicious, unbroken animal, Philip ordered Bucephalas to be led away.

Alexander intervened with a wager: if he could not mount and ride Bucephalas, he would pay his purchase price. Philip's friends laughed at the bet. But Alexander had noticed what no one else had seen: that Bucephalas was spooked by his own shadow. Alexander therefore turned Bucephalas toward the sun, so that his shadow would fall behind him; then, running alongside and stroking him gently, Alexander sprang lightly onto his back. When he saw that Bucephalas had been freed of his fears and wanted to show his speed, Alexander gave him his head and urged him forward at a gallop. As Philip and his friends held their collective breath, Alexander reached the end of his gallop, turned under full control, and rode back in triumph. Philip's friends broke into applause. Philip himself, we are told, wept for joy, and said, "My boy, you must find a kingdom big enough for your ambitions. Macedonia is too small for you."

Philip was right, of course. But the real significance of this event was not what it revealed of Alexander's ambition; what really set the young prince apart were his keen powers of observation and his ability to draw the correct inferences from what he saw. As a young man, Alexander applied those powers to combat; he was able to observe and then act upon data—features of topography, for instance—whose implications no one else could understand as clearly or as quickly.

AN EDUCATION FIT FOR A PRINCE

In charge of the nurses, pedagogues, and teachers expected to educate the tamer of Bucephalas was a certain Leonidas, a relative of Olympias, known as a strict disciplinarian. Alexander's pedagogue (or minder, usually a slave) was an Acarnanian named Lysimachus, who pleased his charge by calling Philip "Peleus," nicknaming Alexander "Achilles," and styling himself "Phoenix," the name of Achilles' old tutor.

Once when Alexander was making sacrifice to the gods and was preparing to throw incense on the altar fire with both hands, Leonidas stopped him: only when Alexander had conquered the spice-bearing regions could he be so lavish with his incense. Later, after he *had* conquered

The grove of Mieza, in Macedon, where Aristotle taught Alexander the Great when he was about fourteen years old. *Author's collection*

those regions, Alexander sent Leonidas 500 talents' worth of frankincense and 100 talents' worth of myrrh, explaining that he had sent this abundance so that Leonidas might stop dealing parsimoniously with the gods.

This ending has always appealed to those who have endured a strict teacher. We should attend, however, to the anecdote's opening scene, which provides the real insight into the character of Alexander. Even before he needed their favor to conquer the world, Alexander was extraordinarily pious and generous to the gods.

When Alexander was fourteen years old, Philip brought the great philosopher Aristotle to Pella as Alexander's tutor. In what was probably a consecrated precinct of the Nymphs near the beautiful grove of Mieza, Aristotle tutored the young prince in ethics, politics, and eristics (formal disputation).

Aristotle also annotated a copy of Homer's *Iliad* for Alexander. He took it with him on his campaigns to the East; it was one of the very few material possessions he ever seems to have cherished. During his campaigns he slept with it under his pillow, along with a dagger.

The influence of the *Iliad* upon Alexander cannot be overestimated. To begin with, it supplied a model of a war of revenge against Asia. And Alexander seems to have been deeply moved by the heroic example of his kinsman Achilles: when he visited the site of Troy in the spring of 334, he honored Achilles and the other Greek heroes buried there with sacrifices, and proclaimed Achilles happy in life, since he had, while he was alive, a faithful friend, and after death, a great herald of his fame.

It was Achilles' acceptance of the inevitability of his own death, however, that most inspired Alexander. According to Homer, both Thetis (Achilles' mother) and Achilles knew that once he had avenged Patroklos by killing Hektor, his own death would be near. But in avenging his friend he would win the only kind of immortality available to mortals: excellent glory.

Alexander too seems to have been willing to accept death, at a time of the gods' choosing, in exchange for the everlasting glory that came from achieving great deeds of arms. That acceptance explains best the pattern of Alexander's actions throughout his life. Like Achilles, to gain all, Alexander was willing to risk all. In combat, that was his great advantage over those who wanted to live longer—and therefore were destined to live shorter and less glorious lives.

Homer may have given Alexander some ideas about how to fight as well; Alexander reportedly regarded the *Iliad* as "a handbook of warfare." Since there are no completely convincing examples in the epics of the massed hoplite warfare typical of Greek practice during the fourth century, we can only assume that what Alexander meant by his remark was that, like Achilles, he should fight glorious duels with his enemies out in front of his supporters. This is exactly what he did. And we know that Alexander justified some of his more controversial actions, such as marrying "barbarian" women, with references to the *Iliad*.

As for Aristotle himself, what influence he had on Alexander's thinking otherwise is debatable. According to some sources, he advised Alexander to treat the conquered peoples of his empire like plants or animals. There is really no good reason to doubt this story; the general sense of the advice is completely consistent with known Aristotelian theories about the natural and desirable submission of slaves to masters, and of the conquered to their conquerors. Fortunately for the conquered peoples of Asia, Alexander ignored his teacher's counsel, preferring to treat at least some of them as human beings.

From between the lines of Plutarch's predictive account of Alexander's early years, then, a picture of the young prince comes into focus: a competitive and ambitious young man, pushed and pulled between equally strong-minded parents, blessed with keen intelligence, pious in a traditional fashion, sensitive and well educated, but with an independent streak, and, most important, fired by a passionate engagement with Greece's heroic past. Much of that past had been defined by violent encounters with Greece's powerful neighbor to the east, Persia.

CHAPTER 2

Ahuramazda's Plan

IMPIETY FOR IMPIETY

The tribes of northern Greece had surrendered in 480 B.C.E. without a fight. The Thebans and the Boeotians had offered earth and water—the ancient tokens of submission. The Spartan king Leonidas and 300 of his city's bravest lay dead in the pass at Thermopylae. Now, as the enormous host of the Persian king Xerxes neared Athens, the Athenians abandoned their city.

Only a few temple stewards and poor old men remained on the Acropolis, huddled together in the temple of Athena Polias. They had barricaded the gates to the Acropolis with some planks and timbers, trusting in the oracle from Delphi, which had promised that "the wooden wall would not be taken."

But some Persians discovered a way up the steep cliffs of the Acropolis by the shrine of Kekrops' daughter Aglauros. They flung open the gates to their fellow soldiers. All those who had taken refuge inside the sanctuary were slaughtered. The Persians looted Athena's temple and then burned the entire Acropolis to the ground.

By the will of the wise god Ahuramazda, Xerxes had punished the Athenians for giving aid to the Ionian rebels almost twenty years before. Truth had triumphed over falsehood. The world had been put back in order.

The Athenians and their Greek allies saw the destruction of the temples rather differently. The Persians had committed perhaps the gravest impiety in history. Such sacrilege required revenge; and the Greeks swore a solemn oath to the gods not to rebuild the sanctuaries, but to leave them as a reminder to coming generations of the impiety of the "barbarians." True to their oath, the Athenians did not begin to rebuild the temple of Athena until 447, by which point they had been fighting Persia for nearly half a century. Even then, many considered that the Persians still had not paid for what they had done. Almost exactly 150 years after Xerxes destroyed the temples on the Athenian Acropolis, a young Macedonian king burned down the palaces of Ahuramazda's divinely selected rulers, returning impiety for impiety. His name was Alexander.

AHURAMAZDA'S PLAN

From a Persian perspective the destruction of the Greek temples was a part of the remarkable imperial expansion that they had accomplished with Ahuramazda's help. The empire's founder, Cyrus II, "the Great" (559–530), had brought first the Medes (550), then Lydia and the Greek cities of Asia Minor (540s), next Babylonia (539), and finally Bactria and Sogdiana, under Persian rule.

After Cyrus' death and burial in the new royal center of Pasargadae (in central Fars) his son Cambyses II (530–522) added Egypt to the Persian empire. A constitutional crisis followed Cambyses' death; it ended in the elevation of the usurper Darius I (522/21–486) to the throne. Now northwest India, several Greek islands including Samos, and the western part of Thrace (c. 513) came under Persian rule, as Darius attempted to consolidate the empire's frontiers.

By the end of the sixth century Persia had become the largest and most successful empire in the long history of the ancient Near East, a success its kings attributed to the will and power of their great god. On a trilingual inscription carved into a cliff at Behistun in the Zagros Mountains, along the main road from ancient Babylon to Ecbatana, Darius, for instance, claimed to have fought nineteen battles and captured nine kings in one year under the protection of Ahuramazda.

The Persians believed that Ahuramazda had made the Persian kings lords over the lands and peoples of the earth to carry out his plan for human happiness and perfect order. It was the duty of the Persian king to help maintain that order for the sake of all humanity. Those who disturbed the order or caused commotion were rebels against Ahuramazda's divine plan and had to be "put down."

In 499, though, Ionian Greeks living on the coast of Asia Minor strayed from Ahuramazda's plan by revolting against Persian rule. Led by the city of Miletos, and with limited naval support from Eretria and Athens, on the Greek mainland, the rebels managed to burn down Sardis, the local center of Persian control, and its temple of the native goddess Cybele. By 494, however, the Persians had subdued both the islands and the cities on the coast of Asia. Miletos was captured, its men were killed, its women and children were enslaved, and the sanctuary of Didyma, which housed the oracle of Apollo, was plundered and burned. Apollo had paid the price for the destruction of Cybele's sanctuary.

Darius then sent a punitive expedition against Eretria and Athens for the help their crews had given to the Ionians. Although outnumbered, the Athenians and the Plataeans defeated that Persian force at Marathon in late September 490.

Ten years later, however, Darius' son and successor, Xerxes, led a much larger force back to Greece, and this was the occasion when the Athenian Acropolis was burned. Yet, it was not Ahuramazda's will that Xerxes should make the mainland Greeks part of the divine plan for order: in September 480, the Greek fleet decisively defeated the Persians and their allies in the Straits of Salamis. Soon Xerxes himself retreated to the Hellespont, leaving his general Mardonius to engage the Greek army on land. But Mardonius' army succumbed to a Spartan-led force at Plataea in 479.

PERSIA AND GREECE, 479–346

Despite these Greek victories, the Persians remained in control of many of the islands in the Aegean as well as of Thrace and the coast of Asia Minor. The Athenians, at the head of the Delian League (a naval league of city-states), then fought for almost three decades to drive the Persians back across the Aegean and out of Asia Minor. In 450 hostilities were brought to an end by the Peace of Kallias, by whose terms the Greek cities of Asia were left to live under their own laws. But while the Persian kings temporarily may have given up on bringing the Greeks into obedience, over the course of the next century the Greeks themselves provided Xerxes' successors with plenty of opportunities to influence Greek affairs, as the city-states exhausted themselves fighting inconclusively for supremacy in Greece.

Thus, when the Peloponnesians (led by the Spartans) finally triumphed over the Athenians at the end of the so-called Peloponnesian War of 431–404, it was largely as a result of the financial subsidies provided to them by Cyrus, the son of the Persian king Darius II. In that war's aftermath, pro-Spartan oligarchies were set up to control the former members of the Athenian alliance. While many Greek cities were left to govern themselves, rule over the Ionians of Asia Minor reverted to the Persians. After 387, this situation was formally recognized in the so-called King's Peace of the Persian ruler Artaxerxes II (405–359).

During the early fourth century, even the autonomy of the major Greek cities thus was authorized by the Persian king. That guarantee, however, turned out to be a license for Spartan intervention into the affairs of other Greek city-states, particularly the great old city-state of Thebes.

The Spartan seizure of Thebes, and then the attempted seizure of Athens' port of Piraeus by a Spartan governor, led to the formation of an Athenian-Theban alliance against Sparta. The Athenians then organized another naval league, called the Second Athenian Confederacy. Hostilities continued after a peace conference held in 371 failed to satisfy the Thebans.

In that year, a Theban army of 6,000 heavily armed hoplite infantry and 1,000 cavalrymen, led by Epaminondas and Pelopidas, defeated a Spartan army of about 9,000 hoplites, plus cavalry, at Leuctra. The keys to the Theban victory were the massing of their hoplites on the left side of their battle formation to a depth of fifty shields, their advance at an oblique angle of attack, and the shock provided by the so-called Sacred Band, an elite unit of 150 pairs of select hoplites, who camped out, lived together as lovers, and fought together as a unit to the point of death. In the battle, a thousand Spartan citizens were killed, including 400 of the officer class.

It was a devastating defeat, and Sparta's Peloponnesian allies—or subjects—sought their freedom. In 362, on the plain of Mantinea, Epaminondas met another anti-Theban army, led by the Spartans but including soldiers from Achaea, Elis, and Athens. Using the same tactics he had deployed at Leuctra, Epaminondas once again defeated the Spartans, but he was killed in the battle. Although his victories had broken Sparta forever as a military power, his death left a leadership vacuum in Thebes, and in Greece generally.

Unrest also arose within the second Athenian naval alliance. The strategically vital city of Byzantium had been detached from the alliance by Epaminondas before he died; and the important islands of Rhodes, Cos, and Chios revolted in 357.

By 355 or early in 354, with the new Persian king, Artaxerxes III Ochus (359–338), threatening Athens, the Athenians made peace, with the independence of Byzantium, Chios, Rhodes, and Cos recognized. Soon Lesbos and other important member states broke away from the alliance as well.

THE THREAT FROM THE NORTH

By the middle of the fourth century, the most important city-states of Greece—Sparta, Thebes, and Athens—were all crippled by their attempts to gain the upper hand against one another, and Persia remained the arbiter of Greek affairs, particularly with respect to the Greek cities of Asia Minor. There was no need for the Persian king to put down the Greeks; they had managed that for themselves. In 346 Persia's imperial prospects in the West were brighter than they had been at any time since before the battle of Salamis.

A single threat to Ahuramazda's divine plan for human happiness loomed. After decades of political instability, the kingdom of Macedon, on Greece's northern border, was showing ominous signs of vitality and aggressiveness under the leadership of its charismatic king, Philip II. Should he manage somehow to unite his own divided kingdom, while dividing the Greeks, a very great disturbance to the perfect order might arise. For Macedon was a land like no other.

CHAPTER 3

The Emergence of
a Superpower

LOWER AND UPPER MACEDONIA

For most of its early history, Macedonia was a fitfully slumbering super-power. All it required to wake up and take the leading role in the Greek world was the strong and dexterous hand of the right king, one who could master its land's fiercely independent tribes and harness its rich resources. Philip II, the father of Alexander the Great, was that king.

The sheer size of the Macedonian kingdom, far larger than the territory of any single Greek city-state, potentially made it the dominant power in the Greek world. For ancient Macedonia consisted of two distinct geographical regions. Lower Macedonia was, essentially, formed from the alluvial plain created by the Haliacmon and Axius Rivers, which flowed into the Thermaic Gulf. Upper Macedonia consisted of the uplands and mountains that stretched northwest toward Illyria and Epirus.

The climate of Lower Macedonia was basically Mediterranean, with short, rainy winters and long, dry summers suitable for the production of cereal grains and olive trees, at least along the coast. The grapevine also flourished in Lower Macedonia, and the Macedonians were enthu-siastic wine drinkers. Well watered by the Axius and Haliacmon, the

The Haliacmon River in Lower Macedon, one of the few year-round rivers in Greece. *Author's collection*

fertile plains of Lower Macedon could sustain a large population. Here also were found Pella, Macedon's largest city and its fourth-century capital, and Aegae (modern Vergina), the burial place of the Temenid kings.

The Temenid kings supposedly were descended from the legendary Temenus of Argos, and through him from Herakles. A descendant of Temenus, either Perdiccas or his son Archelaus, founded the royal house of Macedonia.

The mountainous hinterlands of Upper Macedon bore deep forests of deciduous and evergreen trees, and rich mineral deposits. Pine was used for shipbuilding and construction. Oak was forested for ships' keels.

Eastern Macedonia was rich in mineral wealth, including large quantities of silver and especially gold, mined during the reign of Philip II from the region of Mount Pangaion. The mountains were ideal, too, for the transhumance of flocks. Here the climate was essentially continental—that is, marked by cold winters and warm summers. In these hinterlands lived tribes who had been resisting the political control of the Argead kings of Lower Macedon for nearly 200 years.

Macedon's kings were faced with two rings of external rivals and potential enemies as well. In the first and closer ring, there was Thessaly to the south, Thrace and the Chalcidian League to the east, Paeonia to the north, and Illyria and Epirus to the west. To the outer ring belonged the Greek city-states to the south and in central Greece, and the mighty Persian empire to the east. Until the Macedonian kings were able to control rival dynasts within Lower and Upper Macedonia and to fend off aggressive neighbors, they would not be able to entertain broader ambitions. Unleashing the potential of Macedon would require two centuries of warfare and the development of what looked to many fourth-century Greeks like a very different society from their own.

THE MACEDONIAN STATE

In fact, many Greeks did not think the Macedonians were Greeks. Although the Argead kings, such as Alexander, could speak and read Greek, Greeks could not understand the Macedonian dialect; indeed, modern scholars still debate whether it really was a form of Greek or not.

In other ways, too, fourth-century Macedon differed dramatically from the Greek city-states. Although kings still ruled in some of the latter, in most, assemblies, or councils of citizens, elected their political leaders, usually for limited terms. The exercise of power by elected officials was limited by law.

In Macedon, the Argead kings essentially *were* the state, with no constitutional limitations on their powers. While the army might acclaim a new king and had the right to judge the guilt of nobles prosecuted for treason, the king designated his own successor, served as the prosecutor in treason trials, appointed all officers in the army, made all grants of land, and responded in his own name to all petitions. The powerful position of the Argead kings will help us to understand certain actions of Alexander that otherwise might seem arbitrary or despotic.

Nor was there any bureaucracy in Macedon. Rather, the kings lived among their picked noble companions—fighting enemies, both domestic and external, usually in person on the battlefield; hunting; drinking heavily; and marrying as many women as they wished (often to cement political alliances with their neighbors). Their wild, licentious parties were famous. Few Macedonian kings before Philip II died in their sleep.

Many died in battle. Others fell victim to conspiracies. Ancient Macedonia really was an autocracy tempered by assassination. Its atmosphere was that of a tribally based frontier society.

For all the tumult, though, in the two centuries before Philip's reign, the Argead kings gradually had managed to consolidate their power, sometimes at the expense of their Greek neighbors. During the Persian invasion of Greece in 480, for instance, Alexander I of Macedon (c. 498/7–454) personally led the Macedonian contingent, allied to the Persians, against the Greeks. After the Persians' expulsion from Greece in the 470s, the Macedonian kings incorporated the highlands of Upper Macedon into their kingdom and also seized control of the silver-mining region between the Axius and Strymon Rivers. The successors of Alexander I, particularly Archelaus (413–399), used some of the resulting wealth to open up the Macedonian court to wider artistic influences. Greek craftsmen were brought in to help build Archelaus' new capital at Pella, and Greek artists and writers also came to Macedon; the Athenian tragedian Euripides wrote his last and most disturbing play, the *Bacchae*, there between 408 and 406. In spite of what Athenian orators claimed, Pella was no intellectual or cultural backwater by the late fifth century. Alexander the Great would grow up there at a royal court that had been attracting leading Greek writers, musicians, and artists for decades.

Despite Macedon's growing strength and the Hellenization of its court, the threat of political instability remained. Between 400 and 360, nine kings ruled Macedon. In 360/59, one of those kings, Perdiccas III, was killed fighting the Illyrians, along with 4,000 soldiers and many Macedonian nobles. After this disaster, the Illyrians and Paeonians prepared to invade, while the Athenians and Thracians supported rival claimants to the throne. Perdiccas' infant son Amyntas IV was too young to walk, let alone face such a crisis. That left Perdiccas' brother, Philip II, as the sole surviving Argead adult male able to lead the kingdom—or to watch it fall apart. The latter was the more likely outcome, given the situation.

Philip II of Macedon, born perhaps in 382, met this crisis vigorously and eventually became the master of the sneering Greeks. After stabilizing his kingdom by defeating the Athenians in what amounted to no more than a skirmish, and then buying off threatening Paeonians and Thracians, Philip embarked upon military reforms that resulted in the creation of the first truly professional army in Greek history. In short order, he introduced improved torsion catapults for siege warfare, and he reorganized the Macedonian infantry and cavalry.

PHILIP'S NEW INFANTRY

Greek infantry hoplites took their name from the protective armor they wore in battle, particularly the characteristic Argive-style shield (*hoplon*). Traditionally, in the citizen armies of the Greek city-states, hoplites fought shoulder to shoulder in lines, holding their shields with one arm and their seven-foot-long spears with the other. Depending upon how many hoplites were available, they were organized in lines or rows, one behind another, usually eight to ten men deep. The entire unit of infantrymen fighting in close order with thrusting spears constituted a phalanx.

In Macedon, the heavily armed infantry of the phalanx were known as the Foot Companions (*pezhetairoi*), as a kind of counterpoise to the title of the aristocratic cavalrymen, who were called the Companions (*hetairoi*). By such honorific titles group solidarity, always an important element in the creation of a successful fighting force, was affirmed.

The Macedonian Companion infantrymen (*pezhetairoi*) formed the nucleus of the army with which Alexander conquered the Persian empire. The infantryman depicted here wears a Thracian-style helmet, a cuirass, and greaves. Although Macedonian infantrymen carried swords for close-quarter combat, their primary offensive weapon was the famous *sarissa*, a sixteen-foot-long pike.

During the fourth century, the infantrymen in the front ranks of the Macedonian phalanx usually were equipped with some kind of metal helmet, either of the *pilos* (conical) or of the Thracian type; the rear ranks wore the *kausia*, a broad-brimmed hat made of straw.

The cuirasses (breastplates) of the hoplites were made of layers of linen. Attached to the linen cuirass was a kind of pleated skirt, which protected the lower abdomen and groin. Sheathed in a waistband attached to the cuirass or the skirt, Macedonian infantrymen carried a short, cutting sword for close combat.

Each infantryman was equipped with a slightly concave, circular bronze shield, the *aspis*, with a diameter of about two feet; it was held by an elbow grip, combined with a baldric (strap) slung over the left shoulder. The shield was rimless, to allow the frontline troops to grip the new weapon Philip provided for them, the *sarissa*.

The *sarissa* was a long, heavy pike that required two hands to wield. At a length of sixteen feet or longer, it was at least twice as long as the seven-foot spear that traditional Greek hoplites held with one hand. A pike of such length weighed around fourteen pounds; wielding it effectively with two hands, in formation, required training and a high level of physical fitness. The infantry *sarissa* could not be used effectively by amateur, citizen soldiers; its introduction presumed a high degree of professionalization.

The *sarissa* also had implications for the organization of the tactical unit of the Macedonian phalanx; it was so long that those carried by the first five ranks or rows of infantrymen projected out in front of the infantry line, as the second century B.C.E. Greek historian Polybius observed.

It was the job of the infantrymen in the ranks behind the fifth row to hold their pikes either at an angle over the men in front of them or directly up in the air. The hoplites in these back ranks used their pikes to deflect missiles shot at them and applied their weight to the forward charge of the men in front.

Philip not only equipped the Macedonian hoplite infantrymen with what proved to be a devastatingly effective new weapon but also, and most importantly, reorganized the Macedonian infantry as a unit.

In 334 B.C.E., there were around 24,000 Macedonian Foot Companions, brigaded into tactical units of at least 1,500 men, each called a *taxis*.

At least three (and probably all) of the six Macedonian infantry brigades that went with Alexander to Asia were recruited on a regional basis within Macedonia. Brigading the infantrymen on the basis of local recruitment must also have contributed to unit loyalty, as it was later to do in the locally mustered units of the Scottish regiments of the British army.

In addition to the brigades of the Foot Companions, Philip (and Alexander subsequently) also made use of another corps of heavy infantry, known as the *hypaspistai*, or Shield Bearers. The *hypaspistai* developed out of the old infantry bodyguard of the Macedonian kings; its elite unit, the *agema*, protected the kings when they fought on foot. Under Philip, the *hypaspistai* were organized into three *chiliarchies*, in principle, groups of 1,000 infantrymen. They were used in coordination with the Foot Companions against hoplite phalanxes and also against lightly armed enemies. The *hypaspistai* were highly skilled and flexible infantry warriors. Philip used not only the two types of Macedonian heavy infantry but also large contingents of allied Greek infantry, and of Thracians, Triballians, and Illyrians.

Philip (and then Alexander) also made frequent and effective use of light infantry. One group of javelin men known from Alexander's reign was commanded by an officer named Balacrus and may have consisted of Macedonians. There were lightly armed Thracian and Agrianian *taxeis* of javelin men, as well; the Agrianians were recruited from the upper Strymon River area and were used in actions calling for "rapid movement on difficult terrain." Often associated with the Agrianians were archers from Macedon or Crete, eventually organized into chiliarchies.

In traditional Greek phalanxes, the line had been eight ranks deep; under Philip (and later Alexander) that increased to sixteen or even, at times, thirty-two ranks, which gave the Macedonian infantry additional weight as it crashed into the lines of its enemies. The Macedonian infantrymen were positioned more or less closely together, depending upon tactical requirements. The "locked shields" (*synaspismos*) formation, for instance, with the infantrymen no more than a foot apart, was used to meet attacks or to make a decisive offensive thrust. Alexander would use it at the battle of the Hydaspes River to break the Indian king Porus' otherwise impenetrable defensive screen of elephants.

Discipline was vital to the success of the Macedonian infantry. Above all, it was crucial for each infantryman to remain in his position in line and not to lose contact with the men to his left and right. Any break in the line could have disastrous results for the entire formation, for once a line was broken, it was difficult for infantrymen to stay in order and fight as a tactical unit.

Overall, if Greek hoplite warfare of the fourth century typically resembled a rugby scrum much more closely than it did modern infantry combat, the reforms Philip made to the Macedonian infantry gave it a huge advantage over the units of other armies. Those who dared to do battle with Philip's new infantry were confronted by what must have looked like a giant porcupine—with sixteen-foot quills. Moreover, even if Philip's new infantry could not force a break in the enemy line, they could await a devastating attack by their cavalry. Although Macedon always had produced excellent riders and cavalrymen, here too Philip made dramatic improvements.

THE MACEDONIAN AND ALLIED CAVALRY

Fourth-century Greek cavalry warfare is hard to compare with the mounted warfare of modern or early modern times. First, the horses the Greeks or Macedonians rode were smaller (around 52 to 55 inches at the withers) than modern mounts. Second, ancient riders never benefited from the use of full modern saddles or stirrups, which did not become common until the Middle Ages; instead, they used harsh bridles or bits to control their horses. So ancient cavalrymen had to rely on their own riding skills to control their mounts in combat. Men who grew up in lands more suited to the breeding of horses (such as Alexander in Macedon, which had large, fertile plains) would have had an enormous advantage over those who had not grown up riding every day.

Under Philip II the traditional Macedonian cavalry, which always had been drawn from among the wealthy landowners of Macedonia, was expanded and reorganized into a devastating fighting force of about 3,300 riders—the *hetairoi*, or Companions, mentioned above. They were divided into eight squadrons (called *ilai*), one of which, the Royal Squadron (*ile*), provided the bodyguard of the king himself when he fought on horseback. Apart from the 300 members of the Royal Squadron,

This line drawing of a member of the Macedonian Companion cavalry (*hetairoi*) shows the rider armed with a sword and a lance, and protected by a bronze corselet and greaves. It is most important to note that he rides without the benefit of a saddle or stirrups, which were not widely used until the Middle Ages. Rather, Alexander's cavalry troops controlled their mounts by means of bits or bridles. Fighting effectively required superior riding skills.

who were courtiers of the king, the rest of the *hetairoi* were recruited regionally.

The *hetairoi* were armed with a nine-foot lance made out of tough cornel wood. The lance was tipped with a leaf-shaped blade, with a larger blade at its back end, and was held by a strap attached at its central, balance point. It could be thrown or used as a devastating thrusting weapon. *Hetairoi* also usually carried a reserve of javelins and perhaps a small shield, but not much in the way of body armor. Unlike the frontline infantry, the cavalrymen wore the Macedonian hat, the *kausia*. What protected them was speed and maneuverability.

The Greek city-states typically deployed their cavalry on the flanks of their hoplite infantries and used them to envelop an enemy flank or cover a retreat. Philip had his *hetairoi* trained to fight in a wedge formation (shaped like the Greek letter delta, Δ), with their leader at the front, so that the cavalry could be thrust like a spearhead into the enemy's weak points.

Associated with the Companion cavalry were the mounted advance scouts, the *prodromoi*. Divided into four squadrons of 150, these scouts, recruited from Macedon itself, conducted reconnaissance missions, but also could be detailed to fight in advance of the main cavalry during pitched battles. Lightly armed during reconnaissance missions, on other occasions (unlike the Companion cavalry) the *prodromoi* carried a much shorter, lighter version of the infantry *sarissa*, to be used against other

TYPICAL CAVALRY FORMATIONS

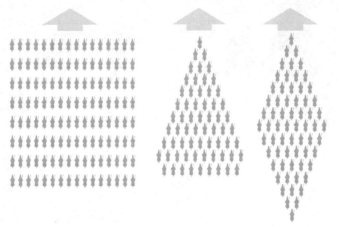

While Greek city-states trained their cavalry to fight in a square formation (*left*) Philip II and Alexander used the squadrons of the Macedonian cavalry as an offensive strike force; for this purpose the delta- or wedge-shaped formation (*center*), which perhaps was based upon Scythian precedents, proved to be most effective. The Thessalian cavalry usually fought in a diamond or rhomboid formation (*right*); because it allowed the Thessalians to turn and fight in any direction quickly, it was ideal for defensive warfare.

more lightly armed cavalry units. Lightly armed scouts from Paeonia and Thrace were deployed alongside them.

The Macedonian army included allied cavalry from Thessaly, commanded by a Macedonian officer. Its numbers were about the same as those of the *hetairoi*, and it usually was stationed on the left wing of the Macedonian line. Its main job was to protect the left flank of the infantry. Divided into *ilai*, the Thessalian cavalry fought in a diamond-shaped formation, which could fend off attacks from any direction and so was especially suited to defensive combat. It would be difficult to say whether they or the *hetairoi* were the best in the world. Other contingents of allied cavalry from central Greece and the Peloponnesus played a much less significant role. Mercenary cavalry played a rather more important role than allied cavalry, and their numbers increased as the Macedonian kings gained the resources to be able to pay them.

Overall, what Philip created was a fearsome military force, one trained and equipped to fight in any tactical situation throughout the year in any season on any terrain. During the 350s and 340s, at the head of his reorganized army, Philip was able to defeat first the Phocians, then the Thessalians, the traditional rival of the Macedonians (whose wonderful cavalry thereafter served with the Macedonians), and the Phocians yet again in 346, to end the (third) so-called Sacred War. These victories brought Philip into the middle of the second ring of Macedon's rivals, the city-states of Greece.

THE BATTLE OF CHAERONEA

Within a few years Philip and the key city-state of Athens were at odds over a variety of issues, including Athenian attacks upon Philip's allies in Cardia and his territories in Thrace. During his siege of Byzantium in 340, Philip captured a fleet carrying grain to Athens. Athens, which depended on grain shipped from the wheat-rich lands of the Crimea through Byzantium, had little choice but to fight.

Thus, late in the summer of 338, the Athenians, the Thebans, and their allies gathered on the plain of Chaeronea to confront Philip and his new, professional army. The Greeks fought with great bravery, but were no match for the Macedonian pikemen, who had been trained to a peak of fitness and discipline. At the decisive moment in the battle, Philip's eighteen-year-old son, Alexander, led the charge that broke through the allies' line. More than a thousand Athenians perished, as did the entire "Sacred Band" of Thebes.

The battle was a turning point in history. Philip not only had awakened Macedon; he had put the Greeks into a deep military and political sleep. Though they received their prisoners of war back without ransom, the Athenians were forced into a treaty of friendship and alliance with Macedon. The Thebans lost control of the rich agricultural region of

Ivory portrait head of Alexander III of Macedon from the royal tombs at Vergina. *By permission of the Thessaloniki Museum*

Boeotia, and an oligarchy was imposed on them. Sparta had taken no part in the battle, but had refused to become a Macedonian ally in its aftermath; its territory was therefore invaded. Macedonian garrisons also were installed in Thebes, in the key commercial city of Corinth, in Ambracia, and in other strategic locations. These garrisons were the chains with which Philip shackled the Greeks.

THE GENERAL ALLIANCE AND DECLARATION OF WAR

Philip then imposed a general alliance on the Greeks in the autumn of 338. An assembly of representatives was established by the spring of 337. The decisions taken by the assembly were sent out not for debate, but for implementation.

In the same year, the new allies voted for an offensive and defensive alliance binding them to Macedon for all time. All then turned to the question of whether to declare war on Persia. Before the vote, Philip made it known that he wanted to go to war on behalf of the Greeks to punish the Persians for the destruction of the temples during the invasion of 480.

Unsurprisingly, the allies voted for war and elected Philip to lead the joint forces. By the spring of 336 an advance force commanded by three Macedonian officers, including Philip's best general, Parmenio, had reached Asia Minor to commence preliminary operations. Born around 400, Parmenio was already an important presence at the royal court in Pella when Philip became regent. Later Philip was quoted as remarking that whereas the Athenians elected ten generals every year, in many years he himself had only ever found one, Parmenio.

Philip himself was to follow Parmenio with the main force in the autumn of the same year. Whether Philip planned to take Alexander with him to Asia is debatable. Indeed, as we shall see shortly, given what had transpired between father and son in the years leading up to Chaeronea, Alexander's presence at that decisive battle would have seemed unlikely only a few years earlier.

CHAPTER 4

The Assassination of
Philip II

DEATH AT SUNRISE

Greece had never quite seen the likes of Philip II of Macedon. Tough, capable, cunning, battle-scarred and battle-hardened, Philip had raised Macedon by his own arms from the brink of dissolution to preeminence in Greece in just over twenty years. Passed off as a charming if ruthless opportunist by pretentious Athenian orators, Philip in fact could out-fight, out-drink, and out-think any man or woman from Epirus to the Bosphorus. Philip was the ideal Machiavellian prince—except, perhaps, for one fatal misconception about human nature. Philip believed that every man's honor had a price and that once that price had been met, all accounts were settled. This error cost him his life.

In the dewy cool of an October morning in 336, before the sun had risen, Philip entered a theater packed with guests who had come to celebrate the wedding of his daughter to King Alexander of Epirus. As he did, a man whose honor could not be bought stepped out from the shadows of Philip's past and plunged a knife deeply into the king's side, killing him instantly. Seconds later, Philip's guards speared the assassin to death as he tried to make his escape. The stunned spectators were left to wonder: Who was the assassin? Why had he killed Philip? And—the question on everyone's mind—was he part of a wider conspiracy?

Ivory portrait head of Philip II
of Macedon from the royal
tombs at Vergina, c. 350–325
B.C.E. *By permission of the
Thessaloniki Museum*

The story of Philip's murder is a tawdry affair. The consensus among
the ancient writers was that there had indeed been a wider plot.
Whether it included Olympias and her son was hotly disputed, and remains so to this day. What is certain is that Philip's death was a defeat for
those who wanted his successor to be a "legitimate" Macedonian. In the
aftermath of the assassination, powerful figures who had supported such
a succession were systematically eliminated. Just as it seemed that Alexander had been effectively pushed aside, Philip's murder reversed his
fortunes. Rarely in history has a father's death presented a son with a
larger or more timely opportunity.

A LEGITIMATE HEIR

In 337 Philip had determined to marry again, to wife number eight.
Most of Philip's previous marriages had been made to secure alliances
with Macedon's neighbors. But this time Philip had fallen in love, with a
young Macedonian woman named Kleopatra, the niece of Attalus, a nobleman and officer in the Macedonian army. Such a marriage, which
might someday produce another potential heir to the throne, was bound
to create trouble between Philip and Olympias—who unquestionably
wanted Alexander to succeed his father—as well as between Philip and
Alexander. The brawling broke out even before the marriage was consummated.

At the wedding banquet, after drinking too much, Attalus called
upon the Macedonians to pray "that the union of Philip and Kleopatra

might bring forth a legitimate heir to the throne." This was a reference, not to Alexander's illegitimacy (for Philip had married Olympias) but to his ethnicity. Olympias was a Molossian princess, so her son was only half Macedonian—an important fact in Alexander's world, and one never sufficiently emphasized in ancient or modern biographies of Alexander. Attalus proposed a toast to an heir who would be fully Macedonian, and, not coincidentally, a relation of his.

Alexander, however, interpreted Attalus' toast as an insult to his legitimacy. "Wretch, do you take me for a bastard, then?" he shouted, and hurled his wine cup at Attalus.

Incensed, Philip himself then drew his sword and would have killed his own son right there and then, but was so drunk and enraged that he tripped and fell. Alexander scoffed: "Look, men, here is the man who was getting ready to cross from Europe to Asia, and who cannot even cross from one table to another without falling down."

After this scandalous incident, Olympias upbraided Philip for attempting to kill Alexander. Soon Philip and Olympias were irreconcilably alienated. Predictably siding with his mother, Alexander took Olympias away to her homeland in Epirus; he himself left for Illyria.

There matters stood for a time, until Philip came to his senses. Persuaded by his friend Demaratus of Corinth, he initiated a reconciliation with the son who was by far his most promising offspring. But more trouble between father and son soon followed. Philip hoped to cement an alliance with one Pixodarus, the Persian governor of Caria, a strategically important mountainous area along the southwestern coast of Asia Minor that eventually would be vital to his plans for the conquest of Asia. So Philip offered Philip Arrhidaeus (Alexander's mentally impaired half brother) as a husband for the satrap's eldest daughter. Learning of the proposal, Olympias and her friends reported to Alexander that Philip was planning to replace him as heir (with his brother). Alexander then sent a friend, the tragic actor Thettalus, to Pixodarus to offer himself (Alexander) as the bridegroom instead.

When Philip found out about this, he reproached Alexander for behaving so ignobly as to wish to marry the daughter of a "mere Carian," the slave of a barbarian (the king of Persia). He then took his anger out on Thettalus, whom he had put in chains, and on Alexander's closest friends, Harpalus, Nearchus, Erygius, and Ptolemy. All were exiled.

At this high cost, Alexander's ploy succeeded. Seeing the divisions within the Macedonian royal house, Pixodarus prudently withdrew the offer of his daughter's hand. Philip's diplomacy was scuttled.

Behind the stories of the breach between father and son, which Plutarch insists Olympias widened, lay the undeniable fact that Alexander was only half Macedonian. His claim to the throne, whatever signs of precocious brilliance he had displayed, always would be subject to dispute. Indeed, Philip's next moves could only have increased Alexander's sense of isolation.

By the spring of 336, Philip had sent the expeditionary force commanded by Attalus, his new wife's uncle, and by Parmenio across the Hellespont, honoring them with the order to liberate the Greek cities of Asia Minor, and thus to begin punitive operations against the Persians. Philip planned to lead the main invasion force over to Asia the next year, but, wanting to make certain of divine approval, he stayed behind to inquire of the Pythia (the priestess of Apollo at Delphi) whether he would conquer the king of the Persians. The Pythia gave the following answer:

"Wreathed in the bull. All is done. There is also one who will smite him."

Philip understood this response as ambiguous, but finally decided to take it in a sense favorable to himself: namely, that the Persian king would be slaughtered like a sacrificial victim. Like many a Greek king before him, Philip had fatally misinterpreted the utterance of the god.

In the summer of 336, on the very eve of his departure for Asia with the main expeditionary force, Philip arranged a marriage between Olympias' and his own daughter Kleopatra, and Alexander, king of Epirus (Olympias' brother and thus the bride's uncle). Olympias already had been replaced in Philip's bed by Attalus' niece Kleopatra. Now, her brother Alexander—Philip's new son-in-law—would replace her as Philip's political link to Epirus. Her brother's wedding was Olympias' political funeral.

THE WEDDING OF KLEOPATRA AND
ALEXANDER OF EPIRUS

Philip had invited his personal guest-friends from throughout the Greek world to the wedding of his daughter in Aegae and had ordered the members of his court to bring as many of their acquaintances from abroad as they could. He planned brilliant musical contests and lavish banquets, too, determined as he was to show himself an amiable man and worthy of the honors conferred on him when he was appointed commander of the war against Persia.

From all directions, crowds flocked to the festival in Aegae. Notable persons and representatives of important cities such as Athens came bearing golden crowns to honor Philip. When the herald announced the Athenian award, he declared that if anyone plotted against Philip and fled to Athens for refuge he would be delivered up for trial.

At the state banquet, the actor Neoptolemus sang an ode appropriate to Philip's imminent crossing to Asia. The song mocked the wealth of the Persian king, great and famous as it was, suggesting that fortune could someday overturn it. Addressing his song directly to Darius, Neoptolemus intoned:

> *Your thoughts reach higher than the air:*
> *You dream of wide fields' cultivation.*
> *The homes you plan surpass the homes*
> *That men have known, but you do err,*
> *Guiding your life from afar.*
> *But one there is who'll catch the swift,*
> *Who goes a way obscured in gloom,*
> *And suddenly, unseen, overtakes*
> *And robs us of our distant hopes—*
> *Death, mortals' source of many woes.*

Finally the drinking was over; the start of the games was set for the following day. While it was still dark, the spectators hastened into the small theater at Aegae for the opening ceremonies. The theater was set below the royal palace, and from their seats the guests had a beautiful view of the broad fields of Lower Macedon. As the sun rose, the parade formed. In the procession Philip included statues of the twelve gods of Olympus, along with a thirteenth—of himself.

Philip appeared near the entryway to the orchestra, dressed in a white cloak. Once the theater was full, his bodyguard stood away from him by his order and followed only at a distance: the leader of the pan-Hellenic alliance wanted to show publicly that he was protected by the goodwill of all the Greeks and had no need of a guard of spearmen. Philip walked between his son Alexander III (the Great) and his new son-in-law, Alexander of Epirus.

Just as Philip was directing his attendant friends to precede him into the theater, one of the guards, a certain Pausanias from Orestis, seeing the king alone, darted forward and pierced him through the ribs with a Celtic dagger. Philip died on the spot.

Pausanias ran for the gates and the horses that had been prepared for his flight. One group of bodyguards hurried to the body of the king, while three others, Leonnatus, Perdiccas, and Attalus, pursued the assassin. As Pausanias leaped for his horse, his boot caught on a vine, and he fell. His pursuers slew him with their javelins. Alexander III, mean-

Remains of the theater at Aegae, in which Philip II of Macedon was assassinated by the bodyguard Pausanias in October 336 B.C.E. *Author's collection*

while, was rushed into the safety of the royal palace by another Alexander, the son of a man named Aeropus, from the Upper Macedonian canton of Lyncestis.

PAUSANIAS THE ASSASSIN

Once the assassin's identity was revealed, his motive was soon surmised. At one time, Pausanias had been beloved of Philip, because of his beauty. But Philip then had become enamored of another Pausanias. Pausanias the guard then insulted his replacement, calling him a hermaphrodite, quick "to accept the amorous advances of anyone."

Unable to endure such insults, the second Pausanias, having confided to his friend Attalus what he proposed to do, determined to bring about his own death in a spectacular fashion. A few days later, when Philip was fighting a battle against Pleurias, king of the Illyrians, Pausanias stepped in front of Philip and received the fatal blows meant for him.

The dead Pausanias' friend Attalus, though, was the uncle of Philip's Macedonian wife Kleopatra (and the general later sent to Asia with the Macedonian advance force). Attalus invited the first Pausanias, the guard, to dinner. When his guest was thoroughly drunk, Attalus handed him over to his muleteers to abuse—that is, to be gang-raped. Attalus thus avenged his friend.

Pausanias charged Attalus before Philip; but, needing Attalus' services, Philip did not punish him. Instead he gave Pausanias presents and advanced him in honor among the guards. Pausanias accepted the gifts and the promotion but, encouraged by a sophist named Hermocrates, he apparently still yearned to revenge himself both on the one who had done him wrong and also on the one who had not avenged him.

At first glance, the story of Pausanias' dishonor and ultimate revenge seems far-fetched. The gang rape took place in 344, eight years before Pausanias assassinated Philip. If Pausanias was nursing a grudge, he certainly nursed it for a very long time.

However, there is also the testimony of Aristotle to consider. In his *Politics* Aristotle cites Pausanias' attack on Philip as an example of revenge for hubris—meaning, in this case, insolence, violence, or rape. While it is not certain that Aristotle witnessed Philip's murder, he certainly knew

Philip, Alexander, and the Macedonian court exceptionally well. Aristotle, who was in a position to know, believed that a gang rape, even one that had taken place eight years before, was motivation enough for Pausanias. But if thinking men believed that Pausanias' motive was plausible, they also believed in a wider conspiracy. Who were the supposed conspirators?

One was the very man (Alexander of Lyncestis) who had led Alexander into the palace after the assassination. He was the brother of two other men (Heromenes and Arrabaeus), "both of whom had a part in the murder of Philip" and who, with the three sons of Pausanias, were executed at the tumulus of Philip. (It was standard Macedonian practice to execute the close male relatives of those who had plotted against the king.) Perhaps because he was the first to hail Alexander as king, Alexander of Lyncestis escaped his brothers' fate. But later, when Alexander was in Asia Minor, he received a report that the surviving Lyncestian brother was plotting against him, and the brother was placed under arrest.

At least one other person was considered culpable in some way. A tantalizing fragment of a papyrus from Oxyrhynchus, in Egypt, indicates that someone, possibly a soothsayer (*mantis*), was crucified following the assassination. The soothsayer may have been crucified for pronouncing it safe for Philip to enter the theater in Aegae on that fateful October morning. But the papyrus text is unfortunately too fragmentary to allow us to understand clearly why the soothsayer was executed.

Sparse and vague though the evidence is, it does make clear that the Macedonians believed that there had been a wider conspiracy. We have no explicit information about what the conspirators' motives were thought to be. It is at least possible, though, that the Lyncestian brothers were planning a coup d'état, either on their own behalf or in the interests of the Persians.

THE PERSIAN THEORY

Later, at any rate, in a letter to Darius after the battle of Issos in 333, Alexander accused the Persian king of organizing the murder of his father. Philip, Alexander claimed, was murdered "by assassins whom, as you openly boasted in your letters, you yourselves had hired to commit the crime."

Although scholars usually have dismissed Alexander's letter as propaganda, the accusation is not intrinsically implausible, especially since, by the spring of 336, the Persians were already feeling the military and political effects of the Macedonian expeditionary force under Parmenio and Attalus. Darius had very good reasons for wanting Philip II dead. But no independent evidence supports Alexander's allegation.

OLYMPIAS AND ALEXANDER?

Others suspected that the conspiracy had been hatched much closer to home. Plutarch reports that Olympias was chiefly blamed, because she encouraged Pausanias and incited him to his revenge. It also was implied that Alexander knew of this incitement or shared in it: when Pausanias met him and complained about the injustice he had suffered, Alexander quoted the lines from Euripides' *Medea* in which Medea threatened "the giver of the bride, the bride, and the bridegroom"—Creon, Creusa, and Jason, that is. Plutarch's classical readers would have understood what Alexander was trying to suggest: that Pausanias should follow Medea's example.

The historian Justin supports and expands upon the case against Olympias and Alexander. Olympias was grieved at her divorce and at Kleopatra, who was preferred to her, more deeply than Pausanias was at his disgrace. Alexander also feared that his brother, supported by his stepmother, had designs on the kingship; hence the quarrel at Philip's wedding banquet.

Furthermore, Justin alleges, Olympias had pressed her brother Alexander, the king of Epirus, to go to war against Philip; she would have succeeded had not Philip married his daughter to him and (thereby) gained control of his son-in-law. It was Olympias, too, who had the horses prepared in advance for the fleeing assassin, Justin claims, and when she hastened to the funeral under the pretext of paying her last respects, she placed a golden crown on the head of the crucified Pausanias. A few days later, she cremated the murderer's body and made a sepulchral mound for him, which she took care of every year. And there was more: Olympias forced Philip's young Macedonian widow to hang herself, but not before killing Kleopatra's daughter at her mother's breast. The dagger with which the king had been stabbed she consecrated to Apollo under the name Myrtales, the name she herself had borne in youth. All these things were done so openly, Justin says, that Olympias seemed to fear being proven innocent.

Independent of Justin's bald assertions, however, there is no proof whatsoever that Olympias either incited Pausanias or provided logistical help for the assassination. That Pausanias was killed as he fled toward "horses" (plural, in the Greek text of Diodorus) does suggest either a co-conspirator or more likely a change of mounts; minimally, "horses" proves that Pausanias planned to flee; he did not intend Philip's murder to be a suicide mission.

But Justin offers no proof that it was Olympias who arranged for the horses to be waiting, and no other source corroborates this assertion. Nor can any of Olympias' actions after Philip's death be used to convict her of the crime. She had every reason to celebrate Philip's death; but her joy, however unseemly, cannot be used as evidence of guilt.

Much the same applies to Alexander; indeed, it is implausible that he knew of the plot. Alexander would have been well aware that he and his mother would be suspects, given what had occurred among father, mother, and son in the years before Philip's death. Had credible evidence existed that Alexander was involved, surely he would have shared the fate of the Lyncestian brothers. Although he (and others) greatly benefited from Philip's death, Alexander has, by the vast majority of scholars, been judged not guilty.

CUI BONO?

The army at Aegae proclaimed Alexander king the day after Philip's death. As so often in Macedonian history, the transfer of power led to further bloodshed and a new political order. Olympias, as we have seen, had the pleasure of supervising the deaths of Kleopatra and her infant. Attalus was assassinated on the instructions of Alexander; a single toast had cost him his life. Parmenio, placed in the position of having to choose between protecting his own son-in-law and fellow commander in Asia (Attalus) or risking his own life by opposing Alexander's assassins, chose life. Years later, he perished in circumstances eerily similar to those in which Attalus had died. Amyntas, the rightful heir to the throne, promptly disappeared, never to be heard from again. With the help of his noble patron Antipater, one of Macedon's most experienced soldiers, Alexander emerged in October 336 as the sole descendant of the Argead kings mentally and physically capable of leading the alliance against the Persians.

Philip's assassination had left Alexander in a position to show the world something great and spectacular, just as he had told the other boys he would. Now, as ruler, Alexander immediately sent for the close friends whom Philip had exiled after the Pixodarus fiasco: Ptolemy, son of Lagos, from Eordaia in Macedonia; Harpalus, the son of Machatas, possibly from Elimiotis in Macedonia; Erigyius, son of Larichos, a Mytilenaian by birth; Laomedon, son of Larichos, from Mytilene; and Nearchus, son of Androtimos, from Crete. Subsequently, Alexander advanced them to some of the highest positions in the Macedonian army and administration. What bound these men together was not Alexander's devotion to a multi-ethnic ruling class, of course, but their loyalty to Alexander. Nevertheless, Alexander's inner circle always included men who were not purely Macedonians. Eventually Alexander's inclusion of "barbarians" into that circle would lead him into further conflicts with Attalus' ideological heirs.

ALEXANDER'S ACCESSION AND THE DESTRUCTION OF THEBES

In Athens, the news of Philip's assassination was greeted with public rejoicing. Elsewhere, the Aetolians recalled those who had been exiled because of Philip. The Ambraciots and the Thebans expelled Philip's garrisons. In the Peloponnese, the Argives, the Eleians, and the Spartans "moved to recover their independence." As for the new king of Macedon, now twenty years old, he was not so much underestimated as ignored.

Alexander's first response to the situation was diplomatic. He won over the Thessalians, then the Amphictyons, and the Ambraciots with reminders of ancient kinship and with flattery. The Athenians prepared for war but also sent envoys, asking Alexander's forgiveness for their "tardy recognition of his leadership."

Alexander then called Greek envoys and delegates to another meeting in Corinth, where he persuaded them to declare him chief general of Greece and to join in an expedition against Persia. Alexander thus officially took over the leadership of the pan-Hellenic campaign of revenge that his father had planned.

While he was in Corinth, Alexander also reportedly met the philosopher Diogenes of Sinope. Diogenes was famous among the Greeks for living in accordance with the supposedly natural life of primitive man or even animals. Diogenes' "natural" lifestyle entailed dressing in a simple cloak, begging for food, and urinating in public. It was from such doglike behavior that his followers, who even copulated in public, acquired the name "Cynics," after the Greek word for dog (*kuon*).

Most Greeks were scandalized by Diogenes; Alexander was curious, especially because, while many philosophers and politicians came to congratulate him on becoming head of the pan-Hellenic alliance, Diogenes remained aloof. So Alexander decided to pay a visit to the "dog" philosopher.

Alexander and a group of his friends found Diogenes in a suburb of Corinth, lying out in the open, sunning himself. Hovering over the philosopher, Alexander asked if Diogenes wanted anything. The philosopher asked Alexander only if he could stand a little out of the sun. The king was reported to have said to his friends who were mocking Diogenes, "If I were not Alexander, I would be Diogenes."

Some have portrayed Alexander's response to Diogenes as an indication of Alexander's noble sense of perspective: while he was King of Macedon and now leader of the pan-Hellenic alliance, the student of Greece's most famous philosopher understood that a life of doglike simplicity was preferable to the complicated and dangerous existence of a great warrior king. If the meeting and the famous exchange did take place, however, it is more likely that it reveals Alexander's admiration for the dog who did not follow the pack, regardless of convention. In Diogenes, one alpha dog recognized another.

Whatever the significance of Alexander's statement, even as Alexander was obliging Diogenes, the ever-restive Triballi and the Illyrians in the north had risen up in rebellion, and the king had to leave Corinth soon to settle affairs in Thrace.

While Alexander was doing so, the Thebans revolted, having been persuaded to rebel by returned exiles who claimed that Alexander had died in Illyria. But within thirteen days, with what proved to be characteristic speed, he and the Macedonian army had marched down from the north 250 miles into Boeotia itself. Even so, the organizers of the revolt continued to maintain that Alexander was dead. Some other Alexander must have arrived in Boeotia. But, as the Turkish proverb goes, nothing is ever certain, especially when it is certain: the real Alexander appeared suddenly at the walls of Thebes, like some malevolent demon in a recurring nightmare. The Thebans should have learned their lesson at Chaeronea.

Alexander surrounded the city but did not initiate action; he only requested the surrender of those who had incited the revolt, and he promised their pardon in return. The reply was a spectacularly ill-judged insult: the Thebans counterdemanded that Alexander surrender Philotas and Antipater. Philotas was the son of Parmenio, Macedon's greatest general, and Antipater (as we have seen) was Alexander's chief supporter and patron within the old guard of Macedonian nobles. Alexander was as likely to hand them over as the Spartans were to become pacifists, which the Thebans well knew.

Thus, before Alexander even gave the order, the Macedonians, led by Perdiccas, later one of Alexander's most trusted officers, stormed into the city, killing more than 6,000 Thebans. More than 30,000 were captured; the rest were sold into public slavery. Only priests and priestesses, a few guest-friends of Macedon, the descendants of the poet Pindar (whose poetry Alexander admired), and those who opposed the revolt were spared. In the bloody annals of Greek history, rarely had a Greek city and its population been annihilated with such savage precision.

Alexander extended his sense of moral selectivity to one Theban family. During the battle, a Thracian leader fighting on the Macedonian side had raped a Theban noblewoman named Timokleia. The Thracian then demanded to know whether she had any gold or silver hidden. Timokleia directed him to a well in her garden and, when he peered down the shaft, she pushed him into the well and stoned him to death. Enraged, the Thracians brought her before Alexander.

Timokleia proceeded to inform the king that she was the sister of Theagenes, who had commanded the Theban army against Philip at

Chaeronea and who had fallen fighting for the liberty of Greece. Filled with admiration at Timokleia's defiance, Alexander immediately gave orders that she and her children should be freed and allowed to leave Thebes.

As for that city, in accordance with a decree of the pan-Hellenic council, Alexander then razed it, except for the house of Pindar. Thebes' terrible fate was intended as a warning to others who might contemplate rebellion while Alexander was away in Asia.

CHAPTER 5

The Spear-Won
Prize of Asia

SACRIFICES AND MUSTERING OF THE ARMY

Returning to Macedon in the spring of 334, Alexander sacrificed to the gods at Dium and held nine days of dramatic contests in honor of Zeus and the Muses. Before and after every important event of the subsequent campaigns, Alexander would make similar sacrifices and hold celebratory games. Perhaps some intellectuals of the time questioned the very existence of the Greek gods and goddesses; Alexander did not share such doubts.

After the games were completed Alexander departed Macedon, leaving Antipater with 12,000 infantrymen and 1,500 cavalry, to keep the peace among the Greeks. Alexander and his army advanced over 300 miles from Macedon to the city of Sestos in twenty days. Sestos, on the European side of the Hellespont, had been selected as the army's departure point to Asia. Diodorus reports most reliably that the invasion force totaled 32,000 foot soldiers and approximately 5,100 cavalry. Of the infantrymen, 9,000 were Macedonian *pezhetairoi* and 3,000 were crack *hypaspistai*. In addition, several thousand Macedonians were already in Asia with the advance force. There was also a relatively small fleet: 160 warships, and a flotilla of cargo vessels, to provide logistical support.

This force certainly was one of the largest Greek or Macedonian armies ever assembled for an invasion. From Philip, Alexander had inherited something far more valuable than a palace full of gold: the best-equipped, best-trained, and best-led army in Greek history. But across the Bosphorus, from Sardis to Samarkand, the armies of all Asia were slowly gathering, preparing to crush the invader. They drank rivers dry; and their campfires turned night into day. Against such odds, what seer would have predicted victory for the Macedonians?

PROTESILAUS AND TROY

While the main Macedonian army was crossing the Hellespont from Sestos to Abydos on the Asiatic coast, Alexander traveled farther south, to Elaeus. It was from this small city on the European side of the Bosphorus that the Achaeans had departed for Troy. Elaeus also was the site of the tomb of the unfortunate Protesilaus. In the famous "catalogue of ships" in book 2 of the *Iliad*, Homer tells us that "plunging ahead from his long ship to be first ashore at Troy of all Akhaians, he had been brought down first by a Dardan spear."

Like Athena's temple on the Acropolis in Athens, Protesilaus' tomb apparently had been plundered by the Persians in 480. Alexander sacrificed at the tomb to ensure better luck for himself than Protesilaus had experienced, we are told. But by such acts Alexander also linked his war against the Persians symbolically to the Trojan War and to the Persians' invasion of Greece in 480. More actions linking the present to the past soon followed.

From Elaeus, Alexander sailed across the Hellespont to the so-called Achaean harbor, taking the helm of the flagship. In the middle of the crossing he sacrificed a bull to Poseidon and poured a libation into the sea to propitiate the Nereids. Alexander doubtlessly meant these pious acts to be seen in contrast to an infamous Persian deed. Xerxes had built a bridge across the Hellespont in 480 on his way to invade Greece, but a storm had destroyed it. Xerxes punished the waters of the storm with 300 lashes and cast into them a pair of fetters.

Before Alexander leaped ashore onto Asian soil, he threw a spear from his ship, fixing it in the ground. The point of this anticipatory act was to claim Asia as a spear-won prize, awarded by the gods. Alexander thus made clear that he intended to become master of Asia by divine will. Throughout the campaigns in Asia Alexander sought, and believed he had received, the sanction of the gods.

Altars also were built and dedicated to Zeus (of Safe Landings), Athena, and Herakles on the spots from which Alexander left Europe and landed in Asia. His crossing to Asia thus was punctuated by a whole series of ceremonies intended to gain the favor of the deities he held most dear: Zeus, whose son he claimed to be; Athena, goddess of wisdom and warfare, whose temple the Persians had destroyed in 480; and Herakles, a kinsman of Alexander who became first a hero and then a god by virtue of his great deeds.

Once ashore, Alexander traveled inland to Ilium (Troy) where Achilles' wrath once had "put pains thousandfold upon the Achaeans, / hurled in their multitudes to Hades' house strong souls / of heroes."

At that site, so imbued with historical and literary resonance for all Greeks, Alexander sacrificed to Athena and poured libations to the heroes. He anointed with oil the column that marked the grave of Achilles, and, in keeping with custom, he and his companions then raced naked past the column and crowned Achilles' grave with garlands. Alexander's friend Hephaestion laid a wreath on the tomb of Patroklos.

Born perhaps in the same year as Alexander, Hephaestion, the son of Amyntor from Pella, was brought up with Alexander and had served as one of Philip's royal pages. Although he was not among those exiled after the Pixodarus affair, he and Alexander were close by the time Alexander reached Asia. Taller than the king and apparently handsome, through Alexander's favor Hephaestion eventually advanced to the highest positions in the empire. This was despite what many considered his quarrelsome nature, which may have annoyed even Alexander. Later, in India, after Hephaestion had argued with Perdiccas, one of Alexander's ablest officers, Alexander reportedly said that Hephaestion was a madman if he did not know that "without Alexander's favor he would be nothing." Still, Hephaestion was known as "the dearest" of all Alexander's friends: unlike others, who loved the king, he was said to have loved Alexander.

During the same visit to Troy, Alexander took from the temple of Athena some of the arms that, dedicated to the goddess, had remained there since the Trojan War. The *hypaspistai* subsequently carried those arms into battle before the king. Later, when he was severely wounded fighting against an Indian tribe called the Mallians, Alexander would be carried off the battlefield on the very shield he had taken from the temple.

Finally, Alexander made sacrifice to Priam to atone for Neoptolemus' sacrilege in slaying him at the altar of Zeus Herkeios; he prayed that Priam's spirit would not vent its anger upon Neoptolemus' descendants (that is, Alexander himself). On the eve of his first confrontation with the Persians in Asia, Alexander did not want the angry spirit of a Trojan king howling for revenge into the ears of the gods.

Some scholars have considered the visit to Troy a relatively unimportant event in Alexander's life and career. But Alexander's identification with the heroes and events of Greece's heroic past went far beyond the cynical construction of a purely symbolic narrative of deeds, meant to justify the Asian campaign. Alexander had internalized at least some of the values of those ancient heroes, and he acted in accordance with those values, at least up to a point. As we shall see, after Alexander achieved a position unprecedented in Greek history, he began to push beyond the values and behavior patterns of those role models; and it could be argued that it was his willingness to move beyond Homer's epic script that led him into conflict with his contemporaries.

THE PRELUDE TO THE BATTLE OF THE GRANICUS RIVER

While Alexander was at Troy, his crossing was reported to the local Persian commanders, who then assembled in force near Zeleia, a small Greek city about eight miles inland from the mouth of the Aesepus River. These commanders included Arsames; Rheomithres; Petines; Niphates; Spithridates, the Persian satrap (or governor) of the provinces of Lydia and Ionia; and Arsites, the satrap of northern (Hellespontine) Phrygia. Serving under them were about 20,000 cavalry levied from Asia Minor, around 20,000 Greek mercenary infantrymen, and also native levies. The Persian infantry thus would be outnumbered substantially by the battle-tested Macedonians. They did, however, have a substantial cavalry force.

Considering the Persians' quantitative inferiority in infantrymen, Memnon of Rhodes, a clever Greek officer serving under the Persian king, advised the Persian governors and generals to avoid military engagement. Rather, he argued, they should burn all the crops in the fields, trample down and destroy all grass and horse fodder, and gut the towns: dearth would expel Alexander from Asia more quickly and with less risk than military confrontation. Memnon could not have known just what sound advice this was: Alexander had come to Asia with only enough money to supply his troops for thirty days. He had to engage the Persians as soon as possible; if there were any delay, he either would have to find more money or go home.

But the Persian governor of the area, Arsites, would not consent to the destruction of a single house belonging to any of his subjects. Suspicious of Memnon because he was Greek, and perhaps made confident by their victories over Parmenio's advance force in the year just past, the rest of the Persian commanders supported Arsites. They voted to cross swords with the Macedonians.

By the time Alexander's scouts located the Persian army, it had taken up a strong defensive position on the east bank of the Granicus River (modern Kocabas Çay), perhaps near the present-day Turkish town of Dimetoka. The Persian cavalry were drawn up along the river's steep bank, but far enough from the edge so that they could charge down upon the Macedonians after they had crossed the river and attempted to make their way up the eastern banks. Behind the Persian riders, and on higher ground, stood the Greek mercenary infantry.

Alexander and the Macedonians reached the river in the late afternoon. Seeing the natural strength of the Persian position, Parmenio advised Alexander to wait and cross the river at dawn, before the Persians could get into position to meet them.

Alexander rejected Parmenio's advice. He would be ashamed of himself, he commented, if a mere trickle like the Granicus were too much for the Macedonians to cross without further preparation, when he had 'had no difficulty crossing the Hellespont. Considerations of shame apart, Alexander probably could see that his overall numbers were superior;

with this in mind, he immediately dispatched Parmenio to command the left wing of the army, while he himself moved to the right of the Macedonian line.

Alexander then stationed his infantry phalanx between his cavalry forces on the wings. On the Macedonian left wing were the Thessalian, Greek, and Thracian cavalry, commanded by Parmenio. Command on the right had been given to Parmenio's son Philotas, with the Companion cavalry, the archers, and the invaluable Agrianian spearmen. Attached to Philotas' troops were Amyntas, the son of Arrabaeus, with the mounted lancers; the Paeonians; and Socrates' squadron (*ile*) from the city of Apollonia. On the left of these were *hypaspistai* commanded by Parmenio's son Nicanor; next the infantry battalions of Perdiccas, Coenus, Craterus, and Amyntas; and finally the troops under Amyntas' son, Philip. So Parmenio and his family held three crucial leadership positions within the Macedonian army at the Granicus.

The advance position on the Macedonian left wing was held by the Thessalian cavalry under Calas, supported by the allied cavalry and the Thracians. On their right were several infantry battalions.

THE BATTLE OF THE RIVER GRANICUS

Among the Macedonians Alexander was conspicuous by his gleaming armor and the large white plume attached to his helmet's crest. Spotting that plume, the Persians had massed cavalry squadrons opposite it.

For some time the forces on both sides of the river remained still and silence prevailed, as both armies dreaded to precipitate the combat. Characteristically, Alexander then undertook the role of the aggressor. He ordered Amyntas, with the advanced scouts, the Paeonians, and one infantry company, and preceded by Ptolemy, son of Philip, with Socrates' squadron of cavalry, to lead off into the water. The depth of the river in the late spring, when the battle was fought, would perhaps have been around three feet. We can assume that Amyntas and his men entered the river and then tried to make their way up the opposite bank at its easiest points, perhaps along the gravel slopes noticed by modern historians, rather than up the steep banks mentioned by Arrian.

Amyntas' mission was to ford the Granicus, absorb whatever Persian attack came, and thereby give Alexander time to get the rest of his right wing across the river in good order, ready to fight in the traditional Macedonian wedge formation. The initial assault group thus was offered up as a kind of pawn sacrifice in pursuit of a more important tactical goal—that of drawing the Persian left wing down into the riverbed, where it could be attacked effectively. A similar operation took place on the left wing, spearheaded by the Thessalian cavalry.

As expected, Amyntas' assault group was forced back into the river, where hand-to-hand combat ensued. The best of the Persian cavalry, and Memnon, with his sons, inflicted most of the Macedonian casualties to this point. The sacrifice of Amyntas' men allowed the rest of the Companions, who had successfully crossed the river, to counterattack where the Persian commanders were stationed and where the serried ranks of Persian cavalry were thickest.

Mithridates, the son-in-law of the Persian king, led a second Persian charge, this time directed at Alexander himself, who by now was up and out of the riverbed, on the east side of the river. Alexander rode out to meet Mithridates and struck him in the face with his spear. The brothers Rhoesaces and Spithridates then rode after Alexander. Rhoesaces sliced off part of Alexander's helmet with his scimitar, slightly wounding him; Alexander killed him with a spear thrust through his cuirass. Spithridates now raised his scimitar, ready to strike a fatal blow at Alexander from behind. But Cleitus, son of Dropidas, nicknamed the Black, who commanded the elite royal squadron of the Companion cavalry, severed Spithridates' arm at the shoulder with a single blow. The whole course of history might have been different if Cleitus' arm, like Cleopatra's nose, had been a bit shorter.

As more Macedonian squadrons followed Alexander across the river, the Persian cavalry was forced back. No less than eight Persian commanders fell fighting. So much for later Greek claims of Asian cowardice; the Persian commanders at Granicus died bravely, defending what they themselves had conquered and believed was theirs.

After hard fighting, however, the Persian center broke. The Macedonians then wheeled on the Greek mercenary infantry, which had taken little part in the battle so far, owing to their position on the higher

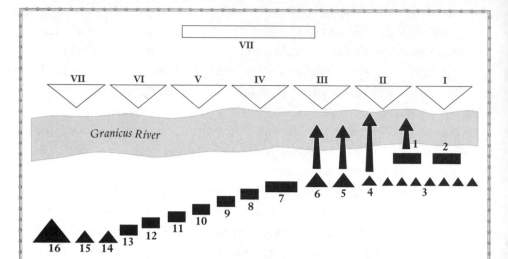

THE BATTLE OF THE GRANICUS RIVER, LATE SPRING, 334 B.C.E.

Opening formations, based upon Arrian, 1.14.1-4

Macedonians

1 Agrianian javelin men
2 Cretan archers
3 Companion cavalry, commanded by Philotas
4 Cavalry squadron (*ile*) of Socrates
5 Paeonian light cavalry
6 Mounted lancers, commanded by Amyntas
7 *Hypaspistai*, commanded by Nicanor
8 Infantry phalanx brigade (*pezhetairoi*) of Perdiccas
9 Infantry phalanx brigade (*pezhetairoi*) of Coenus
10 Infantry phalanx brigade (*pezhetairoi*) of Craterus
11 Infantry phalanx brigade (*pezhetairoi*) of Amyntas
12 Infantry phalanx brigade (*pezhetairoi*) of Philip
13 Infantry phalanx brigade (*pezhetairoi*) of Meleager
14 Thracian cavalry, commanded by Agathon
15 Greek allied cavalry, commanded by Philip
16 Thessalian cavalry, commanded by Calas

Persians

I Cavalry, commanded by Memnon and Arsames
II Paphlagonian cavalry, commanded by Arsites
III Hyrcanian cavalry, commanded by Spithridates
IV Cavalry, commanded by Mithridates and Rhoesaces(?)
V Bactrian cavalry
VI Cavalry, commanded by Rheomithres
VII Median cavalry
VIII Greek mercenary infantry

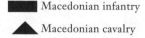

▬ Macedonian infantry

▲ Macedonian cavalry

▭ Persian infantry

△ Persian cavalry

ground at some distance behind the Persian cavalry. Ordering a combined assault by infantry and cavalry, Alexander and the Macedonians proceeded to cut down 90 percent of the mercenaries where they stood, perhaps after they had asked for quarter. Only about 2,000 were taken prisoner.

Some, particularly those who believe the mercenaries asked for quarter, have condemned Alexander for this. But the Greek mercenaries who perished that day were just that: mercenaries in the pay of the Persian king. They had taken the Great King's Darics (Persian coins) and they knew their job was either to kill or die on his behalf. Alexander was under no moral obligation to honor their request, even if they made it, which is not entirely certain.

There were practical reasons, in any case, for Alexander not to spare the mercenaries. At the very beginning of what promised to be a long and dangerous campaign, he had no guarantee that if he let the Greek mercenaries at the Granicus go free, the Macedonians would not end up fighting them another day. Finally, the slaughter on that spring afternoon

Granicus River site in modern Turkey where Alexander fought his first major battle against the Persians in the late spring of 334 B.C.E. *Author's collection*

undoubtedly was intended as a message to other Greeks who might think about fighting for the Persian king: they could expect no mercy.

Yet the massacre was a mistake, albeit one made by a young man in the heat of a battle during which he very nearly lost his life. Those who took Darius' coin thereafter would fight all the harder, knowing they could expect no quarter. A quick learner, Alexander did not repeat this mistake.

On the Macedonian side, casualties were lighter by far. About twenty-five of the Companion cavalry were killed in the first assault led by Amyntas. More than sixty other mounted troops lost their lives, and about thirty infantrymen as well. Bronze statues of the twenty-five *hetairoi* who lost their lives at the Granicus later were executed by Alexander's favorite sculptor, Lysippus, and placed in Dium in Macedonia.

AFTER THE BATTLE

As soon as the carnage was over, Alexander arranged to honor the dead, to reestablish bonds of camaraderie with the survivors, and to send out carefully crafted messages about the progress of the campaign to friends, foes, and various ideological fence-sitters.

By Alexander's order, all the Macedonian dead were buried with their arms and equipment the next day; their parents and children were "granted immunity from local taxes and all forms" of personal service or property dues. The granting of these immunities reveals Alexander's political understanding, if not his basic humanity. In the long history of warfare, far more experienced leaders, and even states, have done far less for the families of those who have given their all. Alexander visited the wounded, too, and listened to them elaborate upon how they had received their wounds. He had a precocious understanding of the need of men who have experienced the trauma of combat to release their emotions by sharing them.

Alexander also gave burial rites to the Persian commanders and the Greek mercenaries who had died. Some scholars have argued that he thus violated the Persians' religious beliefs. But Arrian does not specify exactly how those rites were conducted, and it is hard to see what else

Alexander could have done. He would not have shown more sensitivity to Persian religious traditions if he had left the bodies to rot on the field of battle. Nor could Alexander have given the Persian dead over to their countrymen, for there were none around. Memnon and the Persian survivors of the battle had fled to the friendly city of Miletos.

The surviving Greek prisoners were hauled back to Macedon in chains; there they were condemned to hard labor "for contravening the resolution of the League of Corinth by fighting in a foreign army against their countrymen."

"THE BARBARIANS WHO DWELL IN ASIA"

As an offering to the goddess Athena, Alexander then sent to Athens 300 suits of Persian armor, inscribed "Alexander, son of Philip, and the Greeks, except the Spartans, dedicate these spoils, taken from the barbarians who dwell in Asia."

The armor was dedicated to Athena, the goddess of war, for the favor she had shown Alexander and the Greeks in the battle; the spoils were sent to Athens because the Persians' burning of the Athenian temples in 480 had served as the primary justification for the pan-Hellenic war. It must have given Alexander some pleasure to be able to send the Persian armor to a city that had fought against him and his father and that was, at best, a lukewarm ally.

Because Alexander must have approved the inscription's wording, it is also a key piece of evidence for what he wanted people to believe about the progress of the campaign. Remarkably, Alexander presents himself not as a king, but as the "son of Philip." Why he did so is revealed by the next few words: the subject of the sentence is "Alexander . . . and the Greeks." In this context it was in Alexander's interest to appear not as a king, the son of a king, but as the co-dedicator of the spoils—along with the Greeks, except for the Spartans, who had refused to join the pan-Hellenic crusade unless they led it. Alexander wished to appear as an equal partner in an alliance with the Greeks.

As for the Spartans, their absence rankled because it undermined the official propaganda that this was a pan-Hellenic endeavor. Precisely for that reason, after the first victory of the campaign Alexander singled them out as non-participants in the victory and in the dedication of the spoils.

The second part of the inscription addresses the status of the Persians, "the barbarians who dwell" (not "rule") in Asia. Here Alexander is not even willing to do his enemies the honor of naming them properly; the suits of armor belonged to the "barbarians." While the term "barbarian" in Greek originally only meant someone who spoke a language Greeks could not understand, in 334 Alexander did not use the term as a compliment. It was meant to delegitimize Persian rule of Asia in Greek eyes. Also, given the fact that the Persians still controlled large parts of Asia after the battle at the Granicus, the statement that they *lived* in Asia, rather than *ruled* there, was at best a half-truth.

This confection of propaganda, sarcasm, and contemptuous bravado was intended to be read by Greeks in Greece as an affirmation of the campaign's ideology and as a promise to deliver upon its aims. Those who had chosen not to take part were being left behind.

RISKY VISIONS OF GENIUS

With the battle of the Granicus River, we begin to see why Alexander is considered a military genius. One hallmark of such genius is vision—here, the ability to see a tactical problem and find its solution.

Arriving at the river and seeing the enemy cavalry drawn up in a strong defensive position on the opposite bank, Alexander correctly assessed the tactical problem he faced. He needed to draw the numerically superior Persian riders at least down to the edge of the riverbank, so as to deprive them of what constituted the greatest threat to the Macedonian cavalry: the momentum of their charge.

The tactical solution was the pawn sacrifice of Amyntas' assault group. Once the Persians took that bait, Alexander and the Companions were able to counterattack and fight the Persian cavalry at close quarters, where the superior riding skills and fighting qualities of the Macedonians gave them a decisive advantage.

At the Granicus, Alexander ignored Parmenio's advice because he could see what Parmenio could not, and because he was bold enough to risk what the older man would not. Alexander took that risk because he was not interested in outmaneuvering the Persians. Unlike Parmenio and many others, he had not come to Asia simply to punish the Persians: he had come to rule Asia or die there. Either fate would suit the descendant of Achilles.

CHAPTER 6

The Greek Cities of
Asia Minor

LEARNING THE ARTS OF PEACE

Alexander had demonstrated his military genius and great personal courage. Now, however, the twenty-two-year-old king suddenly had a vast territory in western Asia Minor to rule. This was a different kind of problem from the one he had faced at the Granicus, and it demanded very different skills. Pawn sacrifices and cavalry charges were not likely to be effective. Having barely survived his first battle in Asia, Alexander needed a policy. How he decided to treat his new subjects helps us to understand both his leadership style and his attitude toward the conquered peoples of his empire.

THE MISSION OF ALCIMACHUS

Immediately after the battle at the Granicus, Alexander appointed a certain Calas to the Hellespontine satrapy previously held by Arsites, and gave him orders to maintain taxes at the same level as before. These taxes would have applied both to Greeks and non-Greeks. To the small Greek city of Zeleia he granted pardon, choosing to regard its collaboration with the Persians as a matter of compulsion rather than conviction. But, on the other hand, no special privileges were given to this Greek city, either. Parmenio then was sent to take over Dascylium, the satrapal capital.

Alexander's next objective was the famous city of Sardis, at the foot of a fortified, precipitous hill in the Hermos Valley. This city had been the political center of the Lydian dynasty under Croesus before its capture by Cyrus the Great in 546, and subsequently it had become the capital of the most important northwestern Achaemenid Persian province.

Somewhat surprisingly, Mithrines, the Persian officer in command of the inner fortress of Sardis, and the leading men of the city surrendered the city to Alexander without a fight; Alexander left Pausanias "in charge of the fortress." The king then made Nikias responsible for the organization and payment of the tribute. The governorship of Lydia was given to a Macedonian, Asander, son of Philotas. Argive troops were left in Sardis to garrison the fortress. To Memnon's part of the country (in the Troad) were then sent Calas and Alexander, son of Aeropus, with the Peloponnesians and most of the other allied troops.

Alexander thus permitted the Lydians to observe the customs of their country and gave them their freedom—freedom to pay tribute, to house a garrison, and to enjoy the rule of a new satrap over them. The Lydians had changed masters, not mastery.

Alexander's next stop, Ephesos, the largest and most important Greek *polis* in Asia Minor and the home of the enormous temple of Artemis, which had burned down the night of Alexander's birth, presented a much more complex diplomatic problem. At Parmenio's approach with the Macedonian advance force in 336, the popular party of this ancient Ionian city-state had risen up and overthrown the pro-Persian tyrant in the city, admitting the Macedonians. It was after this that Philip II had become *synnaos* with Artemis; that is, his supporters in the city had installed a statue of the Macedonian king somewhere in her temple.

But Parmenio had suffered some reverses in Asia Minor in 335; the city of Ephesos was retaken by pro-Persian forces, and the statue of Philip was destroyed. Amyntas, the son of Antiochus (a friend of the Amyntas who had been eliminated as a pretender to the Macedonian throne early in 334), was in charge of the mercenary garrison of Ephesos, which confronted Alexander as he approached the city. When news of the devastation at the Granicus reached Ephesos, however, the mercenaries fled.

Upon his triumphal arrival in the city Alexander recalled everyone who had been expelled for supporting him, stripped the governing clique of its power, and restored democratic institutions. All dues previously paid to Persia he transferred to the temple of Artemis. The people of the city were eager to put to death those who had called in Memnon and smashed up the statue of Philip. Syrphax and his son Pelagon, and all his nephews, were dragged from the temple and stoned. Only Alexander's direct intervention halted further bloodshed.

Alexander then wanted to dedicate Artemis' newly rebuilt temple, but the Ephesians (or the temple administration) declined: it was inappropriate, they said, for a god to dedicate offerings to gods.

While Alexander was in Ephesos, envoys from Magnesia on the Maeander and Tralles (both on the border of the mountainous region to the south known as Caria) came and invited Alexander into their cities. Parmenio was sent with 2,500 allied foot soldiers, 2,500 Macedonians, and 200 Companion cavalry to accept the offer. A similar force under the command of the Macedonian officer Alcimachus, brother of the later-famous bodyguard and king Lysimachus, was dispatched to the Aeolian and the Ionian cities still subject to the Persians. Throughout the country he dispossessed the ruling factions and established popular (democratic) governments in their place, allowing each community to enjoy its own laws and customs and to discontinue payment of the taxes it previously had paid the Persians.

At Ephesos, then, Alexander established his policy with respect to the Greek cities of Asia. It was the arrival in Ephesos of the envoys from Magnesia and Tralles that led to the change. These cities had freed themselves of their Persian garrisons and set up democracies. Democracy and autonomy for Greek cities now were raised by Alexander to the level of general principles, and the Persian tribute was abolished. The policy apparently was instituted because it was the democratic parties in the cities (Magnesia and Tralles) that had been willing to get rid of the Persians.

Before Alcimachus' mission, there is no indication that Alexander had democracy and autonomy in mind for the Greeks of Asia. He had come to Asia to punish (or supplant) the Persians, not to free the Greeks or to set

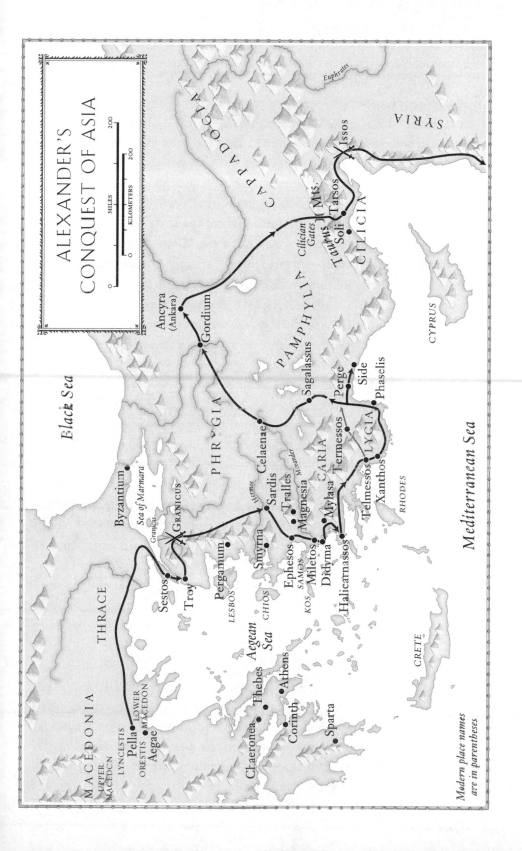

ALEXANDER'S
CONQUEST OF ASIA

MILES
0   200

KILOMETERS
0   200

Black Sea

MACEDONIA
UPPER
MACEDON
LYNCESTIS
ORESTIS
Pella
Aegae
LOWER
MACEDON

THRACE

Byzantium
Sea of Marmara
Sestos
Troy
Granicus
Granicus

Pergamum
LESBOS
Smyrna
CHIOS
Ephesos
SAMOS
Miletos
KOS
Didyma
Halicarnassos

Chaeronea
Thebes
Athens
Corinth
Sparta
Aegean
Sea

CRETE

Sardis
Tralles
Magnesia
Maeander
Mylasa
Termessos
Telmessos
Xanthos
CARIA
LYCIA
RHODES

Celaenae
PHRYGIA
Hermos

Gordium
Ancyra
(Ankara)

CAPPADOCIA

Euphrates

SYRIA
Issos
Tarsos
Soli
Cilician
Gates
Taurus Mts.
CILICIA
PAMPHYLIA
Sagalassus
Perge
Side
Phaselis

CYPRUS

Mediterranean Sea

Modern place names
are in parentheses

up democracies. In fact, he probably had no general policy toward the Greeks of Asia Minor at all before the campaign began in earnest. The new policy grew out of Alexander's appreciation of the political situation he confronted. As in warfare, where Alexander first read the topography of the battlefield and then adjusted his tactics accordingly, so too in politics Alexander tailored his policy measures to the lay of the political landscape.

After a sacrifice to Artemis and a splendid procession of troops, Alexander marched on to the important Greek port of Miletos, which in 499 had been the heart of the unsuccessful revolt against Persian rule. By the middle of the fourth century, however, Miletos' famed opposition to its rulers was a distant memory: the city was tightly controlled by the Persians and there were many friends of Persia among its people. Surrounded by the sea on three sides, Miletos might have served as an excellent base for the Persian fleet, which was more than twice the size of Alexander's (400 warships to 160), and whose galleys were manned by superior Cypriot and Phoenician crews. But Alexander seized the offshore island of Lade before the Persian fleet could arrive to assist the city's Persian garrison.

The resistance nevertheless was stiff; Alexander was able to take the city only with the help of siege engines, which were used to knock down a section of the city wall. Miletos surrendered at the last moment. Alexander spared the civilian population of the city because of the city's heroic struggle against the Persians during the Ionian revolt, but most of the defending force was wiped out, aside from 300 mercenaries whom Alexander took into his service. He had learned from his experience at the Granicus. No doubt because of the city's strategic position and pro-Persian sympathies, a garrison and tribute were imposed upon Miletos.

THE DEMOBILIZATION OF THE FLEET

Having proved that he could capture a coastal stronghold from land, Alexander now decided to demobilize his own fleet, except for a small squadron used for transport. He did so for three reasons: first, he lacked the money to pay the crews; second, he knew that his fleet was no match for the Persians' navy; and third, he had no wish to subject his ships or men to the risk of disaster at sea.

Armchair strategists have long debated the wisdom of this decision, which left the Persian fleet alone to become a threat to the Greek islands, to the mainland of Greece, and to the coast of Asia Minor. (Indeed, early in 333, Alexander would be forced to commission a new fleet to deal with the naval threat to his rear.) But from a strategic point of view, Alexander's decision is defensible as a calculated risk. He could rely upon Antipater and the forces back in Macedon to make sure that the mainland of Greece stayed quiet and at least passively loyal, whatever happened in the islands (which would never be decisive anyway). Moreover, with respect to the immediate theater of operations, as long as Alexander could keep the Persian fleet from resupplying itself from bases on the coast, it would not be a threat to him as he progressed. To put it in a nutshell, Alexander planned to defeat the superior Persian fleet by land. It was a brilliant, bold gamble, and totally characteristic of him.

It was also consistent with what perhaps Alexander alone already had identified as the goal of the war. From his very first battle in Asia, he was not only interested in punishing the Persians; his objective was the eradication of Persian rule in Asia, as the inscription on the captured Persian shields from the battle at the Granicus implied.

To achieve that goal, Alexander eventually would have to meet and defeat the Great King himself. Before he did so, Alexander wanted to deprive Darius of the use of as many of his resources along the Mediterranean coast as possible. Alexander demobilized his fleet and marched southward along the coastal road of Asia Minor to bring matters to a head under circumstances that were most advantageous to himself. Better than his critics, Alexander understood the strengths and weaknesses of the forces at his disposal, and he was determined to win *his* war using his own greatest asset: the incomparable Macedonian army.

THE APPOINTMENT OF ADA

After the subjugation of Miletos, Alexander moved south along the coast of Asia Minor to the Persian satrapal stronghold of Halicarnassus in Caria, the birthplace of the historian Herodotus. Around 370 B.C.E., Mausolus, the Persian satrap of Caria, had made the city his capital and endowed it with many spectacular buildings, including his own tomb, the Mausoleum. Halicarnassus was well fortified, and the Persian fleet could resupply it from the sea. Its defense was organized by Memnon of Rhodes, whose prescient, scorched-earth recommendation to the Persian satraps had been ignored before the battle of the Granicus. The capture of Halicarnassus represented a significant challenge, even to a determined and expert besieger of cities.

After apocalyptic back-and-forth struggles (described in great detail by Diodorus), the Macedonians took most of the city, but not the virtually impregnable citadels of Salmacis and Zephyrium; these remained in Persian hands until 332. Alexander, however, deciding to conserve his resources for the sake of his impending confrontation with Darius, moved eastward, leaving a garrison of 3,000 infantrymen and 200 cavalry to keep the defenders in check.

To the governorship of Caria Alexander appointed Ada, who had surrendered to him the strongly defended nearby city of Alinda. Ada had been expelled from Halicarnassus by her brother Pixodarus, the satrap who had offered his daughter in marriage to Alexander's mentally deficient brother. Alexander had reason to be well-disposed to Ada, since her surrender of Alinda had spared him the cost of another siege. She subsequently adopted him as her son, and when the last citadels of Halicarnassus fell into Macedonian hands, Alexander put the whole country under her control. The appointment of a woman to the governorship of such a strategically important region in the middle of a military campaign was unprecedented in Greco-Macedonian history.

ALEXANDER OF LYNCESTIS

From Halicarnassus, in the autumn of 334 Alexander continued his strategic southeastward swing into the region known as Lycia, reaching the city of Phaselis by the middle of winter. At Phaselis, an agent of Darius named Sisines, who had been captured by Parmenio on his way to contact Alexander the Lyncestian, was brought to Alexander. Sisines apparently had been sent to promise Alexander of Lyncestis the throne of Macedon and 1,000 talents if he succeeded in assassinating Alexander.

At the time of the assassination of Philip II, the evidence against Alexander of Lyncestis had looked damaging, it will be recalled, but

Alexander had not prosecuted him, because Alexander of Lyncestis had been among the first to hail him as king. Later, the king had appointed him to command the Thessalian cavalry, a key post in the Macedonian army. However, given the report he had received in 334, Alexander had little choice but to arrest the Lyncestian. Alexander of Lyncestis remained in custody until late in 330, when he was put on trial at the time of another conspiracy against Alexander's life. On that occasion the last of the Lyncestian brothers did not escape execution.

FROM PHASELIS TO THE REVERSAL OF THE NAVAL POLICY

After Phaselis Alexander continued his journey along the coastal road through Pamphylia. As Alexander marched along the narrow coastline a north wind blew waves onto the shore, inspiring his official campaign historian, Callisthenes, to write that the sea was prostrating itself before the conqueror. Years later, the historian would have cause to regret this flattery.

Using the city of Perge as his base of operations in the area, Alexander forced the major city of Aspendos, which had gone back on a previous agreement with him, to hand over the horses bred there as tribute to Darius and also to pay 100 talents. The leading men of the city were surrendered as hostages and the city was compelled to obey the governor appointed by Alexander, to pay an annual tribute to Macedon, and to submit to an inquiry about the ownership of land, which they were accused of holding on to by force.

The harbor city of Side, later a center of the slave trade in Anatolia, also was occupied, and nearby Syllium was besieged. At the beginning of spring in 333, Alexander then moved up north via Termessus, which was attacked with the help of the Selgians, who were old enemies of the Termessians. Sagalassus, whose soldiers were considered the best of all the fine soldiers of the Pisidians (the fiercely independent inhabitants of the mountainous region extending from the plain of Pamphylia to the lakes now called Burdur, Eğridir, and Beyşehir), was not able to withstand the onslaught of Alexander's heavily armed infantry, and the other Pisidian communities were either taken by assault or surrendered.

The satrapal capital of Celaenae, with its citadel sheer on every side, was left to surrender to a policing force led by Antigonus if reinforcements did not show up within sixty days; Alexander himself then hurried on to Gordium, where he was reunited with Parmenio and his troops (who had been sent ahead into central Phrygia to carry out campaigns at the time Alexander had moved into Lycia), and joined also by a force of new levies from Macedon, including 3,000 infantry and 300 horse, 200 Thessalian horse, and 150 men from Elis. Gordium (modern Yassi-hüyük) was the capital of ancient Phrygia and was situated at a strategic point where the Sangarius River was crossed by the Persian Royal Road from the plateau of Anatolia down to the sea.

While Alexander was in Gordium, envoys from Athens arrived to request the release of the Athenian prisoners captured at Granicus. But these were rebuffed; with the war still going on, Alexander thought it would be dangerous to relax his severity toward anyone of Greek nationality who had fought for the "barbarians."

More problematic was the news that Memnon of Rhodes, who had been sent money and appointed the commanding general of the naval campaign by Darius, had captured several cities in the northern Aegean. Afterward, Memnon apparently planned to carry the naval war back over to the mainland of Greece itself, specifically to the strategically located "Long Island" of Euboea, which curled around the eastern and northern coasts of Attica and Boeotia like a giant scythe. The prospect of Memnon's mission alarmed the cities of Euboea and encouraged Persia's Greek friends, notably the Spartans, to believe there might be "a change in the political situation."

Alexander thus was forced to reverse his naval policy in response, sending Amphoterus to the Hellespont area and an officer named Hegelochus to free the islands captured by the Persians. In addition, Proteas, by order of Antipater, assembled a fleet from Euboea and the Peloponnese to give protection to the Greek coast and the islands in the not unlikely event of a Persian attack.

Once again, however, the goddess of fortune smiled upon Alexander—or perhaps some malevolent deity took away Darius' wits. Ignoring the advice of his Athenian adviser and general Charidemus, Darius determined to follow the counsel of the royal Friends, and began to assemble an army, mostly comprising mercenaries, at Babylon. From there he planned to set out in the summer to meet and crush the Macedonian army in one large, pitched battle. Diodorus says that 400,000 infantry and not less than 100,000 cavalry were gathered together in Babylon. This, in fact, was precisely what Alexander wanted.

Resources, especially mercenaries, accordingly were pulled away from the vigorous prosecution of the Persian naval war in the Aegean. Fortuitously, too, for Alexander, Memnon died, probably during the siege of Mytilene. His death was the most serious blow Persia suffered during this period of the war; he had been Darius' most dynamic and imaginative commander. Without his guiding vision and energy, the Persian naval initiative in the Aegean soon collapsed.

THE GORDIAN KNOT

While Alexander was still scrambling to meet the naval threat to Greece, he was irresistibly impelled to visit the palace of King Gordius and his son Midas to inspect the famous wagon of Gordius and the knot that tied its yoke. By legend this was the wagon Midas had driven into Gordium, fulfilling an oracle given to the Phrygians that a wagon would bring them a king who would put an end to their civil strife. The knot's cord was made of tough cornel wood and was so cunningly tied that no one could see where it began or ended. Anyone who could untie it, people said, would rule Asia.

Two versions exist of how Alexander dealt with the knot. In one, Alexander was just as puzzled as everyone else, but, unwilling to walk away, he finally drew his sword and cut the knot, exclaiming, "I have untied it." Aristobulus, on the other hand, claims that Alexander removed the pin from the shaft of the wagon (which held the knot together), thus pulling the yoke free. Either way a public relations disaster was avoided, just.

Afterward there was a general feeling that the oracle had been fulfilled, and that night there was thunder and lightning, always interpreted by the seers as a sign from the gods. The next day Alexander sacrificed to the gods who had showed him how to undo the knot.

Now, after a brief trip to Ancyra (modern Ankara) to establish order in Galatia, Alexander made his way through Cappadocia's enchanted landscape of rock pillars and caves. Leaving Sabictas as governor there, Alexander marched to the Cilician Gates, the main pass through the majestic Taurus Mountains. Leading an assault team of guards (*hypaspistai*) and the Agrianes, he literally scared the Persian defenders out of the pass. Arsames, the Persian governor, left Tarsus, the satrapal capital of Cilicia (and the birthplace of Paul the Apostle more than three centuries later), with alacrity at Alexander's advance.

Having settled matters inland to his satisfaction, in the late summer of 333 Alexander and the Macedonians were now back near the seacoast, hoping, like Darius himself, to bring matters to a head. For his part, by the will of Ahuramazda, Darius believed that he was about to restore order in his empire. Alexander, on the other hand, had just received a sign from his gods that one day he would be the ruler of Asia. Soon, Darius and Alexander would learn how their respective gods intended to fulfill their plans.

CHAPTER 7

The Battle of Issos

DOCTOR'S ORDERS

Alexander reached Tarsus by the end of the summer of 333. Whether he was exhausted, or because of the intense summer heat, Alexander could not resist taking a dip in the inviting waters of the Cydnus River. Unfortunately, the waters of the Cydnus ran down directly from the snowy peaks of the nearby Taurus Mountains and were very cold, even in summer. After his frigid swim Alexander was seized by a convulsion, followed by a violent fever and sleeplessness.

His doctors despaired for his life, except for Philip, a native of Acarnania in northwestern Greece, who prescribed a purgative drink. As Philip was preparing it, Parmenio handed Alexander a note that read, "Beware of Philip, I hear that he has been bribed by Darius to poison you."

Alexander handed the note to Philip and promptly drank the medicine. Philip read the note without any sign of alarm and simply advised Alexander to continue to follow his instructions: if he did, Philip told him, he would recover. The patient did as he was told and made an astonishing recovery. Alexander subsequently honored his doctor with magnificent gifts and assigned him to the most loyal category of friends. As for Parmenio, there is no indication that the incident damaged his relations with Alexander or shook the king's confidence in him. Indeed, shortly thereafter Parmenio was dispatched with the allied infantry, the Greek mercenaries, the Thracians, and the Thessalian cavalry to secure and hold the other passes between Cilicia and Syria (most importantly, the Beilan pass through the Amanus Mountains).

THE PRELUDE TO THE BATTLE OF ISSOS

Alexander himself moved south to Anchialus, a city supposedly built in one day (along with Tarsus) by the legendary Assyrian king known to the Greeks as Sardanapalus. In Anchialus Alexander may well have seen the famous tomb and statue of the king clapping his hands, with its cuneiform inscription in verse below:

"Sardanapalus, son of Anakyndaraxes, built in one day Tarsus and Anchialus. You, stranger, eat, drink, and be merry, for everything else in the life of man is not worth this."

And "this" was understood to be the sound of a handclap. Arrian informs us that the word for "be merry" in the inscription was a euphemism for the original Assyrian word.

It probably was around this time that a much-debated incident took place. Alexander's boyhood friend and treasurer, Harpalus, fled. Harpalus, it will be recalled, had been exiled with Alexander's other friends in the wake of the Pixodarus debacle. Now he apparently had been persuaded to flee by an adventurer named Tauriscus. Perhaps Harpalus did not fancy Alexander's chances of recovering from his illness or surviving his impending encounter with Darius. Whatever his motives, he spent a year in Greece, in the Megarid, and then returned to his position as Alexander's treasurer in the spring of 331. Some have hypothesized that he had committed treason, or had stolen from Alexander; but in that case, it is hard to see how he would have been welcomed back. Others have argued that he was on some kind of secret mission for Alexander. The entire episode is steeped in mystery.

While the Macedonians presumably speculated about the curious disappearance of Alexander's friend, in Babylon Darius finally had mustered his grand army. Arrian reports that Darius' whole force numbered 600,000 fighting men. Plutarch concurs, while Diodorus and Justin give the number as 400,000. Curtius Rufus gives the number of Greek mercenaries alone as 30,000.

These numbers probably were enlarged to enhance Alexander's subsequent glory, but there are indications that Darius did indeed assemble a very large army. Arrian confirms that Darius had 30,000 Greek mercenaries in the van of his heavy infantry and that these were supplemented by 60,000 Persian hoplite infantry (the so-called Kardakes).

Whatever the exact numbers, Alexander's army clearly was outnumbered, perhaps by a very wide margin, and this time the Persians would be led by the Great King himself. Having rejected the counsel of his adviser, Charidemus, who advised him to divide his forces and let Charidemus attack the Macedonians with the smaller force, Darius decided to lead his entire army against Alexander. The Great King had cast the die.

Ever since, historians have debated whether Darius was right to risk his army and his life in one great battle. The outcome went against him, but his decision to wager all cannot be judged by the result. So why did Darius do it? It undoubtedly was important to the prestige, and even to the legitimacy, of his kingship (which had come into being only after a messy dynastic struggle) for Darius to be seen as willing to lead the Persians into battle and to fight for his empire. The Great Kings of Persia, favored by Ahuramazda, simply did not hide from upstart twenty-three-year-olds, leaders of former slaves, who once had paid earth and water to Darius I. Therefore, by September 333, Darius and his army had marched down to Sochi, in the Amik Plain, on the edge of the Amanus Range, ready to take on Alexander and the Macedonians. To make the immense force more mobile, its enormous baggage train was sent south to Damascus.

Alexander, meanwhile, marched along eastward, first to Magarsus, then northward to Mallus (where he learned that Darius was at Sochi), next northeast to Castabulum, and finally to Issos. Leaving his sick and wounded there, Alexander went on past the Pillar of Jonah, all the way to Myriandrus, perhaps in search of Darius, or to lure Darius into battle somewhere in the coastal narrows, with the Pillar of Jonah at his back and the sea and the Amanus Range on his flanks for protection. Given the Persians' numerical superiority, which he must have anticipated, it was clearly in Alexander's interest to fight in a confined space, where Darius would find it more difficult to maneuver.

Darius, on the other hand, probably wanted to meet Alexander somewhere on the Amik Plain, where the country was open and flat, a good terrain for cavalry action and for maneuvering his vast infantry. If the Persians at Sochi marched down through the Belen pass and confronted Alexander somewhere near Myriandrus, they would end up meeting Alexander on a smaller battlefield, and one of Alexander's choosing to boot.

After a delay of as much as two weeks to see who would move first, Darius finally took the initiative. His decision to leave Sochi, thus losing the potential advantage of meeting Alexander on the Amik Plain, has puzzled some historians. But the Persians had sent most of their supplies to Damascus, and they could not be resupplied from the area of the plain for very long. So Darius could not wait forever, while Alexander and the Macedonians, in a pinch, could be resupplied from the sea.

When Darius set out, however, he did not advance in the direction the Macedonians perhaps expected. Instead of coming down through the closer Belen pass, he marched north at least a hundred miles, then through the Bahçe pass, and finally down through the Toprakkale narrows to the coastal plain north of Issos.

In Issos, Darius made his first significant mistake of the campaign: he tortured, and then put to death, every invalid Macedonian whom Alexander had left there. Strangely, some who have criticized Alexander severely for his decision not to spare the Greek mercenaries at the Granicus have passed over this shameful massacre in silence. The Macedonian rank and file, however, surely must have been made aware of what had happened to their defenseless comrades, and would have been enraged by Darius' actions. Throughout the history of warfare, the torture or execution of prisoners of war very often has come back to haunt the perpetrators.

The Persians were now north of Alexander, cutting him off from his newly acquired land bases in Cilicia. Alexander, at first disbelieving the news, sent a galley of Companions back to Issos to have a look. They quickly confirmed the report: Darius was indeed behind the Macedonians. Alexander may have been invincible, as the Delphic oracle proclaimed; the Pythia never said he was omniscient. Necessity now relieved Alexander of the embarrassment of choice; cut off by land from his bases, he would have to fight Darius as soon as possible.

Leaving the allied infantry to keep an eye on the southern passes, Alexander and the rest of the army marched back up north, spending the night before the coming battle on safe, high ground at the top of the Pillar of Jonah.

South of the Pinarus River, the Persians formed up in a defensive position, so that Darius could get the main body of his army into formation safely. Alexander's official historian, Callisthenes, later recorded that the field of battle was 2.59 kilometers from the sea to the foothills of the Amanus Range; that would make the battlefield about 1.75 miles wide. The relatively narrow width of the battlefield would give Alexander's much smaller army something of an advantage, as it greatly reduced the chances that the Macedonians would be enveloped by the larger Persian force. Nevertheless, Alexander would have to make sure that the Persians did not get up and around his flank on the inland side or break through his line on his left (seaward) flank, and the complex movements of infantry and cavalry he directed as the Macedonians moved into position are a testament to his understanding both of the topography of the battlefield and the tactical exigencies.

THE BATTLE FORMATIONS

When Darius discovered that Alexander was moving forward at last, he sent 30,000 mounted troops and 20,000 light infantry across the river Pinarus to give himself a chance to get his main army into position. The Greek mercenary infantry made up the center of the Persian line; they were supported on each flank by the 30,000 Kardakes. Another division of 20,000 was sent up into the hills to work their way around to Alexander's rear. A great mass of light and heavy infantry supported the main force from the rear. These were organized according to their countries of origin and were drawn up in depth greater than was likely to prove of much service—inevitably so, in view of the numbers involved.

Alexander meanwhile made an impassioned speech to his infantry and cavalry commanders and to the allied officers. We are told that he emphasized the differences between the Greeks and the Persians—"We are free men, and they are slaves"—and that he reminded his soldiers that the Persians were fighting for pay, while they were fighting for

Greece. Alexander then ordered his men to eat and to rest, albeit on the rocky ground. Many battles have been lost because one side fought on an empty stomach or got no sleep at all the night before. Alexander always took care that the Macedonians went into battle well fed and rested.

Just before daylight, the Macedonians marched down from the pass, the infantry leading the cavalry. The infantry was deployed in a formation thirty-two deep, but as the phalanx spread out into the plain its ranks were thinned to a depth of eight men.

Reaching open ground, Alexander sent three battalions of guards under Nicanor to his right wing on the nearby rising ground, with Coenus' battalion on their left, in close touch with Perdiccas' men. On the extreme left were Amyntas' troops, and in touch with them, working toward the center, Ptolemy's battalion and then Meleager's. Command of the infantry on the left side of the line was given to Craterus. Overall command of the left wing belonged to Parmenio. His orders were to see to it that the Macedonians were not outflanked on their left, the seaward side.

As soon as Alexander found the ground in front of him opening up a little more, he brought up the Companion and Thessalian divisions of cavalry from the rear to the right wing under his command, and he sent the Peloponnesians, and other allied divisions, around to Parmenio on the left.

Darius, once his main infantry was in position, recalled the mounted troops he had sent across the river and moved them over to his right to threaten Parmenio on the seaward side of the plain. Darius himself took up a position in the center of the formation, the traditional station of the Persian kings in battle.

Alexander sent the Thessalian cavalry to counter the threat on his left, concealing their movement by having them pass behind his infantry battalions. At the other end of the line, he threw forward his advance scouts under the command of Protomachus, the Paeonians under Ariston, and the archers under Antiochus. The Agrianes under Attalus were then ordered out toward the high ground at an angle to the front line of the main army, where they were to engage the Persians who had worked their way up onto that high ground.

Observing a weakness in his own line, Alexander withdrew two squadrons of Macedonian cavalry from his center and ordered them over to his right, once again concealing the movement. He also strengthened his right by the addition of a contingent of Agrianes and Greek mercenaries, and so outflanked the Persian left. A raiding party of Agrianes and archers drove the Persians in the hills higher up, allowing Alexander to return to his main attacking force the men he had intended to check them with.

After Alexander had completed these realignments, the Macedonians advanced slowly and deliberately, halting now and then, at Alexander's order, to give the Persians the impression that time was on their side. Darius and his army waited on the opposite riverbank, which was steep in places and strengthened elsewhere with stockades.

THE BATTLE OF ISSOS

Once the battle began, the combat was furious and the issue decided relatively quickly. As soon as Alexander was within missile range, he rode at a gallop into the stream at the head of his own troops on the right wing. The left of the Persian line collapsed the moment Alexander was upon them—an indication that the Persians had never before faced such a ferocious attack.

In the center of the battlefield the combat did not go as well for the Macedonians. The Macedonian infantry phalanx was much slower off the mark than Alexander, who rode into battle. Some of the Macedonian infantry broke away toward the right, leaving a gap in the line. In a number of places, the steep banks of the stream prevented the phalanx from maintaining a regular and unbroken line. Darius' Greek mercenaries attacked at precisely the spot in the Macedonian line where the gap was widest. A violent struggle ensued.

Arrian tells us that the Greek mercenaries of the Persians fought to save the day for their left wing, which was already in retreat at the shock of Alexander's charge, while the Macedonian phalanx was determined to equal Alexander's success, which they could see on the narrow battlefield. The fierce clash of the infantries was further fueled by the old ethnic

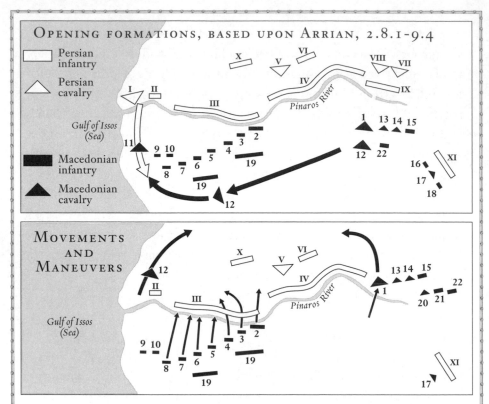

THE BATTLE OF ISSOS, 333 B.C.E.

Macedonians

1 Companion cavalry, commanded by Philotas

2 *Hypaspistai*, commanded by Nicanor

3 Infantry phalanx brigade (*pezhetairoi*) of Coenus

4 Infantry phalanx brigade (*pezhetairoi*) of Perdiccas

5 Infantry phalanx brigade (*pezhetairoi*) of Meleager

6 Infantry phalanx brigade (*pezhetairoi*) of Ptolemy

7 Infantry phalanx brigade (*pezhetairoi*) of Amyntas (Simmias)

8 Infantry phalanx brigade (*pezhetairoi*) of Craterus

9 Cretan archers

10 Thracian javelin men, commanded by Sitalces

11 Greek allied cavalry

12 Thessalian cavalry

13 Mounted scouts (*prodromoi*), commanded by Protomachus

14 Paeonian cavalry, commanded by Ariston

15 Macedonian archers, commanded by Antiochus

16 Agrianian javelin men, commanded by Attalus

17 Detachment of cavalry

18 Macedonian archers

19 Greek infantry mercenaries

20 Two squadrons of Companion cavalry, commanded by Peroedas and Pantordanus

21 Agrianians

22 Greek mercenary infantry

Persians

I Nabarzanes' cavalry

II Slingers and archers

III Greek mercenary infantry

IV Kardakes (heavy infantry)

V Persian King Darius with bodyguard

VI Persian infantry guard

VII Hyrcanian and Median cavalry

VIII Persian cavalry

IX Slingers and javelin men

X Massed infantry levies

XI Detached infantry of 20,000

rivalry between Greeks and Macedonians. During this phase of the battle about 120 Macedonians of distinction lost their lives.

Alexander and the Companion cavalry, however, having shattered resistance on the Persian left, then turned left, toward the center, forcing Darius' mercenaries back from the river. Outflanking the Persian left, Alexander then delivered a devastating flank attack on the Persian mercenary infantry. The Companion cavalry was soon cutting them to pieces.

On the far left of the Macedonian line, the Persian cavalry had refused to stay on the far side of the river; they charged across in a furious onslaught against the Thessalian cavalry, breaking off from this attack only when they saw that the Greek mercenaries were being destroyed by Alexander's infantry, and that Darius himself was in headlong flight. The attack by the Persian cavalry here, which took them away from the center of the Persian line, was perhaps the key tactical blunder of the engagement. Or, to put the case another way, it was the successful defensive action fought by Parmenio and the Thessalians that gave Alexander time to break the Persian left wing and then roll up the Persian center, too.

Arrian reports that Darius fled in a panic the moment the Persian left went to pieces under Alexander's attack. But both Diodorus and Curtius tell a very different story. In Diodorus' account, Alexander, after shattering the Persian left, rode hard with his cavalry directly at the Persian king himself. By now the rest of the cavalry on both sides was engaged, and many were killed as the battle raged indecisively. Some of the fiercest fighting took place around Darius' royal chariot. Many of his most famous generals fell fighting before the very eyes of their king; all of their mortal wounds were in the front of their bodies. The violent deaths of these men in combat once again confirm the bravery of Darius' governors and officers and also indirectly support the thesis that Darius did not flee at the beginning of the battle. These Persian commanders died in a desperate fight focused on Darius himself; indeed, we are told that Darius' horses were covered with wounds, and Alexander himself received a dagger wound in the thigh. It was only when Darius' horses, pierced by lances and distracted with pain, began to toss their yokes and were about to hurl the king from his chariot that Darius, frightened that he might fall into his enemies' hands, jumped down and mounted a horse to escape.

Most of the literary evidence thus does not support Arrian's claim that Darius fled as soon as the Persian left collapsed. Moreover, Diodorus' and Curtius' accounts are perhaps broadly supported by the scene depicted on the famous "Alexander Mosaic" now displayed in the National Archaeological Museum of Naples.

The magnificent mosaic itself is usually thought to have been created c. 120–100 B.C.E., but it was inspired by a contemporary painting of the battle of Issos, probably by the famous artist Philoxenos of Eretria. Philoxenos' painting was based upon eyewitness accounts. Although it obviously was not a photograph of the battle, but an artistic interpretation of one moment during the engagement, if the Alexander Mosaic in Naples is in any sense a faithful representation of the fourth-century painting, it could be argued that the starting point of the painting's compositional assumptions coincides with the narrative accounts of Diodorus and Curtius Rufus, rather than that of Arrian.

If Arrian is right about the way the battle unfolded, Alexander and Darius never got close enough for their eyes to meet, as they do in the Alexander Mosaic. In the mosaic, Alexander and Darius are shown within close striking distance of each other, as both Curtius Rufus and Diodorus report. Thus, Darius could not have fled at the moment when the left of the Persian line was shattered (by Alexander's charge). That charge certainly took place long before Alexander could have gotten close to the Persian king, stationed, as we know Darius was, in the middle of the Persian battle formation.

We also know from later Greek sources that Darius had a reputation among the Persians for personal bravery. So it is likely that he left the battle of Issos only after the issue had been decided, perhaps to ensure that the all-important connection between the divine and human worlds, which the Persian king embodied, should not be broken. It was unacceptable for Ahuramazda's divinely selected king and representative to be killed on the field of battle.

Whatever the timing of Darius' flight, it led to a general rout. Tens of thousands of Persians tried to escape through narrow passes, and the whole countryside was soon covered with bodies. Ptolemy, who was present, wrote that the Macedonians crossed a ravine on the bodies of the Persian dead. Some have considered Ptolemy's description a literary exaggeration. But it is not implausible. At Issos something like 100,000 soldiers were killed on the Persian side, including no fewer than 10,000 cavalry.

Reports of Macedonian casualties vary widely. A low figure of 504 wounded, with 32 infantry and 150 cavalry dead, appears in Curtius. Diodorus gives similar totals of 300 infantry and 150 Macedonian or allied cavalry casualties. These figures may be deflated, but before we dismiss the vast disproportion of fatalities in the armies' losses, we should keep in mind that the battle at the Issos was not a prolonged, equal struggle, but a short, fierce clash followed by a total rout. At no time are soldiers more vulnerable to outright slaughter than when they simply turn their backs and flee.

The Persian survivors fled in all directions as quickly as possible. This was no organized, tactical retreat, but flight, pure and simple. Darius, first with a few of his personal retainers, and then gradually joined by about 4,000 Persians and mercenaries, pressed on to Thapsacus and then to the Euphrates. The surviving Persian cavalrymen made their way to Cappadocia, where they tried and failed to recapture Phrygia for the Persian cause. Another group, led by Macedonians or Greeks who had deserted to Darius, fled into the hills with 8,000 mercenaries. Finally, other mercenaries probably sailed to Crete, where they were hired by the Spartan king Agis to help him prosecute his war against the Macedonians and their allies there.

The news of Alexander's victory at Issos shattered the morale of the Persian fleet around Chios; by the early spring of 332 it ceased to exist as a significant fighting force. The Aegean coast was freed from Persian rule. As had been the case on the mainland of Asia Minor, democracies were established by the Macedonians.

THE FRUITS OF VICTORY

Despite the intelligence failure that had put the Macedonians in a vulnerable position south and east of the Persian army, Alexander's careful logistical preparations, movement and positioning of forces, and heroic leadership on the battlefield at Issos had made the difference between victory and defeat. Nor should the contribution of the Thessalian cavalrymen be overlooked. If the Persian cavalry had broken through their lines, it might well have been Alexander who was depicted fleeing from the battle on a "Darius Mosaic." As it was, however, Parmenio's indomitable Thessalians had held, and Alexander now had an opportunity to taste the fruits of victory.

Although the Persians had sent most of their baggage to Damascus (which Parmenio soon captured), in the Persian camp the Macedonians found that Darius' mother, his wife, his infant son, and two of his daughters, as well as 3,000 talents, had been left behind. There also was a great wealth of possessions, which the Macedonian soldiers plundered with great enthusiasm.

After visiting the wounded on the day after the battle, Alexander gave a splendid military funeral to the dead before the whole army. He also buried those Persians who had distinguished themselves by their courage. Sacrifices to the gods for the victory followed. Balacrus was made governor of Cilicia, and Polyperchon was promoted to command the battalion of Ptolemy, son of Seleucus, who had been killed during the battle.

His duties to man and gods discharged, Alexander prepared to relax. Darius' bath and dining tent had been reserved for his use. When Alexander entered the bath he saw that the basins, the pitchers, the tubs themselves, and the caskets were made of gold and elaborately wrought. The whole room was also marvelously fragrant with spices and perfumes. Passing from this bath into a spacious and lofty tent, he observed the magnificence of the dining couches, the tables, and the banquet that had been set out for him. Taking it all in, Alexander turned to his companions and remarked, "This, so it seems, is what it means to be king." This victor did not yet belong to the spoils.

On that same night, hearing the voices of Darius' mother, wife, and children as they mourned Darius' death, Alexander sent the officer Leonnatus to tell the royal ladies that Darius was alive and that they were to retain all of their marks, ceremonies, and titles of royalty.

Another story was reported about the aftermath of the battle. The next day, we are told, when Alexander and Hephaestion visited the tent of the Persian royal women, Darius' mother, Sisygambis, immediately prostrated herself before Hephaestion, supposing the taller of the two visitors to be the king. When one of her attendants silently pointed to the shorter Alexander, Alexander simply remarked that Sisygambis' error was of no account, for Hephaestion was an Alexander, too—a protector of men. Arrian comments, "If it really happened, I cannot but admire Alexander both for treating these women with such compassion and for showing such respect and confidence towards his friend."

The Persian royal women who fell into Alexander's hands after the battle at Issos were indeed treated with great deference throughout the rest of the campaign. Although Alexander refused to ransom these women back to Darius, he later referred to Sisygambis as his mother, and when Stateira, Darius' wife, died in 331, she was given a royal funeral.

CHAPTER 8

Master of Sieges

DARIUS' FIRST OVERTURE

Leaving Cilicia and northern (lowland) Syria in the hands of Balacrus and Menon, Alexander marched on to northern Phoenicia, where Straton, crown prince of the island city of Aradus, surrendered it. Alexander then proceeded to Marathus, where he received envoys with a verbal request and a letter from Darius.

The letter accused Philip of unprovoked aggression, claimed that he, Darius, had taken the field in defense of his own country and ancestral home, and asserted that the battle of Issos had been decided as some god—not, presumably, Ahuramazda—had willed it. Darius then requested the return of his wife, his mother, and his children in exchange for friendship and alliance.

In reply, Alexander cited the Persians' invasion of Macedonia and Greece: he had invaded Asia because he wished to punish Persia for this act, just as had been proclaimed at the pan-Hellenic congress in Corinth. He accused Darius of hiring assassins to kill Philip; of murdering the legitimate Persian king, Arses, with Bagoas' help; of illegally seizing the throne; and of supplying money to the Greeks, money that only the Lacedaemonians were willing to accept. This explained their unwillingness to join their fellow Greeks on the campaign.

But, Alexander's letter went on, only when Darius' agents corrupted Alexander's friends and tried to wreck the peace he had established in Greece did Alexander take the field against Darius. Now, with Zeus' help, he was master of Darius' country. Therefore Darius should come to Alexander as he would to the lord of all Asia.

Darius could come and ask for his mother, his wife and his children, and anything else. He would give Darius his family and anything else Darius could persuade Alexander to give him. But, in future communications, Darius should address Alexander as the king of all Asia and should not write to Alexander as an equal. Everything Darius possessed now belonged to Alexander; if Darius wanted anything, he should address Alexander properly, or Alexander would take steps to deal with him as a criminal. If, on the other hand, Darius wanted to dispute the throne, he should stand and fight for it and not run away. Wherever Darius might hide, Darius should be sure that Alexander would seek him out.

Alexander's letter echoed the justifications for the war declared at Corinth, but also advanced a new claim: Darius was a usurper. If it had not been clear before, it was now: Alexander was, in his own view, the rightful king of all Asia. He had no intention of negotiating with Darius on an equal basis, and he was not interested in alliance. In such haughty terms was Darius' first peace overture rejected.

Setting aside the rhetoric and posturing of both kings, however, we should consider their real positions. Alexander now held all the money and goods Darius had left behind at Issos and Damascus, as well as Darius' mother, wife, and children, and many other noble ladies. He commanded the superb Macedonian army, which was very largely intact. He also now ruled a large part of what had been the western half of the Persian empire.

Darius, on the other hand, led the shattered remnants of his army. Huge quantities of money and bullion remained untouched in the Persian capital of Persepolis, the accumulation of decades of tribute from the empire. He still ruled the Persian heartland and the eastern part of the empire, which stretched, in terms of effective political control, nearly to the Indus River. To replenish his resources he now could draw from Persia proper and from the eastern provinces.

Although he had suffered a terrible defeat, Darius had some reasons for optimism, which may be why his overture to Alexander was not com-

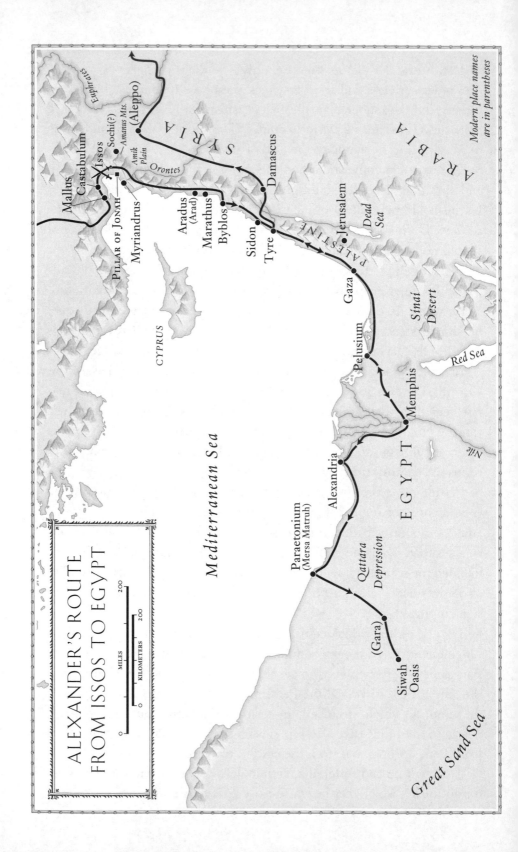

ALEXANDER'S ROUTE
FROM ISSOS TO EGYPT

MILES
0   200

KILOMETERS
0   200

pletely conciliatory. Moreover, Alexander's decision to march farther south along the Phoenician coast, rather than to pursue Darius at once to the east, gave the Persian king a two-year breathing period during which he could build up and train a new army to meet his nemesis on a field of battle that suited him.

Alexander's decision not to pursue Darius into Persia immediately to administer a deathblow to his demoralized force has been debated. But to follow Darius deep into Persia while Persian allies or neutral parties were left unconquered behind him along the eastern Mediterranean coast invited a strategically dangerous war on two fronts. In broad terms, Alexander and his generals appreciated their strategic situation far better at the time than do most of their modern critics. If Alexander intended to become the king of all Asia, he needed to conquer all of Persia's western possessions first. Then, and only then, would it be safe to strike at the heart of Persia.

THE SIEGE OF TYRE

Thus, heading farther south, Alexander received the surrenders of Byblos and Sidon, deposing the pro-Persian king of the latter, Straton II, and appointing Abdalonymus in his place. From Tyre, a delegation of envoys drawn from some of the city's noblest families, among them the son of the king, Azemilcus, came out to meet Alexander and told him that the government had decided to obey any instructions Alexander might give them.

Yet when Alexander told the envoys that he wished to enter the town and offer sacrifice to Herakles, they balked. This request would have involved Alexander sacrificing at the state temple of the chief city god, Melqart, whom Alexander identified with his divine ancestor Herakles. Such a sacrifice, to be performed perhaps in February 332, would have coincided with the main yearly festival of Melqart. If the Tyrians allowed Alexander to make his sacrifice at the festival in the temple, it would have signified their acceptance of Alexander's sovereignty.

The Tyrians were willing to let Alexander sacrifice on the mainland, in the old city of Tyre, but not in the island sanctuary, to which they denied access to Alexander and the Persians alike. In effect, this was a declaration of neutrality. Diodorus claims that in reality the Tyrians simply wanted to draw Alexander into a protracted siege, to give Darius more time for his military preparations.

Whatever the Tyrians' motives, Alexander certainly was not inclined to accept declarations of neutrality. He was not about to leave a neutral city at his rear as he advanced upon Egypt, particularly one with access to the sea and what remained of the Persian fleet.

The stage was therefore set for one of the most famous sieges in history. It would drag on for seven months and would cost the Macedonians dearly. In the end, however, the Tyrians paid far more.

Alexander's plan to take the formidable Phoenician city was encouraged by a sign from heaven given to him on the night he persuaded his friends and officers that Tyre must be captured. On that night he dreamed that when he approached the city's walls his kinsman Herakles greeted him and invited him in. Alexander's soothsayer Aristander interpreted the dream in the following way: Tyre would be taken, but with much labor, because effort characterized all that Herakles himself had achieved.

Aristander was a true prophet. But like most successful prophets, his prophecies were educated guesses based upon perceived facts. In this case, the essential fact was that Tyre was (in part) an island city, situated about half a mile offshore, defended by strong, lofty walls. In addition, the Tyrian fleet was very strong. Taking the city would be a formidable labor indeed, even for a descendant of the great Herakles.

In fact, just to get into position to lay siege, Alexander had to construct an enormous mole, about 200 feet wide, from Old Tyre on the mainland to the island city. As the Macedonians worked on the part of the mole near the city walls, Tyrian naval raiders attacked them at various points along the mole by sea. To counter such attacks the Macedonians built two towers on the mole. On these towers they mounted artillery, which the Macedonians used to keep the Tyrians away from those who were working to complete the enormous pier.

In response, the Tyrians filled a cattle boat with pitch, sulfur, and other flammable materials and sailed it into the towers. Once the towers were ablaze, the Tyrians swarmed out from behind their city walls and destroyed the siege engines.

Undaunted, Alexander ordered the construction of a wider mole start-ing from the mainland, to give space for more towers, and new siege en-gines. It was at this point that fleets from Cyprus and other Phoenician cities joined Alexander's forces, now that the Persian naval initiative in the Aegean had lost momentum. These reinforcements proved to be crucial to the outcome of the siege. They allowed Alexander to gain control of the sea around the city as the Macedonians worked on the new construction.

While the larger mole was being constructed, Alexander led a raid against the Arabians who lived in the area of Mount Antilibanus. The story of the raid helps to explain why Alexander was so beloved of his friends and soldiers.

Alexander's old Acarnanian tutor, Lysimachus, had accompanied him. When the raiding party reached the mountains, they dismounted and marched ahead on foot. Lysimachus, worn out and weary, could not keep up and was in danger of being left behind. Alexander, however, would not abandon him even as a cold night fell, leaving him with only a few other followers in a rough region, with the scattered fires of the enemy nearby.

Wishing to cheer the Macedonians amid their perplexities, Alexan-der stole away to the nearest campfire, dispatched the two enemy sol-diers sitting around it with his knife, and brought back a firebrand to Lysimachus and the rest. He started a great fire, frightening away some of the enemy and routing others who approached. The rest of the night was then spent without further peril. Long before elite modern army units adopted the motto, Alexander personally lived by the maxim of no man left behind.

On his return from the raid, Alexander found that Cleander had brought 4,000 Greek mercenaries to reinforce the army. Alexander then successfully blockaded Tyre by sea, breaking up and driving back into the harbor what remained of the Tyrian fleet. Now he could bring his ar-tillery into action, both from the better-protected mole (which was now completed) and from ships. Although Tyre's walls were more than 150 feet high in places and strongly constructed of cemented stone blocks, the artillery eventually destroyed a considerable length of the wall.

While triremes attacked Tyre's harbor and other vessels cruised around the city, getting as close as possible, Alexander and an officer named Admetus then brought up two ships loaded with guards and heavy infantry to one of the points weakened by the artillery barrage. In the initial assault on the wall Admetus was killed, but Alexander gained control of a section of the battlement and then pressed on toward the royal quarters.

While Alexander's new Phoenician allies seized the southern harbor, the Cypriots sailed into the undefended northern harbor. Most of the Tyrians who were defending the wall fled to the shrine of Agenor, the city's founder, where they were immediately set upon by Alexander and the Macedonians. The vast majority of the defenders were slain at the shrine, and the fugitives were pursued.

Other sources also provide additional details and anecdotes designed to convey the various moods of besiegers and besieged during the siege. Diodorus, for instance, recounts the marvelous story of the Tyrian man who told everyone that Apollo had appeared to him and informed him that he, Apollo, would leave the city, which led to the man nearly being stoned, but also to the Tyrians tying the image of Apollo to its base with gold cords to prevent the god from deserting the city.

Reviewing the siege of Tyre, some have argued that it reveals the essential brutality of Alexander's campaign. That is indisputable: it was prosecuted vigorously, and when the Macedonians finally entered the inner city of Tyre, they went about their business with savage ferocity. At least 8,000 Tyrians were killed. Alexander had some 2,000 crucified later along the beach as a warning to others who might think about resisting a descendant of Herakles. Another 30,000, perhaps the women and children, were sold into slavery, excluding the king Azemilcus, the dignitaries of the city, and some visitors from Carthage who had come to their mother city to pay honor to Melqart/Herakles according to some ancient custom. These Carthaginians had promised the Tyrians help at the beginning of the siege but could not deliver on their promise because of their own war against Syracuse. The Carthaginians were sent packing, bearing a formal declaration of war.

After the victory Alexander offered sacrifice to Herakles and also dedicated the piece of siege artillery that had breached the wall to the temple. In a revealing act of piety, Alexander also removed the gold chains from Apollo and gave orders that the god was henceforth to be called Apollo Philalexandros, or Apollo, friend of Alexander.

The siege unquestionably was brutal and its outcome horrific. But the Tyrians conducted their resistance in a way that probably guaranteed that no mercy would be shown to them. At one point during the siege the Tyrians had captured some Macedonians who had been sailing from Sidon. The Tyrians dragged them up onto the battlements, cut their throats in full view of the Macedonian army, and flung their bodies into the sea. Modern historians who have condemned Alexander and the Macedonians for the slaughter and enslavement of the Tyrians have failed to mention this Tyrian atrocity, which, Arrian says, particularly aroused the rage of the Macedonians—along with the protracted nature of the siege.

To explain, of course, is not to justify, and anyone who reads Arrian's description of the Tyrians' last stand in front of the shrine of Agenor can only feel pity for them, as the historian intended. Diodorus put it well when he commented that Tyre had endured "the siege bravely rather than wisely, and had come into such misfortunes, after a resistance of seven months."

From Alexander, the Tyrian resistance had elicited perhaps the best example during the entire campaign of his absolute determination to achieve total victory no matter what the practical challenges were. At Tyre Alexander showed the world that, once he had committed himself, he just would not be denied. Very soon he would have an opportunity to make that point again.

THE SIEGE OF GAZA

After Tyre's capture, Alexander proceeded down the coast to the ancient Philistine city of Gaza, the only real pocket of potential resistance before the Macedonians would reach Egypt. Its ruler, a eunuch named Batis, had collected together a force of mercenary Arabs and laid in supplies for a protracted siege. Believing that the town was too well defended to be taken by assault, Batis denied Alexander entry. The predictable siege of this turreted city, which was situated some twenty stades from the sea according to Arrian's reckoning, then ensued, eventually lasting from September to November 332.

The siege was notable for several reasons, including the Macedonians' use of shored mines to undermine the fortification wall of the city, an attempted assassination of Alexander by an Arab mercenary soldier who had thrown himself at Alexander's feet, claiming to be a deserter, only to jump up and strike at Alexander with a sword—Alexander dodged the stroke—and then a serious shoulder wound that Alexander received from a catapult bolt he could not dodge.

Batis in fact believed that Alexander had been killed and began to celebrate his victory; like the Thebans, Batis would learn that his celebration was premature. Alexander was hurt but alive and, ominously, angry.

Once the siege artillery had arrived from Tyre, the Macedonians brought it into action and breached the walls. The Gazans resisted three assaults, but not the fourth. Every Gazan defender fell and all the women and children were sold into slavery.

It was from the spoils of Gaza that Alexander was able to send his old tutor Leonidas sixteen tons of frankincense and myrrh, so that he would not deal parsimoniously with the gods.

Batis himself was captured alive. Perhaps in retaliation for the assassination attempt, Alexander allegedly had him dragged around the walls of Gaza by his ankles at the rear of a chariot, as Achilles had dragged Hektor's corpse around the walls of Troy. A week later, Alexander and the Macedonians arrived at Pelusium in the delta of the Nile River in Egypt, which had been the ultimate object of his march to the south.

CHAPTER 9

The Gift of the River

Alexander and the Macedonians came to the "Two Lands" of Upper and Lower Egypt in 332–31 for strategic reasons. But Alexander's visit to the country Herodotus felicitously called the "gift of the river" nonetheless would mark a turning point in his personal evolution.

As the leader of the pan-Hellenic crusade, Alexander already had led the Macedonians and the Greeks to unprecedented military victories over the Persians. By the winter of 332 Alexander was, in effect, the ruler of the largest empire in Greek or Macedonian history. Alexander had turned history upside down. For hundreds of years Persians had ruled Greeks. Now Macedonians and Greeks were about to rule Persians, Egyptians, Arabs, Jews, Scythians, Bactrians, Indians, and all the other subject peoples of the Persian empire.

Before that happened, though, at a remote oasis in the desert between Egypt and Libya, Alexander was transformed by a visit to the oracular shrine of Zeus Ammon. His consultation of the oracle there apparently confirmed his sense that he was descended from the greatest of the Olympian gods and that he had a divinely sanctioned destiny to fulfill. As we shall see, even after Darius had been killed and all of his possible native successors had been tracked down and executed, Alexander's sense of his unique destiny would lead him ever deeper into Asia—and eventually into conflict with the very men who had made him king of Asia.

It was also in Egypt that Alexander founded Alexandria, the first and greatest of his city foundations. Alexander probably did not found seventy cities, as Plutarch claimed, and many of his real foundations were in essence military garrisons. But the dozens of cities he established from Egypt to the Indus nevertheless became outposts of Hellenism where none had existed before.

In Egypt also, during a brief exchange with a local philosopher, Alexander set out his belief that while Zeus was the father of all mankind, the ruler of Mount Olympus nevertheless had a special preference for the "best" among human beings. It is hard to overestimate the importance of that belief for understanding how Alexander intended to organize his world empire.

Alexander was probably never officially installed as the pharaoh of Upper and Lower Egypt. But somehow, like Lawrence of Arabia at Wejh in April 1917, amid the date palms of an oasis in the middle of a trackless sea of sand, the young Macedonian king began a metamorphosis, from leader of the Greeks into king of all Asia, and finally a god, who intended to extend his belief in his father's love of the best over the entire face of the earth.

FROM PELUSIUM TO MEMPHIS

Egyptian scholars of the Hellenistic period traced a history of thirty dynasties of Egyptian kings who had ruled Egypt from c. 3100 B.C.E. until shortly before Alexander's arrival. In reality, however, the Two Lands of Egypt had been absorbed into the Persian empire in 526–25 after a bloody war of conquest directed by the Persian king Cambyses II. Except for a break from about 401 to 343 Egypt essentially had been a Persian province ruled by Persian governors for almost 200 years by the time Alexander arrived.

Mazaces, the Persian governor in 332, commanded no native troops. He had heard the reports of Alexander's victory over Darius at Issos, and of Darius' flight. The unfortunate governor also had learned that

Phoenicia, Syria, and the greater part of Arabia already were in Macedonian hands: the terrible fates of Tyre and Gaza could not have escaped his notice, either. So Mazaces received Alexander in Pelusium, at the easternmost mouth of the Nile, with a show of friendship, and offered no obstacle to his entry into Egypt. Unlike Napoleon in 1798, after nearly two centuries of intermittent Persian rule, Alexander was welcomed as a liberator.

After establishing a garrison at Pelusium, Alexander then marched about sixty miles through the desert up to Heliopolis while the accompanying fleet sailed up the Nile. Heliopolis—"City of the Sun," in Greek—lay to the west of the Nile, although it was connected to it by a canal. From Heliopolis Alexander crossed the Nile to Memphis.

Memphis, located about fourteen miles south of modern Cairo, had been the administrative center of Egypt from the Old Kingdom period (c. 3000 B.C.E.) and from the second millennium B.C.E. had been a very cosmopolitan city, attracting traders and artisans from around the Mediterranean world. Here Alexander celebrated games with both athletic and literary contests, attended by the most famous performers in Greece.

He also offered a special sacrifice to Apis, the bull of Memphis, sacred to the Egyptian god Ptah. According to Egyptian propaganda, as recorded in the hostile account of Herodotus, the Persian king Cambyses II actually had stabbed the Apis bull. Thus, Alexander's public sacrifice was an expression of piety and respect for Egyptian religious traditions, meant to be seen in contrast to (alleged) Persian sacrilege.

Although in the "Alexander Romance" (the later, essentially medieval compilation of stories about Alexander's fantastic adventures), there is a story of Alexander's official enthronement as pharaoh in Memphis, no reliable contemporary evidence of such an official ceremony exists. In contemporary Egyptian inscriptions, Alexander did receive the nomenclature of the pharaohs, and on the relief of the temple of Amun in Luxor he is depicted offering a libation to the god. But such titles and representations do not necessarily imply an induction ceremony. The Persian kings themselves received such titles from their Egyptian subjects without official induction. Alexander probably did so as well. It was enough for him to be king.

In any case, his stay in Memphis was brief. For, after sailing upstream, Alexander was seized by a passionate desire to visit the oracular shrine of Zeus Ammon in Libya and to consult the god there.

THE VISIT TO THE ORACLE OF
ZEUS AT SIWAH

Greeks had known about the oracle in Siwah for hundreds of years and identified Ammon, the Egyptian-Libyan god of the shrine, with their own Zeus. Indeed, Greeks living in the city of Cyrene, on the Libyan coast to the west of the shrine in Siwah, had spread the good news about Zeus Ammon and his infallible oracles to their relations back in mainland Greece, where shrines of Zeus Ammon subsequently appeared in the harbor city of Sparta and in Olympia. The Theban poet Pindar, whose house Alexander had left standing when he razed Thebes, also had celebrated Zeus Ammon 130 years before Alexander's visit, and the family of the great Spartan general Lysander had connections with the shrine and its god. Moreover, only thirty years before Alexander's visit to Egypt, a temple of Zeus Ammon had been built within the Piraeus, Athens' port. Even before he set out on his pilgrimage, then, Alexander would have had some in-depth knowledge of the famous mother shrine and its god, to whom he felt a lineal connection.

We are told that Alexander sought to visit the oracle because of its reputation for infallibility and because Perseus and Herakles had consulted Zeus Ammon—Perseus en route to slay the Gorgon, and Herakles while in Libya and Egypt searching for Antaeus and Busiris. Alexander wanted to equal the fame of these heroes, whose blood flowed in his veins; and, just as myths traced their descent from Zeus, Alexander believed that he too was descended from Ammon. Thus he undertook the expedition to Siwah to obtain more precise information on the subject—or, at any rate, to say that he had.

Some modern scholars have attempted to explain Alexander's visit to the oracle in more political or pragmatic terms. But the journey to Siwah entailed a long, difficult, and dangerous expedition that Alexander never would have undertaken without genuine, passionate interest. Alexander's piety and sense of descent or connection to the immortals, especially to Zeus, were powerful motives for him.

To begin the journey, Alexander sailed down the Nile from Memphis to Lake Mareotis with a force of light infantry and the Royal Squadron. There, ambassadors from the Greek city of Cyrene on the Libyan coast came to him with gifts, requesting peace and asking that he visit Libya. These envoys may have been sent to help solidify the position of the government they represented, which was facing civil unrest. Unintentionally, they also may have planted in Alexander's mind ideas about further conquests to the west.

At the time, however, Alexander marched westward along the coast through country uninhabited, but not waterless, to the city of Paraetonium (modern Mersa Matruh), now about 200 miles from Alexandria. Proceeding to the village of Apis, Alexander and his entourage turned southward in the direction of the oasis of Siwah, which lay somewhat less than 200 miles from the coast.

This was the truly dangerous and difficult portion of the journey, and several of Alexander's contemporaries, including Aristobulus, Ptolemy, and Callisthenes, wrote accounts of it. Callisthenes' account has been criticized for its blatant flattery of Alexander. But many of the phenomena Callisthenes and the others describe seem to be embellishments of features of the desert, rather than outright inventions.

During the first and second days of the journey south, the difficulties of the march seemed bearable, but then the party reached plains covered by deep sand just as they ran out of water. The land lay parched beneath the sun and the men's throats were dry and burned. Then clouds shrouded the sky and hid the sun, and soon high winds showered down generous quantities of rain. According to Arrian, Alexander attributed this cloudburst to Zeus Ammon himself.

But Alexander's party then lost its way. It was saved, according to Ptolemy, when two snakes suddenly appeared and led the army, hissing as they went. Alexander instructed his party to follow the snakes and trust the divinity, and the snakes led the way to the oracle and back again from it. Aristobulus, supported by Callisthenes' account, says that Alexander's guides were not snakes, but two crows, who flew before the men, acting as guides.

Although we may be skeptical about such miraculous rescues, sudden rainbursts, snakes, and crows are not unknown in the Libyan desert. Ptolemy's focus on the snakes also may be explained in terms of his own political agenda. Ptolemy's account of the visit to the oracle was committed to papyrus after he had established himself first as satrap and then as pharaoh of Egypt, a country in which snakes generally were considered sacred. For example, a cobra, the *uraeus*, visualized as the eye of the sun god Re, was depicted rearing up on the crown of the pharaohs, ready to protect the king. Snakes *may* have led Alexander, Ptolemy, and the rest of the Macedonians safely to the oracle and back. But for Ptolemy, writing decades later, their providential appearance was an early and convenient sign of local, divine favor. The snake story helped legitimize the rule of a pharaoh who in fact was a foreigner.

As for Aristobulus' and Callisthenes' story about the crows, if helpful crows appeared in Callisthenes' account, the story ultimately must have been agreeable to Alexander, who had hired Callisthenes to be the official historian of the campaign. Alexander perhaps was not displeased to have it be thought that the gods had sent along some crows to help him reach the oracle and return safely from it.

Whatever were the difficulties of the journey, Alexander finally reached the oasis of Siwah in eight days. The oasis was supposedly more than six miles wide, and many fine springs watered its copious trees. In the center of the oasis was a garden of olive and palm trees.

There also was a unique spring within the oasis, the Spring of the Sun, a natural phenomenon of great interest to classical historians. At midday the waters of the spring were cold, but as the sun set the waters became warmer, reaching their peak at midnight. After midnight the waters cooled again, until by dawn the waters of the spring were cold again, becoming coldest at noon.

Having reached this well-watered garden with its miraculous spring, Alexander set out to consult the oracle in the central sanctuary on the hill now called Aghurmi. When he was conducted into the temple and had gazed upon the god for a while, the priest who held the position of the god's prophet came out to meet him and said to Alexander, "Greetings, O son; take this form of address as from the god also."

To which Alexander supposedly replied, "I accept, O father; for the future I shall be called your son."

According to Plutarch's sources, however, the priest made a mistake in his greeting. Though he wanted to be polite and address Alexander with the salutation *"O paidion,"* or "O son," because of his poor command of Greek the priest instead greeted Alexander with the words *"O pai Dios,"* which meant "O son of Zeus."

Whether it was a mistake or not, Alexander immediately accepted the prophet's greeting with delight, and the legend began that the priest, the human mouthpiece of the god himself, had greeted Alexander as the son of Zeus. Alexander's intimations of his own divine lineage had been stunningly (if mistakenly) reinforced.

Next, we are told, Alexander asked the prophet whether the god had given him the rule of the whole world (or mankind), and whether Alexander had punished all of those responsible for his father's murder. The priest then presumably went into the inner sanctum of the shrine and put the questions to the god himself.

The infallible god had the form of an *omphalos*, or a large, egg-shaped stone studded with emeralds. This stone god was carried about by eighty priests on a litter in the form of a boat. These priests, bearing the stone god in his boat on their shoulders, walked (or staggered) about, without volition, wherever the god directed them. The prophet then interpreted the movements of the litter as responses to the questions asked of the god. To Greeks accustomed to anthropomorphic representations of gods, Zeus Ammon probably seemed quite exotic and even odd-looking; that was undoubtedly part of his appeal.

In answer to Alexander's first question, the priest cried that the god had granted Alexander his request. To the second question, about the punishment of Philip's murderers, Plutarch tells us that the priest cautioned Alexander to speak more guardedly, since *his* father (Alexander's) was not mortal. But in answer to the question of whether *Philip's* murderers had all been punished, the priest told Alexander that Philip had been avenged. Thus (according to this tradition) the god had pointedly implied that Olympias had told the truth after all: it was not Philip II of Macedon who had slithered into her bedroom on the night Alexander was conceived.

The questions Alexander asked Zeus Ammon and the answers he received have always been a source of fascination. Unfortunately, however, there is no contemporary evidence that the two questions (about world rule and Philip's assassins) were asked by Alexander or heard by anyone who was there at the time.

Rather, the questions may have been invented by later writers, such as Cleitarchus, who wanted to explain subsequent developments, such as Alexander's seemingly endless victories; or by Callisthenes, Alexander's official historian, who wanted to make sure that everyone knew that all of Philip's assassins had been punished, thereby exculpating Olympias and Alexander by infallible, divine pronouncement. Indeed, if we assume that Callisthenes only wrote things pleasing to Alexander, it is interesting that he, and implicitly Alexander, should have felt the *need* to have the king's innocence proclaimed by none other than Zeus Ammon. Whether the story therefore reveals filial devotion—or a guilty conscience—is an open question.

That the asking of the question about Philip's murderers *could* be interpreted in such a way may also explain why Arrian (whose account of the journey to the oracle drew upon Ptolemy and Aristobulus, both of whom went with Alexander to Siwah) simply reports that Alexander put his question to the oracle and received the answer that his heart desired. According to Arrian, no one actually heard (or at least later reported) what Alexander asked the god. And if no one heard the questions, there could be no gossip about the god granting Alexander rule of the whole world or exculpating Olympias and Alexander. If Arrian is correct, this may be all we can know about Alexander's famous consultation of Zeus Ammon.

But there also may be some later evidence that casts light on Alexander's consultation with the god. Years later, when Alexander reached what he believed were the ends of the earth, at the mouth of the Indus River, we are told that he made sacrifice to other gods and with a different ritual, in accordance with the oracle of Ammon. Thus the sacrifice to the other gods at that point must be related to what Alexander had been told by the god at Siwah.

Considering the context, we might deduce that the question Alexander asked the oracle was not whether he would rule over all mankind, but whether he would reach the ends of the earth itself, possibly undefeated when he got there. Unfortunately, Arrian leaves us frustratingly ignorant of what precisely the oracular utterance was that Alexander thought had been fulfilled when he reached the Outer Ocean.

Whatever Alexander thought about himself either before or after he consulted the oracle at Siwah, however, he could not have been displeased by his experience there, for he honored the god with rich gifts before setting back off for Egypt.

THE FOUNDATION OF ALEXANDRIA

After his visit to the oracle, Alexander returned to Egypt by the same route. Along the way, he founded Alexandria, the first and greatest of his cities. The foundation date suggested by later Roman tradition is April 7, 331 B.C.E.

All the sources agree that it was Alexander who personally decided to found a great city in Egypt. Indeed, he designed its general layout, inspired by a dream in which a gray-haired old man of venerable appearance stood by his side, and recited these lines from the *Odyssey:*

> *Out of the tossing sea where it breaks*
> *on the beaches of Egypt*
> *Rises an isle from the waters:*
> *the name that men give it is Pharos.*

Alexander got up the next morning and visited Pharos, then still an island near the Canopic mouth of the Nile, but later joined to the mainland by a causeway. Since there was no chalk, Alexander marked out the plan of his new city with barley meal in the shape of the Macedonian military cloak, the *chlamys.*

Huge flocks of birds, however, descended upon the site and devoured the barley. Alexander took this as a distressing omen. But this seemingly ominous event was interpreted by the seers as a sign that the city would not only have rich resources of its own, but would be the nurse of men of every nation.

This "prophecy" has been seen by some scholars as an anachronistic retrojection from Alexandria's subsequent history as a polyglot city of Macedonians, Greeks, Egyptians, Jews, and others, to the time of its foundation as a specifically Greek city. But the historian Curtius Rufus mentions that Alexander ordered people to migrate from neighboring cities to Alexandria to provide the new city with a large population. It is certain that the peoples of these neighboring cities cannot have been solely Greeks or Macedonians, since there were very few Greeks living in the neighboring areas of the Nile Delta at the time. A new city with a large population cannot have been made up of ethnic Greeks. The first Alexandria undoubtedly was a multi-ethnic city from its foundation, as Alexander intended.

At the same time, Alexandria in Egypt was physically organized as a fundamentally Greek city: Alexander indicated the location of the marketplace (*agora*), the temples to be built, what gods they should serve, including the gods of Greece and the Egyptian Isis, and its circuit wall. Alexandria therefore had the essential topographical layout and the physical structures characteristic of the Greek *polis*, as the spectacular underwater archaeological excavations increasingly have disclosed. That Alexander included a temple consecrated to the Egyptian Isis in his plan is, however, another indication of his respect for the religious traditions of a foreign people.

Although the new foundation had a city wall (as virtually all Greek cities did), Alexandria's fundamental function was not military. Nor was the city established primarily for commercial reasons, despite its later history. Rather, the choice of its name literally speaks for itself: with characteristic immodesty, the first Alexandria was founded to project the name of Alexander spatially, into Egypt, the fabled land of one of history's oldest civilizations, and temporally, into posterity. Indeed, Alexander never named a city after himself that he did not intend to be a permanent establishment. According to one Byzantine-era grammarian, there were finally no fewer than eighteen such Alexandrias dotting the landscape of the Middle and Near East.

THE FATHER OF ALL MANKIND

From the site of his first eponymous city, the king returned to Memphis, where he was visited by deputations from Greece and was joined by a new force of 400 Greek mercenaries and 500 Thracian cavalry. He once again offered sacrifice to Zeus the king and held a ceremonial parade of his troops under arms, followed by games with athletic and musical contests. As so often, a major sacrifice followed recent successes.

It was perhaps at this time that Alexander listened to the lectures of a philosopher named Psammon, who apparently argued that all men were ruled by Zeus, since in each case that which acquires mastery and rules is divine. Plutarch tells us that although Alexander approved of this argument, his own pronouncement on the subject was more philosophical: namely, that while Zeus was indeed the father of all mankind, he nevertheless made the best especially his own. Whether Alexander uttered these words in Egypt at this time or not, no better summation of Alexander's understanding of Zeus' relationship to mankind has ever been made.

Both clauses of Alexander's "more philosophical" pronouncement on the subject can be traced back to Alexander's favorite work of art, the *Iliad*, where Zeus is repeatedly referred to as the father of both men and gods. Moreover, in the epic world the best, the *aristoi* (e.g., Achilles, Hektor, and the other heroes), are especially dear to the gods. Achilles' quest to prove himself the best of the Achaeans is a central, perhaps *the* central, theme of the *Iliad*. The ideas Alexander perhaps enunciated in Egypt about Zeus' relationship to mankind and the best were thoroughly grounded in the theological world of the *Iliad*.

Alexander obviously believed that he belonged to those "best" whom Zeus made particularly his own. From his earliest days, Olympias had encouraged him to believe that he was a descendant of heroes and gods. Nothing he had accomplished would have discouraged this belief. Against all the odds, a king who was not yet thirty had met and defeated in battle the Great King of Persia and taken half his empire away from him. No Greek mortal of any age had accomplished such feats of arms; Achilles, Alexander's model and ancestor, had not even taken Troy. Alexander and his Macedonians had reversed the tides of history itself. By his deeds, Alexander had elevated himself not just to the ranks of the best: he was the best of the best. After what had happened at the Granicus and Issos, who could doubt that Alexander was beloved of the gods, especially of Zeus, who held sway over the entire world? According to the Colophonian natural philosopher Xenophanes, the Thracians, who had blue eyes and red hair, claimed that their gods had blue eyes and red hair. Of course Alexander's Zeus made the best especially his own. He was the father of the best: Alexander!

But Alexander's pronouncement also implied that among the rest of mankind were other *aristoi*, who were also dear to Zeus. Zeus made the best (plural) his very own. Alexander did *not* say that all the best were Greeks or Macedonians; indeed, the logical implication of his reply to Psammon was that the best could come from among all mankind.

If Plutarch has quoted Alexander accurately, what Alexander seems to have been claiming then was that there were men whom Zeus made his very own because they were the best, regardless of their ethnic background or nationality. This is important because it possibly gives us some idea of the theological underpinnings of Alexander's later willingness to incorporate the best of the Persians and some other conquered peoples into his army and the administration of his empire. As we have seen, Aristotle had advised his pupil to treat the conquered peoples of his empire like plants or animals; it is not easy to reconcile such advice with the belief that Zeus is the father of *all* mankind. Alexander's subsequent treatment of the "best" among the conquered peoples, on the other hand, is completely consistent with the beliefs he apparently expressed in Egypt.

LEAVING THE "TWO LANDS"

In addition to giving local philosophers lessons about Zeus' preferences, Alexander also reorganized Egypt politically, leaving two Egyptians as provincial governors (*nomarchs*), and installing garrisons at Memphis and Pelusium. Lycidas, a Greek from Aetolia, was left in charge of the mercenaries. A Companion was left as the secretary of foreign troops and two men of Chalcis were left to superintend the work of Lycidas and the Companion.

Governors of Libya and of Arabia by Heröopolis also were appointed. Peucestas, son of Macartatus, and Balacrus, son of Amyntas, were put in charge of the troops in Egypt. Command of the fleet was given to Polemon, son of Theramenes. Various other promotions in the army also were made.

Alexander was deeply impressed by Egypt and the potential strength of the country: that is why he divided its control among several officers. He did not believe it was safe to entrust the governance of such a rich and important country to one man. The Roman emperors later took a leaf from Alexander's book: they never sent a senator there as proconsul, but always governors and administrators drawn from the class of *equites*, or knights. The Roman emperors feared what a Roman senator might do with the resources of Egypt at his disposal.

As for Alexander, with a renewed sense of confidence in his divinely sanctioned destiny, he and the Macedonians marched out of Egypt in the spring of 331 beneath the shadows of the pyramids, determined to find Darius and his great army wherever they were and to settle the contest for Asia, once and for all.

CHAPTER 10

The Battle of Gaugamela

FROM MEMPHIS TO TYRE

The first order of business after Alexander left Memphis on his way to Phoenicia was a brief punitive campaign in Samaria, the region lying between Judaea and the Galilee. While Alexander was in Egypt, the Samaritans had burned alive Andromachus, whom he had put in charge of Syria. After punishing those held responsible, by summer the army reached Tyre, where the fleet was waiting.

In Tyre, Alexander once again honored Herakles with religious celebrations and games, perhaps a sign that he anticipated great labors. The kings of Cyprus sponsored dithyrambic choruses and tragedies featuring some of the most prominent actors of the day. During the performance of one comedy, Lycon of Scarpheia introduced a line into his character's speech asking Alexander for a present of ten talents. Alexander laughed and gave the enterprising thespian the money.

The matter of Alexander's Athenian prisoners then arose again. The Athenian state galley, the *Paralus*, crewed by free citizens and bearing envoys named Diophantus and Achilles, arrived. The purpose of the embassy was to ask for the return of the Athenians taken prisoner at the battle of the Granicus. Alexander had already denied a similar request two years before, but the strategic situation now was quite different.

Since 332 a war between Macedonian troops and the mercenary army of the Spartan king Agis had been raging on the island of Crete. To deal with this dangerous situation, Alexander dispatched his admiral Amphoterus with the fleet to assist the Macedonians and to help support his allies in the Peloponnese. To keep Athens neutral in the conflict, Alexander now promised to return the Athenian prisoners of war.

Amphoterus was sent with orders to support all the Greek cities that were "sound" on the Persian War and did not listen to the Spartans. Phoenicia and Cyprus supplied a hundred additional ships for the war in the Peloponnese. By the spring of 330, these forces and Antipater would combine to defeat the Spartan king.

DARIUS' SECOND OVERTURE

The summer of 331 brought another overture from Darius as well. After praising Alexander for his generous treatment of his mother and the other royal captives, Darius offered him all the land west of the Euphrates, 30,000 talents of silver, and the hand of one of his daughters in return for a cessation of hostilities. If he accepted, Alexander would become Darius' son-in-law and would share the rule of the whole empire. To judge by the terms of the offer, Darius made his offer to Alexander for both strategic and personal reasons.

Alexander called his friends together into a council and put the alternatives before them. After a silence, Parmenio alone dared to speak up: "If I were Alexander," he said, "I should accept what was offered and make a treaty." To which Alexander replied, "So should I, if I were Parmenio."

Alexander then told the envoys that the earth could not maintain its plan and order if there were two suns, nor could the world remain calm and free from war as long as two kings ruled. If Darius desired supremacy, he should fight Alexander to see which of them would have sole rule. If Darius despised glory and preferred a life of ease, then he should obey Alexander, but remain king over all other rulers, since this privilege was given to him by Alexander's generosity. Such was Alexander's reply.

Moreover, there was more bad news for Darius after he received Alexander's insulting response. Darius' wife Stateira, who had been taken prisoner by Alexander after the battle of Issos, died in childbirth. Alexander provided her with a sumptuous funeral. Plutarch says that the magnanimity and self-restraint Alexander had shown toward her in captivity lessened Darius' agitation and misery at his wife's misfortune.

The difference of opinion between Parmenio and Alexander in 331 was real and revealing. Parmenio may have believed that Alexander and the Macedonians had punished the Persians sufficiently by now, in accordance with the propaganda of the campaign. Moreover, the older, more experienced man may have thought it better to quit while the Macedonians were ahead; all could yet be lost in one battle against the vast numbers that Darius at that very moment was gathering in Babylon.

Alexander, however, clearly had a different personal and strategic conception. Ever since the battle at the Granicus, Alexander apparently was not interested in a simple, punitive campaign. His decision to disband his fleet and his strategy of defeating the Persian fleet on land had proved correct, given his resources and above all his personal objective: to conquer the entire Persian empire. Once the Persian fleet had been eliminated as an effective fighting force after the death of Memnon, Alexander had almost no reason to accept Darius' offer of half the prize he desired.

Just as in battle, in council Alexander pursued his objectives with a ruthless single-mindedness. Unlike Parmenio, he was a risk-taker, and the cards he now held were better than the ones he had played when he stood to gain less. So by midsummer of 331 Alexander prepared to set out from Tyre, to test the gods' favor yet again.

THE GATHERING STORM

Meanwhile, in Babylon Darius was mustering his grand army. Although cut off from the manpower resources of some of his former provinces in the west, he still could call up huge levies from the eastern and northeastern parts of his empire. After Darius sent out the order for his governors and their troops to come to Babylon, vast numbers of warriors did make their way to Mesopotamia. They came from a long list of nations and tribes: tough, battle-tested Sogdians, Bactrians, and Indians from the Bactrian border, especially adept at guerrilla warfare; contingents of the Sacae, a branch of the Asiatic Scythians, who fought in suits of laminated armor; Arachotians and Indian hillmen; and mounted Parthians, Hyrcanians, and Tapurians. From closer to home, Medes had turned up to fight alongside their kinsmen; contingents from the Persian Gulf followed. Uxians and Susiani had come down from their redoubts. Lowland and Mesopotamian Syrians had joined the grand army. Even the Babylonians, known better for their peacetime talents, had taken up arms.

The list of Persian levies was not quite as long as Homer's catalogue of ships in book 2 of the *Iliad*. But the geographical origins of the contingents under Darius' command do give some idea of the spread of Persian rule to the north and east, and of its rich diversity.

Altogether Darius' force consisted of no fewer than 40,000 cavalry and a million infantry, according to Arrian. These totals are perhaps somewhat exaggerated, but there is no doubt that Darius assembled a very large army, one clearly numerically superior to Alexander's forces.

Nor would Darius rely solely on his vast numerical advantage. After facing the *sarissa*-wielding Macedonian phalanx at the battle of Issos, Darius had fashioned for his army swords and lances much longer than those previously carried into battle. Darius also had constructed 200 scythe-bearing chariots to astonish and terrify his enemy. The scythes on these chariots projected out in front of the horses and also from the sides. Finally, Indian troops from the far side of the Indus had brought Darius about fifteen elephants, a terrifying superweapon, by which Darius hoped to stem the inevitable Macedonian cavalry charge.

Darius understood that his infantry was relatively weak compared with the Macedonian phalanx, but that his cavalry was strong. The cavalry on the right side of his line at Issos, after all, might have achieved a local, tactical victory had it not been forced to retreat to help the shattered left wing (and hard-pressed center) of his line. Now he had given his infantry what he hoped would be more effective weapons. He intended to use the scythed chariots to wreak havoc among Alexander's heavy infantry. But he meant to win the battle with his cavalry, which, given adequate space, might be able to envelop the Macedonian line on one or both of its flanks.

Clearly, it was not in Darius' interest to fight Alexander from behind the walls of Babylon. Alexander had shown at Tyre what he could do if his enemy opted to stay behind city walls, even the high, thick walls of a courageously defended island city. So Darius wisely chose to move north to the open plains of Assyria (modern northern Iraq). His plan was to deploy for battle in the area of Nineveh (modern Kuyunjik and Nebi Yunus), where the terrain was well suited to his purpose, affording ample maneuvering room for the huge forces at his disposal.

To give himself time to reach his selected field of battle, Darius sent the satrap Mazaeus forward to discover Alexander's progress and to stop or (more likely) forestall his crossing of the Euphrates. Darius meanwhile made his way with the bulk of his army through the Mesopotamian plain, over the Tigris to Arbela and finally to Gaugamela. There his soldiers literally dug themselves into the plain between the river Bumelus (Gomil) and the Jebel Maqlub, the highest of the hills that together intersect the terrain between the Tigris River and the foothills of the Zagros Mountains.

On the plain the Persians set about smoothing out the ground so that no broken surface might obstruct the movement of cavalry. Military discipline was maintained by continued training and practice. After all of his preparations, Darius was most concerned, however, that confusion might arise in the battle, owing to the different languages spoken by his soldiers. Given the list of combatants he had called up from around the Persian empire, Darius' concern was not unwarranted. Unfortunately, we do not know what measures he adopted to deal with this not insignificant problem. But his other actions show that Darius was a careful commander and would leave nothing to chance.

FROM TYRE TO GAUGAMELA

Alexander, meanwhile, had set out from Tyre and reached Thapsacus (on the upper Euphrates) in August 331. The Macedonians nearly had completed construction of two bridges across the Euphrates River, but had not quite brought them to the farther bank because of the presence of Mazaeus, with his 3,000 mounted troops, waiting there. At Alexander's approach, however, Mazaeus made off, and the Macedonian engineers finished their job. Alexander thus was able to cross the river.

From Thapsacus Alexander and the Macedonian army probably marched to Harran (the Assyrian city in northwestern Mesopotamia) and then eastward along the route from Rhesaena to Nisibis (modern Nusaybin) in northeastern Mesopotamia, and finally on to the Tigris River. Alexander crossed the Tigris without opposition except for the swift current.

While the troops were resting afterward there was an almost total eclipse of the moon, dated to nine P.M. on September 20, 331. Alexander offered sacrifice to Moon, Sun, and Earth, the three deities said to have caused the phenomenon. Alexander's trusted seer Aristander prophesied that the Moon's eclipse was propitious for the Macedonians and Alexander: the impending battle would be fought before the end of the month, and the sacrifices portended victory.

On the fourth day after the crossing, Macedonian advance scouts sighted an advance guard of enemy cavalry in open ground, but their numbers could not be accurately assessed. Alexander himself then led a flying force of the Royal Squadron, one squadron of Companions, and the Paeonian mounted scouts (*prodromoi*) against a thousand (or so) Persian cavalry. Some of these were captured, and it was learned that Darius was not far off, with a powerful force.

Alexander pitched camp and rested his troops for four days. He then moved his army to a base camp below the northern foothills of Jebel Maqlub. From there, leaving behind the baggage animals and soldiers unfit for duty, he took his army across the hills. As his army descended the hills, Alexander saw the enormous enemy host. The sight led him to call an immediate meeting of his general staff officers.

PREPARATIONS FOR BATTLE

Alexander now consulted with his personal Companions, generals, squadron commanders, and the officers of the allied and mercenary contingents. To them he put a question: should they advance at once, or camp where they were and make a detailed survey of the field of battle? The majority urged Alexander to advance immediately with the main infantry. Parmenio, however, advised a careful reconnaissance. For once,

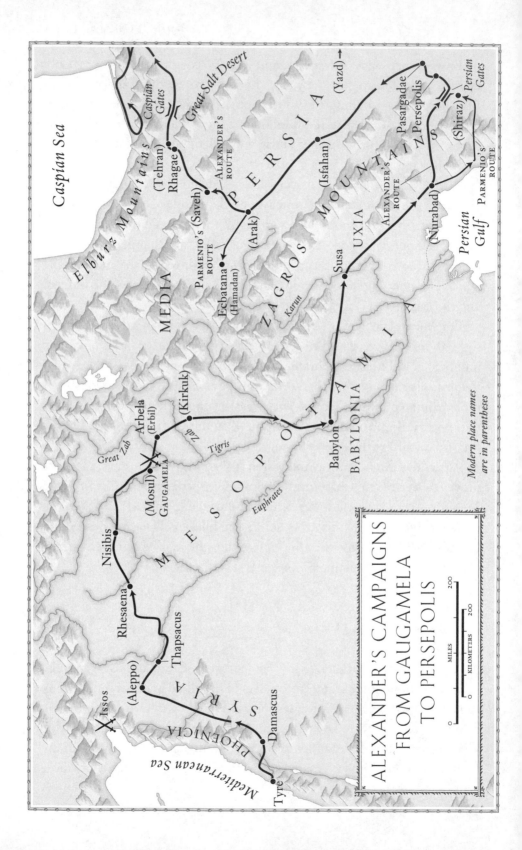

ALEXANDER'S CAMPAIGNS
FROM GAUGAMELA
TO PERSEPOLIS

*Modern place names
are in parentheses*

Caspian Sea

Elburz Mountains

Caspian Gates

Great Salt Desert

(Tehran) Rhagae

(Yazd)→

Pasargadae

Persian Gates

Persepolis

PERSIA

ALEXANDER'S ROUTE

PARMENIO'S (Saveh) ROUTE

(Arak)

(Isfahan)

(Shiraz)

MEDIA

Ecbatana (Hamadan)

ZAGROS MOUNTAINS

ALEXANDER'S ROUTE

PARMENIO'S ROUTE

Karun

UXIA

(Nurabad)

Persian Gulf

Susa

Kirkuk)

Arbela (Erbil)

Zab

(Mosul) GAUGAMELA

Great Zab

Tigris

Babylon

BABYLONIA

MESOPOTAMIA

Nisibis

Euphrates

Rhesaena

Thapsacus

(Aleppo)

SYRIA

Issos

PHOENICIA

Damascus

Mediterranean Sea

Tyre

MILES

KILOMETERS

200

Alexander agreed. Light infantry and Companion cavalry were sent out to inspect the terrain.

After the reconnaissance was completed, a second meeting of commanders was held. At the staff meeting Alexander exhorted his officers to encourage their troops: the sovereignty of all Asia was there and then to be decided, he declared. They should urge each man, in the moment of danger, to keep his place in the line and to heed the requirements of order: to remain perfectly silent when necessary; to shout loudly when it was right to shout; and to howl to inspire fear, when the moment to howl came. Above all, each man should remember that neglect of his own duty would bring the whole cause into common danger, while energetic attention to it would contribute to the common success.

If Arrian faithfully reports here at least the essence of what Alexander said at the time, it is interesting to note that Alexander's speech, rather than focusing on Macedonian successes in the past, concentrated upon what individual soldiers had to do during the impending battle for the army as a whole to be successful. Alexander simply told his soldiers that if they did their jobs, then all would be well. No heroics were needed. As ever, heroics could be left to someone else—Alexander. By such "pep" talks effective military leaders traditionally have helped those under their command to face imminent combat.

In response to Alexander's speech, the assembled commanders assured him that they could be relied upon. Having brought the meeting to a close, Alexander then ordered the army to eat and rest. Parmenio afterward went to Alexander's tent and advised him to attack the Persians at night; the enemy would be surprised, confused, and more prone to panic during a night attack, he suggested. Since others were listening, Alexander replied grandiloquently that it would be dishonorable (*aischron*) to steal a victory (at night). Alexander had to win his victory openly and without stratagem.

While the presentation of Alexander's response to Parmenio probably belongs to the hostile literary tradition that was created by Alexander's publicists after the king and the old general had their falling out, behind the rhetorical flourish lay sound tactical and strategic judgment. Alexander, a student of warfare from the Trojan War to his own day, knew that combat at night was notoriously unpredictable. Stronger attacking forces often had been defeated by weaker ones, contrary to expectation.

Once the element of surprise had been adjusted for, anything could happen.

Alexander also recognized that to become king of all Asia he must capture or kill Darius himself. Nothing less would suffice. If Darius escaped, a distinct possibility given the confusion of warfare at night, Alexander would not have his decisive and final victory. And if the Macedonians came out the worse, they would be alone in a hostile country. Above all, however, if Alexander believed, as he apparently did, that the Macedonians could and would defeat the Persians during the day, there was no reason to risk the uncertainties of a night battle.

Alexander rejected Parmenio's advice because he trusted in Aristander's interpretation of the sacrifices: the Macedonians would win, and they would win before the end of the month. Alexander relied upon the divine inspiration of his seer rather than the seasoned advice of his best and most experienced general. At the defining moment of his life, Alexander placed his ultimate trust in the gods.

Indeed, Alexander spent the night before the battle in front of his tent in the company not of his generals but of his seer, Aristander, with whom he performed sacred ceremonies and sacrificed to the god Fear (*Phobos*), for the first and only time. Some commentators have interpreted this sacrifice as an indication of fear or doubt on Alexander's part. This interpretation represents a fundamental misunderstanding of how Greek religion itself worked. Alexander's sacrifice to the god Fear was a way of giving that god his due lest he visit the Macedonians during the battle and extract his price. Alexander believed that the only thing the Macedonians had to fear was Fear himself. If the Macedonians fearlessly did their jobs, and left the heroics to the hero, they would win, as Aristander promised.

The Persians meanwhile were standing to arms throughout the night, and Darius held a review of them by torchlight. They had no camp surrounding them and they feared a night attack—just as Parmenio suggested. There was no meal or rest for them. This enervating stand to arms and the anxiety that arose during it subsequently told against the Persians more than anything else.

When dawn finally broke, the Persians were still under arms, while Alexander overslept. In fact, it was only with difficulty that Parmenio was able to rouse Alexander after entering his tent, standing by his couch, and calling out his name two or three times.

Finally having awakened Alexander, the astonished general asked the king how he could possibly sleep as if already victorious. Smiling, Alexander replied that the Macedonians already *had* won the battle, now that they had been delivered from wandering about in a vast and desolate country in pursuit of Darius, who heretofore had fled the fight.

BATTLE FORMATIONS

As it happens, we know exactly how the Persians stood to fight, because the Persian order of battle fell into Macedonian hands afterward. On the left of the Persian line was stationed the Bactrian cavalry, supported by the Dahae and the Arachotians. Next to these (from the outside to the center) were the mixed Persian cavalry and infantry, followed by the Susian and the Cadusian contingents. This was the disposition of units up to the center of the entire phalanx.

To the right were the contingents from "Hollow" (lowland) Syria and Mesopotamia, and farther to the right, the Medes. In touch with these were the Parthians and the Sacae, then the Topeirians, and next the Hycanians. Last, closest to the center, were the Albanians and Sacesinians.

In the center of the line was Darius himself with a thousand of his kinsmen, the royal Persian bodyguard with the golden apples on their spear-butts, the Indians, the "transplanted" Carians (who had been carried off from their homeland), and the Mardian archers. Uxians, Babylonians, troops from the Persian Gulf, and Sittacenians were drawn up in deep formation behind them.

In addition, in front of the Persian left wing (facing Alexander's right wing) were the Scythian cavalry, about a thousand Bactrians, and one hundred scythed chariots. The elephants and another fifty chariots were posted in close support of the royal squadron of the king's cavalry.

Another fifty chariots were posted in front of the Persian right wing, as were the Armenian and Cappadocian cavalry. The Greek mercenary infantry was drawn up facing the Macedonian infantry phalanx in two sections, one on each side of Darius and his Persian guard. These Greek

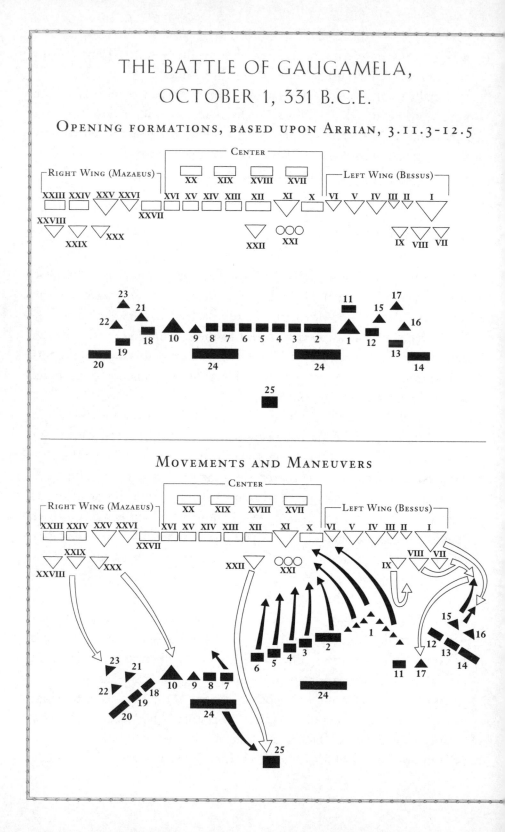

THE BATTLE OF GAUGAMELA,
OCTOBER 1, 331 B.C.E.

Opening formations, based upon Arrian, 3.11.3–12.5

Movements and Maneuvers

Macedonians

1. Companion cavalry, commanded by Philotas
2. *Hypaspistai*, commanded by Nicanor
3. Infantry phalanx brigade (*pezhetairoi*) of Coenus
4. Infantry phalanx brigade (*pezhetairoi*) of Perdiccas
5. Infantry phalanx brigade (*pezhetairoi*) of Meleager
6. Infantry phalanx brigade (*pezhetairoi*) of Polyperchon
7. Infantry phalanx brigade (*pezhetairoi*) of Amyntas (Simmias)
8. Infantry phalanx brigade (*pezhetairoi*) of Craterus
9. Allied Greek cavalry, commanded by Erigyius
10. Thessalian cavalry, commanded by Philip
11. Agrianians, archers and javelin men, commanded by Balacrus
12. Agrianians, commanded by Attalus
13. Macedonian archers, commanded by Brison
14. Old mercenary infantry, commanded by Cleander
15. *Prodromoi*, commanded by Aretes
16. Paeonian cavalry, commanded by Ariston
17. Mercenary infantry, commanded by Menidas
18. Thracian javelin men, commanded by Sitalces
19. Cretan archers
20. Achaean mercenary infantry
21. Allied Greek cavalry, commanded by Coeranus
22. Thracian cavalry, commanded by Agathon
23. Mercenary cavalry, commanded by Andromachus
24. Greek infantry
25. Thracian infantry and grooms

Persians

Left Wing

I. Bactrian cavalry, commanded by Bessus
II. Dahae cavalry
III. Arachosian cavalry, commanded by Barsaentes(?)
IV. Persian cavalry and infantry
V. Susian cavalry
VI. Cadusian cavalry
VII. Scythian cavalry
VIII. Bactrian cavalry
IX. Scythed chariots

Center

X. Greek mercenary infantry
XI. Cavalry with Darius
XII. *Melophoroi* (Golden Apples)
XIII. Greek mercenary infantry
XIV. Indians
XV. Carians, commanded by Bupares
XVI. Mardian archers
XVII. Uxians, commanded by Oxathres(?)
XVIII. Babylonians, commanded by Bupares(?)
XIX. Tribesmen from the Red Sea, commanded by Ocondobates, Ariobarzanes, and Orxines(?)
XX. Sittacenians, commanded by Bupares(?)
XXI. Elephants
XXII. Scythed chariots

Right Wing

XXIII. Coelo-Syrian and Mesopotamian cavalry, commanded by Mazaeus
XXIV. Median cavalry, commanded by Atropates
XXV. Parthian and Sacae cavalry
XXVI. Topeirian and Hyrcanian cavalry, commanded by Phrataphernes(?)
XXVII. Albanians and Sacesinians
XXVIII. Armenian cavalry, commanded by Orontes
XXIX. Cappadocian cavalry, commanded by Ariaces
XXX. Scythed chariots

▭ Persian infantry

△ Persian cavalry

○ Persian elephants

 Macedonian infantry

 Macedonian cavalry

mercenaries were considered the only infantry on the Persian side capable of standing up to the Macedonian phalanx.

Once Alexander was awakened the Macedonian army was marshaled in the most complex formation used thus far. The tactical requirements of the situation demanded no less.

On the right wing was the Companion cavalry, led by the Royal Squadron in front, and commanded by Cleitus the Black. Parmenio's son Philotas was the general officer in charge. The shock troops (*agema*) of the Guards were closest to the Companion cavalry, supported by the rest of the Guards units who were commanded by Nicanor, another son of Parmenio. Next were the infantry battalions commanded successively by Coenus, Perdiccas, Meleager, Polyperchon, and Simmias.

The left of the Macedonian line was held by the infantry battalion of Craterus, who also commanded the entire left of the phalanx. Next to them came the allied cavalry under Erigyius and next to them, on the left wing, the Thessalian cavalry commanded by Philip. Parmenio was the overall commander of the Macedonian left. Close around him were the mounted troops of Pharsalus, the best and most numerous of the Thessalian cavalry. Crucially, behind the front line was a reserve phalanx formation. The officers of this formation had orders to face about and meet any attack coming from the rear.

Half of the Agrianes under Attalus, and the Macedonian archers under Brison were thrown forward at an oblique angle on the right wing next to the Royal Squadron of the Companion cavalry in case it was necessary to extend or close up the front line of infantry. Next to the archers were the "Old Guard" of mercenaries under Cleander.

In advance of these units were posted *prodromoi* and the Paeonians under Aretes and Ariston. At the very front of the oblique formation on the right wing was the Greek mercenary cavalry under Menidas. He and his men had orders to wheel about at an angle and attack the enemy flank if the enemy tried to ride around their wing.

In front of the Royal Squadron of the Companion cavalry were half of the Agrianes and archers, supported by Balacrus' javelin men, who were posted opposite the Persian scythed chariots.

On Alexander's far left, forming another oblique angle to his front, were the Thracian javelin men under Sitalces, supported by the allied cavalry under Coeranus, and then the Odrysian cavalry under Agathon.

At the front of this section were the foreign mercenary cavalry commanded by Andromachus. Thracian infantry guarded the pack animals. Alexander's entire army totaled 7,000 cavalry and about 40,000 infantry.

His battle order obviously was set in order to deal with the Persian numerical superiority and the likelihood of being outflanked on the right or the left or on both wings. Thus, Alexander and his staff presented Darius and the Persian army with a kind of rectangle or tactical square, designed to repel attacks on all four sides. It was a brilliant adaptation to the situation facing the Macedonians.

THE BATTLE OF GAUGAMELA

Before the two armies met, Alexander gave a long address to the Thessalians and the other Hellenes, who shouted for him to lead them against the barbarians. Alexander realized that the role of the Thessalians in the battle would be crucial. If they broke or were defeated on the left of his line, all would be lost. If they held up under the pressure of the inevitable Persian cavalry charge, Aristander's prophecy might come true.

Alexander was wearing a vest made in Sicily and over this a breastplate of two-ply linen taken from the spoils of Issos. The helmet he wore was a work of Theophilos, made of iron. It gleamed like silver and fitted to it was an iron gorget set with precious stones. Around his waist was fastened an elaborate belt, a work of Helicon, given to him by the city of Rhodes. He carried a sword of astonishing temper and lightness, presented to him by the king of the Citieans. Unlike many of the Macedonian riders, Alexander had trained himself to rely chiefly on his sword in battle.

As he had been at the Granicus, Alexander was almost ostentatiously visible both to his own troops and to the enemy as he rode up and down the line, exhorting the officers and anyone else nearby. There could be no doubt who Alexander was and what he was about to do. Readying himself for the attack, Alexander, now mounted on Bucephalas, shifted his lance into his left arm and raised his right hand. The king then called upon the gods and prayed: if he really were sprung from Zeus, let the gods protect and strengthen the Greeks.

Aristander, wearing a white mantle and with a crown of gold on his head, also rode along the lines and fortuitously spotted an eagle that hovered above Alexander's head, apparently directing its flight against the Persians. This was said to have filled the Macedonians with great courage. The Macedonians could have received no better omen: the eagle was the creature most dear to Zeus.

The proper omens found, Alexander sparked the combat, moving to the attack with the Royal Squadron. At once, he was outflanked on his right, and he inclined farther to that side. The Persians countered this move, far outflanking the Macedonian right. During this time the Persian chariots remained on their smooth, prepared ground. However, as Alexander moved even farther out to the right, the Persian mounted troops moved with him, out to their left.

Alexander's initial attack in the battle of Gaugamela, at an oblique angle until his right wing made contact with the Persian left, was a tactical innovation that anticipated by two millennia tactics that would make Frederick the Great the most celebrated soldier of his day. Attacking at an oblique angle allowed Alexander to "economize"—that is, to hold in reserve his other forces until he was ready (as always) to launch his decisive offensive thrust at the head of the Companion cavalry.

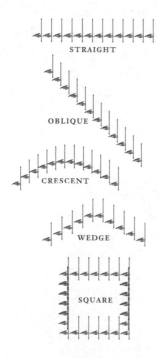

Although the Macedonian Foot Companions (*pezhetairoi*) could be deployed in any formation (straight line, oblique, crescent, or wedge) to suit the requirements of the tactical situation, at the battle of Gaugamela it was Alexander's innovative use of a tactical square that allowed the Macedonians to defeat the Persians despite the Persians' vast numerical superiority.

Alexander then ordered an attack by Menidas and the mercenary cavalry against the Persian mounted troops. This was probably another one of Alexander's tactical stratagems, designed to draw the Persians into committing their cavalry, in preparation for a devastating counterattack. Alexander had used a similar "drawing" tactic at the Granicus, when he had sent Socrates and his squadron down into the riverbed to bring the Persian cavalry down from the high ground into the river. If this was what Alexander intended at Gaugamela, however, it did not work. The numerically superior Scythian cavalry and the Bactrians counterattacked in very good order, driving Menidas' small squadron back, but not into disorder. Thereupon, Alexander put into the action the Paeonians and the mercenaries. There a cavalry engagement ensued in which the Macedonians eventually broke the enemy formation.

Meanwhile, before Alexander could get off the level, prepared ground, Darius sent his scythed chariots into action. They were met by the Agrianes and Balacrus' javelin throwers, who dragged the drivers to the ground and cut down the horses. The Macedonians let other chariots through their formations, to be dealt with by guards and Alexander's grooms. The calm way the Agrianes and the javelin throwers eliminated these terrifying contraptions helps to explain why the Macedonian army never lost a battle while Alexander led it. Alexander was a visionary genius of warfare commanding men as brave and as competent as any soldiers of any era.

On the far left wing, however, the Macedonians fared less well. Mazaeus, who commanded the best of the Persian cavalry on the right side of the Persian line, killed a number of Alexander's men during the first onslaught. He also sent 2,000 Cadusians and 1,000 picked Scythian horsemen around Parmenio's flank to the Macedonians' camp to capture the baggage. When the Scythians stormed into the camp, most of the captive Persian women rushed out to welcome them; Sisygambis, the mother of Darius, however, did not. She neither trusted the turns of fortune nor wished to tarnish her gratitude toward Alexander, we are told. Less colorfully, but more important, using his superior numbers, Mazaeus pressed his attack and the Macedonians on the left of Alexander's line gave ground.

But what proved to be the decisive action of the battle took place on the Macedonian right. As more Persian cavalry were sent to help their

comrades who were attempting to encircle the Macedonian right, a gap
was opened up in the Persian front. Into that gap, at the double, with a
loud battle cry Alexander rode with the Companion cavalry in its famous
wedge formation, along with the part of the phalanx stationed there,
straight in the direction of Darius himself. This was the one drop—or
wave—that made the vessel run over, the moment in the engagement
when, as Napoleon observed in another context, a single maneuver was
decisive and gave the victory to one side. A close struggle ensued, with
the Macedonians thrusting at the Persians' faces with their spears and
the phalanx, bristling with pikes, adding irresistible weight. At some
point during this fierce encounter Darius took fright and rode for safety.
Meanwhile, Aretas and his men broke up a Persian outflanking party.

The infantry battalion under Simmias, however, was unable to join
up with Alexander as he pursued the Persians; it was forced to stand and
fight on the spot, especially because the Macedonian left still was having
difficulties. Between Alexander's force and Simmias' a gap opened up in
the Macedonian line. Some of the Indian and Persian cavalry burst
through this hole and advanced to the place where the pack animals
were held. The reserve phalanx then sprang into action and dealt with
these Indians and Persians. Alexander's tactical square had functioned
just as designed.

On Alexander's far left, however, the Persians were pressing home
the attack against Parmenio's forces. Eventually Parmenio was compelled to send a dispatch rider or riders to Alexander to report that his
troops were in distress and needed help.

But, according to one account, Parmenio's riders found that Alexander was already in pursuit of Darius, and the messengers gave up hope of

The *hypaspistai* (whose name in
Greek meant literally, "under
the shield,") were heavy infantry,
commanded by Nicanor, the son
of Parmenio, at the battle of
Gaugamela. Its elite unit, the
agema, protected the king when
he fought on foot.

reaching him. Parmenio and the Thessalians were left to face Mazaeus and his cavalry on their own. Fighting brilliantly, they eventually emerged victorious against an enemy disheartened by Darius' flight. Indeed, Parmenio eventually took possession of the Persian camp including all of its baggage, elephants, and camels. Alexander meanwhile pursued Darius to Arbela but could not overtake him; once again he captured Darius' chariot, his shield, and his bow and arrows, but not the Persian king himself.

By an alternative tradition, Alexander did receive the message from Parmenio; he at once broke off his pursuit of Darius and came to the aid of the Thessalians. Encountering first the enemy cavalry already in flight, and then the Parthians, the Indians, and the Persian cavalry, the most numerous and best of the enemy forces, Alexander and the *hetairoi* then fought the fiercest cavalry engagement of the whole battle. There was no throwing of javelins or maneuvering of horses. The cavalrymen of both sides sought only to break their way through, giving and taking blows unsparingly. About sixty Companion cavalry lost their lives, and among the wounded were several commanders. But Alexander was once again victorious.

Which of the "messenger" stories is true?

The first story is consistent with what the majority of sources report about the circumstances at the moment when the riders were dispatched. Diodorus tells us that because of the numbers of the Persians, and the thickness of the dust, Alexander could not tell in what direction Darius was fleeing. Confusion and thick dust thus prevented Parmenio's riders from delivering their message. If Alexander did come to the aid of Parmenio and the Thessalians, it was essentially after the engagement on the Macedonian left wing was settled, and perhaps after Alexander had broken off his pursuit of Darius anyway.

The second version, on the other hand, was created by Callisthenes, Alexander's court historian, who was responsible for developing a portrait of Parmenio as sluggish and inefficient in this battle and indecisive elsewhere. So the story of Alexander breaking off his pursuit of Darius to help a beleaguered Parmenio should be seen as propaganda, generated later to justify Alexander's failure to achieve what for him was the primary objective of the battle itself: the capture of Darius. The story of Alexander saving Parmenio was a fig leaf created to cover over or explain

Alexander's failure to capture or kill Darius at Gaugamela and thus to bring the pan-Hellenic campaign to an end.

Nevertheless, the seer Aristander had been right: before the month that saw the moon's eclipse was over, the battle had been fought and Alexander had won it.

THE COSTS OF THE BATTLE

The fulfillment of the prophecy had a dreadful human cost. Diodorus tells us that about 500 Macedonians were killed and very many wounded, among the latter being Hephaestion, Perdiccas, Coenus, and Menidas, some of the most prominent Macedonian officers. Diodorus also gives a figure of 90,000 Persian cavalry and infantry killed.

The risks to Alexander and to the Macedonian army as a whole at the battle of Gaugamela cannot be overestimated. The Macedonians were outnumbered and potentially overlapped on both wings. Moreover, if they had lost the battle, there was nowhere to hide; for them, it was victory or death.

Once again, Alexander had understood perfectly the tactical dangers facing the Macedonians, and he had devised a revolutionary order of battle to meet the challenge. Of the Macedonians, he wisely required only that they do their jobs in their places within his brilliantly conceived tactical square. As the battle unfolded, the Macedonians fought as if there were no tomorrow. Although his opening gambit (the drawing attack of Menidas) failed, Alexander personally led what proved to be the decisive charge into his opponent's line. Despite what Alexander's propagandists later claimed, Parmenio had fought a crucial holding action against the finest of the Persian cavalry. Although Darius' escape was a major setback for Alexander, the victory at Gaugamela against the numbers and the odds had left open the road to Babylon and Persia. At the age of twenty-six Alexander had led the Macedonians and their allies to the greatest military victory in Greek history.

CHAPTER 11

The Sack of Persepolis

BABYLON

For Greeks and Macedonians, Gaugamela was a moment of unprecedented triumph. Not since Plataea in 479 had a Hellenic army so decisively defeated a Persian force. Yet even that famous victory had been achieved against what amounted to an expeditionary force, led by one of the Great King's generals. Now Alexander and his peerless Companions had utterly annihilated Persia's grand imperial army, commanded by Darius himself. After three years of warfare Alexander was the sole ruler of the western half of the Persian empire. Darius, still the ruler of its eastern provinces, had survived Gaugamela, but for how long?

After the battle, Darius made his escape first to Arbela and thence eastward by way of the Armenian mountains into Media with the Bactrian cavalry, some Persians, the royal kinsmen, and a few of the Golden Apples. Media, the homeland of the Medes, comprised the Kermanshah-Hamadan region in the central Zagros along the Khorasan road. During his flight the monarch was joined by around 2,000 of the foreign mercenaries.

Alexander, as we have seen, had pursued Darius to Arbela, but was too late to capture him. Nevertheless, in Arbela Alexander was first proclaimed king of Asia, despite the fact that Darius was still alive. In keeping with the propaganda of the campaign, Alexander then wrote to the Greeks, stating that all tyrannies were now abolished and that henceforth they were autonomous.

He wrote to the Plataeans, too, saying that he would rebuild their city because their forefathers had made their territory available to the Greeks in the struggle for their common freedom (against the Persians in 479). He also sent some of the spoils from Gaugamela to the city of Croton in Italy. In 480, when the rest of the Greeks in Italy had refused to help their fellow Hellenes against the invading Persians, a citizen of Croton, an athlete named Phaÿllus, had equipped a ship at his own expense and sailed to Salamis to share in the common danger. By such gestures Alexander was signaling to the Greeks that at least some of the objectives of the pan-Hellenic campaign had been fulfilled.

Three weeks after leaving Arbela, Alexander reached Babylon (east of the Euphrates River). There he was greeted by Mazaeus, the leader of the Persian right wing at Gaugamela, who had fled to Babylon after the battle. Mazaeus came out as a suppliant, with his adult sons, to surrender himself and the city. Following him was the man in charge of the citadel and treasury of Babylon, Bagophanes, who had carpeted Alexander's road into the city with flowers and garlands and had set up silver altars piled up with frankincense and perfumes at intervals. The gifts to Alexander also included herds of cattle and horses and lions and leopards in cages. After the ingratiating treasurer came the Magi chanting, then the Chaldaean priests, Babylonian priests and musicians, and finally the Babylonian cavalry. Having been conquered many times, the Babylonians knew how to put on a good show for the latest would-be world conqueror.

Once he had settled in the city, Alexander directed the Babylonians to rebuild the temples that the Persian king Xerxes allegedly had destroyed, most importantly the temple of the powerful storm god, Baal. Alexander himself sacrificed to Baal according to the instructions of the Chaldaeans. Mazaeus was appointed to the governorship of the city, with a Greek troop commander and tax collector.

Alexander stayed in Babylon for thirty days because there was plenty of food and the local population was friendly to strangers. Curtius Rufus claims that this was the longest he stayed anywhere and that in Babylon he let military discipline slide, taking advantage of the fact that the Babylonians permitted their children and wives to have sex with strangers as long as it was paid for. The Babylonians also were a bibulous lot, so they and the Macedonians shared common interests.

From the money surrendered to Alexander in Babylon, he gave each Macedonian cavalryman six minas (in Greek currency), while the foreign cavalry received five. The gratuity was equal to about 300 days' pay. The Macedonian infantry received two minas, while the mercenaries got a bonus of two months' pay. There was much more to come.

After Alexander marched out of Babylon, toward the end of November 331 he was joined by reinforcements sent by Antipater, including 6,000 Macedonian infantry; 500 cavalry; 600 Thracian cavalry; 3,500 Trallian infantry; and from the Peloponnese, 4,000 mercenary infantry and 380 cavalry. The horsemen were assigned to the Companion cavalry and the infantrymen to battalions according to their national origins. In each squadron of cavalry two companies were formed, with the companies commanded by Companions appointed by Alexander himself on the basis of proven courage. This reorganization of the command structure signified Alexander's desire to gain more direct control of the Companion cavalry as a whole.

It was also around this time that Amyntas brought fifty young-adult sons of Macedonian noblemen to serve as royal pages. These young men waited on the king at dinner, brought him his horses when he went to battle, and attended him when he was hunting. They also guarded his bedroom while he slept. Before long, some of these royal pages conceived a strong dislike for Alexander and his policies.

SUSA

Alexander now marched eastward along the ancient road through Elam (now southwestern Iran) to Susa, covering the 225-mile distance in twenty days. Susa (modern Khuzistan) had been developed by Darius as one of the capital cities of Persia because of its access to the western parts of his empire. Its satrap, Abulites, greeted Alexander at the river Choaspis with gifts including dromedaries and a dozen elephants, and surrendered the city. In the city, Alexander ascended the throne of Darius and promptly provoked some discreet hilarity: when he sat on the throne, his legs were too short to reach the royal footstool. An alert page saved further embarrassment by placing a table under Alexander's dangling legs.

What was more important, in Susa Alexander came into possession of 40,000 talents of gold and silver bullion and 9,000 talents of minted gold in the form of Persian Darics. This was the largest financial windfall that any Greek or Macedonian had ever gained. Three thousand talents of silver immediately were sent with Menes to the coast, to pay Antipater as much as he required for the Lacedaemonian war.

Of greater symbolic significance, Alexander also recovered the bronze statues of Harmodius and Aristogeiton, the so-called tyrant slayers of Athens. These famous statues had been taken from Athens and brought to Susa by Xerxes after he sacked Athens in 480. Alexander returned them to the Athenians, who set them up in the cemetery called the Kerameikos. The gift was a timely reminder to the Athenians of the justification of the war just as Sparta's King Agis was tempting them to break away from the pan-Hellenic alliance.

In Susa Alexander also sacrificed according to ancestral custom and held torch races and an athletic contest. The sacrifices undoubtedly were made to give thanks to the gods for the singular favor they had shown Alexander and the Macedonians. His very presence in Susa was an unprecedented indication that he was specially favored by Zeus. Certainly no other Greek or Macedonian had ever before been in a position to make such sacrifices in the very heart of Persia.

Abulites was appointed satrap of Susiana. Mazarus, a Companion, was made commander of the garrison in the citadel of Susa, and Archelaus was made general there. Left behind in Susa as well were Darius' mother, Sisygambis, and his children, who were provided with Greek tutors. This measure indicates that Alexander expected Greek to be used near the center of the Persian empire for the foreseeable future.

In addition to providing the queen mother with language lessons, Alexander decided to make a present to her of purple fabric, some Macedonian clothes, and women to teach her and her granddaughters how to make woolen clothes. Unfortunately, as Alexander subsequently learned, nothing was more degrading for Persian women than working with wool. Informed of his cultural faux pas, the king hurriedly apologized for his ignorance while also reminding Sisygambis that he had given her the title of his own mother.

THE UXIANS

By late December 331, Alexander was on his way to Persis, the heartland of the Persian empire itself, despising both the snow that often blocked the passes through the Zagros Mountains, and also the tribesmen who guarded them. Those fierce tribesmen made a living extracting "gifts" from all who wished to pass, including Persian kings. Some of these tribesmen, the Uxian hillmen, sent Alexander a message telling him that they would not let him into Persia unless they received their usual payment. In reply, Alexander invited the Uxians to meet him at the pass, where he would give them what they had demanded.

Alexander then sacked the nearest Uxian villages and advanced to the pass before the Uxians had arrived. Craterus was sent ahead to seize the heights of the mountains to which Alexander believed the Uxians would retreat under his pressure. When the Uxians found Alexander at the appointed mountain pass, they fled without a fight. Those who escaped to the hills were promptly wiped out by Craterus. Alexander had paid the Uxians—in shrouds. Only after Darius' mother pleaded with Alexander on their behalf were the surviving Uxians allowed to keep possession of their land—in exchange for an annual tribute of 100 horses, 500 mules, and 30,000 sheep.

Once the Uxians had been humbled, Parmenio then took the easier main road southward—perhaps through modern Kazerun as far as Firuzabad, and then up to Shiraz and Persepolis—with the Thessalian cavalry, the allied and mercenary units, the more heavily armed units, and the baggage train. Alexander took the more scenic and dangerous route, through the hills from modern Fahlian, with the Macedonian infantry, the Companion cavalry, the Agrianes, archers, and advanced scouts.

Alexander's path initially was blocked at the so-called Persian Gates (perhaps the gorge known as Tang-i Mohammed Reza) by the satrap Ariobarzanes, who had fortified the pass and now lay in wait with 40,000 infantry and 700 cavalry. This was a considerable obstacle; indeed, it is a myth that Alexander was welcomed into Persia. A first assault on the pass was repulsed with losses to the Macedonians, but then Alexander found another way around the pass, and an attack on the defenders was launched simultaneously from above and below their position. Only a few of Ariobarzanes' men survived.

Alexander then pressed on to Persepolis itself, marching so quickly that the garrison there did not even have time to plunder the treasury at his approach. For the first time in history, Greeks and Macedonians were about to enter the capital city of the great Persian empire not in chains, but under arms.

THE SACK OF PERSEPOLIS

Shortly before he reached Persepolis, however, Alexander received a letter from its governor, Tiridates, saying that if he arrived ahead of those who planned to defend the city on Darius' behalf, he (Tiridates) would betray the city to Alexander. Thus, Alexander led his troops on to the Persian capital by forced marches.

But after the Macedonians crossed the Araxes River, their advance was halted by a dreadful sight. About 800 Greeks, most of them elderly, came out to greet Alexander, bearing branches of supplication. These Greeks had been carried away from their homes by previous Persian kings and in captivity had been taught skills or crafts. Afterward their captors had mutilated them, amputating all the extremities they did not need to perform their work. Some lacked hands, others feet, some ears and noses. Others had been branded with letters from the Persian alphabet. The battle-hardened veterans of the Macedonian army pitied the lot of these poor wretches; Alexander was said to have been moved to tears.

Alexander promised to restore these men to their homes in Greece as soon as possible. But they voted to stay together where they were, rather than to be separated into small groups in Greek cities, where their deformities would stand out. To each of these horribly mutilated Greeks Alexander therefore granted 3,000 drachmae, five men's robes, two oxen, fifty sheep, and fifty bushels of wheat. He also made them exempt from royal taxes and charged his officials to make sure that no one harmed them. Diodorus comments that Alexander mitigated the lot of these unfortunates in keeping with his natural kindness. Scholars who have scoured the sources for each and every example of his cruelty have passed over Alexander's humane gesture here in silence. Nor have they addressed the general issue of Persian mutilation of prisoners of war.

Perhaps roused to anger, when Alexander entered Persepolis, the king returned to the vengeful rhetoric of the campaign's ideology. He told his generals that no city was more hateful to the Greeks than Persepolis, the dynastic capital of Persia since the days of Darius I: it was the city from which troops without number had poured forth and from which the Persian kings had waged an unholy war on Europe. To appease their forefathers' spirits, Alexander said, they should blot Persepolis out.

And thus Alexander handed over the Persian capital (except for the royal palaces) to an army that had been deprived of any substantial reward except the gratuity given to it at Babylon. The private homes of the Persians were sacked, the men slaughtered, and the women enslaved in an orgy of plunder and murder, though Alexander did issue an order for the soldiers to keep their hands off the women. Rape was explicitly forbidden.

The sack of Persepolis, according to one historian, was "an act of outrage on a helpless populace and was coldly calculated." But, as we consider that act, it is important to keep in mind that the populace of Persepolis had lived off the fruits of the defeat, suffering, and exploitation of millions of people (including large numbers of Greeks) throughout its history. Persepolis' symbolic role at the center of an empire does not justify a single murder of an innocent Persian civilian, or a single act of destruction to private property. But it probably helps to explain the ferocity with which the Macedonian soldiers took their revenge. Moreover, the Macedonians' recent encounter with hundreds of terribly mutilated Greeks cannot have inspired them to be merciful to their enemies.

Pasargadae, the older Persian capital, in which the tomb of Cyrus the Great lay, was spared such destruction, although its treasury of 6,000 talents was confiscated. Meanwhile, Alexander took possession of the treasury in Persepolis; it contained the absolutely staggering sum of 120,000 talents. He had some of the bullion transported to Susa, while part was kept with the army. Some of the riches eventually ended up with Parmenio at Ecbatana (Hamadan).

Alexander was now not just "rich rich," he was madly rich, the wealthiest man in Greek history, richer than Croesus. The richest man in the world and his men then rested in what was left of Persepolis until Parmenio and his forces rejoined them. One last destructive revel now ensued.

THE BURNING OF THE PERSIAN PALACES

In April 330, after a short punitive raid against the Mardians, Alexander burned the palaces of the Persian kings.

Parmenio had advised against this act on the grounds that it was hardly wise to destroy one's own property. Alexander replied that he wished to punish the Persians for the destruction of Athens, the burning of the temples, and all their other crimes against the Greeks. Thus, the burning of the palace complex in Persepolis was a matter of policy, one directly related to the justification of the pan-Hellenic campaign itself.

But several ancient writers tell a more scandalous tale. In this version, after Alexander held games in honor of his victories, and performed costly sacrifices, there was a feast, followed by drinking. One of the courtesans present, an Athenian named Thais, said that it would be the finest of all the things Alexander had done in Asia if he took part in a triumphal procession, set fire to the royal palaces, and permitted women's hands in a few seconds to wipe out the famous accomplishments of the Persians.

Alexander took up the idea: after the king, the courtesan was the first to hurl her blazing torch into the palaces. The entire palace area was soon consumed, so great was the conflagration. Diodorus comments that it was most remarkable that the impious act of Xerxes, king of the Persians, against the acropolis at Athens should have been repaid in kind after many years by an Athenian woman, and in sport.

Modern historians have divided over the question of whether Alexander destroyed the Persian palaces for reasons of policy or during a drunken revel. But the Macedonians spent at least four months in Persepolis; it is very hard to believe that in all that time the fate of the royal palaces was not considered. The story of Parmenio advising Alexander not to destroy the palaces sounds like an echo of a real debate (albeit one elaborated as part of the later campaign to discredit Parmenio). These considerations suggest that the palaces were burned after a policy decision was taken. That decision was consistent with the justification for the campaign itself, as Arrian explicitly states. The burning of the palaces of the Persian kings was direct retribution for the burning of the temple of Athena on the acropolis of Athens, and it was calculated, at least for several months.

Later, however, after Alexander had become the king of Asia, the policy decision of 330 looked very different. The story of Thais instigating the destruction of the palaces probably belongs to the period after Alexander had returned from India and had taken on his pan-Asian kingship. The blame for what had turned out to be an embarrassing decision was thus shifted onto an Athenian courtesan. Significantly, Arrian does not mention Thais or the drunken party that led to the fire, perhaps because Thais later became the mistress of one of his main sources, none other than Ptolemy.

Either way, Alexander regretted the fire almost as soon as it was set, and he gave orders to extinguish it. Parmenio had been right after all: destroying one's own property was not wise; it was the act of a conqueror, not a ruler. But it was too late. The palaces were in ashes and Darius was still on the loose. Learning that he planned resistance in Media, Alexander made the mountainous land of the Medes his next objective, after appointing a satrap in Persia.

PART TWO

King of All Asia

CHAPTER 12

The Death of Darius

THE HUNT

The Magi taught the princes of Persia how to hunt at a very young age, and many of them pitted themselves against nature's most dangerous predators even after they had attained positions of power within the empire. A relief from a stairway in Persepolis shows either a nobleman or the Persian king himself stabbing a lion as the lion claws its hunter. After Gaugamela, however, Darius had become the prey.

In Macedon, too, the sons of the nobility were taught to track, to corner, and then to dispatch the wild animals that roamed the lofty heights of the kingdom. In his pursuit of Darius, Alexander showed that he had learned his lessons well; he hunted Darius with relentless zeal, care, and swiftness. When, at last, he had Darius cornered, however, Alexander was robbed of the satisfaction of the kill. Darius was cruelly cut down by some of his own pack.

Deprived of his pleasure, Alexander immediately redefined the hunt itself, determining to track down and punish his enemy's killers. Whether he hunted men or beasts, Alexander never permitted anyone to strike the mortal blow—at least, not without punishment—before he took his chance.

THE DEATH OF DARIUS

By the time the dust had settled at Gaugamela, Darius had fled to the Median capital of Ecbatana, one of the royal residences of the Achaemenid Persian kings. Ecbatana had been incorporated within the Persian realm when Cyrus the Great had defeated and captured Astyages in 550 and had long served as the capital of the Median satrapy. Among Greeks, Ecbatana was known for its wealth and the magnificence of its buildings; the columns in the porticoes and colonnades of the royal palace were said to be gold-plated and even the tiles made of silver.

If reinforcements from Scythia (probably in the area of the modern Crimea) and Cadusia in northern Media could reach him in time, Darius had steeled his nerve to face Alexander in battle yet again. But if Alexander marched against him in Media before his nomadic and tribal allies could arrive, Darius had determined to go farther up-country, across the Elburz Mountains into the territory of the Parthyaeans and Hyrcania, in the area along the southern shore of the Caspian Sea. The women and the rest of his belongings were sent on ahead to the Caspian Gates, the defiles that marked the boundary between Media and Parthyene.

Unfortunately for Darius, Alexander was quicker than the Persian king's reinforcements. Having set out from Persepolis in May, along the way he subdued the Paraetacae and placed Oxathres as satrap over them. Three days' journey away from Ecbatana Alexander was met by Bisthanes, a son of Ochus, the previous Persian king, who informed him that Darius had fled four days before with a treasury of 7,000 talents and a force of 3,000 cavalry and 6,000 infantry.

The chase was now truly on. To lighten his load, Alexander dismissed the Thessalian cavalry and other allied contingents with a payment of 2,000 talents to divide among them; he took the Companion cavalry, the advanced scouts, the mercenary cavalry, the Macedonian heavy infantry (except for the sections detailed to guard the treasury), the Agrianes, and the archers. Parmenio was ordered to transfer the Persian treasury to Ecbatana and to hand it over to Alexander's boyhood friend Harpalus for safekeeping, while Alexander pushed eastward in search of Darius. Harpalus was left in charge of it with a guard of 6,000 Macedonians, cavalry, and a few light troops.

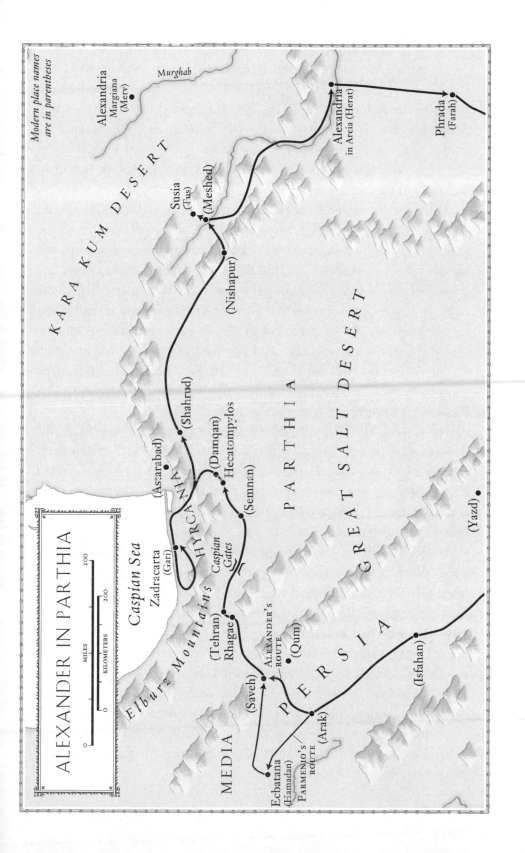

ALEXANDER IN PARTHIA

Modern place names
are in parentheses

KARA KUM DESERT

Murghab

Alexandria
Margiana
(Merv)

Alexandria
in Areia (Herat)

Phrada
(Farah)

Susia
(Tus)

(Meshed)

(Nishapur)

Caspian Sea

GREAT SALT DESERT

PARTHIA

(Shahrud)

(Astarabad)

HYRCANIA

Zadracarta
(Gari)

(Damqan)

Hecatompylos

(Semnan)

Caspian
Gates

Elburz Mountains

(Yazd)

(Tehran)
Rhagae

ALEXANDER'S
ROUTE

(Qum)

MEDIA

(Saveh)

PERSIA

(Isfahan)

Ecbatana
(Hamadan)

PARMENIO'S
ROUTE

(Arak)

MILES   200

KILOMETERS   200

0

On the eleventh day Alexander reached Rhagae (modern Rey), but Darius already had passed through the Caspian Gates. Alexander then rested his force for five days. After passing through the Gates himself, Alexander learned from Bagistanes, a Babylonian nobleman, and Antibelus, one of Mazaeus' sons, that Darius had been seized and put under arrest by Nabarzanes, his own cavalry commander; Bessus, satrap of Bactria; and Barsaentes, satrap of Arachotia and Drangiana.

At this point Alexander made the pursuit team lighter and quicker. Taking with him only the Companions, the advanced scouts, and the very toughest of his light infantry, Alexander set off after the unfortunate prisoner and his captors. Covering about 130 miles in three enervating stages, which included two all-night marches, Alexander reached the camp from which Bagistanes had brought his news, only to find it deserted. Darius had been taken off in a covered wagon. Bessus had assumed power in his place and had received the royal salute from all except Artabazus and the Greek mercenaries. Alexander's exhausted team pressed on; at noon the next day, they reached a village where Darius and his captors had been the day before.

Parmenio's son Nicanor and his guards were instructed to follow Bessus and Darius by the road they had taken. Alexander, led by local guides and accompanied by the fittest of his infantry, who were mounted for the final pursuit, took a shortcut. Covering some fifty miles in the course of the night, Alexander closed in on the fugitives near the city of Hecatompylus (Shahr-i Qumis).

When Alexander was close upon them, Nabarzanes and Barsaentes struck down Darius and then fled with 600 horsemen. Darius died of his wounds before Alexander had seen him. He was around fifty years old at the time of his death. Alexander, we are informed, gave his dead adversary, whom he had insulted so many times while alive, a full royal funeral. Darius' body was then sent back to Persepolis to be buried in the royal tomb, alongside his divinely selected ancestors.

Arrian judged Darius to have been the feeblest and most incompetent of men, although in other spheres of conduct moderate and decent. This is too harsh: Darius clearly was not a complete military incompetent. When his empire was invaded, he led a determined and flexible, if somewhat tardy, defense of his realm.

Unfortunately for Darius, the fates had brought him onto the stage of history at a time when a fierce new light was blazing across the sky, scorching everything and everybody in its path who did not warm to it, and sometimes those who did as well. Thus, although Darius deserved his final resting place among the tombs of the great kings of Persia's proud imperial history, as Alexander understood, he did not merit his exact fate. Whatever Alexander believed, as Darius himself concluded about the outcome of the battle of Issos, it was perhaps as some god willed it.

A NEW WAR OF REVENGE

After the murder of Darius, the last of the Achaemenid kings of Persia, Alexander appointed a Parthyaean named Amminapes as satrap over the Parthyaeans and Hyrcanians and named a Companion, Tlepolemus, to rule in association with him. Alexander had not changed his normal practice of appointing a trusted Macedonian officer to keep an eye on a locally recruited governor.

Meanwhile, we are told, with Darius dead, all of Alexander's soldiers were expecting to return home. In their imaginations, they already were embracing the wives and children they had left behind years before. The pan-Hellenic crusade was over, all of its goals achieved.

Its leader, however, had other ideas; indeed, he apparently always had. Calling an assembly of the soldiers, Alexander pointed out to them that Nabarzanes was still occupying Hyrcania; that the murderer Bessus was not only occupying Bactria, but was threatening the Macedonians; and that most of Persia's eastern subjects or allies remained independent. The moment the Macedonians turned their backs, all of these would be after them. How much greater would the obedience of the Persians be when they realized that the Macedonians' wars were righteous and that their anger was directed against the crime of Bessus and not against the Persian race?

In other words, this was no longer a campaign of national revenge for historical injustices; Alexander and the Macedonians were now to be Darius' avengers, and Alexander was to be king of all the peoples over whom Darius had ruled.

Flushed with victory, the soldiers greeted Alexander's speech with great enthusiasm, shouting for the king to lead them wherever he wished to go. Once Alexander had received the enthusiastic response of his men, the allied troops from the Greek cities were praised for their services, and promptly released from their military duties. Each cavalryman was given a talent and each infantryman ten minas. These rewards signify that the goals of the pan-Hellenic alliance had been achieved in Alexander's eyes. But to those soldiers who would remain with him in the Macedonian royal army to avenge Darius and leave none of his former lands independent, Alexander also gave a bonus payment of three talents each.

In effect, Alexander had disbanded the pan-Hellenic army only to reenlist a large part of it to serve under him as he pursued what was now a war of revenge and conquest. It is nevertheless doubtful that any of the soldiers who called upon Alexander to lead them wherever he wished could have imagined that the next phase of the campaign would last six long years and that Alexander intended to lead them to the very ends of the earth.

THE QUEEN OF THE AMAZONS

It was during this high tide of enthusiasm for further adventures that Alexander supposedly was visited by Thalestris (or Minythyia), the queen of the Amazons. Accompanied by 300 other women, she had traveled for thirty-five days to meet Alexander. Her appearance and the purpose of her visit aroused general surprise, we are informed; she was strangely dressed for a woman and she came to have a child by the king. Alexander allegedly paused for thirteen days to oblige the queen, leaving only when she thought she had conceived.

The story has been rejected as fiction by many modern historians, but its main features are recorded by Diodorus, Curtius, Justin, and Plutarch. Even the usually skeptical Arrian reports that a Scythian king offered the hand of his daughter to Alexander in marriage. Somewhere on the borders of Hyrcania Alexander perhaps left behind a curly-haired offspring among the one-breasted warrior women of Scythia.

FIRST MOVES

Presumably recovered from chasing Darius and being pursued by mythical queens, Alexander now led the Macedonians after Darius' murderers. Dividing his forces into three columns, Alexander made his way first over the lofty peaks of Mount Elburz (about 18,550 feet), toward the Hyrcanian capital of Zadracarta (probably modern Sari).

Along the way, Nabarzanes, Darius' cavalry commander and one of the men responsible for Darius' death, Phrataphernes, satrap of Hyrcania and Parthia, and other high-ranking officers came to Alexander and gave themselves up. Autophradates, the satrap of Tapuria, also surrendered and was returned to his post. Artabazus, who had refused to betray Darius, also came to Alexander with his three sons; he was treated with respect and honor. To the representatives of the Greek mercenaries, who came to him begging for terms, Alexander replied harshly: he would make no compact with them. Men who had fought with the barbarians against the decrees of the Greeks were guilty of grave injustices. They were ordered to surrender, leaving themselves to Alexander's mercy, or to take what steps they could for their own safety. There were approximately 1,500 of these Greek mercenaries, and Alexander sent Artabazus and Andronicus to them to inform them of their options.

Alexander then made a five-day expedition against the warlike Mardians, who were driven quickly from their passes into their mountain strongholds. Those who surrendered were placed under the authority of Autophradates, satrap of Tapuria.

THE ABDUCTION OF BUCEPHALAS

While Alexander was wasting the surrounding countryside, some of the inhabitants made a surprise attack upon the royal pages who were looking after Bucephalas and made off with Alexander's horse. Having been tamed and won by Alexander in his famous bet with his father, Bucephalas had carried Alexander into every one of his major battles in Asia, and when he was caparisoned he allowed no one but Alexander to mount him. Horse and rider were literally inseparable.

After Hephaestion, and perhaps his mother, there was no living creature on earth Alexander loved more than his Thessalian horse. Alexander was so infuriated by Bucephalas' abduction that he ordered every
tree in the land felled. Through native interpreters he also proclaimed
that if the horse were not returned, the natives would see the countryside laid waste to the greatest extent possible, and the inhabitants would
be slaughtered to a man. As he began to carry out these threats the locals
returned Bucephalas, along with gifts; fifty men were also sent to beg for
forgiveness. Later, when Bucephalas died in India of old age and exhaustion after the battle of the Hydaspes Alexander named a city after
him.

MERCENARIES, ENVOYS, AND REBELS

Returning to his camp, Alexander found the Greek mercenaries, whom
he had ordered to surrender or to look out for their safety, waiting to
give themselves up. The mercenaries who had joined Darius before the
establishment of the pan-Hellenic alliance in 337 were demobilized.
Those who joined after the congress at Corinth were merely ordered to
serve Alexander at the same rate of pay.

The contrast between Alexander's relatively lenient treatment of
these mercenaries and his refusal to accept the surrender of most of the
Greek mercenaries at the Granicus is easily explained. The battle of the
Granicus took place at the beginning of the war, when the guiding principles of the pan-Hellenic expedition were in full force. After the death
of Darius, those principles had become moot, and Alexander needed experienced troops for his new campaign. His employment of Darius' surviving Greek mercenaries represented neither a betrayal of principle nor
a sudden change of heart. It was self-interest, pure and simple, dictated
by the requirements of his new goals.

Self-interest also explains Alexander's treatment of some Spartan and
Athenian envoys to Darius who now fell into his hands. The envoys had
been dispatched before the news of Darius' death had reached their
cities. These representatives of Alexander's foremost Greek enemy and
least enthusiastic ally were arrested and put into custody, a prudent
measure at a time when Alexander believed that the war against the

Spartans was still raging. Representatives from the small city of Sinope, on the coast of the Black Sea (a city that was not a member of the pan-Hellenic League of Corinth), who also had been captured on their way to Darius, were released, on the grounds that it was not unreasonable for them to have been sent on an embassy to their own king.

These issues addressed, Alexander then returned to Zadracarta, Hyrcania's largest city, where he stayed for fifteen days in August 330, sacrificing to the gods and celebrating games. For the moment it looked as if he had gained acceptance as the new ruler both from those who had instigated (or participated in) the murder of Darius and also from those who had refused to take part. Bessus remained the outstanding threat to the new order. Thus Alexander moved first back into the territory of the Parthyaeans and from there to the borders of Areia. At the city of Susia (near modern Meshed), Satibarzanes came to Alexander and was confirmed in his office of satrap of the Areians. He was sent back with Anaxippus, with forty mounted javelin troops.

However, just when all seemed well, some Persians arrived with a report that Bessus was wearing his tiara upright, was dressing in royal attire, was calling himself Artaxerxes instead of Bessus, and was proclaiming himself king of Asia. He had with him the Persians who had made their escape into Bactria, as well as many Bactrians, and was expecting additional forces from Scythia. Alexander was now faced with a full-fledged nationalist resistance.

ORIENTALIZING

Alexander immediately set out for Bactria with his whole force, joined now by the mercenary cavalry, the Thessalian volunteers, and allied troops. It was at this point, according to some of the ancient sources, that Alexander lost control of his appetites and degenerated into arrogance and dissipation.

First, Alexander installed Asian-born ushers in his court and ordered the most distinguished Persians to act as his guards, including Darius' brother Oxathres. He then put on the Persian diadem and dressed himself in the white robe, the Persian sash, and the other things except for the trousers and the long-sleeved upper garment.

He gave cloaks with purple borders to the Companions, too, and out-fitted their horses in Persian harness. Finally, he added concubines to his retinue in the manner of Darius, in number not less than the days of the year, and outstanding in beauty as selected from all the women of Asia. Each night these women paraded about Alexander's couch so that he might select the one with whom he would lie that night.

Curtius Rufus and other ancient writers represent Alexander's adoption of Persian dress and customs simply as a slide into luxury and extravagance. But Alexander's actions can be seen and explained in a different way.

The news that Bessus was wearing the tiara of the Persian kings and had declared himself king of Asia created some complex military, political, and cultural problems for Alexander. The solution to the military problem was thought to be the easiest: Bessus had to be hunted down and killed.

The political and cultural problems were far trickier. If Alexander was, as he himself had declared, king of Asia, he had to act, and be seen to act, as a king of Asia traditionally had done. Alexander had little choice then but to dress like the Persian king and to adopt at least some of the ceremonials of the Persian court. To do so would help to legitimize his rule over all of Persian Asia. To be the king, Alexander had to play the king.

Unfortunately, the more realistic his performance was, the greater was the risk he ran of alienating the Macedonian veterans, who had been persuaded to fight the Persians by speeches deriding the latter as barbaric and effeminate. Now, suddenly, Alexander had become the object of his own ridicule. Alexander was becoming the barbarian.

Although the veterans of Philip displayed an open revulsion toward the extravagance and adoption of foreign customs, at this point Alexander faced no open opposition, only grumbling in the ranks. Resistance to his policies came only later, after a series of setbacks that undoubtedly damaged the army's morale.

The army was proceeding toward Bactria, pursuing Bessus and pacifying all the areas that had at least nominally been under Persian rule, when Nicanor, a son of Parmenio, and the commander of the hypaspists, suddenly died. Because of a shortage of supplies, Alexander could not halt the main army to attend the funeral. Philotas, Nicanor's brother, was left with 2,600 men to conduct his brother's last rites, while Alexander hastened on after Bessus.

But while Alexander was en route, more bad news came: Satibarzanes had murdered Anaxippus and the forty javelin men with him. He was arming the Areians and concentrating them at Artacoana (on the border of modern Afghanistan), and had decided to join Bessus and to assist him in attacking the Macedonians wherever an opportunity should arise. Suddenly, there were two rebellions.

In response, Alexander, leaving Craterus in command on the spot, marched seventy-five miles in two days to Artacoana with the Companions, the mounted javelin men, the Agrianes, and the battalions of Amyntas and Coenus. But by the time he reached Artacoana, Satibarzanes had fled. After killing and enslaving as many of those who had a hand in the revolt as he could catch, Alexander appointed a new governor of Areia.

Craterus and his troops now rejoined Alexander, who marched on to the Drangian capital of Phrada (modern Farah, in western Afghanistan). This region had been under the control of Barsaentes, one of the conspirators who had mortally wounded Darius. When Barsaentes had learned of Alexander's approach, he had run away to the Indians living to the west of the Indus, but they arrested him and returned him to Alexander, who had him put to death for his treachery to Darius. That took care of one problem, but soon Alexander was to face a much more deadly threat.

CHAPTER 13

Anticipation

THE CONSPIRACY OF DIMNUS

It was at Phrada in October 330 that Alexander learned of a plot against his life. The revelation of the plot, its investigation, and its aftermath would leave several of the highest-ranking officers in the Macedonian army, including Philotas, the commander of the Companion cavalry, and his father, Parmenio, Macedon's greatest general, dead. Ever since, historians have debated whether Philotas actually was involved in some kind of conspiracy. Some have made the case that Alexander himself initiated a plot against Philotas and Parmenio at Phrada to get rid of powerful officers who had been closely associated with his father, Philip.

Although all the main sources report the episode, almost predictably, Curtius Rufus, who lived and wrote during the early Roman imperial period, provides the fullest account, complete with speeches from Craterus (who had commanded the left of the phalanx at Issos and Gaugamela); Alexander; Philotas; and Amyntas, a commander of the phalanx. When reading Curtius, we should never forget that he wrote his history of Alexander during an era when ghastly treason trials dominated the Roman political scene.

In Curtius' account, Dimnus, a man of slight influence with the king, revealed to his young boyfriend Nicomachus that a plot to assassinate Alexander had been hatched. The assassination was to take place in two days' time. Dimnus also confided in his young friend that he was involved in the plan, along with some brave and distinguished men.

Pressed by Nicomachus, Dimnus named the conspirators: Demetrius, one of Alexander's personal bodyguards; Peucolaus; Nicanor (not Parmenio's son); Aphobetus; Iolaus; Dioxenus; Archepolis; and Amyntas (not the phalanx commander).

Nicomachus soon divulged what he had been told to his brother Cebalinus. Alarmed, Cebalinus immediately determined to inform the king. Not being permitted to enter the royal quarters right away, Cebalinus told his story to Philotas and insisted that it be reported to Alexander without delay.

But Philotas did not tell Alexander. The next day Cebalinus made the same request. Philotas replied that he was seeing to it, but still he did not report the existence of the plot to the king.

Having lost patience, Cebalinus revealed the story of the conspiracy to a young nobleman named Metron, who was in charge of the armory. Metron promptly hid Cebalinus amid the shields and swords. When Alexander happened to enter the armory, Cebalinus accosted him and at last betrayed the plot to the king. Guards were dispatched at once to arrest Dimnus, but Dimnus killed himself (or was killed, according to other sources) during his arrest.

Alexander then ordered Philotas into the royal quarters and asked why he had not reported Cebalinus' story. Philotas said that he had feared that reporting an argument between a male prostitute and his lover would make him an object of ridicule.

Alexander consequently held a meeting of his closest friends, including Craterus, to whom Nicomachus was induced to repeat his story. Craterus, who perhaps was hostile to Philotas because of their competition for advancement in the army, pointed out that while Philotas always could plot against Alexander, Alexander would not always be able to pardon Philotas.

Alexander's other friends argued that Philotas would not have suppressed evidence of a conspiracy unless he was one of the ringleaders or at least an accomplice; any loyal soldier would have run to the king on hearing such charges. The unanimous decision of Alexander's friends was that Philotas should be interrogated under torture to force him to name his accomplices in the crime.

Cavalrymen then were posted at all the entrances to the camp with orders to block the roads so that no one could slip off secretly to Philotas' father, Parmenio, who was governor of Media at the time, in charge of strong forces. A man named Atarrhias with 300 attendants was sent to arrest Philotas. As the shackles were being placed upon him, Philotas is reported to have said, "Your majesty, the bitter hatred of my enemies has triumphed over your kindness."

THE TRIAL OF PHILOTAS

The next day, Philotas was put on trial before 6,000 soldiers. In keeping with traditional Macedonian procedure, the king acted as the prosecutor in the case. The body of Dimnus was brought out. Alexander accused Parmenio of heading the plot against his life, and charged Philotas as an accomplice who had suborned Peucolaus, Demetrius, and Dimnus. Philotas' silence about the plot masked his criminal intent, he alleged.

Arrian, whose source Ptolemy was there in Phrada at the time, reports that this was the most damning proof of Philotas' guilt: he admitted that he had some knowledge of the plot against Alexander, but had said nothing about it, despite the fact that he visited Alexander's tent twice a day.

Alexander also produced a letter Parmenio had written to his sons Nicanor and Philotas, advising them to take care of themselves and their people, for this was how they would accomplish their purpose. Curtius comments that the letter did not seem to contain evidence of a dangerous plot.

Alexander's accusations were supported by speeches made by Amyntas, son of Andromenes, and Coenus, Philotas' own brother-in-law, who accused him of being a traitor to king, country, and army.

In his defense, Philotas pointed out that Dimnus had never mentioned him among the conspirators. He argued that he had been silent about what he had been told because he thought that what was coming to his ears was only a lovers' quarrel.

A lesser officer who had risen from the ranks, Bolon, then got up and reminded the army of Philotas' high-handed manner, his wealth, and his rejection of Alexander's divine parentage. Bolon's speech aroused the assembly, and the trial was adjourned until the next day. That night, under torture led by Craterus, Philotas implicated Parmenio in a plot to kill Alexander, a plot hatched after Darius' defeat but unconnected to Dimnus' plot. Parmenio was said to have been inspired by a certain Hegelochus, a great-nephew of Attalus, who had objected to Alexander's adoption of Zeus as his father.

ANTICIPATION

The next day Philotas' confession was read out to the assembly. Demetrius the bodyguard made a confident and vigorous defense. Philotas, unable to walk, but able to speak and accuse others, implicated a certain Calis, who confessed on the spot that he and Demetrius had planned the crime. When the signal was given, all those named by Nicomachus were stoned to death according to the Macedonian customary practice.

Philotas' death, however, did not put the matter to rest. It was at this time also that Alexander the Lyncestian was put on trial for treason. Having survived, seemingly against the evidence, when his two brothers were executed for their involvement in Philip's death, he had been charged subsequently with plotting against the king but had been kept alive for three years under guard.

His hearing had been delayed because of his relationship to Antigonus (or Antipater, in Curtius). But now he was brought before the Macedonians and executed, "lacking words to defend himself." Amyntas, the son of Andromenes, and his brothers, Polemon, Attalus, and Simmias, also were brought to trial for conspiracy on the grounds of their closeness to Philotas. Most people were inclined to believe them guilty, particularly because Polemon had fled at the arrest of Philotas. But Amyntas made a vigorous defense and the brothers were acquitted. Amyntas then went off and retrieved Polemon. Amyntas died of an arrow wound during the siege of a village shortly thereafter. From his acquittal all he gained, said Arrian, was that he died with his good name intact. (His younger brothers survived Alexander's reign.)

Alexander also had to deal with Parmenio. Polydamas, a friend of Parmenio, indeed one of the dispatch riders sent by Parmenio to Alexander during the battle of Gaugamela, was ordered to hasten to Ecbatana by racing camel, along with two Arab companions, with a letter from Alexander addressed to Cleander (commander of mercenaries and Coenus' brother), Sitalces, and Menidas. Two letters also were sent along to Parmenio. One was a letter from Alexander; the second was a forged letter from the now dead Philotas. After Parmenio read the letter from Alexander and while he was reading the forged letter from his son, Cleander and the others stabbed him to death. The letter addressed to Cleander, Sitalces, and Menidas had informed them of the plot and ordered them to assassinate Parmenio.

Those who subsequently expressed regret at Parmenio's death or sent letters home expressing anything contrary to the king's interest Alexander then formed into a single unit called the *atakton tagma*, or "Disciplinary Company." In addition, the Companions (cavalry) were split into two separate divisions, with Hephaestion and Cleitus appointed as *hipparchs* (cavalry commanders) of the two divisions. Ptolemy was appointed a royal bodyguard in place of the executed Demetrius. Phrada, where the plot was exposed, examined, and exterminated, Alexander renamed Prophthasia, "Anticipation."

THE DEATHS OF PHILOTAS AND PARMENIO

The story of the conspiracy at Phrada and the executions of Philotas and Parmenio have provoked widely varied reactions. Some historians have concluded that there was indeed a plot against Alexander's life at Phrada; that Philotas was part of it; and that Parmenio's assassination was a brutal and unfortunate, but necessary, consequence of Philotas' implication.

Others, while not doubting that there was some kind of conspiracy afoot, nevertheless have argued that there is no evidence that Philotas was part of the plot hatched by Demetrius and Calis. He was never named as a conspirator by Nicomachus or Cebalinus, and only implicated himself and his father under torture. Indeed, some modern historians have argued that the whole affair was a cunning plot by Alexander to get rid of Philotas, and especially Parmenio, whom Alexander wanted to replace because he believed that the old general might serve as a light-ning rod for opposition to his adoption of Persian customs.

Dimnus' suicide (or his death resisting arrest) strongly suggests, however, that there was a real plot against Alexander's life at Phrada in the autumn of 330. Furthermore, that one of Alexander's personal body-guards, Demetrius, was apparently one of the conspirators, shows that the plot was serious and potentially lethal to Alexander. Demetrius had immediate, easy, and continuous access to the king. Alexander could hardly have forgotten that his own father, Philip, had been assassinated by another guard (Pausanias).

Moreover, according to Curtius Rufus at any rate, Philotas had been told by Cebalinus *what he had learned* about the plot from his brother Nicomachus. What he had learned very likely included the information that Demetrius the bodyguard was one of the conspirators. Although there is no evidence of Philotas' direct involvement in the actual con-spiracy, his failure to disclose the fact that one of Alexander's elite body-guards allegedly was plotting against the king really was more than just "passive disloyalty." It was treason.

If a minor officer in the U.S. Army reported the existence of a con-spiracy to assassinate the president, a conspiracy that allegedly included a member of the presidential security detail, to one of the Joint Chiefs of Staff and the chief did not disclose the contents of the report immedi-ately and in full, and this fact was subsequently discovered, the chief would be removed from command and court-martialed without delay. So Philotas was arrested, put on trial, and executed according to tradi-tional Macedonian procedure and customary law for his treasonable fail-ure to disclose to Alexander what he had been told.

THE REVENGE OF ATTALUS

The judicial assassination of Parmenio was a terrible and sad conse-quence of his son's treason. Parmenio had been Philip's one and only general, and he was as responsible for the Macedonian victories at the Granicus, Issos, and Gaugamela as Alexander himself. If Parmenio and the Thessalian cavalry under his general command had not fought so tenaciously at those three major battles, inevitably against the best of the Persian cavalry, Alexander never would have had the opportunity to launch his decisive Companion cavalry thrusts.

To the aged general Parmenio, Alexander and the younger Macedonians owed more than they ever could repay. Parmenio was, in some sense, Alexander's second father; he certainly was the godfather of his great victories in battle. Of all the Macedonians, he alone could—and did—check Alexander's impulsiveness.

But Parmenio's murder after Philotas' execution does not prove that Alexander had been plotting against Philotas and Parmenio, let alone that the king concocted the whole story of the Dimnus conspiracy to entrap Philotas. Even *if* Alexander had arranged for Philotas to be told a story about a plot to assassinate himself in order to entrap his cavalry commander, he never could have known that Philotas would *not* have reported the story to him immediately. In that case, Philotas would have emerged as a hero for having alerted the king to the existence of a dangerous plot against his life.

Alexander did not plot against Philotas or Parmenio, whose execution could not be avoided after Philotas' execution. In Ecbatana, Parmenio commanded at least 5,600 Greek mercenaries and had a huge treasury at his disposal. The likelihood is vanishingly small that Parmenio would have understood or agreed with the decision of the Macedonian army assembly that his son had been guilty of treason. Alexander could not safely pursue Bessus in Afghanistan while Parmenio was alive in Ecbatana.

Parmenio certainly did not deserve to be murdered, tricked into a false sense of security by the arrival of a trusted friend bearing a (forged) letter from his only surviving son, and then cut down by his own trusted commanders as he read the news from Phrada. It certainly would have been more just if the old warrior had died on the field of battle, with all of his wounds in front. The only explicit evidence that Parmenio was involved in a conspiracy against Alexander was the confession of his son, extracted under torture. Parmenio's death, although cloaked in Macedonian legal garb, was an expedient murder made necessary, from Alexander's point of view, by Philotas' treason. Before we condemn Alexander for Parmenio's murder, however, we should keep in mind that, but for Cebalinus' sense of loyalty and persistence, it might have been Alexander who was murdered in faraway Phrada.

At Phrada, Alexander had to choose between his own safety and Parmenio's—just as Parmenio once had had to choose between Attalus' salvation and his own. Perhaps influenced by jealous officers and friends, Alexander made exactly the same choice that Parmenio had made in 334. Somewhere perhaps, Attalus' shade greedily lapped up Parmenio's blood.

CHAPTER 14

The Massacre
of the Branchidae

CROSSING THE HINDU KUSH

After leaving "Anticipation," Alexander marched south to the rich lands of the Ariaspians, where the army stayed for sixty days, requiting the Ariaspians (also called the Benefactors) with a large sum of money for their outstanding loyalty to Cyrus the Great. Impressed by their claim to follow justice, Alexander granted them freedom and augmented their territory from the lands of their neighbors. Freedom, however, did not preclude the appointment of a satrap to govern them, as well as the tribes of Gedrosia to the south.

Alexander then received the alarming news that Satibarzanes, who had returned to Areia from Bactria with a large force of cavalry, had instigated a second revolt in Areia. Artabazus, Erigyius, Caranus, and Andronicus were sent to suppress the rebellion; the satrap of Parthyaea, Phrataphernes, also was ordered to help the Macedonians put down the revolt. As always, Alexander took care to secure his rear before proceeding to his overall objective.

Back in Areia in the spring of 329, troops under the command of Erigyius and Caranus fought Satibarzanes and the rebels in a fierce battle that was decided when Erigyius killed Satibarzanes in hand-to-hand combat, striking him in the face with a spear. Only then did the rebels turn and flee. Alexander's white-haired old friend Erigyius later personally displayed Satibarzanes' head to the king.

By that time, Alexander was in the territory of Arachosia, the region around modern Kandahar. There, perhaps in December 330, Alexander was joined by the army that had been under Parmenio's command, which included 6,000 Macedonians, 200 noblemen, and some 5,600 Greeks. There was no opposition, and as usual Alexander installed a satrap and left a garrison of 4,000 infantry and 600 cavalry.

Alexander and the Macedonians then marched up the Helmand Valley, entering into the area of Parapamisadae, centered on the Kabul Valley of modern Afghanistan, by March 329. As the Macedonians moved through the harsh environment, they faced terrible hardships: lack of provisions, fatigue, and wild temperature swings. (In the area of Kabul today the temperature varies between –6 and 101 degrees Fahrenheit, and temperature variations of fifty degrees over a twenty-four-hour period are not unknown.) Like so many invaders of Afghanistan, the Macedonians suffered at least as much from the elements as from the local tribesmen. On the verge of despair, they found relief only when they came into a more cultivated area, where the troops finally got a plentiful supply of provisions.

At the foot of the mountain where Prometheus was said to have been bound by Zeus (perhaps located near modern Begram), Alexander founded a new city, Alexandria-in-the-Caucasus, which was settled by 7,000 natives and 3,000 camp followers, as well as other volunteers from among the mercenaries. Alexandria-in-the-Caucasus therefore was intended to be another one of Alexander's ethnically mixed foundations. After Alexander conducted one of his customary sacrifices, the army then crossed the "Caucasus Mountains" (the Hindu Kush) in seventeen days in the spring of 329.

Crossing the famous Hindu Kush with a large army at any time of year under any conditions would be a magnificent logistical achievement; making the trek in the spring through thick, snow-covered mountain passes, which reached heights of 10,000 feet, without significant losses, was a miracle of leadership, endurance, and determination. Bessus, we are told, was terrified by the speed with which Alexander and the Macedonians pursued him.

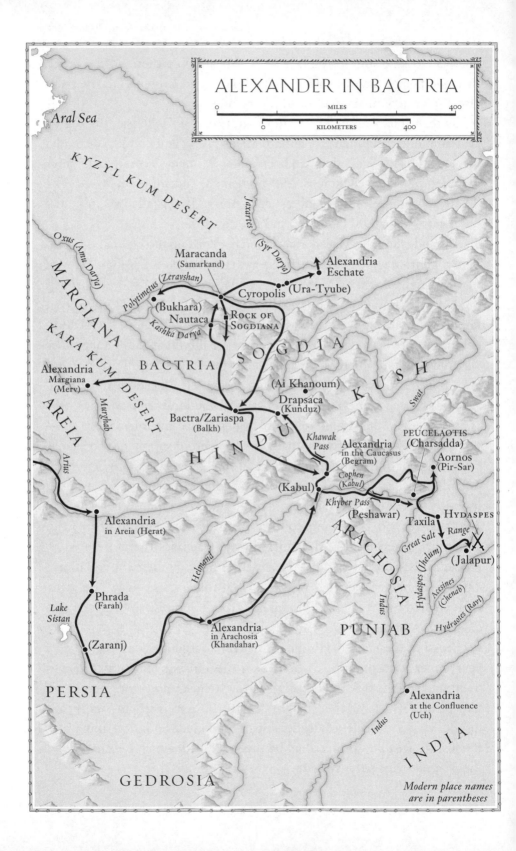

ALEXANDER IN BACTRIA

MILES   0 — 400

KILOMETERS   0 — 400

Aral Sea

KYZYL KUM DESERT

Jaxartes (Syr Darya)

Oxus (Amu Darya)

MARGIANA

Maracanda
(Samarkand)

Alexandria
Eschate

(Zeravshan)

Polytimetus

(Bukhara)
Nautaca

Cyropolis   (Ura-Tyube)

ROCK OF
SOGDIANA

Kashka Darya

KARA KUM DESERT

Alexandria
Margiana
(Merv)

BACTRIA   SOGDIA   KUSH

(Ai Khanoum)

Murghab

Drapsaca
(Kunduz)

Bactra/Zariaspa
(Balkh)

HINDU

*Khawak
Pass*

Swat

PEUCELAOTIS
(Charsadda)

AREIA

Artius

Alexandria
in the Caucasus
(Begram)

Aornos
(Pir-Sar)

*Cophen
(Kabul)*

(Kabul)

Alexandria
in Areia (Herat)

Khyber Pass
(Peshawar)

Taxila

HYDASPES

ARACHOSIA

Great Salt Range

Hydaspes (Jhelum)

(Jalapur)

Helmand

Acesines (Chenab)

Phrada
(Farah)

Lake
Sistan

Indus

PUNJAB

Hydraotes (Ravi)

(Zaranj)

Alexandria
in Arachosia
(Khandahar)

PERSIA

Alexandria
at the Confluence
(Uch)

Indus

GEDROSIA

INDIA

*Modern place names
are in parentheses*

Despite the conditions and Bessus' attempts to impede his progress by ravaging the countryside, Alexander and the Macedonians arrived at Drapsaca (perhaps modern Kunduz, in northern Afghanistan) in Bactria, where Bessus had put on the Persian royal tiara and was trying to raise an army.

The cavalry Bessus was able to mobilize, however, amounted to no more than 7,000 or 8,000. As a result, he was forced to retreat across the Oxus River (Amu Darya), where he planned to continue resistance by guerrilla warfare. He was accompanied by followers of Spitamenes and Oxyartes, with horsemen from Sogdiana (Uzbekistan/Tadjikistan), and by the Dahae from the Tanais (the Don). But the Bactrian cavalry dispersed when they learned that Bessus was planning to flee. This enabled Alexander to occupy the chief towns of Bactria without a fight, and Artabazus was made the governor of the region.

In pursuit of Bessus, Alexander now pressed on to the Oxus, reaching the river after a difficult march of forty miles across the desert in the midsummer heat of 329. Alexander and his army got across the river, which was approximately half a mile wide and also deep and fast-flowing, on rafts made of hides stuffed with chips and dry rubbish. It took five days to get the whole army across the river.

THE MASSACRE OF THE BRANCHIDAE

On the far side of the river, the Macedonians found the town of the so-called Branchidae, descendants of the priests and caretakers of the oracular shrine of Apollo near the Greek city of Miletos in Asia Minor. In 479 Xerxes had destroyed the temple and demanded that the Branchidae surrender to him the treasury of the shrine; the Branchidae had complied and then accompanied Xerxes back to Persia. They eventually ended up settling in this distant eastern satrapy, as far away from their angry Greek kinsmen as they could be while still living within the borders of the Persian empire.

The actions of the Branchidae in 479 were infamous and were seen as treasonable by many Greeks. The Milesians, whose city had been burned to the ground once by the Persians, bore a particular grudge. Alexander initially left the decision about what to do with the Branchidae to the Milesians in his army. When they divided on the question, he settled it: the town should be sacked because it provided a refuge for traitors. The adult male population of the town was slaughtered to a man. The women and children were sold into slavery.

The decision to massacre the male population of this unfortunate town was not taken out of frustration, but after debate, and Alexander made it. Why did he decide to slaughter the Branchidae, and how are we to square such a decision with the actions of a man who treated many war captives with exemplary mercy?

The crucial point lies in the nature of the Branchidae's alleged crime. Without attempting to justify Alexander's decision, we should remember that the war against Persia had been undertaken and justified on the basis of Xerxes' sacrileges against the Greeks. From the point of view of Alexander and many Greeks, the Branchidae were complicitous in Xerxes' sacrileges and crimes. Moreover, the religious pollution that such sacrileges conferred upon the perpetrators was, according to Greek religious tradition, handed down over the generations. This may be the reason why Alexander made his awful decision to wipe the polluted off the face of the earth.

THE DEATH OF BESSUS

Some time after the destruction of the town of the Branchidae, Spitamenes and Dataphernes sent a message from Sogdia to Alexander: if a body of troops under the command of an officer came to them, they would arrest Bessus and hand him over. Alexander responded immediately, dispatching Ptolemy and an advance force. By the time they reached the village where Bessus was being held, Spitamenes and his men had left. Nevertheless, Bessus was handed over to Ptolemy, who conveyed him to Alexander. On his orders Bessus was first stripped and then led along in a dog collar to the place in the road by which Alexander and the Macedonians would pass.

Seeing Bessus on the road, Alexander asked him why he had treated Darius, his king, his relative, and his benefactor, so shamefully, first seizing him, then leading him about in chains, and finally murdering him. Bessus reportedly replied that the decision had not been his alone. All of those close to Darius at that time had shared in the decision, and their goal was to gain Alexander's favor and thus to save their lives.

In response Alexander ordered Bessus scourged. At every lash a crier repeated the words of reproach he had used when he was asked the reason for his treachery. After this humiliating punishment Bessus was sent away to Bactra for execution. He eventually was handed over to Darius' brother Oxathres to be hung on a cross. First, his ears and nose were to be cut off and then he would have arrows shot into him. This was the traditional Persian punishment for rebels.

The most prominent and dangerous of Darius' murderers now had been captured and was about to endure a gruesome punishment for his hand in the regicide. It remained for Alexander to assert his royal authority over the far eastern possessions of his Asian empire. Already in Bactra Alexander had shown that a relentless, swift, and, at times, merciless hunter had arrived on the scene. Soon even the nomads on the other side of the Oxus would learn to fear his very name.

CHAPTER 15

The Wrath of Dionysos

GROWING RESISTANCE

All of the Persian nobles who had taken part in the betrayal and murder of Darius had been captured (Nabarzanes) and executed (Barsaentes), or were awaiting execution (Bessus). But the nationalist rebellion was not quite over. While Satibarzanes, the leader of the second revolt, in Areia, had been killed by Erigyius, Spitamenes and Dataphernes were still at large, and soon most of the Sogdians, some of the Bactrians, and even the Scythians from the unexplored steppes of the north rose up against Alexander.

It would take him nearly two years to crush them all; to do so Alexander was forced to adapt his fighting tactics to those of his nomadic adversaries in a new and difficult environment. As usual, he was up to the tactical challenges, for the first time in history using catapults as field artillery to cover his assaults on the nomads. By the spring of 327 these proud nomads from beyond the known world would be only too happy to have a secure border between themselves and the son of Zeus.

But Alexander's "pacification" of Sogdiana was not accomplished without one shocking military disaster. That catastrophe may have resulted from Alexander's policy of orientalizing, including his practice of assigning commanders from different ethnic groups to command troops.

Opposition to that policy in the autumn of 328 certainly led to an ugly and violent confrontation in Maracanda (Samarkand in modern Uzbekistan) between Alexander and Cleitus, perhaps the best general officer in the Macedonian army.

It was also at the end of this difficult period that Alexander got married for the first time—to a young Bactrian woman, whose name, Roxane, in Persian meant Little Star. Alexander's marriage to the daughter of a Bactrian nobleman was consistent with the orientalizing policy and may have been a fundamentally political act. It is more likely, however, that Alexander was motivated to taste bread from the same loaf with his new Bactrian father-in-law (the defining ritual of the Macedonian marriage ceremony) by a less calculated and stronger impulse: the passionate desire for a beautiful young woman.

ALEXANDRIA ESCHATE

After Bessus had been disposed of, Alexander proceeded on to the Sogdian royal city of Maracanda. While assaulting the mountain refuge of natives who had killed some Macedonian foragers, Alexander was shot through the leg with an arrow and his fibula was broken. Even so, Alexander captured the fugitives' position; not more than 8,000 out of the 30,000 there survived.

Alexander then advanced to a river called by locals the Jaxartes (the modern Syr Dar'ya). The Macedonians, on the other hand, thought it was the European river they knew as the Tanais (now the Don). This identification was based upon contemporary Greek geographical speculation about the geography of eastern Asia. Aristotle maintained that the Araxes (Jaxartes) arose in the Hindu Kush and sent off a branch river that became the European Tanais. It was assumed by some that the Tanais formed the boundary between Asia and Europe. The steppes north of the Tanais constituted the edge of the inhabited world.

The Jaxartes, in fact, did not form the boundary between Europe and Asia, but that error has important implications. By the autumn of 329, Alexander very well may have believed that he had come to the border between Asia and Europe, and perhaps he saw the Jaxartes as the northeastern border of his empire.

While recovering from his leg wound, Alexander received deputations from the Abian and European Scythians, and concluded a pact of friendship with the latter. He did not attempt to make these peoples subject to his rule. This decision confirms that Alexander had decided that the Jaxartes was going to be the border of the empire, at least for the time being.

As if to underscore that point, on the south bank of the river Alexander began to lay out the foundations of a new city to serve as a base for a possible future invasion of Scythia and as a defensive position against raiding tribes from across the river. The city was christened Alexandria Eschate, "Alexandria the Furthest." Its name signified that it marked the frontier of the empire at the time.

This Macedonian foundation has been identified with modern Khujand (former Leninabad) in Tajikistan. The new settlement was constructed as a walled city (of about eight miles), to be populated by Greek mercenaries, local tribesmen, and some time-expired Macedonians.

THE MASSACRE AT THE POLYTIMETUS RIVER

While Alexandria Eschate was still in the planning stages, however, a major revolt broke out among the tribes along the Tanais/Jaxartes, most of the people of Sogdiana, and some of the Bactrians as well. Fear of Alexander may have motivated it; Alexander had issued an order for the leading men of the country to meet him at the city of Zariaspa (modern Balkh in northern Afghanistan). The order may have been perceived as concealing some sinister purpose.

The seven major towns in the vicinity were pacified first, although not before Alexander himself received a violent blow from a stone on his head and neck and Craterus was wounded by an arrow at the storming of Cyropolis (modern Kurkath), a city supposedly founded by Cyrus the Great. At least 8,000 rebels perished at Cyropolis alone.

At the same time, however, a force of Asian Scythians had gathered at the Jaxartes, and a report also reached Alexander that Spitamenes was blockading the troops who had been left behind at Maracanda. To deal with him, Alexander sent Andromachus, Menedemus, and Caranus, along with a force of 60 Companions, 800 mercenaries (commanded by Caranus), and 1,500 mercenary infantry. Also attached to the troops was Pharnuches, a Lycian interpreter who was supposedly skillful in dealing with the local peoples.

Having dispatched the relief force, Alexander then fortified Alexandria Eschate with alacrity and then set about securing his rear. While these preparations were taking place, he was heckled by Scythians on the opposite bank of the river: if Alexander dared to touch them, he would learn the difference between the barbarians of Asia and the Scythians, they shouted. Alexander ignored two sets of unfavorable omens (which his prophet Aristander interpreted as portending danger to him personally) to lead a punitive attack on the Scythians across the Jaxartes. The river crossing was achieved under cover of a volley of missiles launched from catapults, a first in the history of warfare.

Once on dry land again, Alexander quickly adjusted to the encircling tactics of the nomadic cavalrymen, throwing together a mobile force of archers, Agrianians, light troops, and cavalry that prevented the Scythians from using their favorite tactic of wheeling around as they were being assaulted simultaneously by the rest of the cavalry. About 1,000 of the Scythians fell and 150 were taken prisoner; but dysentery, brought on by drinking the bad water of the region during the hot pursuit, prevented Alexander from pursuing and wiping out the rest. Alexander, in fact, had to be carried back to camp in serious danger. Aristander had been proved a true prophet, but Alexander had put an end to the Scythian insults.

Scythian envoys soon appeared, blaming the whole incident on brigands. What had happened, they said, was not the policy of the Scythian community. Their king also expressed a willingness to carry out whatever instructions Alexander might give. In reality, Alexander had won a brilliant victory against the nomads, and their leaders now wanted to be left alone.

Matters went far less well at Maracanda. Spitamenes broke off the siege at the approach of the relief force, but during his retreat was joined by 600 Dahae, the westernmost of the Sacae nomads.

Now reinforced, Spitamenes waited for the pursuing Macedonian force to catch up to him. Once the Macedonians came into contact, the

Scythians wheeled around and went on the offensive. The Scythians rode around and harassed the Macedonian infantry until the latter were forced to retreat in a square to the river Polytimetus (Zeravshan).

Caranus, in command of the cavalry, attempted to cross the river to safety with his men, but failed to inform Andromachus. Spitamenes' cavalry and the Scythians attacked them as they emerged from the river and while they were still in the water. All of these were shot down, and the few prisoners who were taken were quickly put to death, too.

According to another ancient account, the Macedonians had been caught in an ambush. The Scythians were concealed in a wooded park and fell upon the Macedonians when they were already engaged. To make matters worse, at that very moment Pharnuches, the translator, was trying to surrender his command to the Macedonian officers sent with him, on the grounds that his job was to establish relations with the locals, not lead troops in battle, since he was altogether ignorant of military tactics.

Pharnuches' colleagues, Andromachus, Caranus, and Menedemus, refused to accept the command, in order to avoid responsibility for a personal decision not covered by Alexander's orders. They did not want to incur individual blame in case of defeat and they did not want to expose themselves to the charge of poor leadership. While this argument was going on, the Scythians pounced, and only 40 cavalry and 300 infantry survived.

When Alexander received the news of this debacle, he marched an astonishing 185 miles in three days with half the Companion cavalry, the Guards, the Agrianes, the archers, and most of the infantry, looking to settle accounts with Spitamenes, who had returned to besiege Maracanda once again. When Alexander appeared close to the city at dawn on the fourth day, Spitamenes promptly vanished, leaving Alexander to take revenge on the local natives who had joined in the attack on the Macedonians. These were butchered.

Alexander then spent the depth of the winter of 329–28 at Zariaspa in Bactria, where Arsaces and Barzanes, who had been appointed satrap of Parthia by Bessus, were brought to Alexander by Phrataphernes and Stasanor. Reinforcements totaling around 19,000 men also arrived, including infantry mercenaries and cavalry, Lycians, Syrians, and Greeks sent by Antipater.

His force thus augmented, as soon as the weather permitted, Alexander set about a pacification program in the foothills along the Oxus Valley and then into Sogdiana. North of the Oxus, six military garrisons were established to serve as strongpoints for the occupying forces to be left behind. Then Alexander headed once again toward Maracanda after dividing his forces under the command of himself, Hephaestion, Ptolemy, Perdiccas, Coenus, and Artabazus. These commanders systematically crushed all opposition in Sogdiana.

THE ROCK OF SOGDIANA

It was during this campaigning season in the summer of 328 that Alexander and the Macedonians captured the Rock of Sogdiana, a sheer citadel that rose up to a height of 18,000 feet. No fewer than 30,000 Sogdians had fled to the rock, which Arimazes was occupying as commander. Among the refugees were Oxyartes, his wife, and his daughter Roxane. According to the men who took part in the campaign, Roxane was the loveliest woman in Asia, save Darius' wife.

Alexander had sent Arimazes a message, urging him to surrender. Arimazes had replied with a question: could Alexander fly? The king was so incensed that he told his friends that by the following night the barbarians would believe that Macedonians indeed could fly.

He then detailed 300 expert rock-climbers to scale the Rock of Sogdiana, promising twelve talents to the first man up. Although thirty men lost their lives during the ascent, the climbers finally made it to the very peak, above Arimazes. They signaled their success to Alexander below by waving linen flags. Alexander then sent his messenger back to Arimazes. Pointing out Alexander's soldiers on the summit, the messenger triumphantly declared to Arimazes that, as he could now see for himself, Alexander's soldiers did have wings. Arimazes promptly gave up.

When Alexander saw Roxane among the captives, he fell in love with her immediately, we are told, and decided to take her in marriage. For the moment, however, the wedding had to be delayed; he still had business in Maracanda.

At the end of the summer of 328, Alexander's forces returned to Maracanda to regroup. There the king was visited by envoys from the

European Scythians and the king of the Chorasmians. Friendship and alliance with the Scythians were cemented. Pharasmanes' offer to guide Alexander if he wished to subdue the various peoples between the Scythians and the Black Sea, however, was put on hold; the king's thoughts were occupied with India. Once India was his, Alexander replied, he would return to Greece and then make an expedition to the Black Sea by way of the Hellespont and the Propontis. At that point he would take Pharasmanes up on his offer. So, by the summer of 328 at the latest, Alexander was planning the conquest of India.

THE DEATH OF CLEITUS

Unfortunately, Maracanda proved to be an ill-fated city for Alexander and his friends. After an enormous hunt in the game reserve of Bazaira, during which he killed a lion with a single stroke, Alexander returned to Maracanda in the autumn of 328 and assigned Artabazus' province of Bactria to Cleitus, who had served as a commander of the Companion cavalry since 330. Artabazus had asked to be relieved on the grounds of advanced age.

Instead of sacrificing to Dionysos on the customary day, we are told that Alexander then sacrificed to Castor and Polydeuces, the Dioscuri. Cleitus, meanwhile, was ordered to prepare to march the following day; he was then invited along to one of Alexander's early-starting banquets.

At the banquet heavy drinking ensued, in the course of which the topic of the Dioscuri came up in conversation, particularly the now common attribution of their parentage to Zeus instead of to Tyndareus.

Some of the company declared that there was no comparison between the deeds of the Dioscuri and Alexander. During the drinking others did not refrain from making invidious comparisons with Herakles. Only envy deprived the living of the honors due to them from their friends, they suggested.

At that point, Cleitus, who for some time had been aggrieved by Alexander's adoption of a "more barbaric style" and by the words of Alexander's flatterers, intervened. He said that he would not permit Alexander's flatterers to show such disrespect for the divine power, or to belittle the deeds of heroes of old to do Alexander a favor that in fact was none. In any case, they exaggerated the nature of Alexander's achievements, Cleitus opined, none of which were mere personal triumphs. On the contrary, those great deeds were the work of the Macedonians as a whole.

Undeterred, some of the guests, hoping to gain favor with Alexander, brought up the subject of Philip, and suggested that his achievements were neither great nor marvelous.

At this Cleitus could no longer govern his emotions. He spoke up in favor of Philip's achievements, making light of Alexander and his deeds and reminding him that he, Cleitus, had saved his life during the cavalry battle at the Granicus River.

"This very hand," Cleitus cried, while raising his right hand, "saved you, O Alexander, at the time."

To this ugly and painful scenario of flattery, drunken insults, and anger, Plutarch adds even more explosive details. At the banquet a singer began to sing the verses of a certain Pranichus (or Pierio), lines written to shame and mock the generals who recently had been defeated by the barbarians. It is very likely that the commanders who had led the ill-fated mission to relieve Maracanda the year before were the subject of the singer's ridicule.

Among those commanders was a man named Andronicus. Almost certainly, this Andronicus was the husband of Lanice, Alexander's childhood nurse. Much more importantly, we know that Lanice was also the sister of Cleitus. Andronicus, in other words, was Cleitus' brother-in-law, his sister's husband. Thus, Cleitus and his friends among the older Macedonian officers may have had personal, as well as political and cultural, reasons for reacting to the mocking verses of the singer as they now did.

The older members of the party understandably were offended by Pranichus' song and displayed their resentment of both poet and singer. But Alexander and those around him listened with pleasure and urged the singer to continue.

Cleitus then shouted out that it was not well done for Macedonians to be insulted among barbarians and enemies, even if they had met misfortune, for they were better men than those who were laughing at them.

Alexander replied that if Cleitus was trying to disguise cowardice as misfortune, he must be pleading his own case. Alexander, in other words, was asserting that the commanders at Marcanda had died because of their own cowardice. This barb also neatly shifted the responsibility for the disaster away from Alexander, who had sent the relief force out, perhaps without a clear structure of command, and onto the commanders themselves. Cleitus, however, heard only a painful insult to himself and to his family.

To Alexander Cleitus replied,

"Indeed, this cowardice saved your life, you who call yourself the son of the gods, when you were turning your back to Spithridates' sword. And it is by the blood of these Macedonians and by their wounds that you have become so great that you disown your father Philip and make yourself the son of Ammon."

Alexander's reaction was incendiary.

"Wretched fellow," he cried out, "do you think that you can keep on speaking of me like this, and cause trouble among the Macedonians, and not pay for it?"

Cleitus replied,

"But we do pay for it, Alexander! Just think of the rewards we get for our efforts: the dead are the happy ones, because they did not live to see Macedonians beaten with Median rods or begging Persians for an audience with our king."

Alexander's friends then jumped up and began to abuse Cleitus, while the older men tried to calm everyone down. Alexander then turned and asked two of the guests at the banquet, Xenodochus of Cardia and Artemius of Colophon, "Do not the Hellenes seem to you to walk about among the Macedonians like demi-gods among wild animals?"

But Cleitus refused to stand down, indeed called on Alexander to say whatever he had to say in front of the company or else not to invite freeborn men to dinner who spoke their minds. Better, Cleitus said, for Alexander to live among barbarians and slaves, who would bow down before his white tunic and his Persian girdle.

At this remark, Alexander threw an apple at Cleitus and looked around for his sword. One of his bodyguards wisely had moved the weapon away, and others begged Alexander to be quiet. But Alexander leapt up, and in the Macedonian dialect shouted for the guards to turn out. Alexander's use of his native tongue meant that he now considered this to be a moment of personal peril. When no one obeyed his order,

Alexander cried out that "he had come to the same pass as Darius, when he was led prisoner by Bessus and his confederates, and that he had nothing now left but the name of king."

Alexander then ordered the trumpeter to sound (the alarm). When he refused, Alexander struck him with his fist. Cleitus' friends managed to shove Cleitus out of the room, but he soon came back through another door. When he returned, Cleitus recited a line spoken by Peleus in Euripides' drama the *Andromache:*

"Alas, in Hellas what an evil government!"

The context of the line was one in which Peleus observed that while it was the army which set up the victory trophy over an enemy, it was the general who received the honor.

This apposite quotation cost Cleitus his life. For Alexander knew his Euripides just as well as Cleitus did. After he heard what Cleitus had said, he grabbed a pike from one of his guards, met Cleitus just as he was drawing aside the curtain before the door, and ran him through.

When Alexander realized what he had done, his first reaction was to try to kill himself, because "it was not honorable for him to live after killing a friend in his cups." But his guards stopped him. Alexander then took to his bed and lay there mourning, crying out the names of Cleitus and Lanice, who had nursed him when he was young. What a fine return he had given for Lanice's nursing now that he was a man, he lamented. She had seen her sons die fighting for him and now, with his own hand, he had killed her brother. Again and again calling himself the murderer of his friends, for three days Alexander refused all food or drink and neglected all bodily needs.

At last worn out, Alexander lay speechless, groaning deeply. Alarmed, his friends forced their way into his quarters. To what most of them said, he paid no attention. But Aristander reminded Alexander of a vision of Cleitus he recently had seen, and of an omen, assuring Alexander that these events had long ago been decreed by fate.

The story was that, some days before Cleitus' death Alexander had called Cleitus away from a sacrifice he was conducting to look at some fruit he, Alexander, had been brought; three of the sheep on whom libations preparatory to their sacrifice had been poured followed Cleitus. Aristander and Cleomantis, a seer from Lacedaemon, pronounced this interrupted sacrifice a bad omen for Cleitus, and Alexander promptly

166 Narrative King of All Asia

had ordered a sacrifice for Cleitus' safety. Two days before that, Alexander had had a dream in which he had seen Cleitus sitting with the sons of Parmenio in black robes; all were dead.

Callisthenes and the philosopher Anaxarchus were also brought in to help Alexander conquer his shame. Callisthenes reportedly skirted the subject to spare Alexander's feelings. Anaxarchus, on the other hand, made the argument that just as Zeus had justice and law at his side, so what the king did was lawful and just. By these arguments, Plutarch comments, Anaxarchus relieved Alexander's suffering, but made him more proud and lawless than before.

It is hard to know how seriously to take these reports of how Aristander, Callisthenes, and Anaxarchus managed to help Alexander restore his own self-image after such a horrific and inexcusable crime. As so often, Arrian perhaps provides the most insight into the man at this low point. He reports that Alexander's soothsayers suggested that the god Dionysos was angry because Alexander had failed to offer him sacrifice; and that when at last Alexander was persuaded by his friends to take food and attend in some measure to his bodily needs, he did offer the neglected sacrifice. Doubtless, Alexander was not unwilling to have his deed attributed to the wrath of a god. But, as Arrian also reports, he did not attempt to justify his crime. Rather, he simply admitted that, being no more than human, he had done wrong.

Alexander's admission of wrongdoing is indeed a historically rare example of a man in a powerful position admitting to making a grave mistake; and it is especially remarkable when we consider that Alexander easily could have pleaded that both he and his friend had drunk too much wine and that Cleitus had provoked him—which was true.

But, to his credit, Alexander made no excuses for his crime. Even if he had not taken responsibility for the disaster at the river Polytimetus, Alexander took his full share of the blame for the murder of the man who had saved his own life.

What could not be avoided either by sophistry or repentance, however, was the public revelation of the trouble in the Macedonian camp that had led to the crime. At the fatal dinner party, simmering tensions between the older generation of Macedonian soldiers and their younger counterparts, including many of Alexander's closest friends, finally boiled over into public brawling and violence. After his sense of self-esteem was restored, Alexander undoubtedly recognized that there was deeply felt opposition both to his personal beliefs and to his policy of orientalizing. Within a year that opposition would give rise to another conspiracy against his life.

CHAPTER 16

The End of the Revolts

THE BURIAL OF CLEITUS

Those who opposed Alexander's policies might have rallied around Cleitus' murder. But no such thing occurred. Indeed, the Macedonians formally declared that Cleitus' death had been justified and even would have refused him burial had not Alexander himself ordered it to be done. Ordinary Macedonians saw Cleitus' death as the unfortunate outcome of a drunken brawl, one of the all-too-predictable results of the ritual drinking parties frequently celebrated by the Macedonian nobles.

Amyntas, the son of Nicolaus, was appointed to replace Cleitus as governor of Bactria. The Macedonian soldiers marched onward. There was campaigning to be done and, on the whole, the Macedonians were better fighters than drinkers. Or, at least, campaigning resulted in more casualties among their enemies than among their friends. Alexander and the Macedonians therefore turned their attention toward those who had been responsible for the massacre at the Polytimetus.

THE DEATH OF SPITAMENES

While Alexander and the Macedonians drank themselves senseless in Maracanda, Spitamenes and the Massagetae had had some successes in the north, capturing one of Alexander's garrisons and besieging Zariaspa (Balkh). A few of the Companion cavalry, eighty mercenary cavalry, and some of the royal pages who had been left at Zariaspa attacked Spitamenes, stripping him and his forces of their booty, but they were ambushed on their way back from the punitive raid. Seven Companions and sixty mercenaries lost their lives. Aristonicus the harpist also died there, "with more courage than a harpist might have."

Craterus was sent out to track down the Massagetae and, in a fierce engagement, 150 of the Scythians were killed before the survivors fled into the desert.

With two battalions of the Macedonian phalanx, four hundred Companion cavalry, the mounted javelin men, and the Bactrians and Sogdians attached to Amyntas, the commander Coenus was ordered to winter in Sogdiana, to protect the region, and to try to ambush Spitamenes. Gathering up an additional force of poverty-stricken Scythian horsemen from around Gabae (on the border of Sogdiana and the land of the Massagetae), Spitamenes attacked Coenus but was decisively defeated, losing 800 cavalry. Most of the surviving Sogdians and Bactrians with Spitamenes then surrendered to Coenus.

Alexander himself had marched on southward to Nautaca (probably Karshi in modern Uzbekistan), about halfway between Maracanda and the Rock of Sogdiana, where the army was rested during the winter of 328/7. Sisimithres, the local ruler, had established his forces in a strong defensive position, blocking the defile that gave access to the plains. The Macedonians built a causeway across the defile at its narrowest point using trees and rocks, and when they brought up their siege towers and engines, Sisimithres and his followers gave up. Alexander sacrificed to Athena Nike (Victory) and restored Sisimithres to his rule of the area. While Alexander was engaged with mopping up the remaining rebels in the area, Philip, the brother of Lysimachus, died; so too did Alexander's old friend Erigyius. When Alexander returned to his camp both men were given magnificent funerals. Erigyius' grave was a long way away from his native Mytilene.

As for Spitamenes, his wife, grown tired of a life on the run, decided to take matters into her own hands. After Spitamenes attended a banquet, he was carried into his room half asleep, torpid from excessive drinking and eating. As soon as his wife saw that he was sound asleep, she drew the sword she had hidden under her clothes and cut off Spitamenes' head. She then handed over to a slave her ex-husband's head.

With the slave in attendance, Spitamenes' wife, her clothes still drenched in blood, then went to the Macedonian camp. She sent a message to Alexander saying that there was a matter about which he should hear from her own lips. Alexander immediately had her escorted in.

Seeing her spattered with blood, Alexander had assumed that she wanted to complain about some kind of assault. He told her to state what she wanted; she asked only that the slave, whom she had told to stand in the doorway, now be brought in. The slave, we are told, had aroused some suspicion because he seemed to have something concealed under his clothes. When the guards searched him, he showed them what he was hiding: Spitamenes' head. Pallor, however, had disfigured Spitamenes' features so that a firm identification was not possible.

Arrian tells a different but no less chilling version of the story. Putting self-interest ahead of loyalty, the Massagetae themselves cut off Spitamenes' head and sent it to Alexander. They hoped by this act to keep Alexander away from them.

CLEANING UP

Dataphernes, the other ringleader of the rebellion, was imprisoned by the Dahae, who surrendered him and themselves to Alexander. By midwinter Stasanor and Phrataphernes returned to Nautaca, having successfully suppressed the rebels in Parthia and Areia. Phrataphernes was sent to the Mardians and Tapurians with orders to bring back the satrap Autophradates, who had been sent for by Alexander but had ignored the summons. Stasanor was dispatched to the Drangians as governor, and Atropates was sent along to Media as satrap to replace Oxydates since

Alexander believed that Oxydates was willfully neglecting his duty. Stamenes also was sent back to Babylon since Mazaeus was reported to have died. Sopolis, Epokillos, and Menidas were ordered to return to Macedon, to bring back a new force.

These measures are worth noting in detail for two reasons. First, they imply that Alexander now believed that the revolts in Bactria and Sogdiana had been snuffed out after two years of fighting. They also signify, already in the winter of 327, Alexander's insistence that governors do their jobs as ordered. After his return from India, Alexander replaced or executed more governors, whom he accused of maladministration, and this period has been called a reign of terror. But, in fact, there was no such discrete phase. Alexander was never willing to put up with insubordination or administrative incompetence, and he was making that clear by 327.

To keep the restive indigenes of Bactria and Sogdiana quiet, Alexander established a large garrison under the satrap Amyntas, who was given 10,000 infantry and 3,500 cavalry to keep the peace. The king also incorporated natives into his own cavalry and in 327 gave orders for 30,000 native youths, the so-called *epigoni*, or successors, to be taught Greek and to be trained to use Macedonian weapons for eventual service in a native phalanx. The establishment of this indigenous levy shows that by the spring of 327 at the latest Alexander was planning to incorporate "barbarian" troops into his army for future use. He was no mere military adventurer, interested only in fleecing Asia, as he often has been portrayed. Even in 327, Alexander was planning for the future conquest of the rest of Asia and Europe, and he meant to do it with mixed levies of European and Asian troops.

THE MARRIAGE TO ROXANE

Now that military matters had been resolved for the time being, it was the moment, just before he embarked upon his invasion of India, for Alexander to settle affairs of the heart. In the spring of 327, in his twenty-ninth year and thousands of miles from home, Alexander married Roxane, the beautiful daughter of the Bactrian nobleman Oxyartes.

Oxyartes and his daughter, it will be recalled, had been taken captive after the fall of the Rock of Sogdiana in 328.

The ceremony was performed in Macedonian style. Bread, the sacred symbol of betrothal among the Macedonians, was brought in and then cut with a sword. Alexander and his new Asian father-in-law then tasted bread from the same loaf.

Historians have rightly pointed out the political advantages of this marriage for Alexander: his new father-in-law was an important and powerful ally in a restive area of his empire. To violate his daughter would have been out of the question and would not have been consistent with Alexander's general attitude toward women. A marriage to the daughter of an Asian noble also might have been intended as a signal to both Macedonians and Asians, in the wake of the murder of Cleitus, that Alexander had no intention of backing away from his policy of oriental-izing, even on a personal level. As always, Alexander led by example. But the purely political or pragmatic explanation for Alexander's first mar-riage is not persuasive.

Alexander certainly could have married any Macedonian, Greek, or Persian woman (or women) he had met before or after 336. Marriage to any one or more of these women might have brought greater political benefits at times when Alexander's prospects were far less secure. And yet he had chosen not to marry any of the many noblewomen he had en-countered from Greece to Bactria.

Nor can it be maintained that Alexander did not marry until it was politically necessary because he was not attracted to women. Since 332 he had kept a mistress, Barsine (the daughter of Artabazus and the ex-wife of Memnon), by whom he now had a son, Herakles. He also had re-tained the services of Darius' harem after the Persian king's death. Although Alexander probably had sexual relationships with men, it is a myth that he was not sexually attracted to women as well. Clearly he was. The question is why, given all of his opportunities, Alexander chose to make Roxane his first wife.

Moreover, Alexander's first wife was a foreigner, and a "barbarian" (though possessed with a dignity "rare" among the barbarians). Such a marriage was bound to provoke grumbling, and it did. In response, Alexander was careful to point out to the grumblers that Achilles himself had shared his bed with a captive, Briseis. The simple explanation here is most convincing: this was a love match; Roxane in fact had caught Alexander's eye when she was performing in some kind of dance at a banquet. Since he would not, and could not, simply take her, he decided to marry her. There is also no doubt that the marriage was consummated, for they had a son, Alexander IV, whose name indicates that Alexander intended him to be his heir and the inheritor of his empire.

In the future, Alexander would marry more foreign women, using their native marriage ceremony. Moreover, he would make it worth the while of his friends to do so in turn. A true son of Zeus could break the molds, even if those around him could not understand why—or did not want to. But that particular mold would be broken only four years later, when the king returned to Persia. First, however, Alexander prepared to take his new bride on what promised to be one of the most exotic but dangerous honeymoons in nuptial history: the conquest of India.

CHAPTER 17

One Kiss the Poorer

THE CALM BEFORE THE STORM

Alexander now spent two months in winter quarters, presumably enjoying the pleasures of married life (328/7). During this hiatus, Alexander and his officers probably put together the detailed plans for the invasion of India. Once these plans had been fleshed out in the late spring of 327, Alexander led his forces into the region called Gazaba. On the third day out the army was caught in a lightning storm followed by a torrential cloudburst that showered them with hail. Finally the men broke ranks and wandered about aimlessly through the woods. The storm, we are told, claimed the lives of 2,000 soldiers and camp followers.

Sisimithres brought pack animals and 2,000 camels plus sheep and herds of cattle to help relieve the army. After giving him a public commendation, Alexander ravaged the land of the Sacae and gave 30,000 head of cattle to Sisimithres in recompense for saving the army.

After defeating the only rebels left in Pareitacene, Alexander headed south toward Bactra. Craterus' forces too made for Bactra after subduing some local rebels. In the spring of 327 Bactra was to be the assembly point for the Macedonian invasion of India.

PROSKYNESIS

In Bactra, Alexander attempted to introduce the custom of *proskynesis*, or prostration, to his court. In Persia, the act of what the Greeks called *proskynesis* might involve bowing forward and blowing a kiss from the tip of the fingers (as depicted on a Persian treasury relief), or it might entail actually prostrating oneself before the king. Prostration of either kind was understood in Persia as a fundamentally social and secular gesture, performed by all social inferiors to their social superiors right up to the king.

In the Greek tradition, *proskynesis* was usually done by individuals who were standing up with their arms raised to the sky and their palms forward. Sometimes, however, prostration was performed kneeling. Among the Greeks, however, *proskynesis* was understood as a sacred act, only to be performed before gods (or their images).

It is not clear that all Greeks understood the social and secular significance of the Persian practice of prostration. Some Greek authors, such as the early fifth-century Athenian tragedian Aeschylus, seem to have believed that the Persian form of prostration was an act of worship. Later writers clearly understood it as a social custom—which nevertheless evoked feelings of disgust and superiority among Greeks. Indeed, Alexander's teacher Aristotle regarded the Persian form of prostration as a specifically barbarian act.

There also was a strong imperative in Greece against performing the act in front of another man, even a king. When Spartan ambassadors visited the court of the fifth-century Persian king Xerxes, for instance, and were being pressured to prostrate themselves (in the Persian style) before the king, they replied that it was not their custom to prostrate themselves before any human. Greek authors such as Xenophon regarded the Persian form of prostration as inconsistent with the freedom of a citizen.

With this background in mind, we now can turn to the two versions of what happened when Alexander attempted to introduce prostration in the late spring of 327. The first version involves a private drinking party, at which, Alexander's chamberlain Chares records, after he [Alexander] had drunk, [he] passed the cup to one of his friends, who took it and rose so as to face the shrine of the household; next he drank in his turn, then made obeisance to Alexander, kissed him and resumed his place on the couch. All the guests did the same in succession, until the cup came to Callisthenes. The king was talking to Hephaestion and paying no attention to Callisthenes and the philosopher, after he had drunk, came forward to kiss him. At this Demetrius, whose surname was Pheido, called out, "Sire, do not kiss him; he is the only one who has not made obeisance to you." Alexander therefore refused to kiss him, and Callisthenes exclaimed in a loud voice, "Very well then, I shall go away the poorer by a kiss."

To this basic account Arrian adds the important detail that Alexander had passed the cup first to those with whom an agreement about the act of prostration had been reached ahead of the party. Hephaestion later claimed that Callisthenes had been among those who had promised to perform prostration, but that the historian had reneged on his agreement at the party.

Whether Callisthenes went back on his word or not, clearly the introduction of prostration at this private symposium was orchestrated in advance, although perhaps not everyone was informed about what was to take place. The introduction of prostration was a kind of trial balloon, popped by an overly observant diner.

The plot of the second version depends entirely on prostration being planned in advance. It had been agreed by Alexander with the sophists and the Persian and Median noblemen that the subject of prostration should be broached at another drinking party. Anaxarchus began the discussion. He declared that

Alexander had a better claim upon them to be considered divine than Dionysos or Herakles. The reason for this was not merely his brilliant and successful career, but also the fact that neither Dionysos nor Herakles was connected with Macedon. Dionysos belonged to Thebes and Herakles to Argos—the latter's only connection to Macedon was through Alexander himself, who had his blood in his veins. That being so, there would be greater propriety in the Macedonians paying divine honors to their own king. In any case there was no doubt that they would honor him as a god after he had left the world; would it not, therefore, be in every way better to offer him this tribute now, while he was alive, and not wait until he was dead and could get no good of it?

Those who were in on the plan then expressed their approval of what Anaxarchus said and were willing to begin prostrating themselves right away. The Macedonians—or most of them—who were present strongly dissented but kept quiet.

It is crucial to our understanding of what Alexander actually intended on this occasion to note that the idea of introducing prostration was brought up in the context of a discussion about divine honors for Alexander.

Moreover, Callisthenes' reply to Anaxarchus similarly implies that he too connected the introduction of prostration with the question of whether Alexander deserved divine honors. Callisthenes replied to Anaxarchus:

> For my part, I hold Alexander fit for any mark of honor that a man may earn; but do not forget that there is a difference between honoring a man and worshipping a god. The distinction between the two has been marked in many ways: for instance, by the building of temples, the erection of statues; the dedication of sacred ground—all these are for gods; again, for gods sacrifice is offered and libations are poured; hymns are composed for the worship of gods, while panegyrics are written for the praise of men. Yet, of all these things not one is so important as this very custom of prostration. Men greet each other with a kiss; but a god, far above us on his mysterious throne, it is not lawful for us to touch—and that is why we proffer him the homage of bowing to earth before him.

After berating Anaxarchus for introducing the idea of paying homage to Alexander, Callisthenes then turned his criticisms to the king himself:

> Not even Herakles was accorded divine honors by the Greeks when he was alive—nor when he was dead either, until the command to do so was given by an oracle of Apollo at Delphi. Well, here we are in a

foreign land; and if for that reason we must think foreign thoughts, yet I beg you Alexander to remember Greece; it was for her sake alone that you might add Asia to your empire, that you undertook this campaign. Consider this too: When you are home again, do you really propose to force the Greeks, who love their freedom more than anybody else in the world, to prostrate themselves before you? Or will you let the Greeks off and impose this shameful duty only on the Macedonians? Or will you make a broad and general distinction in the matter, and ordain that barbarians only should keep their barbarous manners, while Greeks and Macedonians honor you honorably as a man, according to the traditions of Greece?

It is said that Cyrus, son of Cambyses, was the first man to receive the homage of prostration, and that this humiliating custom thereafter became an accepted thing in Persia. So be it; none the less you must remember that the Great Cyrus was cured of his pride by the tribe of Scythians—poor men but free; that Darius was humbled by Scythians too, as Xerxes was by Athens and Sparta, and Artaxerxes by the Ten Thousand of Clearchus and Xenophon. And now Alexander has robbed another Darius of his pride—though no man has yet bowed to earth before him.

Callisthenes' long speech angered Alexander profoundly, but the Macedonians found it very much to their liking. Recognizing this, Alexander told the Macedonians not to think about prostration further.

But that was not the end of the story.

There was an awful, embarrassed silence after Callisthenes' speech. Then, in turn, the senior Persian officials rose from their seats and prostrated themselves on the floor before Alexander. Thinking that one of the Persians had bowed down in an ungraceful way, Leonnatus, one of Alexander's officers, mocked his posture. In one late version of the story, it was Polyperchon who ridiculed the hapless Persian, telling him to beat the ground harder (with his chin). Dragging Polyperchon off his drinking couch, Alexander threw him face-first on the floor; "You see," said Alexander, "you are doing just what you laughed at in another a moment ago." Then the king ordered Polyperchon to be arrested and the banquet came to an end.

Thereafter, the custom of prostration was dropped for Greeks and Macedonians; it applied only to Alexander's non-Greek or non-Macedonian subjects. In return, up to the mutiny at Opis several years later, only Persians ever received a kiss from Alexander.

This episode has left historians with more questions than answers. Most important, why did Alexander do it? He must have been aware that to require prostration from Greeks and Macedonians would cause grave offense, religious and civic. The fact that prostration was introduced not once but twice may suggest that Alexander anticipated dissent and perhaps even opposition.

Some have speculated that the reason Alexander decided to go ahead anyway was the need for a uniform court ceremonial. As the ruler of all Asia, Alexander had to be seen by his Asian subjects as receiving the same acts of social deference that the Persian kings had received. Otherwise, Alexander's Asian subjects might not see Alexander as the true successor of Darius. To require the Asians, but not the Macedonians and the Greeks, to prostrate themselves would be to suggest that the Asians were of a lower social status. This was not an option, given Alexander's policy of adapting himself and his army to the customs of the East. After careful preparation, Alexander conceivably introduced the practice, hoping to convince the Macedonians and the Greeks to view prostration the way the Persians did, as an essentially secular and social custom.

If this was what Alexander had in mind, he had seriously misjudged the strength of the opposition to the practice. Even if Alexander had persuaded the Macedonians to accept prostration as a social custom, most Greeks and Macedonians would still have perceived it as an affront to their own sense of social status. Prostration was incompatible with the Macedonians' sense of being free men. And Alexander surely knew that no Greek or Macedonian wanted to bow down in front of him the way that they believed slaves or barbarians did. So, the hypothesis that Alexander hoped to sell prostration to the Macedonians as a social custom is not convincing.

Rather, we should recall that both attempts to introduce prostration took place in the context of discussions about divine honors. The logical explanation for Alexander's introduction of prostration is not that Alexander wanted to convince the Macedonians that the Persian custom was only a secular act, which should not offend their secular sensibilities, but that the Macedonians were quite correct about what prostration before Alexander implied. Alexander introduced prostration because he wanted the Greeks and Macedonians to think of him as a real son of Zeus, just as he had been claiming since his visit to Siwah.

That he dropped the idea does not prove that Alexander wished to introduce prostration for "pragmatic" reasons of unifying court ceremony, changed his mind about his own divine son–ship, or believed that he was not worthy of the honors accorded to divinity. After he returned from India, Alexander demanded far more than prostration from the Greeks, with all that prostration implied to Greeks. Only official declarations of his divinity then would do. The introduction of prostration in the spring of 327 was a logical (mis)step along the road to Alexander's eventually successful demand for divine honors.

THE CONSPIRACY OF THE PAGES

Many of the ancient sources connected Alexander's introduction of prostration in 327 with the so-called conspiracy of the royal pages, both because the conspiracy evidently took place shortly after the unsuccessful introduction of prostration and also because Callisthenes played a central role in both episodes.

The plot had its origins in a hunt during which Alexander was charged by a wild boar. Before the king could strike, one of the royal grooms, a certain Hermolaus, the son of Sopolis, dispatched it. Angry because he missed his opportunity, Alexander ordered the groom to be whipped in front of the other boys and then took his horse away from him.

Outraged by this treatment, Hermolaus told his boyfriend Sostratus that life would no longer be worth living until he had revenge on Alexander for this assault. He easily persuaded Sostratus to lend a hand in planning it. Several other pages, including Antipater, Epimenes, Anticles, and Philotas, consented to help.

It was agreed among them that when Antipater's turn to guard Alexander at night came around, they would murder the king in his sleep. Because of the duty rotation of the pages, however, it took thirty-two days for the planned opportunity to arise.

According to some writers, that night, Alexander sat up drinking until dawn. Aristobulus claimed that as Alexander was returning to his tent, a Syrian woman—thought by some to be gifted by the gods with second sight, but by others to be just plain mad—begged him to go back and drink the night out. Alexander, believing this intervention to be a divine sign, took her advice—and lived.

The next day one of the conspirators, Epimenes, told the whole story to his boyfriend Charicles. Charicles in turn related the story to Epimenes' brother Eurylochus, who passed the information on to Ptolemy. Ptolemy, perhaps mindful of Philotas' downfall, told Alexander right away.

All the boys were arrested. Questioned under torture, they openly admitted their guilt and implicated others, too. Aristobulus and Ptolemy both claimed that Callisthenes had urged the pages to commit the crime. Most authorities had a different version—namely, that Alexander was ready anyway to believe the worst about Callisthenes because he already hated him and because Hermolaus was close to the sophist.

At his trial, Hermolaus confessed, but declared it was no longer possible for a free man to bear Alexander's hubris. The young page then went on to give a list of Alexander's crimes: the lawless killing of Philotas, the arbitrary execution of Parmenio and the other officers put to death at the time, the murder of Cleitus, the assumption of Persian dress, the introduction of prostration, the heavy drinking, the drunken sleeps that followed. These were things no longer to be borne and from which he wished to free himself and the Macedonians.

The outcome of the trial was predictable. Hermolaus and the other prisoners were stoned to death on the spot by the assembly or were transferred back to their own military units to be tortured to death.

As for Callisthenes, Plutarch, writing during the Roman empire, claims that even under torture, not one of Hermolaus' accomplices denounced him. Curtius, too, explicitly denies that Callisthenes was part of any plot to kill the king.

Yet Plutarch does relate that Callisthenes may have encouraged Hermolaus to undertake the deed. When the page asked Callisthenes how he might become a most illustrious man, Callisthenes is said to have replied, "By killing the most famous." Supposedly, too, he remarked to Hermolaus that he should not be overawed by Alexander's golden couch, but should keep in mind that he was approaching a man subject to sicknesses and wounds like anybody else.

The issue of how Callisthenes died is no clearer than the question of whether he was part of the conspiracy of the pages. Ptolemy recalled that Callisthenes was racked and then hanged. If Ptolemy's memory was correct, the manner of Callisthenes' death perhaps is a sign that he was judged to have been a member of the conspiracy, an indicted co-conspirator. Aristobulus, on the other hand, wrote that Callisthenes was bound in fetters and carried around with the army until he eventually died from sickness. This account leaves open the question of whether Callisthenes was thought to have been guilty of conspiring to murder Alexander; his house arrest can be compared to that of Alexander of Lyncestis.

Curtius claims that Callisthenes was tortured to death although he was innocent of any plot to kill the king. Torture was the standard way the Macedonians attempted to extract information from suspected plotters.

Chares, the court chamberlain, says that Callisthenes was kept in chains for seven months so that he could be tried by the Council of the League of Corinth in Aristotle's presence. But he died (when Alexander was wounded in India) from obesity and the disease of lice.

In assessing Chares' story, some historians have focused upon Alexander's apparent desire to prove Callisthenes' guilt to Aristotle, Callisthenes' kinsman and Alexander's teacher. The more important point, however, is that, if Chares is right, Callisthenes' slow demise perhaps can be attributed to his citizenship. According to customary procedure, Macedonians charged with treason were tried by the Macedonian army with the king acting as prosecutor, but not as the judge or jury.

But Callisthenes was not a Macedonian and therefore did not have the dubious constitutional privilege of a trial in front of the Macedonian army. Rather, he was a Greek from Olynthos. The point of dragging him around in chains until he could be tried by the Council of the League of Corinth was not to embarrass Aristotle, but to follow Greek constitutional procedure.

Overall, it is difficult to know what to make of these stories about the fate of Callisthenes. It may finally be impossible to say whether Callisthenes died because of his commitment to freedom of speech or his commitment to Alexander's demise. We may not be any more certain about what motivated the pages themselves.

For we happen to know that Hermolaus' father, Sopolis, who had commanded the Amphipolitan squadron of the Companion cavalry since 335, had been sent back with Menidas and Epokillos to bring new recruits from Macedon in the winter of 328/7. There is no evidence of Sopolis returning to Alexander.

Moreover, the father of another conspiring page (Antipater), a man named Asclepiodorus, had brought reinforcements to Alexander in Bactra in 329/8, and then had not been returned to his governorship of Syria.

So the fathers of two of the admitted conspirators against Alexander seem to have been demoted, effectively. It is significant that the assassination was scheduled for the night when Antipater was to guard the sleeping Alexander. Antipater would not have been the first or the last son to attempt to avenge himself upon a man who had demoted his father.

Whatever motivated the pages who plotted to kill Alexander, there was no rallying around them or their alleged cause. The Macedonian rank and file executed them without hesitation. They were found guilty as charged.

TO INDIA

Alexander had been contemplating the conquest of India since the summer of 328. It was part of his overall plan to conquer all of Asia, return to Greece, and from Greece to make an expedition to the Black Sea region, by way of the Hellespont and the Propontis, with all of his land and sea forces. Although Alexander may not have needed a great deal of encouragement to extend his empire into an area only nominally under Persian control before his campaign, he did get such encouragement from Indian rulers; several came to him inviting him to come to their countries to conquer their neighbors. In Sogdiana, for example, Mophis (or Omphis), the ruler of Taxila, appeared, promising to join Alexander in a campaign against his enemies.

What Alexander and the Macedonians knew about the size of India and what the campaign was likely to entail is another question altogether. It was only when Alexander got to the Hyphasis (modern Beas) that he got any sort of realistic view of what he had bitten off. Of course, the more accurate reports he got about the size of India and of the enemy army waiting for him there did not in any way discourage the king, but they did have a sobering effect upon his less ambitious soldiers.

In the late spring of 327, however, Alexander's thoughts probably were shaped more by the stories told about his semi-mythological predecessors in the region. The Semiramis of Greek legend, for instance, who was the daughter of the Syrian goddess Derceto of Ascalon, reportedly had conquered Bactria; and Dionysos was supposed to have started out on his triumphal march westward from India. Herakles, too, one of Alexander's ancestors and rivals, supposedly had visited India.

Never one to be outdone, Alexander was determined to surpass the accomplishments of Zeus' other sons. They had merely passed through India; he came to establish a lasting empire.

From Bactra, therefore, Alexander and his army marched for ten days back over the Caucasus and reached the city he had founded during his first expedition into Bactria, Alexandria-in-the-Caucasus (modern Begram). There he dismissed the local *hyparch* for governing poorly and then appointed Nicanor as governor of the city. Tyriespis was made satrap of the region of Parapamisadae and the land up to the Cophen River (now the Kabul). More people from the area and all the soldiers declared unfit for fighting were settled in the city. Having settled these matters, by way of Nicaea, where he offered sacrifice to Athena, Alexander then marched for the Cophen toward the plain of the Indus River.

CHAPTER 18

In the Footsteps
of Dionysos

THE FIRST GREAT GAME

For his route to the Indus, Alexander had chosen to pass through the region that more than 2,000 years later would comprise the Northwest Frontier of British India. In that mountainous and inhospitable territory, solitary, brilliant, and often eccentric officers of the Indian army, such as "Bokhara" Burnes, Captain Arthur Conolly, and Francis Younghusband, often disguised as horse traders or Tibetan holy men, played the Great Game against Britain's indigenous and European enemies. Twenty-three centuries earlier Alexander played his own brutally effective game against the local tribesmen.

Before setting out, Alexander divided his army into two columns. Hephaestion and Perdiccas were put in charge of three battalions, half the Companions, and all the mercenary cavalry. These troops were sent along the main road through the Khyber Pass into the territory of Peucelaotis toward the Indus River. Hephaestion's battle group therefore holds the distinction of being the first documented military force to make the thirty-mile trek through the famous pass in the Safed Koh mountains, now on the border between modern Afghanistan and Pakistan.

Alexander, with the Guards, the rest of the Companion cavalry, the phalanx regiments from Upper Macedon, the archers, the Agrianes, and the mounted javelin men, took a more northerly route, which followed the river Choes (modern Kunar) into the mountain country through Bajaur and Swat (in modern Pakistan).

They assaulted the first town they came upon after crossing the Choes, and here Alexander was slightly wounded in the shoulder by an arrow that pierced his corselet. Nevertheless, he and the Macedonians easily stormed the settlement, and all the prisoners taken in the town were massacred in revenge for Alexander's wound. As usual the Macedonians were particularly ferocious and unmerciful toward their enemies when Alexander was hurt in battle.

The town of Andaca capitulated, and Craterus was left there with the other infantry commanders to destroy any other cities that did not surrender. When Alexander advanced into the territory of the *hyparch* of the Aspasians, the inhabitants burned their city and fled into the mountains. Ptolemy killed the local leader in hand-to-hand combat, and the Macedonians again prevailed.

After Alexander and his men crossed the mountains into the region of Bajaur, they came to the town of Arigaion (Acadira), where they were met by Craterus and his colleagues. The city was now fortified and settled with volunteers from the area and soldiers unfit for duty. Greeks called such a settlement at a strategically or commercially important site *synoikismos*.

At the news that Ptolemy had sighted barbarian fires ahead more numerous than in Alexander's camp, Alexander once again split the army into three columns and attacked the locals after they had descended into the plain. We are told that no fewer than 40,000 men and 230,000 oxen were captured. The finest of the latter were sent back to Macedon. Within weeks Alexander had pacified—by lance and fire—a region the British later struggled to control for more than fifty years.

IN THE FOOTSTEPS OF DIONYSOS

Sometime during the campaign in the Bajaur region, the people of a town named Nysa sent out to Alexander their chief, Acuphis, with thirty envoys, to ask Alexander to leave their city to their god. Acuphis explained that Dionysos had founded their city (with discharged soldiers who were also his Bacchoi) on his return to the Greek Sea after his conquest of the Indians, naming the city Nysa after his nurse.

Alexander bought Acuphis' story, granting freedom and independence to the settlers of Nysa, only demanding that the Nysaeans send 300 cavalrymen to accompany him. The persuasive Acuphis subsequently was appointed governor of the territory.

While he was in the area, a "desire" seized Alexander to see Mount Merus, where the Nysaeans displayed memorials of Dionysos. Ivy and laurel grew there in abundance. Alexander and the Macedonians had not seen these plants, so characteristic of the Greek landscape, in seven years. Alexander offered sacrifice on the spot (presumably to Dionysos), and some of his officers reportedly crowned their heads in ivy and performed a Bacchic revel. Regrettably, none of the sources tell us what the local tribesmen made of the spectacle of drunken, ivy-wreathed Macedonian soldiers roaming the mountainside, crying out *"Euhoi, Euhoi,"* as the women Bacchants in Euripides' last and greatest tragedy had done.

The inhabitants of the kingdom of the Assaceni of the lower Swat Valley, who could claim no life-saving connection to any Greek god, were far less friendly. They had prepared for battle with 2,000 cavalry, 30,000 infantry, and 30 elephants. One by one, however, their fortresses, including Massaga, Ora, and Bazira, were seized, assaulted, or abandoned. The inhabitants of Massaga were cut down, but reportedly only after their mercenaries, whom Alexander had granted leave of the city, appear to have gone back on an agreement with Alexander to join his army.

THE ROCK OF AORNOS

The survivors from these towns fled to the Rock of Aornos (in southern Swat), identified today with Pir-Sar, a flat-topped ridge rising 8,000 feet above sea level, and commanding the Indus about seventy-five miles north of Attock City. Atop the rock there was a perennial spring, as well as wood and arable land. By legend, Herakles himself had tried to capture the Rock of Aornos, but had failed because of an earthquake.

Naturally, a longing seized Alexander to succeed where Herakles had failed. Any labor at which Herakles had come up short was a welcome challenge to Alexander. After appointing a satrap of the region, Alexander therefore advanced toward Aornos, accepting the surrender of towns in the area and establishing garrisons and a supply base at Embolima.

Despite its intimidating history and height, Aornos proved relatively easy to capture. Some of the neighboring people who had surrendered guided Ptolemy, the Agrianes, and other lightly armed units up to the first saddle of the mountain, where they established a stockade and fought off a counterattack. Alexander then brought up the rest of the army.

For four days the Macedonians worked on building up an earthen mound from the crest of the hill they occupied to the level of the Rock itself. From the mound, slingers fired on the Indians, and missiles were flung from the Macedonian siege engines to give cover to the Macedonians as they worked. Alexander's use of artillery to cover field operations (as opposed to siege warfare) was another brilliant adaptation, one that has been copied by virtually every commander since.

Recognizing that defeat was certain once the Macedonians had completed the mound, the defenders of Aornos then used a delay during surrender negotiations to concoct a plan to escape and scatter at night to their homes. Unfortunately for them, Alexander led an assault team of bodyguards and elite guards (hypaspists) onto the plateau itself before they could carry out their plan. The king was the first to scale the Rock. Many of the refugees were killed as they fled. Some panicked and threw themselves over the cliffs of the Rock. Alexander had surpassed Herakles. Altars in honor of Athena the Victorious were duly set up.

Resistance among the Assaceni then collapsed. As he made his way toward the Indus River, Alexander now learned that the Indians of the district had fled to the kingdom of Abisares (to the east of the Indus), but had left their elephants grazing near the Indus. The surviving elephants were captured and incorporated into Alexander's army. Meanwhile, Hephaestion and Perdiccas had pressed along through the Cophen Valley, seriously opposed only by the prince of Peucelaotis, whose capital (modern Charsadda) was stormed after thirty days.

Beating Alexander to the Indus, Hephaestion and Perdiccas had constructed a bridge for the crossing of the great river, perhaps at Ohind (Udabhandapura). For the crossing itself, many smaller boats and two thirty-oar ships had been prepared as well; and awaiting Alexander at the crossing point were gifts from the local Indian ruler, Taxiles, including 200 talents of silver, 3,000 oxen, 10,000 sheep for sacrifices, and 30 elephants. Taxiles also had sent 700 cavalry as fighting allies and had surrendered Taxila (present-day Takshiçila, about twenty miles northwest of Islamabad), the largest city between the Indus and Hydaspes Rivers.

CROSSING THE INDUS

Before crossing the Indus, Alexander sacrificed to the gods whom it was his custom to honor and then held a contest of athletics and cavalry. The sacrifices turned out to be favorable to the crossing.

Exactly how Alexander crossed this immense river—about two and a half miles wide today at its broadest point—unfortunately is not known. Arrian reports only that Alexander crossed with the army and then made customary sacrifices on the far side of the river. Alexander certainly was the first (and last) Greek or Macedonian ever to reach India at the head of a large army.

Once across the mighty Indus, Alexander made his way first to Taxila, where he granted Taxiles' son Mophis (who took the name Taxiles after his father's death) and the Indians of the district as much of the territory bordering on their own as they asked for. This, of course, was a reward for the gifts that Taxiles had left for Alexander. In Taxila Alexander also received representatives from Abisares, king of the Indian hill tribes east of the Indus (modern Kashmir), who brought presents but also the somewhat alarming news that Abisares kept two snakes, one 80 cubits in length and the other 140 cubits. This was a reminder to Alexander and the Macedonians that they were a long way from home; it should have been a warning, too.

Perhaps Alexander's presence unnerved Taxiles/Mophis, for he kept up a shower of gifts: 56 elephants, large numbers of sheep, and some 3,000 bulls. He also revealed to Alexander how much grain he had sup-

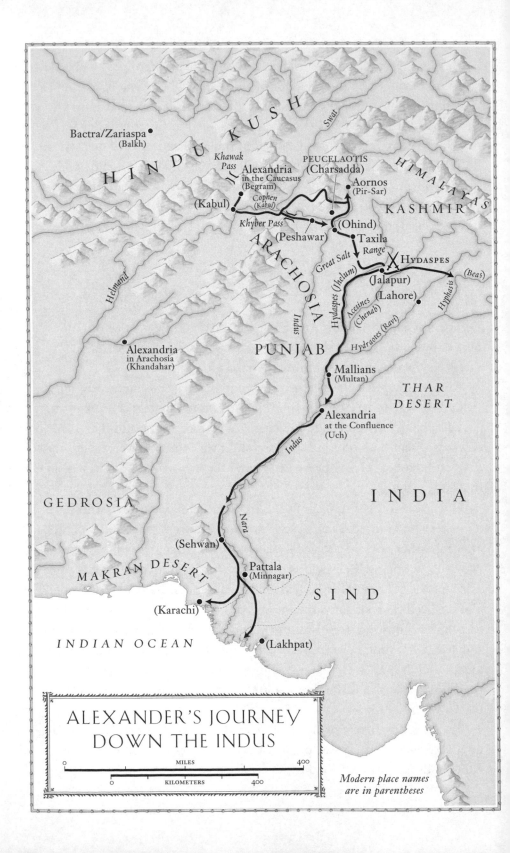

Bactra/Zariaspa •
(Balkh)

HINDU KUSH

Swat

Khawak
Pass

Alexandria
in the Caucasus
(Begram)

PEUCELAOTIS
(Charsadda)

Aornos
(Pir-Sar)

HIMALAYAS

KASHMIR

(Kabul)

Cophen
(Kabul)

Khyber Pass

(Ohind)

ARACHOSIA

(Peshawar)

Taxila
Range

Great Salt

HYDASPES

(Beas)

Helmand

Indus

Hydaspes (Jhelum)

(Jalapur)

(Lahore)

Acesines (Chenab)

Hyphasis

Alexandria
in Arachosia
(Khandahar)

PUNJAB

Hydraotes (Ravi)

THAR
DESERT

Mallians
(Multan)

Alexandria
at the Confluence
(Uch)

Indus

INDIA

GEDROSIA

Nara

(Sehwan)

Pattala
(Minnagar)

SIND

MAKRAN DESERT

(Karachi)

INDIAN OCEAN

(Lakhpat)

ALEXANDER'S JOURNEY
DOWN THE INDUS

| 0 | MILES | 400 |
| 0 | KILOMETERS | 400 |

*Modern place names
are in parentheses*

plied to the forces under Hephaestion, and gave golden crowns to Alexander and his friends. As if all this were not enough, he added eighty talents of coined silver. Alexander was so pleased that he returned all the gifts and added 1,000 talents from his booty, gold and silver dinnerware, Persian clothing, and thirty horses with their trappings. After he had drunk too much at dinner, one of Alexander's Macedonian officers, Meleager, sarcastically congratulated Alexander on having at least found one man in India now worth 1,000 talents. Remembering another party that had ended disastrously, Alexander controlled his anger, remarking that "envious men only torment themselves."

After the usual sacrifices and games, Alexander left Philip as governor of the district, along with any men who were sick or unfit for duty. Alexander and the army, its ranks swelled by the addition of 5,000 Indian troops led by Taxiles/Mophis and the governors of the district, then made their way to the Hydaspes River (the modern Jhelum).

Awaiting them on the far side of the Hydaspes was Porus (Indian Paurava), ruler of the rich and densely populated country between the Hydaspes and Acesines (modern Chenab) Rivers. The geographer Strabo of Amascia later claimed that there were no fewer than 300 cities within Porus' realm.

While in Taxila Alexander had sent a representative, Cleochares, to Porus to instruct him to pay tribute and to meet Alexander at the point of entry to his territory. Porus agreed to be present when Alexander entered his kingdom—but under arms. These "arms" included about 2,000 cavalry, 20,000 infantry, and perhaps 85 war elephants. Because horses will not charge elephants, these last were the greatest threat to the Macedonians. Overall, however, Porus' army was far smaller than the Persian army Alexander had faced at Gaugamela, and was smaller too than the army Alexander now was leading, which perhaps totaled 75,000 combatants.

Once Alexander got to the Hydaspes, Porus was observed on the far bank of the river in a strong defensive position. The exact location of what proved to be the battlefield remains controversial, but Sir Aurel Stein has made strong arguments for the area of Malakwal (on the Jhelum) opposite Haranpur. Once the Macedonians had arrived, Porus himself moved to guard the best crossing point. At the other parts of the river where a crossing was possible, the Indian king had posted guards.

His strategy clearly was to prevent the Macedonians from crossing the river and to attack Alexander if he tried. Overall, Porus was in a very strong defensive position; the problem facing Alexander has been aptly compared to that which faced Napoleon before the battle of Wagram in 1809, when Napoleon was confronted by the Austrian army led by the Archduke Charles on the other side of the Danube. At the Hydaspes Alexander faced the greatest tactical challenge of his career.

CHAPTER 19

The Battle of the Hydaspes

With Porus' position in mind and his forces in view, Alexander planned his counter-measures with great care and skill. The Hydaspes was no mere trickle of water, as Alexander had scornfully called the Granicus. Moreover, Porus would prove a far more formidable adversary than the Persian satraps of Asia Minor.

The flotilla Alexander had used to cross the Indus had been disassembled and transported in carts to the Hydaspes. Grain was also brought from all the territory controlled by Taxiles/Mophis. Alexander divided up his forces into a number of smaller units and moved these up and down the river, destroying any enemy possessions, but all the while looking for a ford.

After a while it was clear to Porus that Alexander meant to remain in the neighborhood of the Hydaspes until the water fell sufficiently to allow Alexander to effect a crossing at any one of a number of places. The low-water point would come in September 326.

But Porus had underestimated his opponent. Alexander was determined to bring matters to a head even before the river reached its high-water mark in late June (when the river would be swollen by the melting snows from the Himalayas and the advent of the monsoon season).

Since the river could not be crossed openly in the face of Porus' forces, however, Alexander decided to get his army across the river by cunning. Unlike Piero Soderini, the Gonfalonier (chief official) of the Florentine Republic, Macedon's greatest prince had learned how to play the Fox as well as the Lion; he knew when to roar and when to deceive. Alexander noisily moved his mounted troops up and down the river every night, until Porus and the elephants got tired of shadowing his movements.

Alexander then discovered a crossing point about seventeen (or so) miles upriver from his base camp, around modern Haranpur. There, at a sharp bend in the river, was a projecting headland of thickly wooded land (perhaps near Jalalpur). Just off the spit was an uninhabited island (Adana).

On the night of the intended crossing, Craterus, perhaps Alexander's most reliable general, was to be left at the base camp with his own cavalry regiment, two mounted contingents, two Macedonian infantry battalions, and 5,000 Indians. His orders were not to attempt to cross the river until Porus had moved to attack Alexander (who would have crossed the river in secret with a strong force at the spit) or until Craterus was sure that Porus was in retreat and the Macedonians were victorious. If Porus opposed Alexander with only part of his forces, Craterus was to stay put. But if the Indian king moved his whole contingent of elephants against Alexander, then Craterus was to attack across the river immediately. Craterus and the men under his command thus were to be used as a "pinning force," positioned to present Porus with one of two equally unpalatable tactical options once he recognized that Alexander was across the river. Porus could confront Craterus or Alexander, but not both, at least effectively.

Between Craterus and Alexander mercenary cavalry and infantry also were posted, to effect river crossings in sections as soon as they saw the Indians engaged in the battle.

Alexander was to take with him to the crossing point a strong "turning" force, comprising the special squadron of the Companions (the *agema*), three Macedonian cavalry regiments, native contingents from Bactria and Sogdiana, the Scythian cavalry, the mounted archers, the infantry units of the Guards, two Macedonian infantry battalions, archers, and the invaluable Agrianes. In all, this force numbered 6,000 foot and

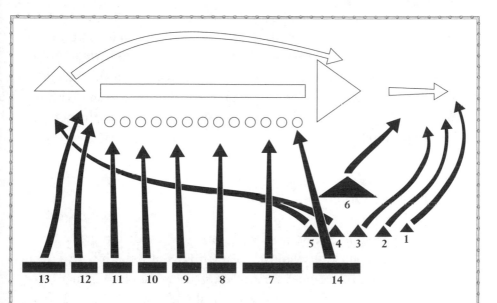

THE BATTLE OF THE HYDASPES, MAY/JUNE 326 B.C.E.

OPENING FORMATIONS AND MOVEMENTS, BASED UPON ARRIAN, 5.15.3–18.1

Macedonians

1 Agema of Companion cavalry, led by Alexander
2 Cavalry hipparchy, commanded by Hephaestion
3 Cavalry hipparchy, commanded by Perdiccas
4 Cavalry hipparchy, commanded by Demetrius
5 Cavalry hipparchy, commanded by Coenus
6 Dahae horse archers and Bactrian, Sogdian, and Scythian cavalry
7 *Hypaspistai,* commanded by Seleucus
8 *Asthetairoi,* brigade of "Coenus"
9 Infantry phalanx brigade *(pezhetairoi)* of Cleitus
10 Infantry phalanx brigade *(pezhetairoi)* of Gorgias
11 Infantry phalanx brigade *(pezhetairoi)* of Attalus
12 Infantry phalanx brigade *(pezhetairoi)* of Meleager
13 Archers, Agrianians, and javelin men, commanded by Tauron
14 Archers, Agrianians, and javelin men

▭ Indian infantry	▰ Macedonian infantry	
△ Indian cavalry	▲ Macedonian cavalry	
○ Indian elephants		

5,000 cavalry troops. Alexander then brought the assault force to the crossing point at some distance back from the river to hide their movement from Porus. Before the night of the crossing the skin-floats and the thirty-oared galleys had been brought up near the point of embarkation and concealed in the trees. A fortuitous deluge drowned out the noise of final preparations.

THE BATTLE OF THE HYDASPES

Just before dawn, after the wind and rain had subsided, the operation was initiated. The cavalry embarked upon rafts and the infantry were loaded into boats. Alexander himself crossed in one of the galleys, accompanied by three officers of his personal bodyguard—Ptolemy, Perdiccas, Lysimachus—as well as by Seleucus and half of the hypaspists. It was now time to play the Lion.

Indian mounted scouts spotted the crossing party and immediately rode off to Porus with the news of their approach, but the crossing was a success. Alexander, the first ashore, promptly began to put the disembarking cavalry into battle order. The only problem was that, from want of local knowledge, he and the rest of the Macedonians had not landed on the river's opposite shore, but on an island separated from the far bank by a stream. "Intelligence" had let the Macedonians down—as it had before the battle of Issos, when Darius and the Persians were able to circle back behind Alexander and cut the Macedonians off from their Cilician supply bases. Now, on an island in the middle of a rain-swollen river, thousands of miles from home, came the test of Alexander's leadership.

Finding another fording point from the island to the far bank, the assault group calmly reassembled and crossed over. The water rose to the men's armpits and to the necks of the horses during the second crossing.

Having reached the opposite bank of the river, Alexander then marshaled his forces again. The Royal Squadron and the rest of the best cavalry were put on the right wing, with mounted archers in front. In the rear of the cavalry was the Royal Regiment of Guards under Seleucus, then the Royal Regiment of heavy infantry, in touch with the other Guards regiments. The archers, the Agrianes, and the javelin men were stationed on the wings of the infantry phalanx. Alexander's men had regrouped flawlessly under terrible conditions, a tribute to his leadership and their own professionalism.

Alexander then ordered the turning force to advance, with the cavalry leading the way, the archers following them, and then the infantry. In effect, therefore, he had deployed his cavalry as a kind of screen for his infantry. At this point, our sources diverge. According to one contemporary account, the landing on the bank was initially opposed by Porus' son with sixty chariots; this force promptly drove right past the Macedonians' landing point and was put to flight by the mounted archers. Other writers state that Porus' son did fight Alexander at the landing point, wounding Alexander and striking the blow that killed Bucephalas.

Ptolemy, however, who fought in the battle, later recalled that Porus' son did indeed come, not just with 60 chariots (an improbable number, for it would be insufficient to challenge Alexander, and too many for reconnaissance) but with 2,000 mounted troops and 120 chariots. The purpose of this attacking force must have been to disrupt Alexander's landing or to prevent the Macedonians from forming up in good order. In either case, it was not successful. Alexander routed it with a cavalry attack, with the Indians losing 400 mounted men, including Porus' son. The chariots with their teams were captured in the subsequent retreat; they had driven rather heavily and had been useless in the action itself because of the mud.

News of his son's defeat (or failure) was conveyed to Porus, who now saw that the pinning force left with Craterus was beginning to cross the river. Caught in a classic pincer movement, Porus wisely determined to confront the strongest part of the Macedonian army, which was led by Alexander himself. Leaving behind a small force with a few elephants to spread alarm among Craterus' cavalry as they crossed the Hydaspes, Porus then marched out to meet Alexander on his side of the river with around 2,000 cavalry, 85 elephants, 240 chariots, and 20,000 infantry.

After reaching a place that was sandy (rather than muddy), level, and solid, and therefore suitable for cavalry maneuvers, Porus positioned his elephants along his battle formation at intervals of fifty feet, screening the whole body of his infantry (and intending to terrify the Macedonian cavalry). Behind the screen were set the foot soldiers, slotted into the intervals between the elephants. Infantry were posted on the wings as well, stretching out beyond the line of elephants. Mounted units, each with a screen of war chariots, provided additional protection on the flanks.

After allowing his infantry to catch up with his cavalry and then to re-form and rest, Alexander moved the majority of his cavalry to his right wing (opposite Porus' left). Philotas' brother-in-law, Coenus, with his own and Demetrius' cavalry regiments, was sent over to Porus' right with orders that when Porus sent his cavalry over to his own left to face Alexander's massed cavalry, he should stay behind them. The heavy phalanx infantry units under Seleucus, Antigenes, and Tauron were ordered to hold off from engagement until the Indians were thrown into confusion by the (usual) Macedonian cavalry charge.

Alexander commenced the attack with an assault by 1,000 mounted archers against Porus' left wing. This assault was followed by a charge of the Companion cavalry led by Alexander against the Indian left, before their cavalry could mass.

The Indians meanwhile were removing all of their cavalry from their line to meet Alexander's charge. These cavalrymen were followed by Coenus and his men, who began to appear at the rear of the Indian cavalry as it followed Alexander out to the right. The Indians therefore split their forces to deal with Alexander and Coenus.

In that instant, when the Indian cavalry split, and part of it changed direction to meet Coenus, Alexander charged into the Indian line facing him. The Indians immediately fell back into their screen of elephants.

At this point the Macedonian infantry advanced, hurling javelins at the drivers of the elephants, and, surrounding the elephants, volleyed upon them from all sides. The elephants then charged out into the line of infantry, devastating the infantry of both sides, whichever way they turned. The Indian cavalry, seeing that the action had settled down into an infantry battle, regrouped and charged again into the Macedonian cavalry. Once again, however, the strength and experience of the Macedonians told, and the Indian cavalry was pushed back into the elephants.

By this time the elephants too had been crowded back into a narrow space where they trampled to death as many friends as enemies. The Macedonians, with more room to maneuver than the Indians, gave ground when charged or went after the elephants with their javelins when the opportunity arose.

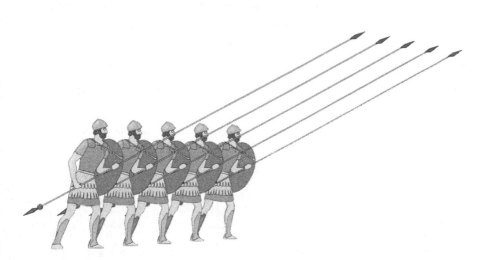

The Macedonian infantry adopted a close-order formation when they were about to make contact with enemy infantry. Within such a formation, the pikes of the infantry men in the first few rows projected out in front of the phalanx, like the quills of a porcupine, but at different heights. While the shields-locked formation of the infantry (*above*) was primarily a defensive formation, it could also be used offensively as it was during the final stages of the battle of the Hydaspes River.

When the elephants grew tired of charging and backed away, retreating like ships backing water, Alexander surrounded the whole lot, elephants, horsemen, and all, and signaled the infantry to lock shields (*synaspismos* formation, in Greek) and move up in phalanx order. Most of the Indian cavalry were cut down in the resulting action. Some of the infantry escaped only to be met by Craterus, who had successfully crossed the river and taken over the pursuit of the survivors from Alexander and his men.

No fewer than 12,000 Indians were killed in the battle, including both infantry and cavalry, and 9,000 were taken prisoner. Of Porus' force of elephants, eighty were captured alive. All of the Indian war chariots were destroyed. On the Macedonian side, 280 cavalry and 700 infantrymen lost their lives.

Alexander and his multi-ethnic force had prevailed against a brave and tenacious foe who was fighting on his home ground from a superior defensive position. The king had used deception to effect a difficult river crossing under dreadful conditions. Despite the mistake of landing on the island in the middle of the river, he and the Macedonians had executed the pinning and turning operation flawlessly. As usual, Alexander had led the cavalry charge that decided the outcome of the battle. The Hydaspes was a complex triumph of operational planning, deception, and execution. If Alexander's major battles can be compared to symphonies, this was his *Jupiter*, his masterpiece, and like the *Jupiter*, it was to be his last.

THE FATE OF PORUS

Porus himself was not among the Indian casualties. Mounted on the largest elephant, more than seven feet tall himself, the king had fought on. He had refused to surrender, although he was wounded in his right shoulder and he could see that his cavalry had been slaughtered, most of his infantry had been killed, and his elephants had been cut down or were wandering about without riders. At last persuaded to listen to a message from Alexander brought by an Indian friend named Meroes, Porus dismounted and drank some water. Then the towering Indian king was brought to Alexander.

"What do you wish me to do with you?" Alexander asked. Porus replied, "Treat me, O Alexander, like a king." Impressed, Alexander restored Porus to his sovereignty and even enlarged his realm.

Alexander then founded two new cities (*poleis*). The first, sited on the east bank of the Jhelum where the battle took place, was named Nikaia (Victory), in honor of Alexander's victory over Porus and the Indians. The second city stood on the west bank, perhaps on the spot where Alexander had initiated his crossing; it was christened Bucephala, in memory of his beloved horse, who had died there (at the age of thirty) not wounded by anyone, but from exhaustion and age.

THE EULOGY OF BUCEPHALAS

Of Bucephalas and Alexander, Arrian wrote:

> In former days, he had shared with Alexander many a danger and
> many a weary march. No one ever rode him but his master, for he
> would never permit anyone else to mount him. He was a big horse,
> high-spirited—a noble creature. He was branded with the figure of
> an ox-head, whence his name—though some have said that the name
> came from a white mark on his head, shaped like an ox. This was the
> only bit of white on his body, all the rest being black. In Uxia, once,
> Alexander lost him, and issued an edict that he would kill every man
> in the country unless he was brought back, as he promptly was. The
> story is evidence both of the fear which Alexander inspired and of his
> devotion to Bucephalas. But I must say no more: what I have written
> in Bucephalas' praise, I have written for Alexander's sake.

CHAPTER 20

The Mutiny at the
Hyphasis River

THE MARCH TO THE HYPHASIS RIVER

After respects had been paid to those who had fallen at the Hydaspes, Alexander performed customary sacrifices of thanksgiving to the gods for the victory. A contest of athletic and cavalry games also was held on the bank, at the spot where Alexander first had crossed the river with the turning force. Such games were celebrated throughout the campaigns when bonding mechanisms or reaffirmations of solidarity were deemed necessary—especially, it should be noted, after Alexander and his soldiers had witnessed the deaths of many of their friends.

Alexander also used commemorative objects to keep morale high and to promote his own version of events. Later, his mint in Babylon issued a series of coins marking his great victory over the Indians, including one that showed an elephant on the reverse and an Indian archer on the obverse, and a much larger coin that featured Alexander himself on horseback with a pike in his hand attacking two Indians riding an elephant.

While the king advanced against the Indians across the border of Porus' kingdom to the northeast (in what is now Kashmir), he left Craterus, with part of the army, to build and fortify his new cities.

He clearly intended to continue the march eastward until the conquest of India was complete, just as Alexander already had revealed to Pharasmanes in the summer of 328. The advance, however, soon turned into a journey, if not quite into the heart of darkness, then certainly close enough to it to persuade the majority of the Macedonians to refuse to go any farther before the end of the summer of 326.

The name of the tribe of Indians Alexander first encountered on the march was the Glauganicac or Glausae. The thirty-seven towns of these Indians that Alexander captured were handed over to Porus, who thereby was immediately paid off for his new alliance with Alexander. Taxiles, having been reconciled with Porus and supplanted by him in Alexander's esteem, was then sent home.

From the timber of nearby mountains Alexander then had built a large number of ships, which he meant to use later to sail down the Indus after the conquest of India. In this region Alexander and his men also encountered a large number of snakes; some were twenty-four feet long. Others were small and multicolored. Many were venomous, and until the locals showed the Macedonians a root that could be used to treat their deadly bites, the Macedonians slept uneasily at night in hammocks slung from trees.

The Macedonians also marveled at the wide variety of monkeys found in the region. Among these were the famous monkeys who had taught the Indians how to entrap them. Because of their strength and cleverness these monkeys could not be captured simply by force, but had to be tricked. The Indian hunters, making sure that they were within the sight of the monkeys, would smear their own eyes with honey, fasten sandals upon their ankles, and hang mirrors on their own necks. The hunters then departed, having attached fastening to the sandals they left behind, having substituted birdlime for honey, and having attached slip nooses to mirrors. When the monkeys imitated what they had seen the Indians do, their eyes were stuck together by the birdlime, their feet were bound fast in the sandals, and their bodies were held immovable by the slip nooses. After disabling themselves, the monkeys were easier to catch.

Having learned all about the local fauna, Alexander and the Macedonians then turned their attention to the human opposition in the area.

Very soon Alexander received envoys from Abisares, including his own brother, who finally brought treasure and a gift of forty elephants. Alexander sent a message to Abisares ordering him to come and threatening that if he did not, Abisares would soon see him with his army—an unpleasant sight.

There also came to Alexander representatives from the autonomous Indians and from Porus' cousin, confusingly also named Porus. Porus the cousin initially had offered submission to Alexander but then had fled across the Hydraotes River (Ravi) with his army. Alexander then marched off eastward in pursuit of Porus' cousin.

Alexander made it to the Acesines River (Chenab) without much opposition, but the crossing of the river, which was a little under two miles wide, was difficult. It was the time of the summer solstice (326), and the river was still swollen from the monsoons. Although Alexander apparently crossed the river at its widest point, where the current was slower, nowhere were the waters of the rivers completely calm, and there were large, sharp rocks in the bed of the river. For those who crossed the river on hides the way across was easy. But many of those who crossed in boats lost their lives when their vessels crashed upon the rocks and were wrecked. Crossing the tributaries of the mighty Indus was as dangerous as combat itself.

Once Alexander himself had made it across, Coenus with his brigade was left at the river to supervise the crossing of the remainder of the army and to gather wheat and other necessities from the part of India that Alexander already ruled. Porus (of the Hydaspes) was sent back to his kingdom with orders to bring the most warlike of the Indians and any elephants he had to Alexander. Porus had proved his mettle and Alexander now trusted his former adversary.

The campaign eastward from the Acesines River to the Hydraotes (Ravi), and finally to the Hyphasis (Beas in India), now was fought in the worst conditions the Macedonians ever had faced. It rained for seventy days straight. The heavy rains were accompanied by continuous thunder and lightning. For the time being, however, the iron discipline of the Macedonians carried them along. Overrunning the lands of Porus' cousin, they left guards at the most strategic points along the route to the Hydraotes so that the troops with Coenus and Craterus might safely search for provisions. Hephaestion was then left with two phalanxes of infantry, his own cavalry regiment, Demetrius', and half the archers to consolidate the conquest while Alexander crossed the Hydraotes and attacked the stronghold of the Cathaei (Kathas) at Sangala (perhaps between modern Lahore and Amritsar).

Despite the construction of a triple defensive ring, the fortifications of the Cathaei were to prove no match for the Macedonians. Alexander once again personally led the attack of phalanx infantry that dislodged the Indians from the (third) outer ring of wagons. The phalanx then forced them back from the second, denser formation. The Indians did not even attempt to defend the innermost line, but retreated and shut themselves up behind Sangala's walls.

At this point, Alexander had a double stockade built around the town, and several attempts to break out of the besieged town were interdicted by Ptolemy and the Guards under his command. Porus arrived with his elephants and 5,000 Indian troops, and Alexander then had the siege engines brought up to the city walls; but before any part of the wall was battered down, the Macedonians undermined the wall, set up ladders all around, and captured the city by assault. At least 17,000 Indians were killed and 70,000 taken prisoner. The short siege cost Alexander 100 men killed in action, with 1,200 wounded, including Lysimachus, one of Alexander's personal bodyguards.

Alexander now dispatched his secretary, Eumenes of Cardia, to the two towns that had rebelled at the same time as Sangala to announce that Alexander would not treat them harshly if they stayed where they were and received him peacefully. But the inhabitants of the towns had fled at the news of Sangala's capture. The refugees were pursued, but most escaped. Those who were too infirm (or sick) to flee were executed, to the number of 500, an atrocity that recalled Darius' mutilation of Alexander's wounded at Issos, even if the inhabitants of the Indian town were viewed as rebels. As for Sangala, it was razed and its territory was given over to those formerly self-governing Indians who had surrendered. Porus was sent to set up garrisons in those cities.

Alexander and the army now advanced on to the Hyphasis to conquer the Indians there. As long as there was any hostility at all, he felt that there could be no end to the war. Alexander's appetite for combat seemed to grow with the fighting. The Macedonian soldiers, on the other hand, felt differently. Since leaving the Hydaspes River two months before and some 390 miles to the west, they had been fighting in dreadful conditions, literally destroying everything and everyone in their path who did not surrender. Unlike Alexander, the Macedonians at last had had enough of the carnage, at least under such dreadful conditions.

THE MUTINY AT THE HYPHASIS RIVER

At the Hyphasis, the local ruler, Phegeus, told Alexander how far it was to the Ganges River and described the foes he would encounter on the other side of the river. It was twelve days' march through desert to the Ganges, and he reported that the river was four miles wide and by far the deepest of all Indian rivers. On the eastern bank of the Ganges, Phegeus said, the kings of the Gandaridae and the Praesii were waiting for Alexander with 80,000 cavalry, 200,000 infantry, 8,000 chariots, and 6,000 fighting elephants.

Alexander doubted these reports but Porus confirmed them. Porus added, however, that the king of the Gandaridae was a common and undistinguished fellow, the son of a barber. His father had been a good-looking man who was greatly loved by the queen. After she had her husband murdered, the kingdom fell to the barber's son.

Naturally Alexander was undeterred by the reports about the size of the enemy force. He had faith in the courage of the Macedonians and in the oracles he had received. He remembered that the Pythia had called him "invincible" and that Ammon had given him the rule of the whole earth.

But the Macedonian soldiery had a different point of view. They had spent nearly eight years amidst toils and dangers. Many had been the losses among the soldiers and there was no end in sight. The horses' hooves had been worn thin by marching. The arms and armor of the soldiers were just about worn out and their Greek clothing was altogether gone. They were wearing recut Indian clothes. This was also the season of the unremitting rains. The monsoons had been pelting down rain upon the Macedonians without respite. And then there were the snakes.

Sensing the mood at the camp, Alexander shrewdly allowed the men to pillage locally, hoping thereby to raise their spirits. To the soldiers' wives he gave a monthly ration, and disbursed to the children a service bonus scaled to their fathers' military records.

Nevertheless, soldiers grumbled about their present fate. Some maintained that they would follow no farther, not even if Alexander himself should lead them.

Hearing of the grumbling, Alexander called a meeting of the army and announced his grand plan: he intended to go beyond the Ganges even, to the eastern ocean, and from there, around from the Persian Gulf to Libya as far as the Pillars of Herakles. All of Libya and the lands eastward, as well as Asia, would be theirs. There would be no boundaries to the empire but what Zeus himself had made for the whole world.

Thus Alexander confirmed what many must have long suspected, namely, that while Zeus reigned over the gods on Mount Olympus, his son intended to rule over the whole earth. The war would not end until Alexander had conquered the world.

Alexander's speech was a spectacular flop. For a long time there was silence. Then Coenus, one of the phalanx commanders and a very well-respected soldier, who had seen action at every major battle, finally spoke up. He urged Alexander to set some limit to the present enterprise. Alexander should return to Greece, he said, and put right its affairs. If he wanted to begin another expedition against the Indians of the east, or to the Black Sea, or to Carthage and the Libyan territories beyond, he should do so with other Greek and Macedonian troops.

Last, Coenus made a memorable point: it was a noble thing to exercise a sense of self-restraint when all was going well. In other words, Alexander still needed to learn when to stop.

Coenus' speech was greeted with applause. Some men wept. None seem to have rallied to Alexander's call to world conquest.

The next day Alexander called another meeting and declared that although he would pressure no Macedonian to accompany him, he himself was resolved to go on.

"I shall have others," he said, "who will need no compulsion to follow their king. If you wish to go home, you are at liberty to do so—and you may tell your people there that you deserted your king in the midst of his enemies."

And, with that defiant proclamation, Alexander retreated to his tent to sulk for three days, and to wait and see if emotional blackmail would work after an appeal to self-interest had failed. But the silence was total, unbroken, and presumably deafening. Perhaps recognizing that he had gone too far, and certainly realizing that he needed a way of saving face, Alexander ordered sacrifices to be made for the crossing of the river to determine the will of the gods.

The sacrifices fortuitously proved to be unfavorable. The gods, not the Macedonians, had stayed Alexander's steps. On hearing the news, most of the troops wept and came to Alexander's tent calling down every blessing upon him for allowing them to prevail. It was the only defeat Alexander ever suffered. The long march eastward was over.

In hindsight, what is remarkable about the mutiny at the Hyphasis is not that it happened, for many armies have rebelled when they have suffered too many casualties, or gone hungry for too long, or had to march too far through mud or snow. What is astonishing about the mutiny at the Hyphasis is rather that it took so long to happen. The Macedonians had followed Alexander for the better part of a decade, over thousands of miles, in every season, over every kind of terrain, against countless foes, all of whom they had vanquished in every kind of warfare. It was only when they finally understood that Alexander would never stop until he reached the ends of the world that the Macedonians refused to take one step farther away from their homeland. Yet there was no violence or even the threat of it against Alexander or any of his generals. Rather, the Macedonians through Coenus essentially begged Alexander to stop for their sake, which Alexander did, if somewhat grudgingly. So deep was the bond between the Macedonian soldiers and their king.

No doubt Alexander was deeply disappointed at the loss of his chance to march to the Ganges and conquer India. He might have done it, too; Sandracottus, the eventual Indian ruler of the area Alexander had intended to invade, remarked that Alexander was within a step of conquering the whole country, since the king who ruled it then was hated and despised on account of his base character and low birth.

But there is no evidence that after the mutiny Alexander bore a grudge against his soldiers, as some historians have imagined, which caused Alexander to punish the Macedonians by leading them into suicidal battles or on marches for which they were ill-prepared. Both before and after the mutiny at the Hyphasis, Alexander and the Macedonians fought desperate battles against formidable foes, and the conditions they faced on their march homeward were different from those on the journey out, but no less dangerous. Moreover, as we shall see, Alexander did everything humanly possible to provide for his soldiers under the worst conditions. That he failed cannot be used as evidence for his intentions—which are truly unknowable.

Thinking how best to mark the limits of his realm at the Hyphasis, Alexander had the soldiers build altars to the twelve Olympian gods, each seventy-five feet high. On them were inscribed the following words: "To Father Ammon and his brother Herakles, and to Athena Providence, and to Olympian Zeus, and to the Kabeiri of Samothrace, and to the Indian Sun, and to the Delphian Apollo."

These altars were dedicated to give thanks to the gods and goddesses who had promised and brought Alexander his unprecedented and unbroken string of successes. Neither the altars nor the inscriptions have been found.

Alexander then offered sacrifice upon these altars, as was his custom, and held a contest of athletics and cavalry exercises. He also had built a giant camp three times the size of a normal one, with huts containing huge beds and horse mangers twice the normal size, in order to leave the locals evidence of men of huge stature.

Now Alexander began to prepare for the long march westward, back to Macedon. All the territory as far as the Hyphasis he gave to Porus to rule over. Abisares was given the governorship of his province, while Arsaces was joined to the administration of Abisares. Tribute also was imposed, a sign that Alexander was not simply abandoning the area. He fully intended to enjoy the profits of his empire.

THE DEATH OF COENUS

Alexander made his way back toward the Hydaspes River, reaching it probably by late summer of 326. At the Hydaspes, Coenus, who had given voice to the soldiers' discontent at the Hyphasis, died by an illness. The timing of his death has given rise to speculation that Alexander somehow was involved in Coenus' death. But there is no concrete evidence for that. The worst that can be said is that although Alexander gave Coenus a magnificent funeral, he also is reported to have remarked, somewhat uncharitably, that "it was merely for the sake of a few days that Coenus had made his long speech, as if he were the only one who would see Macedonia again." At most, Coenus' opportune death perhaps suggests that Alexander really was favored by at least some gods.

PART THREE

When They Were Happy

CHAPTER 21

The Meed of Great Deeds

SOUTHBOUND

Using his new cities of Bucephala and Nikaia as twin bases, Alexander marshaled his forces for the long, difficult journey southward. Including recent reinforcements from Greece, Thrace, and Asia, Alexander now led about 120,000 men. Around 13,000 of these were cavalry and there also were 55,000 front-line infantrymen. This was unquestionably one of the largest and most powerful Greco-Macedonian forces ever assembled.

To convey the horses and provisions of this huge army down the Indus, Alexander had constructed an equally impressive fleet. It consisted of no fewer than 80 thirty-oared galleys, while the total number of boats of all sorts was not far short of 2,000. The armada was considerably smaller than the Allied fleet of 5,333 ships that brought 175,000 men to the beaches of Normandy on June 6, 1944, but far larger than any other Greek fleet ever assembled.

The ships were manned by crews picked from the Phoenicians, Cypriots, and Egyptians who had followed the expedition. Ionians and men from the Hellespontine region also provided nautical expertise. Commanders of the triremes (a largely honorary title) were appointed from among Alexander's Macedonian, Greek, and Persian officers and friends. Overall command was put into the hands of Nearchus, Alexander's boyhood friend from Crete. Onesicritus of Astypalaea was selected as the helmsman of the royal flagship.

Contests of art and athletics were celebrated and victims for sacrifice were given to the whole army before the fleet set out. The embarkation began at dawn, probably at the beginning of November 326. Alexander sacrificed to the gods following his custom, and made a special offering to the river Hydaspes, in accordance with the seers' instructions. Then, having embarked from the bows, he poured a libation from a golden cup into the water, invoking the river and joining with its name the name of Acesines, which he knew to be the greatest of its tributaries, and calling upon the Indus, too. He also offered a libation to his ancestor Herakles and to Ammon, and to the other gods he usually honored. Another great labor had begun; at its conclusion the fulfillment of Ammon's oracle might still come.

Alexander then ordered the bugle to sound for their departure. As the blast of the bugle pierced the early morning quiet, the fleet started out in due order, the oars of the triremes rhythmically dipping into the brown waters of the immense river.

Alexander was joined on the ships by the Guards, the archers, the Agrianes, and the special squadron of the Companion cavalry. As the huge armada made its way down the Hydaspes, Craterus marched with part of the infantry along the right bank, while Hephaestion proceeded along the left bank with the best fighting troops and 200 elephants. Hephaestion's battle group had been ordered to march to the kingdom of Sopeithes. Philip, governor of the territory on the Bactrian side of the Indus, had orders to wait for three days and then to follow up with his troops, mopping up whatever resistance survived the three-pronged advance of Craterus, Alexander, and Hephaestion.

On the fifth day out, the fleet reached the dangerously narrow junction of the Hydaspes and Acesines. Although some ships suffered damage from the disturbed waters, repairs were quickly made, and Alexander was rejoined by Hephaestion, Craterus, and Philip with their troops. That took place at a prearranged meeting point and indicates the care that went into planning the advance downstream. On the first leg of the journey downriver, the Macedonians suffered little loss of life or property; now, though, they would encounter fierce resistance to their progress, and they in turn would bring death or enslavement to all who opposed them. If this part of the campaign were merely a "raid," as some Indian historians have claimed, it was surely one of the most devastating raids in human history.

THE MALLIANS

Nearchus now was instructed to bring the fleet down south from the Acesines to the territory of the Mallians (Malavas), while Craterus and Philip (under Craterus' command) were detailed to lead a column down the right bank of the river. Hephaestion and Ptolemy were ordered to take two other army groups down the left bank, Ptolemy following Hephaestion's advance after three days, to intercept stragglers.

Alexander himself then led a formidable force of hypaspists, archers, Agrianes, a heavy infantry battalion, the mounted archers, and half the Companion cavalry out into the desert against the Mallians. The ensuing campaign was as brutal as any waged thus far, and it nearly turned out to be fatal to Alexander.

Marching toward the Hydraotes over mostly waterless country, Alexander surprised the first Mallians he encountered and then stormed their towns. Those who fled the city that Perdiccas had been ordered to capture were overtaken and massacred, except for some who found refuge in local marshes.

Crossing the Hydraotes, Alexander pursued other refugees across the river and slew many of them. Others were captured, and Peithon captured a stronghold to which some of the rest of the Mallians had escaped. Those who were not killed in Peithon's first assault were enslaved.

Alexander himself then led an attack upon a city of the Brahmans, where some of the surviving Mallians were ensconced. These Brahmans were members of an ascetic religious sect. Alexander was the first to climb up and hold one of the walls that the Macedonians had successfully undermined. The rest of the Macedonians, feeling shame, followed Alexander's example and finally captured the citadel. Owing to their brave defense of their homes, up to 5,000 of the Indians fell, with only a few survivors captured alive.

The residents of the largest Mallian cities abandoned their homes and took up a position on the bank of the Hydraotes, intending to prevent Alexander from crossing. Eventually dislodged from the bank by the Macedonians, the Mallian forces, numbering around 50,000, then took refuge in the most strongly fortified of the cities nearby.

The next day Alexander divided up his army; giving command of half to Perdiccas and leading the other half himself, he began his attack upon the wall of the city to which the surviving Mallians had fled. After the Mallians abandoned the outer wall and fled into the citadel, Alexander and his troops penetrated into the city, while those under Perdiccas' command fell behind, having difficulty getting over the wall. Most of Perdiccas' men were not carrying ladders, apparently because they believed that the city already had been captured. However, when it became obvious that many of the enemy were still fighting from within the citadel, some of the Macedonians began to undermine the wall. Others (now better equipped) set up ladders where they could and tried to force their way into the citadel of the city.

Alexander, considering that the Macedonians who were bringing up the ladders were hanging back, grabbed a ladder from someone, reared it up against the fortress wall, and climbed up, crouching underneath his shield. Peucestas, one of the hypaspists, managed to climb up after, carrying with him the sacred shield that Alexander had received from the temple of Athena at Troy. Peucestas was followed by Leonnatus, one of Alexander's seven personal bodyguards. Abreas, a veteran on double pay for his exemplary service, also scampered up by another ladder.

By this time Alexander was up by the battlement. Leaning his shield against it, he pushed some of the Indians off the wall and slew others with his sword, clearing that part of the wall of its defenders. Down below, the Guards, fearing for the king's safety, tried to make their way up the ladder he had used. Their combined weight promptly broke it. The soldiers on the top rungs tumbled down. Now no one could ascend the wall to help. Alexander was virtually alone.

The Indians on all the neighboring towers and the defenders within the city (positioned on some kind of mound nearby), recognizing Alexander on the battlement by the splendor of his arms, let loose a barrage of arrows and spears at their solitary target. None, however, dared to approach the king.

At this moment, we are told, Alexander felt that if he remained where he was he would be in danger while achieving nothing of note. But if he leapt down within the wall he might, by that very action, frighten the Indians. Moreover, if he must be endangered, at least he would not die ignobly, but after accomplishing great deeds. In an instant, Alexander made his decision: he jumped down from the wall into the citadel itself.

If the Mallians were stunned by Alexander's bold action, they recovered admirably. Almost immediately they attacked Alexander from every direction with every kind of weapon available. His back to the wall on his left, and with a tree providing some protection on his right, Alexander fought off these attacks, including one by the commander of the Indians. Two other Indians were driven off by well-aimed stones. All who charged him were dispatched. After seeing this, the rest of the Indians had second thoughts about close-quarter combat and held off. Surrounding the king at a safer distance from all sides, they hurled every kind of missile at Alexander.

Fortunately for Alexander, at this moment Peucestas, Abreas, and Leonnatus, who had made it up to the top of the battlement, also jumped down from the wall, and began to fight in his defense. Almost immediately, however, Abreas was shot in the face by an arrow and killed. Next Alexander himself was struck; the arrow went right through his corselet and entered his body above the right breast. In his old age, Ptolemy recalled that air together with blood shot out from the wound. Soon there was a violent hemorrhage, and Alexander pitched over his shield, giddy and faint. Peucestas stood over Alexander, protecting his body with the sacred shield from Ilium. Leonnatus warded off attackers while receiving a shower of missiles. Alexander was on the verge of fainting from his loss of blood. He would have died there and then had not these men protected him.

The Macedonian assault force, meanwhile, having seen Alexander leap down into the town, used every means to get up and over the wall. Some hammered pegs into the clay wall; others stood on their comrades' shoulders. Finally, someone managed to get up over the wall and reinforced Peucestas and Leonnatus, who were still protecting Alexander. Alexander was now lying on the ground, clearly near death. At this sight, first there was a lament, followed by the Macedonian battle cry. A fierce battle then erupted over the fallen king, as first one Macedonian and then another held his own shield over Alexander.

Eventually the bar that secured the gate between the city's towers was severed and the fortress was laid open. The Macedonians, believing that Alexander was dying or dead, slaughtered everyone they met, including men, women, and children. No one was spared.

Once the Macedonians controlled the citadel, Alexander was carried away on his shield. Some writers report that Critobulus, a doctor from the island of Cos, cut out the arrow that had wounded Alexander, first severing its shaft, then enlarging the wound, and finally removing its barbed head. Others wrote that since there was no surgeon available, at Alexander's express order, Alexander's bodyguard Perdiccas cut the wound with his sword, and then pulled out the arrow. It was three feet long and three inches thick. No one thought Alexander could live.

Indeed, a rumor quickly spread throughout the Macedonian camp that he had died. The news brought distress and grief to the soldiers. Lamentation, however, quickly gave way to fear: without their king the Macedonians despaired of getting home safely. They were surrounded by warlike nations, some of whom had not yet surrendered. Others were certain to revolt, if the fear of Alexander's name were removed.

When word was brought to the Macedonians that Alexander was alive, few believed it. Even after a brief letter came to the soldiers from Alexander himself, saying that he would shortly come to camp, many of the soldiers were unconvinced: surely the letter was a forgery made up by Alexander's bodyguards and officers.

Alexander, realizing that a breakdown of discipline might ensue if the news of his death were not squelched, had himself carried down to the bank of the Hydraotes. From there, he was borne by ship downstream to the confluence of the Hydraotes and Acesines, where the troops were assembled. As soon as the vessel drew near the camp, he ordered the awning over the stern to be taken off so that everyone on the shore might see him. Still, many of the troops thought that they were being shown Alexander's corpse.

The ship was then brought up to the bank of the river. Seeing his soldiers, Alexander slowly raised a hand in greeting. In relief, many of the soldiers burst into tears. As he was being taken off the ship, some of the guards brought out a stretcher to carry the king ashore. Alexander ordered his horse to be brought alongside instead. Once on shore, Alexander arose and mounted the horse. In awe, the whole army clapped their hands again and again, and the sound reverberated up and down the river along the banks and glens. Alexander rode through his soldiers toward his quarters. Near his tent he dismounted from his horse and began to walk. But the men rushed toward him from all sides, touching his hands, his knees, and his clothes. Others just looked on from near at hand. Some cast wreaths in his path, some the flowers that bloomed in India at the time.

Later, after Alexander had recovered somewhat, his friends rebuked him for running so great a risk. Alexander in turn was reported to have been angry at his friends because they had upbraided him for playing the role of a soldier rather than that of a commander. Arrian comments that Alexander was upset with his friends' reproaches because he knew that they were true. But Alexander could not help himself. Just as some men are overcome by some pleasure, because of his enthusiasm for battle and passion for glory, Alexander simply was not strong enough to keep out of dangers.

Nearchus also claimed that an old Boeotian man, perceiving that Alexander was angry about his friends' criticism, came up to the king and said, "O Alexander, noble deeds are men's work." He then added an iambic verse along the lines that suffering was the meed (reward) of him that does a great deed. The old man was thereby said to have won Alexander's instant approval and closer friendship.

Both Arrian and the Boeotian were right. Although he was a king, with all the responsibility that position entailed, Alexander was also at heart a warrior. Indeed, to judge by his actions, Alexander belongs to that very rare class of warriors who not only are superbly talented professionals, but who also enjoy the combat itself. As someone who clearly relished combat and was willing to risk all, Alexander had an enormous advantage over adversaries whose main goal was to survive. In boxing, counter-punchers often win matches in the late rounds. In hoplite warfare, there usually were no late rounds: the advantage belonged to the aggressor, and Alexander was always the aggressor. It is no accident at all that most of the eight wounds he suffered during his campaigns came from missiles or rocks thrown at him from a safe distance. No one who engaged Alexander in close combat ever survived, in part because Alexander was always the one who initiated the action.

To many, the idea that there are such warriors, who enjoy the practice of their craft, is repulsive. But there have always been such men and there always will be. To identify Alexander as belonging to that elite, history's virtuosos of violence, is not the same thing as celebrating the fact. But before we condemn Alexander for his aptitude in this dark zone of human capacity, we should also keep in mind that we often disparage such men—until the next time they are needed. Alexander at least was willing to pay the price that accomplishing great deeds in combat has always required. He never sent out anyone to do what he himself would not dare to venture. That is much more than can be said of many of the modern tyrants to whom he has been fashionably compared.

THE BRAHMANS

While Alexander was recovering from his wound, envoys from the surviving Mallians and another local tribe, the Oxydracae (Kshudraka), came to surrender, the latter bringing a gift of 500 chariots. This gift was an implicit token of surrender. The Oxydracae had learned from the Mallians' experience. Alexander appointed Philip as governor over them and the Mallians. New river craft also were built, and 1,700 Companion cavalry, light infantry, and up to 10,000 heavy infantry embarked upon the ships. Still convalescing, Alexander and the fleet then set off down the Hydraotes, first to its confluence with the Acesines (Chenab), and following that to the Acesines' intersection with the Indus.

Here Perdiccas and his army joined Alexander, having received the submission of the Abastani on the way. Philip, with all the Thracians and enough troops to garrison the country, was left there in command, and was ordered to found a city at the juncture of the rivers. Alexander also ordered dockyards to be built there so that the river should become a profitable conduit for trade. At this time Roxane's father, Oxyartes, also visited; he was made governor of Parapamisadae (Afghanistan). The appointment was predicated upon the removal of Tiryaspes from the governorship of the province because Tiryaspes had conducted his office ineffectively. Yet again Alexander had shown that he had no patience with maladministration.

Craterus was then sent over to the left bank of the Indus with the elephants and most of the troops, while Alexander sailed down the river to the royal palace of the Sogdai. Another new city was built and fortified there, along with dockyards, while repairs were made to the damaged boats. Peithon and Oxyartes were appointed to govern the country from the juncture of the Acesines and the Indus to the sea, along with the coastal region of India. The size of this territory was an indication of how much Alexander trusted his father-in-law. Desire aside, Alexander had married well.

Alexander then sailed with the fleet down to the kingdom of Musicanus, reportedly the richest realm in India. Thus far, Musicanus had ignored Alexander. But when the Macedonians suddenly appeared, he wisely offered submission. Alexander allowed him to retain his sovereignty, although Craterus was ordered to fortify the citadel in his city (perhaps Alor, the capital of Sind during the Middle Ages), and a garrison was installed in it.

After quickly subduing some neighboring cities, ruled over by a certain Oxycanus, Alexander set off after Sambus, Musicanus' local enemy and the governor of the Indian hill tribes. When Alexander approached Sambus' capital, Sindimana, Sambus' relatives opened the gates to Alexander, bringing out Sambus' treasure and all of their elephants. Sambus himself had fled; his relations explained that his flight was due, not to any personal enmity, but to Sambus' alarm at the clemency Alexander had shown toward his enemy Musicanus. For the moment Alexander seemed to accept their story.

Other cities that had revolted Alexander then captured and then enslaved the inhabitants. Afterward he put to death a large number of the local Brahmans, who allegedly had been responsible for encouraging the revolt. At least 80,000 Indians were killed and many captured (and then enslaved) in this campaign. Meanwhile, despite his earlier acquiescence, Musicanus had revolted, too. He was captured almost immediately by Peithon. Alexander had Musicanus and the Brahmans who had instigated the revolt executed.

Harmatelia (or Harmata), the last independent city of the Brahmans, at first resisted Alexander, its defenders fighting back fiercely with arrows smeared with the venom of snakes. All those struck by the poisoned arrows died horrible deaths after suffering numbness, sharp pains, vomiting, and gangrene. Ptolemy apparently was wounded by one of the poisoned arrows. His life was saved after he drank an infusion from a plant that Alexander had seen in a dream being carried by a snake in its mouth. Once Alexander had discovered this remedy, all the Macedonian wounded were cured, and the army prepared to besiege Harmatelia. The Brahmans, however, having lost their secret weapon, came out of the city with suppliant branches. Alexander spared them. It might have been a very different story if Ptolemy had died.

It was amid these encounters, fatal to so many of the Brahmans, that Alexander's helmsman Onesicritus met Dandamis, an Indian philosopher. According to some sources, Dandamis' only words to Alexander consisted of the question "For what reason did Alexander make such a long journey hither?" It was a somewhat strange inquiry given the clear evidence of what the Macedonians recently had done to Musicanus and the Brahmans. Alexander certainly had not come in peace.

CALANUS

Alexander himself, we are told, received the Indian philosopher Sphines, called Calanus by the Greeks because he greeted everyone he met, not with the Greek greeting of *Chairete*, but with the Indian word *Cale*.

The Indian sage tried to teach the Macedonian king the doctrine of good government. Throwing a piece of dried and shrunken hide on the ground, Calanus put his foot on the outer surface. The hide was pressed down at that point, but rose elsewhere. This happened wherever Calanus stepped on the edge of the hide. But when Calanus placed his foot on the center of the hide, it finally lay flat. The demonstration was supposed to show Alexander that he should concentrate the weight of his authority on the center and not go meandering around on the borders. It was an idea with which most of the Macedonian army fully agreed. Somewhat oddly, Calanus himself then chose to accompany Alexander and the Macedonians on their journey back toward that "center." Ironically, the Indian sage never made it to Macedon itself. His death, however, achieved in spectacular style, would leave a permanent impression upon Alexander, the Macedonians, and Western literature.

CHAPTER 22

Fulfillment of an Oracle

The ruler of Pattala (Bahmanabad, about fifty miles northeast of Hyder-abad), who controlled the area of the Indus Delta, now came to Alexander and turned himself and all his possessions over to Alexander. At the same time, Alexander chose to divide his army, sending Craterus back to Carmania by way of Arachotia and Drangiana, with three battalions of the infantry, some archers, the elephants, and Macedonian units deemed unfit for service, including members of the Companion cavalry. Their task was to solidify Macedonian rule in the areas through which they would pass. Hephaestion was given command of the rest of the army except those units who were to sail with Alexander down the Indus to the sea. Alexander would lead these men southward to the Outer Ocean and then westward along the coast.

Peithon, with the mounted javelin men and the Agrianes, was conveyed across the river, with orders to settle the towns that already had been fortified, and to deal with any signs of trouble among the Indians before meeting Alexander at Pattala.

When Alexander had been on the voyage downstream for three days he received news that the chief of Pattala had fled along with the majority of his tribesmen. The country around Pattala was reportedly now virtually deserted. And, indeed, when Alexander and the Macedonians arrived, around the middle of July 325, they found both Pattala and the territory around it empty. By this time Alexander's name alone inspired terror.

The king sent out light troops to pursue the fugitives, who were urged to return without fear. Pattala was theirs to live in and the country was theirs to till, the messengers announced. Many of them eventually did return.

Meanwhile, Alexander began preparing for the army's passage along the Makran coast (the southwest coast of Pakistan). As usual, Alexander planned carefully. Hephaestion fortified the citadel of Pattala, and wells were dug in the surrounding desert. A harbor and dockyards were also built there.

At Pattala the Indus split into two large streams that eventually flowed into the Outer Ocean (the Indian Ocean). After arranging for Leonnatus to lead a land force of 1,000 cavalry and 8,000 heavy and light armed infantry along the riverbank, Alexander lowered his ships into the Indus' westerly stream. Before leading the army southward and westward, Alexander had determined to find the easiest and safest route down the Indus to the Outer Ocean.

TO THE OUTER OCEAN

This proved a surprisingly formidable task. The day after the fleet weighed anchor, a storm blew up and damaged most of the ships, so that the sailors had to beach them and build new ones.

After securing some local pilots, Alexander's fleet set out once again, sailing into a hard wind and waters so rough that they were forced to seek refuge in a side channel. There they were left high and dry by the receding tide. This was a considerable surprise to Alexander's men. Having grown up like frogs around the calm Mediterranean pond, they had never experienced a real tide.

Eventually, however, the Macedonians reached the island of Cilluta. With the best sailors Alexander then went to the far side of the island to see if it offered a safe passage out to the sea. Sailing out about 200 stades from Cilluta they saw another island right out in the sea itself. Having seen it they returned to Cilluta, and anchoring at the headland, Alexander sacrificed to those gods whom, he used to say, Ammon had ordered him to so honor. Whatever Alexander had been told at Siwah, it was now, in Alexander's view, that the oracle had been fulfilled.

On the following day Alexander sailed down to a second island, the one in the sea, went ashore, and once more offered sacrifice, this time to other gods and with a different ritual, though still, by his own account, in accord with the oracle of Ammon.

THE OUTER OCEAN

Then leaving the mouths of the Indus River behind him altogether, Alexander set sail for the open ocean to see, as he said, whether there was any land nearby. Out on the open ocean the king sacrificed bulls to Poseidon and cast them out to sea. He poured a libation from a golden cup and flung the cup and golden bowls into the sea as thanks offerings. Finally, Alexander prayed that Poseidon might safely conduct the fleet that he proposed to send later to the Persian Gulf and to the mouths of the Tigris and Euphrates under Nearchus' command.

The son of Zeus had reached the great Outer Ocean—as Zeus Ammon perhaps had promised in Siwah. Although he had stayed his steps at the Hyphasis, to this point Alexander had not lost a single battle. As of yet, he was invincible.

But Zeus' brother Poseidon ultimately denied Alexander's prayer, or at least decided to make Nearchus' subsequent journey an odyssey rather than the well-provisioned cruise Alexander had meticulously planned.

Alexander himself then returned to Pattala, where he directed Hephaestion to make preparations for fortifying the harbor and installing docks. Pattala was being prepared for a prosperous future. Alexander then undertook a second voyage down to the ocean, this time by the eastern arm of the river. His object was to learn which branch of the Indus was safer. On his way down Alexander came to a great lake. The passage by this branch proved easier (but slower). Having landed on the shore, Alexander arranged for wells to be dug along the coast to supply the fleet with water.

After he returned to Pattala, Alexander set out once more down the eastern stream and then had another harbor and more docks built at the lake he had discovered on his way down the first time. Leaving a garrison there with four months' supplies for the troops, he prepared all other things for the coastal voyage. The way was now prepared for the Macedonian fleet and army to begin sailing and marching westward for the first time since 335.

THE CONQUEST OF INDIA

Alexander's campaign down the Indus in just over six months had been an astonishing feat of planning, coordinated movement, and arms. Alexander had directed the campaign despite suffering a wound that almost killed him. Somewhere, very deep inside of Alexander's heart, there was a will or self-belief that simply would not let him give up his spirit to the arrow of an Indian tribesman. His story would not end inside the walls of an unnamed mud-brick fort.

At the same time, we must not overlook the sheer brutality of Alexander's conquest of the region—as well as the ferocity of the resistance, which continued long after Alexander left the Indus Delta. While the Indians who capitulated immediately usually were spared, those who did not were subjected to ferocious attacks in which soldiers and civilians were slaughtered, often without distinction. Tens of thousands were enslaved, as they always had been after battles in the ancient world. Alexander may have brought the Indians "peace and with it the promise of economic development," but the price was very, very high. Alexander's conquest of the lower Indus Valley was not genocide by any definition of that modern word. He did, however, intend to conquer and rule the Indians. If they were unwilling to accept his rule, he felt no qualms about killing them by the thousands.

Some have argued that because Alexander later withdrew his governor Peithon from the Indus Delta and transferred him (along with his troops) to the northwestern satrapy (where direct Macedonian control was maintained from the central Hindu Kush to the Indus Valley), the campaign in India proper was a failure. But after that transfer, Macedonian interests between the Indus and the Hydaspes were secured by a native prince (Eudamus) who was supported by an army commanded by a Macedonian officer, and Alexander's great ally Porus ruled over the

enormous area from the Himalayas to the Indian Ocean. By these measures Alexander adjusted the administration of his empire to the circumstances, as he always had done. If that constitutes failure, rarely in the
history of imperialism can a conqueror be said to have failed so successfully.

WESTWARD

If Zeus Ammon had revealed to Alexander that he would reach the ends
of the world unconquered, then his prophecy had come true. Soon,
however, Alexander would embark upon another conquest, this one not
so much of peoples, but of a landscape, the fabled deserts of Gedrosia
(the modern Makran, comprising the southwestern coastal area of Pakistan). Gedrosia had a legendary history of vanquishing those who
attempted to cross its waterless dunes. Although Alexander and the majority of his army would survive their march through the desert, many of
the army's camp followers would not. For that reason Alexander's march
through Gedrosia has been compared to Napoleon's disastrous Russian
campaign. But whether Alexander bears full responsibility for the disaster is debatable.

CHAPTER 23

Death in the Desert

THE OREITAE

Alexander himself left Pattala, perhaps in late August 325. He brought with him half the Guards and the archers and the brigades of the Companion infantry, the special squadron of the Companion cavalry, a squadron from each cavalry regiment, together with the mounted archers. Hephaestion was left with the rest of the army. Between them the two men led at least 30,000 combatants and non-combatants (wives, concubines, children).

For the time being, the fleet also stayed behind; the plan was for it to remain in Pattala until the southerly winds of the monsoon subsided, sometime in early November.

But the hostility of the locals was such that the admiral, Nearchus, was forced to leave with the fleet while the stiff breezes were blowing hard, probably early in October. Moreover, he sailed, not down the eastern stream of the Indus River as Alexander had planned, but down the western stream, perhaps because the Indians had destroyed the docking facilities Alexander had constructed on the easier, eastern branch of the river.

The army meanwhile marched along first "by the foothills of the Kirthar Range to the mouth of the Arabis River" (probably the modern

Hab, west of Karachi). From there, Alexander turned toward the ocean, keeping it on his left. He meant to dig wells along the way for the army that was sailing along the coast and to make a surprise attack upon an independent and hostile Indian tribe in the area called the Oreitae.

Soon Alexander launched his attack. Those who resisted were cut down by the cavalry, but many surrendered. The remaining Oreitans and the Gedrosians, who sought to block Alexander's advance into Gedrosia, either fled or gave up. The Oreitans then were put under the governorship of Apollophanes. One of Alexander's personal bodyguards, Leonnatus (who had fought at Alexander's side within the Mallian town), also was left behind with the Agrianes, archers, cavalry, and mercenaries to wait for the fleet when it passed, to build a new city, and to put everything in order. After Hephaestion arrived with his force, Alexander proceeded in early October toward the territory of the Gedrosians.

THE PLAN

To reach Pura (modern Iranshahr in Iran), the capital city of the Gedrosians, Alexander first had to cross a desert region (now called the Makran) well known in antiquity for its heat and lack of water and food. Alexander, however, did not choose the route in ignorance of the difficulties involved. He chose it, we are told, because, with the exception of Semiramis, returning from her conquests of India, no one had ever brought an army successfully through it. Indeed, Semiramis had "succeeded" in getting twenty survivors through the desert, while the Persian king Cyrus the Great supposedly had lost all but seven of his men when he crossed it. Alexander knew about these stories, and they had inspired him to emulate—and hopefully surpass—Cyrus and Semiramis.

Alexander thus thought he knew what he, his army, and his fleet would face as they made their way westward; and, on the basis of that knowledge, he had made his usual, careful preparations. As we have seen, for the sake of the fleet a secondary harbor had been constructed on the lake along the eastern stream of the Indus down to the sea. In addition, a four-month grain supply had been laid on to meet provisioning demands before Nearchus sailed.

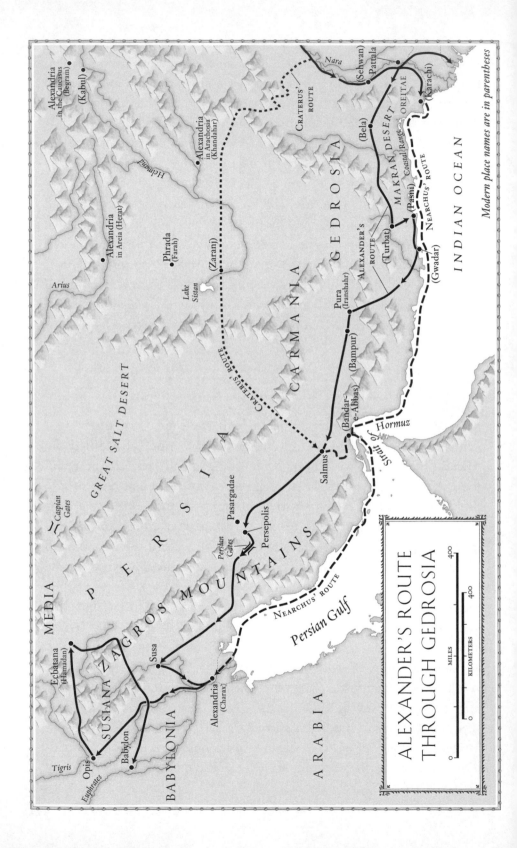

ALEXANDER'S ROUTE
THROUGH GEDROSIA

Modern place names are in parentheses

INDIAN OCEAN

Nara

Patrala
(Karachi)
(Sehwan)
ORITAE
(Bela)
MAKRAN DESERT
Coastal Range

CRATERUS'
ROUTE

GEDROSIA

Alexandria
in the Caucasus
(Kabul) (Begram)

Helmand

Alexandria
in Arachosia
(Khandahar)

Alexandria
in Areia (Herat)

Arius

Phrada
(Farah)

Lake
Sistan

(Zaranj)

NEARCHUS' ROUTE
(Gwadar)
(Pasni)
(Turbat)
ALEXANDER'S
ROUTE

Pura
(Iranshahr)

CARMANIA

(Bampur)

Bandar-
e-Abbas
Strait of
Hormuz

GREAT SALT DESERT

Caspian
Gates

P E R S I A

CRATERUS' ROUTE

Salmus

Pasargadae

Persepolis
Persian
Gates

Z A G R O S   M O U N T A I N S

NEARCHUS' ROUTE

Persian Gulf

MEDIA

Ecbatana
(Hamadan)

Susa

SUSIANA

Alexandria
(Charax)

A R A B I A

Tigris

Opis

Babylon

Euphrates

BABYLONIA

MILES
0   400

KILOMETERS
0   400

During the crossing of the Makran itself, Alexander's plan was for the (land) army to dig wells for the fleet at points along the coast to supply it with water during the coastal voyage, and also to make provision for a market or anchorage. The fleet thus would be supplied with adequate water from the land. The parallel plan perhaps was for the transport ships to furnish the army with whatever food provisions Alexander and the land forces might not be able to carry along their route inland.

These provisions would supplement both what Alexander and the army carried into Gedrosia and also what they might be able to forage from the countryside; for Alexander also had timed his entry into Gedrosia, in early October, to coincide with whatever local harvest there might be. The monsoon rains would have guaranteed that whatever crops could have grown in the Makran region at the time would have been growing as Alexander made his way westward. Alexander did not take the Macedonian army through the Makran in ignorance of its dangers or without a plan.

THE MARCH THROUGH GEDROSIA

No doubt based upon local intelligence, at the outset of its march the army avoided the particularly inhospitable coast, instead taking the inland route through the valleys between what is now called the Central Makran Range and the Coastal Range. Here, too, however, supplies were lacking and the army found no water. The men marched great distances at night to avoid the heat. This was done in spite of the fact that, as we have seen, Alexander was anxious to work along the coast to find anchorage and to assist the fleet by digging wells. Under the circumstances, Alexander could not risk bringing the army down to the coast.

Nevertheless, at one point, a party of mounted troops under the command of a certain Thoas was sent to the seacoast with a few cavalrymen to find out if there might be any anchorage for ships, or any fresh water near the sea, or anything else of use to the fleet. But all Thoas found were a few fishermen living in stifling huts built out of shells fastened together and roofed by the backbones of fish. For drinking water these wretched souls scraped away the gravel, and even this was not exactly sweet. These fishermen became known to the Greeks as the

Ichthuophagoi, or Fish Eaters, because they subsisted on the fish left by the receding tide. Among other quirks of personal hygiene the Fish Eaters let the nails of their fingers and toes grow from birth to old age, and also let their hair grow until it was matted like felt. For clothes they wore animal skins. Such men certainly could not adequately resupply the army—and were hardly worth conquering.

When Alexander (and the army) finally reached a slightly more fertile area (perhaps the oasis of Turbat in southwestern Pakistan), he collected what supplies he could and sent them down to the coast (perhaps at modern Pasni). But the guards bringing the supplies, near starvation themselves, broke open the provisions and shared them out.

Though Alexander rarely tolerated violations of military discipline, he understood that to punish men for saving their own lives would have disastrous effects upon morale. Taking into account their grave necessity, Alexander pardoned those who had broken into the provisions.

It was after Alexander and the army entered lands even less affected by the monsoon, however, that they really began to suffer. The deep sand, the blazing heat, and lack of water along the march caused great suffering and many casualties both among the soldiers and the baggage animals. The horses and the mules struggled across high hills of sand. When the provisions began to give out, the men gradually killed and ate most of the animals, telling their officers that the horses and mules had died of thirst or collapsed from fatigue. The officers chose to look the other way. The sick and those who could not keep up were left behind to die in sandy graves. No Lawrence was along to unwrite what had been written for them.

Alexander, who cannot have fully recovered from his arrow wound, nevertheless led the men on foot through the scorching sands. At one point, some of the light armed troops found a small water hole from which they gathered up a helmetful of water. They brought this to the king. Alexander thanked them—and then poured the water out into the sand in full sight of the troops. We are told that the army was so heartened by this act that it was as if every man had drunk the water that Alexander had poured away.

Cruelly, when the army managed to bivouac at one point near a small stream (to take advantage of its life-giving waters), the stream, swollen by a sudden rainstorm, which took place out of sight of the army, flooded the camp, drowning most of the women and children who had followed the army, and sweeping away the royal tent.

Despite this last disaster, pushing along from Pasni down to the coast at Gwadar and from there inland to Pura, the capital of Gedrosia, the army finally rested after a march through the desert that took sixty days. In Pura, the troops were given a rest and were somewhat relieved by food sent on racing camels by Stasanor, satrap of Drangiana. Nevertheless Alexander pushed on to Carmania (in Iran) itself, where he received more food from Drangiana and elsewhere.

REPREHENSIBLE AMBITION?

Alexander had surpassed the achievements of Semiramis and Cyrus, but at a dreadful cost. The camp followers in particular were devastated by the heat, the lack of water and food, and by the flash flood. Some of the Roman-era sources claim that the king was overwhelmed by both grief and shame at being responsible for such a disaster.

Following their lead, modern historians have gone so far as to argue that Alexander put the army through the hellish march across the desert of Gedrosia for its mutiny at the Hyphasis River, "to expiate its contumacy." Others have judged that "his prior knowledge of the coast was inadequate and the egotism of his ambition reprehensible."

If Alexander intended the march as a punishment, however, it is difficult to understand why he traveled at night across the desert and prepared as well as he could for the navy, either by digging wells or by making provision for a market or an anchorage. Or why, when he finally obtained provisions, he distributed them among the baggage train. Nor would he have sent Thoas on his mission down to the coast. Above all, when he had a golden opportunity to punish his men for breaking into what limited supplies there were, he chose to ignore what they had done. All of these actions simply are not consistent with a speculative hypothesis about what Alexander was thinking—for which there is little or no evidence in any case. Alexander's motives can only be judged by his actions. Those actions show that he did everything possible to relieve the suffering of his followers. Thus, Alexander did not lead the Macedonian army through Gedrosia to punish it for what had happened at the Hyphasis.

Nor was Alexander guilty of relying upon inadequate intelligence. It was precisely because he understood that the coastline was a desert that he led the army inland, between the Central and Coastal Makran Ranges, where conditions, though harsh, were better.

As for Alexander's reprehensible ambition to cross the Makran itself, which led to such suffering, there is no doubt that the land army suffered greatly, although Plutarch's figure of an army reduced to a quarter of its initial size (starting out from impossible figures of 120,000 infantry and 15,000 cavalry) cannot be accepted at face value.

Terrible as the casualty figures were, Alexander cannot be blamed for casualties that resulted neither from faulty intelligence nor from inadequate preparations. Even a king who claimed to be the son of Zeus had no control over winds, rains, heat, or floods. A flood, the result of a rainstorm that could not be seen as it approached the Macedonians' camp, not Alexander's ambition, killed the camp followers. But for completely unpredictable weather conditions there would have been no disaster in Gedrosia and no debate about Alexander's ambition.

As in the past, Alexander had made careful preparations for a combined land and sea crossing of the south coast of Gedrosia based upon largely accurate information. Unfortunately, factors over which he had no control destroyed his plans and an unknown (but significant) proportion of his army and its followers. For once, the gods to whom Alexander sacrificed had not accepted his offerings.

CHAPTER 24

The Reign of Terror?

THE REVEL IN CARMANIA

Whatever Alexander believed about his own culpability for what had happened in Gedrosia, the news brought to him in Pura about the administration of his empire was not destined to make him any happier. The details must be situated carefully in their context if we want to decide whether his response to the reports constituted a "reign of terror," as some historians have claimed.

Because he believed that Apollophanes, the governor of the Oreitae, had failed to carry out all of his orders, Alexander initially replaced him with Thoas. (In fact, Apollophanes was already dead, having been killed in a battle against the rebellious Oreitae.) When Thoas became ill and died, Sibyrtius was appointed in his place. Sibyrtius recently had been appointed satrap of Carmania, but now was given the governorship of both the Arachotians and the Gedrosians.

On his way to Carmania Alexander also learned that Philip, the governor of India (from west of the Indus to Parapamisadae), had been assassinated by his own mercenaries. All the assassins were eventually killed by Philip's Macedonian bodyguards. Until a new governor could be sent out, Eudamus and Taxiles were put in charge of Philip's satrapy.

Despite the fact that he had been suspected of advocating rebellion while Alexander was in India, Astaspes, who had been serving as the satrap of Carmania, came to meet Alexander. For the moment concealing his anger, Alexander greeted Astaspes in a friendly way and let him keep his job until he could review the reports about him.

In Carmania, Craterus, with the rest of the army and the elephants, rejoined Alexander. Craterus, who had taken the northern and easier route back westward, also brought along Ordanes, who had been captured after he revolted. Massive supplies of food and livestock from the northern satrapies also arrived. Bowls of wine and huge jugs were set out on the thresholds of houses for the army by the Carmanians.

Alexander and the survivors of Gedrosia then went on a seven-day drinking binge in imitation of the *komus*, a celebratory procession in honor of Dionysos. The king and his drinking companions supposedly rode in a cart weighed down with golden bowls and huge goblets, while the army joined the revels in decorated wagons. In this way the army spent "seven days on a drunken march, an easy prey if the vanquished races had only had the courage to challenge riotous drinkers."

There is no mention of this revel in the accounts of Ptolemy or Aristobulus (who were there), but this does not mean that the drunken binge did not happen. Ptolemy may not have thought it an important episode, and Aristobulus consistently underplayed Alexander's drinking. But whether there was a full-scale Dionysian revel or just a long party during which the army attempted to drink away the memory of Gedrosia, more serious issues soon interrupted the festivities, as Alexander began to address the charges brought against various governors and officers.

THE "REIGN OF TERROR"?

Among the first to be judged was Astaspes, the governor of Carmania. After Alexander examined the reports about him, Astaspes was executed. About Astaspes' execution by Alexander, Curtius commented that it showed that "luxurious living and base cruelty are not mutually exclusive." But Curtius offers no proof of Astaspes' innocence either.

Next up in Alexander's docket were Cleander, Sitalces, Heracon, and perhaps Agathon, officers who had been left behind with Parmenio in charge of the forces in Ecbatana. Coenus' brother Cleander and Sitalces, who commanded the Thracian javelin men, had been involved in the assassination of Parmenio. These commanders brought the greater part of their troops with them to Alexander. Both locals and serving soldiers brought many charges against Sitalces and Cleander and their soldiers. These accusations included plundering temples, rifling ancient tombs, and committing unjust acts against the inhabitants of the province. Even Curtius admits that these men had assaulted noblewomen, and Cleander, it was said, had raped a virgin and then given her to his slave as a concubine.

Sitalces and Cleander were found guilty of these crimes and were executed to put fear into any other satraps or governors: if they committed like crimes, they too would suffer the same fate. These executions kept in order the tribes that had surrendered to Alexander, for they proved that Alexander would not tolerate abuse of his subjects by his governors.

We are informed that 600 of the common soldiers (from Ecbatana) were also executed for carrying out their commanders' orders. If the commanders had not been guilty of the crimes they were accused of, and if their soldiers were not thought to be guilty of assisting them, it is very hard to see how Alexander could have expected that his own troops would carry out so many executions of fellow soldiers. The evidence must have been compelling.

Moreover, Alexander did not simply conduct Stalinist "show trials" of bad apples, at which carefully prepared confessions of guilt were read out by the accused. Heracon, another one of the generals from Ecbatana, was initially acquitted of the charge brought against him. It was only later, when he was convicted on a second, separate charge (robbing a temple in Susa) that he was executed.

Finally, on the same day that the 600 troops from Ecbatana were executed, two men brought in as ringleaders of the Persian insurrection, Zariaspes and Ozines (perhaps to be identified with the man called Ordanes by other sources), were also put to death.

In Carmania, therefore, there were no innocent victims of Alexander's suspicious temper and there was no "reign of terror." Nor did Alexander use the allegations against Sitalces and Cleander as a convenient way of getting rid of the generals who had carried out the assassination of Parmenio. Sitalces, Cleander, and their henchmen were executed for crimes committed against Alexander's subjects after the death of Parmenio. None of the ancient sources dispute their guilt. Astaspes, Ordanes/Ozines, and Zariaspes were put to death for insurrection while Alexander was away in India. None of the sources claim that these men were *not* plotting rebellion.

THE DISMISSAL OF THE MERCENARIES

Many scholars have connected the trials in Carmania to Alexander's order that all of his governors and commanders in Asia should disband their mercenaries at once. The order has been interpreted by some historians as an attempt by Alexander to strip his generals and governors of troops who might have protected them from Alexander. Indeed, if some governors or generals were worried about how they had discharged their responsibilities while Alexander was away in India, such an order probably did inspire fear. Their sense of anxiety, however, cannot be used as evidence to explain why Alexander decided to disband, or, rather, release the mercenaries from service.

For we know that the mercenaries Alexander ordered to be disbanded were not to be demobilized. Rather, they were to be transferred to service in Alexander's army. Because Alexander had left so many of his own mercenaries in city foundations and garrisons in Asia, he issued the order primarily to bring his own levy of mercenaries back up to an acceptable level.

At the same time, Alexander cannot have intended to deprive all of his satraps in Asia of all troops. These governors needed troops to keep order. They were expected to raise new levies, as Peucestas did when he was made satrap of Persis early in 324.

Alexander's order, nevertheless, had unanticipated effects. Rather than embarking upon a long march to join him, many of the mercenaries simply fled and joined bands of free-roaming brigands. Others eventually found their way to the Athenian Leosthenes, who delivered them to Taenarum in the territory of Sparta, a notorious depot for the hiring of mercenaries.

Moreover, although Alexander probably did not issue the order so as to deprive his governors of all forces, it did alarm at least some of his satraps and generals. Some who had mercenary troops under their command revolted against the king's authority. Others got together what money they could and fled.

Most famously, after the trials and executions in Carmania, Alexander's old friend and treasurer, Harpalus, fled from Babylon and Alexander (for the second time), this time taking with him 5,000 talents of silver and 6,000 mercenaries.

THE SECOND FLIGHT OF HARPALUS

Perhaps assuming that Alexander would never make it back from India alive, Alexander's boyhood friend had settled down to a life of luxury in Babylon, a city that afforded wide scope to a man with well-defined and expensive tastes. At first occupying himself with illegitimate amours with local women, Harpalus then squandered much of the treasure under his control on more expensive pleasures. Great quantities of delectable fish were brought from the Red Sea.

Pythonice, the most dazzling courtesan of the day, was fetched from Athens, and as long as she lived she received gifts from Harpalus worthy of a queen. When she died, she was given a magnificent funeral and a costly monument of the Attic type.

After her death, a second Athenian courtesan, Glycera, whose name in Greek could be translated as Honey, was brought out to keep Harpalus company amid Babylon's hanging gardens. She too was kept in exceeding luxury, provided with a way of life that was madly expensive. Meanwhile, the treasurer made regular (cash) benefactions to Athens; whatever were his assumptions about Alexander's long-term prospects, Harpalus had the born survivor's sense to keep in mind a rainy day.

The clouds began to gather when Alexander, like Dionysos before him, suddenly returned from the east, determined to show his power. The long party was finally over, and it was time to pay the bill. Harpalus, who knew exactly what happened to those whom Alexander suspected of disloyalty or regal pretensions, slipped out of town with his money and his mercenaries, first to Athens (where he perhaps hoped to incite a revolt), then on to Taenarum after he escaped from Athens with the help of the orator Demosthenes, and finally to Crete. There, on the most beautiful of all the Greek islands, Alexander's refined bagman was done in by a certain Thibron, but not before leaving a long and messy trail of political infighting, accusations of bribery, and the inevitable lawsuits (even then) in his wake.

Harpalus was one of the few men who ever crossed Alexander, not once but twice, and lived, at least for a while, to talk about it. While Alexander may have been extremely shrewd about human nature in general, to his boyhood friends he remained endearingly loyal, and even vulnerable, to the end of his life, never wanting to believe that his own absolute fidelity was not reciprocated. Harpalus, on the other hand, clearly preferred the charms of Pythonice and Honey to those of friendship.

CHAPTER 25

Nabarzanes' Gift

THE EUNUCH BAGOAS

Finally, toward the middle of the winter of 325/4, Alexander reached Salmus (perhaps near Khanu), the capital of Carmania. Here he made sacrifices for the Indian victory and on behalf of the army for its safe passage through Gedrosia; this was perhaps a kind of backhanded admission that he had underestimated the challenge after all. He also held artistic and athletic competitions. Peucestas, who had guarded Alexander with his shield in the Mallian city, was made Alexander's eighth bodyguard and was appointed as the future satrap of Persia.

During the general festival, Alexander reportedly attended some contests in dancing and singing where his "favorite," Bagoas, won the prize. This Bagoas was the handsome young Persian eunuch who had been brought to Alexander by Nabarzanes in Hyrcania as a kind of gift, and whose pleas had induced Alexander to pardon Nabarzanes for his part in the betrayal and murder of Darius.

After winning his prize, Bagoas, still in his performer's costume and wearing his victor's crown, came across the theater and seated himself beside the king. At the sight the Macedonians applauded loudly and shouted for Alexander to kiss the winner. At last the king put his arms around Bagoas and kissed him.

Some historians have denied that this episode even took place. But there seems no good reason to question its historicity. Alexander did kiss the eunuch Bagoas in a theater filled with Macedonians and Greeks in the capital of Carmania. What that kiss signified about their relationship is less clear.

The Greek word Plutarch uses to describe Bagoas in the relevant passage of his biography of Alexander (*eromenon* in the accusative case) previously had been used by Athenian writers of the fifth and fourth centuries to describe a younger man who was involved in a relationship with an older man (*erastes*). Such a relationship was partly educational and cultural, but also frequently included a sexual or erotic component. These kinds of relationships seem to have been popular and fashionable especially among the well-to-do. In classical Athens the expectation also seems to have been that the erotic dimension of the relationship would end by the time the younger man reached his early twenties, at the latest. Otherwise, both men might become subjects of gossip or criticism. Such a relationship conformed to only one pattern and set of protocols among a variety of same-gender attractions and relationships described in ancient texts and also represented pictorially during the classical and Hellenistic periods.

If Plutarch used the term *eromenon* to describe Bagoas in the way that the term was sometimes employed by earlier classical authors to describe a beloved younger partner in an intimate relationship, the conclusion must be that Plutarch believed that Alexander and Bagoas had some kind of intimate relationship. The relationship may have included an erotic element. The historian Curtius Rufus certainly believed that there was a sexual relationship between the two men.

Whatever Alexander's relationship to Bagoas was, however, it apparently caused the Macedonians no alarm; rather, we are told that when Alexander kissed Bagoas, the spectators cheered. This should not surprise us. Whatever conventions applied to relationships between younger and older men in Athens, they did not apply in Macedon. It will be recalled that Alexander's father, Philip, while in middle age and after marrying a number of women and siring a number of children, also had at least two erotic relationships with men, the most significant of which was with the guard Pausanias. The death of Philip's second lover led directly to Philip's assassination by the first. Before that, according to one fourth-century historian, at Philip's court were gathered "companions" who shaved themselves and made themselves smooth, mounted each other, although they had beards, and caroused with two or three companions. That Alexander had kissed a handsome young Persian boy in a theater in Salmus after that young man had won a prize at a festival was hardly likely to shock men who had seen Philip stabbed to death in another theater by his former lover.

ALEXANDER'S SEXUALITY

Based upon Plutarch's account of the incident in Salmus, and the scattered and ambiguous evidence for Alexander's relationship to Hephaestion, many scholars have concluded that Alexander the Great was a homosexual. Other scholars, pointing out that Alexander married three times, sired at least two children, and also maintained a harem of 365 women, have argued that Alexander essentially was a heterosexual.

But modern sexual categories such as "homosexual" and "heterosexual" cannot be usefully applied to describe the sexuality of Alexander. He belonged to a culture in which the erotic impulse (*eros*) was not necessarily assumed to be confined to feelings or acts directed to either men or women that, if they were consummated, thereby placed individuals exclusively in one sexual category or another. Rather than striving to fix Alexander within one modern sexual camp or another, it is far more illuminating to examine the evidence for the trajectory of the erotic impulses he acted upon.

If we look at Alexander's sexuality historically, it is striking that the farther he got from Macedon, the stronger and more varied his impulse toward erotic expression became. At the same time, a consistent thread can be discerned. Alexander was drawn to physical beauty without regard either to modern sexual categories *or* ancient prejudices about ethnic origins.

To begin at the beginning: whatever the truth is about the report of Athenaeus that because Alexander seemed to have little appetite for sex of any kind when he was young, Olympias and Philip conspired to have the beautiful prostitute (*hetaira*) Kallixena go to bed with Alexander to make sure that he was not effeminate, or whether we can credit Aelian's statement that a certain Pancaste was the first woman with whom Alexander had sexual relations, Alexander's first intimate relationship seems to have been with the tall and handsome Hephaestion. That said, the unambiguous evidence that sex was central to the relationship is conspicuously absent.

After his victory at Issos Alexander took as his mistress Barsine, the beautiful ex-wife of Memnon of Rhodes. They subsequently had a son named Herakles. Following the battle of Gaugamela Alexander acquired Darius' harem of concubines. These concubines had been selected for their beauty. In Bactria Alexander immediately fell in love with Roxane, the daughter of a Bactrian nobleman, who, after Darius' wife, was said to be the most beautiful woman in Asia. Bagoas apparently had been a court favorite first of Darius, then of Artabazus, and finally of Alexander himself—and not because of his martial prowess. Finally, after he returned from India, at Susa, Alexander married both Darius' eldest daughter, another Barsine, and Parysatis, the youngest daughter of Artaxerxes III Ochus. As we shall see, he fully expected these marriages to produce heirs.

Unlike the last Ottoman sultans, whose harems grew larger as the number of their provinces diminished, for Alexander sex apparently was not a form of compensation for military incompetence. Rather, the more Alexander conquered, the more he was conquered, by men, women, and a Persian youth, all of whom had been gifted by the gods with physical beauty. Indeed, casting his eyes over the Persian women captured after the battle of Issos, Alexander is said to have remarked jestingly that Persian women were a torment for the eyes. The plain did not excite Alexander's erotic impulse. If sex, along with sleep, made Alexander aware that he was mortal, as we are told, then his sense of his own mortality increased dramatically as he made his way from the Haliacmon to the Indus River.

THE RETURN OF NEARCHUS

When Alexander was celebrating at Salmus he also received the joyous news that Nearchus and the fleet at long last had arrived at Harmozeia, the main port of Carmania. Nearchus was able to give Alexander the good news in person, although Alexander apparently barely recognized him because of his briny, fatigued state. Nearchus' account of the difficult voyage, which Arrian used extensively in his short work entitled the *Indike*, emphasized the difficulties of the voyage and helped to explain to Alexander what at first glance had looked like irresponsibility or disobedience on the part of some of his generals or governors.

From Nearchus Alexander learned the following: as soon as Alexander had left Pattala, its inhabitants and the people around it had turned on the troops left behind. It is very likely that they destroyed the harbor installation Alexander left at the lake on the eastern stream of the Indus. Nearchus therefore was compelled to sail down the western stream, but he left earlier than anticipated, probably in early October, well before the southern wind had died down in early November.

Sailing down the western stream of the Indus to reach the Outer Ocean, Nearchus was forced to make a cut through the coastal sandbar. After this, the winds compelled him to land on an offshore island, where he remained for twenty-four days, until they finally died down.

By the time Nearchus had reached the territory of the Oreitae, Leonnatus and his troops had killed 6,000 of the Oreitae in battle, but Apollophanes, the satrap of Gedrosia, had fallen during the engagement. This was the reason why Apollophanes had not carried out Alexander's orders—not due to any negligence on the satrap's part. Apollophanes' reputation was saved for posterity by Nearchus' account. Despite the victory, which made the coastal region safe for the fleet, Nearchus did not begin his voyage off the south coast until late October or early November 325 at the earliest.

As we have seen, Alexander himself had left the territory of the Oreitans in early October, perhaps as much as a month before Nearchus and the fleet got there. Marching westward in early October, Alexander certainly would have been much too far ahead of Nearchus for the fleet to catch up to him at the pre-arranged wells and food drops along the coast. Nor could Alexander have stopped to wait once he realized what the conditions were really like. If Alexander stopped, he risked starving the army.

Thus Alexander was forced to accept Nearchus' account of his voyage, replete as it was with fantastic stories of encounters with the Fish Eaters and a school of whales that spouted water up into the air to great heights, terrifying the Macedonians. To scare the whales away, Alexander was told, the sailors had shouted with all their might, blown trumpets, and beaten the water with their oars.

Despite all of the adventures, the fleet lost only one vessel, an Egyptian galley and crew that strayed too close to the island called Nosala. By legend anyone who touched this island, which was sacred to the Sun, instantly disappeared. Nearchus himself landed on Nosala to search for the galley's crew, but found no one.

It was also said of this island that a Nereid lived there, luring any sailor who approached. But if he were foolish enough to respond to her advances, she would turn him into a fish and throw him into the sea. The Sun eventually grew annoyed at these shenanigans and forced the Nereid to vacate the island; pitying the sailors she had piscified, he turned them into the Fish Eaters Alexander had encountered along the south coast.

Whatever Alexander thought of these sailors' yarns, he must have been genuinely relieved to see Nearchus and the fleet. They had been at sea for sixty days and had traveled nearly a thousand miles through uncharted waters since leaving the Indus. Now Alexander sent them onward: he ordered Nearchus to continue his voyage from Harmozeia to Susia, and then from there on to the mouths of the Tigris, where he would rendezvous with the army.

THE TOMB OF CYRUS

As for the land army, from Carmania in December 325 Alexander now ordered Hephaestion to proceed to Persia by the coastal route, with the elephants, the baggage train, and the greatest part of the army. Accompanied by the most mobile infantry units, the Companion cavalry, and a part of the archers, he himself took the direct road to Pasargadae.

When he reached the Persian frontier, Alexander discovered that the governor Phrasaortes had died and that the satrap's position had been undertaken or usurped by Orxines, a descendant of Cyrus the Great. Orxines' wealth was partly inherited and also had been augmented during the long period when he had served as a satrap.

Apparently recognizing the precariousness of his position, Orxines greeted Alexander with herds of horses, chariots trimmed with silver and

Tomb of Cyrus the Great, at Pasargadae in Persia. *Slides collection of the Joint Library of the Hellenic and Roman Societies*

gold, costly furniture, jewels, gold vessels, purple garments, and 3,000 talents of silver coins. Alexander already had designated his new body-guard Peucestas governor of Persia, but Orxines' lavish gifts kept him alive, for the moment. Others were not as fortunate.

In the district of Pasargadae Alexander also found Atropates, governor of Media, who brought with him a Mede named Baryaxes. Baryaxes had been put under arrest for wearing his cap upright and calling himself king of the Medes and Persians. He and all of his associates were promptly put to death, as was one Phradates (or Autophradates), suspected of having designs on the throne.

At the city of Pasargadae itself, Alexander also found that the gabled tomb of Cyrus the Great had been robbed, its famous inscription having failed to protect it. The inscription read:

"O man! I am Cyrus son of Cambyses, who founded the Persian empire and ruled Asia. Grudge me not my monument."

Of all the treasures in the tomb, only the coffin of Cyrus and a divan remained. The robbers even had opened up the sarcophagus and thrown out the body of Cyrus.

Alexander had the Persian priests (Magi) who served as tomb guards arrested and tortured to find out the names of the culprits. But even under torture, the Magi neither confessed nor implicated others. At length, none the wiser, Alexander let the Magi go without discovering who had been responsible for the sacrilegious treatment of the tomb.

Aristobulus, however, was personally instructed to put the tomb in a state of thorough repair, to restore Cyrus' body to its sarcophagus, and to replace with exact replicas every stolen object. As Cyrus' putative successor, Alexander had good political reasons for repairing Cyrus' tomb. At the same time, Alexander, the conqueror of a great empire himself, must have been distressed by the ill treatment of the remains of another great king.

Finally, however, it was Orxines who was hanged for the crime, after Bagoas implied to Alexander that the satrap was the guilty party. As Orxines was led away to be executed, we are told, the satrap looked at Bagoas and was said to have remarked that he had heard "that women once were rulers of Asia," but that this was something new, a eunuch as king.

But many other Persians also brought accusations against Orxines, and Orxines was convicted not only of robbing temples and royal tombs but of putting many Persians to death illegally.

With Orxines dead, Peucestas now took up his appointment as satrap of the Persians. As soon as Peucestas entered the office he adopted Median dress and learned Persian. The Persians, we are told, were delighted that at least one Macedonian preferred the customs of their country to his own. The problem for Alexander was that Peucestas was the exception rather than the rule.

CHAPTER 26

Marriage: Persian Style

THE SUICIDE OF CALANUS

Either in Pasargadae or on the borders of Persia and Susiana, after living for seventy-three years in perfect health, Alexander's Indian friend Calanus developed an intestinal disorder of some kind and decided to end his own life. Alexander tried to talk the philosopher out of his decision, but to no avail. Ptolemy therefore was ordered to build a funeral pyre.

By the time the pyre was built, Calanus was too ill to walk to it. A horse was provided, but Calanus could not mount it. He had to be borne on a litter lying down. A procession of horses, soldiers in armor, and people carrying incense to throw on the flames escorted the sage.

The horse Calanus was to have ridden was of the royal breed of Nysaia; before he mounted the pyre, he gave it as a gift to Lysimachus, one of his students in philosophy. To his other pupils and friends Calanus distributed the draperies and cups Alexander had ordered to be burned on the pyre in his honor. Calanus' head was wreathed with garlands in the Indian fashion, and on his way to his death he sang hymns of praise to his country's gods.

When the fire was kindled Alexander ordered the trumpets to be sounded. The troops raised their battle cry, and even the elephants bellowed out their war cry in Calanus' honor. Calanus slowly climbed up on the pyre as the whole army watched. Alexander himself felt that the spectacle was unseemly, especially in the case of a man who was dear to him. But the rest were simply astonished to see Calanus give no sign of flinching from the flames. Some thought he was mad, others that his ability to bear the pain was a form of vanity. Others marveled at his bravery and contempt for death. Calanus' end made a deep impression upon all who witnessed it, and his name became proverbial for calm courage in the face of death.

THE CROWN OF PROMACHUS

There followed a less dignified event. After leaving the funeral pyre, Alexander invited a number of his friends and officers to dine with him and proposed a contest in drinking neat wine—no doubt to help everyone forget what they had just witnessed. The prize was a crown worth a crown. The winner, Promachus, drank four pitchers (about twelve quarts) of fortified wine. Promachus unfortunately survived just three days to enjoy his victory. According to Chares, who, as chamberlain, was in a position to know, forty-one other competitors from the contest also died from the effects of the wine, having been seized with a violent chill after the debauchery ended. The episode should have been a warning sign to Alexander. But the road of excess usually does not lead to the palace of wisdom; more often, it has brought its travelers directly to the Elysian fields.

HONORS FOR BRAVERY

Alexander now took the army along the royal road to Susa, which he reached by March 324. Just before he entered the city, Nearchus appeared once more, having safely brought the fleet from Harmozeia.

Alexander now offered sacrifices for the safety of his ships and men, and contests were celebrated. Awards of golden crowns for conspicuous bravery during the campaign in India also were made: to Peucestas for saving the king's life; to Leonnatus for saving Alexander, service in India, his victory in Oria, his defeat of the Oreitae and their neighbors, and settling affairs in Oria; to Nearchus for his voyage from India; to Onesicritus, master of the royal galley; and to Alexander's friend Hephaestion and the other members of the bodyguard.

THE MASS MARRIAGE AT SUSA

A larger and more significant ceremony followed. After the battle of Issos Alexander had pledged to Darius' mother, Sisygambis, that he would provide for the marriage of her captive daughters even more generously than her son had promised to do. How Alexander now fulfilled that promise was not perhaps quite what the queen mother, the royal daughters, or especially the Macedonians themselves would have envisioned.

For at Susa the royal daughters of the Persian king and many other royal ladies were wedded to Alexander and ninety-one of his Companions and friends. Alexander himself married Barsine (Stateira), Darius' eldest daughter, and also, according to Aristobulus, Parysatis, the youngest daughter of Artaxerxes III Ochus.

Thus Alexander was linked through matrimony to both branches of the Persian royal family. To Hephaestion, Alexander gave Drypetis, another of Darius' daughters and the sister of his own wife Barsine, so that Hephaestion's children should be Alexander's nephews and nieces. Amastrine, daughter of Darius' brother Oxyartes, was wedded to Craterus. To Perdiccas was given the daughter of Atropates, governor of Media. Ptolemy married Artacama, the daughter of Artabazus, and Eumenes was joined to her sister Artonis. Nearchus married the daughter of Barsine and Mentor, and Seleucus wed Apame, the daughter of the Bactrian Spitamenes. And so it went, with Alexander's officers being given young Persian and Median noblewomen as brides.

More significantly, however, the weddings were conducted in Persian style. Chairs were set for the bridegrooms in order. After toasts to health had been drunk, the brides came in and sat down next to their bridegrooms, who took them by the hand and kissed them. Alexander performed the ceremony first.

If the Persian ritual was notable for its simplicity and dignity, Alexander's arrangements for the wedding party were not. Bridal chambers for all the newlyweds were set within a specially constructed pavilion, and in it were one hundred couches, each adorned with nuptial coverings made of silver. Alexander's couch had supports of gold. The pavilion was decorated sumptuously with expensive draperies and fine linens. Underfoot there were purple and crimson rugs interwoven with gold.

The nuptials lasted for five days, with entertainment provided by Indian jugglers, rhapsodes, harp virtuosi, singers, flautists, dancers, and the most famous actors of the day. Ambassadors and guests gave wedding presents worth 15,000 talents. Alexander himself provided a dowry for each couple. Ten thousand other Macedonians had married Asian women, and now every one of those men received a wedding gift from Alexander.

The mass marriage ceremony at Susa has elicited strikingly contradictory interpretations. Arguing against the idea that Alexander wanted to fuse the Macedonian and Persian aristocracies into one, the Australian scholar Bosworth has hypothesized that, in the wake of the execution of Orxines and the other Iranian pretenders, Alexander may have been leery of giving Persian nobles the prestige of a royal marriage. Alexander did not want Persian noblemen marrying Sisygambis' daughters or other Persian noblewomen because of his fears of insurrection. In support of this hypothesis, it has been observed that, with two exceptions, all of the grooms were Macedonian or Greek, and all the brides were Persian or Median. As far as we know, no Persian noblemen married Macedonian or Greek women as part of the ceremony. Thus, the mass marriage ceremony was not an equal fusion of the two aristocracies, but rather the absorption of the Persian aristocracy into the Macedonian ruling class.

On the other hand, the ceremony needs to be seen in its ancient context. We are hard-pressed to find another example of a mass marriage of Greek or Macedonian officers or royalty to women of any other ethnic group. In fact, previously Alexander had set the precedent of marrying outside his ethnic or national group with his first marriage, to Roxane, a Bactrian woman. Yet Alexander's wedding to Roxane had been celebrated according to the Macedonian or Greek form. The marriage ceremony at Susa was that of a conquered people. Such an accommodation to the customs of the Persians would have been unthinkable only a few years before. No one would have missed the significance of the choice of ceremony. The weddings at Susa were not a fusion of cultures on an equal basis, but did represent an accommodation that displayed the present and future political order. Although virtually all the grooms at the wedding were Macedonian or Greek and all the women were Persian or Median, the future ruling class of Alexander's empire—the issue of the marriages at Susa—would be one of mixed Macedonian and Persian blood. Shortly, Alexander would make it crystal clear that a joint Macedonian-Persian ruling class was exactly what he had in mind for the administration of his world empire. The majority of the Macedonian soldiers understood this very well, and they were far from pleased about it.

THE PAYING OFF OF THE DEBTS

The Macedonian soldiers' dissatisfaction with the weddings in Susa helps us to understand their suspicious reaction to an extraordinary gesture of generosity. Seeing that many of the soldiers somehow had fallen into debt during the campaigns, Alexander decided to pay off all those debts. At first the troops were reluctant even to register to have what they owed paid off, thinking that Alexander was trying to identify the spendthrifts among them.

Learning of these apprehensions, Alexander had banking tables set up in the camp. The king told his accountants at the tables to cancel the debts of all who produced any bond, without so much as registering their names. The lowest figure given by the sources for the total debt Alexander paid off was 9,870 talents, the highest 20,000. Much of the money apparently was owed by the soldiers to Asian traders. By paying off the vast debt, Alexander was doing a good deed on behalf both of the debtors and their creditors.

The incident is significant both for the amount of debt it reveals the soldiers to have accumulated during the campaigns, despite the gratuities paid to them, and also for the suspicion of Alexander among the rank and file that the episode clearly betrays. As so often, generosity did not breed gratitude, but resentment.

THE RETURN OF THE SUCCESSORS

The growing displeasure of the Macedonian soldiers was further inflamed by the sudden arrival of the governors of the new cities that

Alexander had founded and of the provinces he had captured. These governors brought with them the 30,000 "Successors," young Persian men from the eastern satrapies, selected for their grace and strength before the Hyphasis mutiny. Since their selection they had been taught Greek, trained along Macedonian military lines, and given Macedonian battle dress. Upon their arrival in Susa they gave a splendid display of their skill and discipline in the use of their weapons; Alexander warmly praised their performance. The reaction of the battle-scarred, graying Macedonian veterans does not need to be imagined: later, the Macedonians jeered at Alexander's "ballet-soldiers."

But the real object of the Macedonians' simmering anger was not the Successors. Rather, it was the king himself.

From the Macedonians' point of view, the appearance of the Successors was only another example of Alexander's many efforts to lessen his future dependence upon his own countrymen. Alexander's Median clothes also had caused pain, and the weddings in the Persian style had not been to the Macedonians' taste. The Macedonians also were not happy about Peucestas, the satrap of Persia, imitating the Persians in dress and speech, and the inclusion of foreign mounted troops, including Bactrians, Sogdians, Arachotians, Zarangians, Areians, Parthyaeans, and Persians, in the units of the Companion cavalry. Moreover, a fifth cavalry regiment now was being added, not "wholly barbarian" but with some of the "barbarians" picked to serve in it. Some foreign officers also had been posted to the Royal Squadron (*agema*); their commander, Hystaspes, a Bactrian, and the foreign troops were all equipped with Macedonian lances in place of their native javelins. All this caused deep indignation among the Macedonians, who felt that Alexander's whole outlook had become "barbarized" and that he no longer esteemed Macedonian customs or the Macedonians themselves.

Soon the resentment boiled over into a second mutiny. This time, however, the king had prepared the ground and would emerge victorious. What had happened at the Hyphasis may have been forgiven after what the king and his men endured together in Gedrosia, but it was not forgotten. Like his Homeric role model, Alexander did not strive to finish second, even to his own soldiers.

CHAPTER 27

The Mutiny at Opis

A NEW ALEXANDRIA

The Macedonians departed from Susa in the spring of 324. Hephaestion, leading the majority of the infantry brigades, traveled directly down to the Persian Sea (Gulf) by land. Alexander sailed down the Eulaeus (modern Karun) to the sea with the hypaspists, the Royal Squadron, and a few of the Companion cavalry, and then took the fastest ships along the coast to the mouth of the Tigris. The other ships made their way up the Eulaeus to the canal that joined the Eulaeus with the Tigris and passed through it (into the Tigris).

Alexander then navigated up the Tigris to the rendezvous point where Hephaestion was waiting with the army. At the confluence of the Eulaeus and the Tigris Alexander paused to found another Alexandria, possibly the later Spasinou Charax. Although part of the population of the settlement was drawn from a native town (Durine), an elite of Macedonian veterans also was settled there in a special quarter known as Pellaeum, an obvious reference to the Macedonian capital of Pella.

From the newly founded city Alexander then went up the Tigris River with the whole army to Opis. On the way he destroyed the artificial cataracts the Persians had constructed along the river to make it impassable to invading fleets. Such preparations indicate that Alexander was not exhausted. Nor had he lost his desire for future conquests. On the contrary, just as he had done before his expedition to the Outer Ocean from Pattala, Alexander was carefully preparing the logistical groundwork for the next phase of his plan to conquer the world.

THE MUTINY AT OPIS

By midsummer of 324 Alexander and the army had reached the city of Opis. Opis had important links to both Babylonian and Persian history; there, in September 539, Alexander's imperial predecessor Cyrus the Great had conquered the Babylonian king Nabonidus and become the ruler of Nabonidus' immense empire.

In Opis Alexander summoned the Macedonians and announced that all men unfit for duty by reason of age or disablement were to be discharged from the army and sent home. He also promised to give them when they left enough to make them the envy of those in their homes and also to encourage others to come out and take part in similar dangers and toils.

Undoubtedly contrary to Alexander's expectations, his announcement pleased neither the veterans who were being discharged nor those soldiers who were staying on. The Macedonians vehemently protested. He had used them up in every kind of service and now he was turning them away in disgrace and throwing them upon their cities and parents, no longer the same men he took with him. Why not send them all away and write them off as useless, since he had these young ballet-soldiers with whom he could go on to conquer the world?

The troops who were to remain picked up on the call for general demobilization. They demanded release for themselves too. Further, they loudly insisted that their years of service should be counted, rather than their ages; it was only fair, they argued, that those recruited together should be released at the same time. The mutineers then mockingly told Alexander to go to war by himself, along with his father Ammon, since he did not respect his soldiers.

Alexander's response was ferocious. For the first time, the Macedonians now faced an enraged Alexander, the same Alexander whom Asians had come to know and fear from the Hellespont to the Indus. The king leaped down from the platform on which he had been standing. Pointing out the ringleaders of the mutiny, he ordered his guards to arrest them on the spot. By some accounts, Alexander seized the instigators with his own hands. Thirteen soldiers were arrested immediately and executed without delay.

To the rest of the Macedonians Alexander then made an impassioned speech, telling them to go wherever they wanted. At the Hyphasis he had endured Coenus' long speech; now the Macedonians would have to listen to his side of the story. He reminded them that his father had found them a tribe of impoverished vagabonds, most dressed in skins, pasturing a few sheep and fighting (without much success) to keep them from their neighbors, the Illyrians, the Triballians, and the Thracians. Philip had made the Macedonians dwellers of cities, annexed Thrace, subjected Thessaly to Macedonian rule, and humbled the Phocians.

The men of Thebes and Athens, who once had exacted money or obedience from the Macedonians, now looked to them for their salvation. Philip had put everything in the Peloponnese into order, and when he was made supreme leader of all Greece for the war against Persia, he had won this glory not for himself alone, but for the Macedonian people.

Yet the services of his father were small compared with his own: he had inherited a handful of gold and silver cups, and less than sixty talents in the treasury; there was eight times that amount in debts. He had had to borrow a further 800 talents. Nevertheless, his cavalry had crushed the satraps of Darius at the Granicus and made the Macedonians the masters of the gold of Lydia, the treasures of Persia, and the wealth of India. From all this, what was left to Alexander was only the purple—and the diadem.

Alexander then asked if any man believed that he had suffered more for Alexander than Alexander had for him. He challenged them to strip and show their wounds; he would show his. No part of his body save his back was without scar. He bore the mark of every weapon a man could grasp or fling.

Through every land and sea, across rivers, mountains, and plains, he had led them, a victorious army.

He had married as they had married.

He had paid their debts.

The dead had been given illustrious burials. Their parents were held in high honor, and had been freed of all taxes and services. Now he had it in mind to dismiss men no longer fit for service.

They wished to desert *him*? Let them go. But when they returned home, they should tell all that they had deserted their king, who had crushed everyone, and left him at the mercy of the barbarians they themselves had conquered. When these things were announced, they would win praise among men and a reputation for piety among the gods.

He then ordered them out of his sight.

And with that, Alexander sprang from the speaker's platform and hurried into the palace, where he remained secluded for two days, unwilling to eat, wash, or permit any visitors to enter his quarters.

Yet the men did not budge.

On the third day Alexander sent for the most select Persian officers and divided among them the commands of the brigades. Only those designated as his relatives were now allowed to give him the customary kiss.

On the surface, the situation on the third day of the mutiny at Opis resembled the state of affairs at the Hyphasis. Alexander had announced his policy, and the men had balked. As before, Alexander had retreated to his quarters to sulk and wait. But there were crucial differences in 324. Now the Successors were present and fully trained. The Macedonians really could be replaced. Nor was there now a Coenus around, an officer respected by all in the army, who could give voice to the demands of the rank and file.

Alexander knew all of this. This time, Alexander was not bluffing. He could conquer Arabia without most of the Macedonians. No face-saving sacrifice to the gods was needed. The king had decided, and his decision was final.

When the ranks heard that commands were being given to Persian officers, that foreign troops were being drafted into Macedonian units, that a Persian Corps of Guards was being called by a Macedonian name, that the Persian infantry was being given the title of foot-companions, and that there was to be a brigade of Persian Silver Shields and mounted Companions, and even a (Persian) Royal Squadron (*agema*), they broke. Running all together at the double to the palace, they threw down their arms, offered to give up the leaders of the mutiny, and swore that they would not move by day or night until the king took some pity on them.

Alexander hastened out to meet them and stepped forward to speak, with tears in his eyes. But one of the soldiers, Callines, an officer of the Companion cavalry notable for his age and rank, anticipated him.

"O king," he cried, "this is what hurts the Macedonians, that you have made Persians your kinsmen—Persians are called 'Alexander's kinsmen' and they are allowed to kiss you. But no Macedonian has tasted this honor."

"But all of you," Alexander interjected, "I regard as my kinsmen, and so from now will I call you."

Thereupon, the old veteran Callines came up and kissed Alexander. And so did all the others who wished to. The Macedonians then picked up their weapons and went back to the camp, shouting and singing the victory paean.

But, of course, it was Alexander who had won the garland of victory. Kissing your kinsman was, as Callines implied, a Persian custom. Moreover, kissing the king after performing prostration was part of the Persian court ceremonial that Alexander had been forced to abandon when he was in Bactria years before. Now the Macedonians were only too happy to receive a kiss from Alexander. Unlike Callisthenes, none would now go away the poorer by a kiss, but some surely would go away, just as Alexander intended.

THE BANQUET AT OPIS

To mark the restoration of harmony—or his triumph over his men—Alexander offered sacrifice to the gods and then gave a public banquet, at which he sat among all the Macedonians. Next to the Macedonians the Persians had their places, and next to the Persians, "any of the other tribes who had precedence in reputation or any other quality." No fewer than 9,000 people attended.

At the banquet Alexander and those around him drank from the same bowl and poured the same libations, following the lead of the Greek seers and the Persian Magi. Alexander prayed for other good things and also for harmony and fellowship of rule between the Persians and the Macedonians. They all poured one libation and followed it by the paean of victory.

Some have inflated this banquet into a kind of international lovefest, organized by Alexander to celebrate the unity of mankind. But it was nothing of the sort. Rather, it was carefully organized first of all to reconcile the Macedonians to Alexander. The Macedonians were the ones who sat around Alexander, and they dipped their wine from the same bowl and poured libations, following the lead of the Greek and Persian priests.

The guests were seated separately first by ethnicity and then by merit. Ethnic groups were not intermingled at the banquet. Alexander also did not pray for the unity or brotherhood of mankind generally. Rather he prayed for harmony and fellowship of rule between the Persians and the Macedonians alone. In other words, this was a prayer for joint imperial hegemony. Alexander was not Woodrow Wilson, and the banquet at Opis was not the foundation of an ancient League of Nations.

Nor does the evidence for what happened at the banquet support the idea that Alexander believed in the unity or equality of mankind. Rather, as we have seen, he believed that Zeus was the father of all mankind and made the best particularly his own. Like Zeus, Alexander at Opis signified his clear preference for the Persians among the rest of humanity, after the Macedonians. They were the best among the barbarians, and Alexander was now making them especially *his* own. As for the rest of Zeus' sons, they were fit to be ruled by the Macedonians and the Persians. That was the kind of unity Alexander had in mind.

At the same time, Alexander's prayer that the Macedonians and the Persians share imperial rule was quite extraordinary. In Alexander's world, the notion that a conqueror might share rule with the conquered on something approaching an equal basis was virtually unprecedented. Ironically, it was precisely Alexander's willingness to adopt the customs of the conquered, and then to share rule over his empire with them, that had led to his alienation from many of his Macedonian officers and troops.

"NINE MONTHS' LODGING"

After the banquet of reconciliation, 10,000 Macedonians too old for service or somehow unfit were discharged, at their own requests. They were given their pay to date and for the time they would take on their way homeward. They also received a gratuity of one talent.

Alexander also ordered that the children (by Asian wives) of these discharged men should remain in Asia, to avoid trouble back home. For while the Persians might have to accept the children of Macedonian and Greek men with Persian and Median women, the Macedonian families of his soldiers might not make their new family members welcome. Alexander pledged that when these children had grown up he would personally lead them back to Macedonia and hand them over to their fathers.

Craterus, Alexander's most loyal follower, was instructed to take the veterans home. Once there, he was ordered to assume charge of Macedonia, Thrace, and Thessaly, and secure the freedom of Greece. Antipater was to bring out fresh drafts of Macedonians to replace the men sent home.

That order was variously interpreted at the time. On the one hand, Alexander clearly was building up his forces for his next campaign, and the new troops Antipater was supposed to bring out to Asia with him would have been vital to those plans. But because relations between Antipater and Olympias in Macedon had deteriorated notably in Alexander's absence, his order to Antipater also gave rise to the rumor that Alexander was falling under the spell of Olympias' slanders against the regent in Macedon.

Indeed, it appears that Antipater and Olympias had been writing letters to Alexander complaining about each other for years. Antipater had written to Alexander criticizing Olympias' willful nature, her sharp temper, and her constant interference. That Alexander was not completely unsympathetic to this point of view may be inferred from Alexander's famous remark at the time that Olympias was charging him a high price for his nine months' lodging in her womb.

For her part, Olympias complained about Antipater's arrogance, about his forgetting who had put him in his position, and about his expecting to assume every kind of precedence among the other Macedonians and Greeks.

Whatever Alexander made of the war of missives, no deed or word could be attributed to Alexander from which one could conclude that Antipater was not held as high as ever in Alexander's estimation. In fact, Arrian suggests that Alexander may have wanted to get Antipater away from this corrosive situation before he (Alexander) was unable to do anything about the rift between his mentor and his mother.

It is also true, however, that Antipater did not come out immediately to Alexander, as he had been ordered to do. Instead he sent his son Cassander to Babylon. Alexander treated him with such ferocity that Cassander was left with a permanent case of the shakes. Years after Alexander's death, even the sight of an image of Alexander nearly gave Cassander a nervous breakdown.

Whether Antipater's delay was a sign of disloyalty, or perhaps of fear, is difficult to judge. However, the insecurity of his position can be judged by the fact that after Alexander died a story was spread that he and his son Iollas, Alexander's cup-bearer, had been part of a conspiracy to poison the king. This tale may have been invented for political reasons years after Alexander's death by enemies of Antipater and his family. But it would not have been an effective piece of political propaganda unless it was grounded in some kind of reality, namely, the belief that relations between Alexander and Antipater were not as friendly in 324 as they once had been. After Alexander's prolonged absence both men were wary of each other.

With no sign of Antipater, Alexander and his army therefore prepared to move from the heat of Opis to the higher elevations of the Zagros, to spend the autumn at Ecbatana (Hamadan), the summer capital of the Persian kings.

CHAPTER 28

Future Plans

THE DEATH OF HEPHAESTION

In Ecbatana, Alexander sacrificed and held another one of his festivals. As usual, this festival included athletic and artistic contests, as well as more drinking bouts with his companions. For the artistic contests, 3,000 "Artists of Dionysos" arrived from Greece. These were itinerant Greek actors and musicians, organized in guilds, who traveled around Greek cities from the early to mid-fourth century, performing ancient Greek dramas for civic and royal sponsors.

At the time of this festival (perhaps October) Hephaestion came down with a fever. Being a young man used to a soldier's life, he could not bear to remain on the strict diet recommended by his physician, Glaucius. As soon as Glaucius went off to the theater, Hephaestion helped himself to a meal. He ate a boiled fowl and washed it down with a great cooler of wine. His fever then rose quickly. Alexander, who had been attending a race, rushed to his side on the seventh day of his illness, but was too late. Hephaestion already was dead.

Alexander's grief knew no bounds. One of Alexander's companions once had remarked that Craterus was loved by Alexander no less than Hephaestion, but Alexander was reported to have replied that while Craterus was king-loving, Hephaestion was Alexander-loving. Hephaestion was Alexander's closest male friend, probably his lover, another Alexander, in Alexander's own words.

Alexander ordered the manes and tails of all horses and mules shorn and the battlements of all neighboring cities demolished. According to some reports, he also crucified Glaucius—because he either gave Hephaestion the wrong dose of medicine or because he did nothing when Hephaestion kept on drinking heavily—and forbade the playing of any music until an oracle from Ammon arrived permitting him to honor Hephaestion and to sacrifice to him as a hero. With a view to their own futures, many of Alexander's Companions dedicated themselves and their arms to Hephaestion. Eumenes of Cardia, who had quarreled with Hephaestion, prudently initiated at least some of these gestures of mourning.

Alexander planned a funeral pyre for Hephaestion in Babylon at a cost of at least 10,000 talents, and he ordained a period of mourning throughout the East. The funeral pyre as planned would have been something of an architectural and artistic monstrosity: it was designed as a kind of huge brick cube, a stadium square, over 200 feet high. Its base was to be surrounded by the prows of five-oared galleys and its upper walls decorated with five successive friezes.

Perhaps fortunately for our estimation of Alexander's taste in architecture—not to mention the reputation of its architect—this monstrous edifice probably was never begun, let alone completed. Indeed, after Alexander's own death the plans for Hephaestion's pyre and other projects on a similar scale were revealed to the Macedonian troops by Perdiccas, probably with a view to undermining anyone's desire to carry them out.

ALEXANDER'S "LAST PLANS"

Some scholars have dismissed Alexander's "last plans" as forgeries or at best exaggerations of Alexander's future projects. Did he really intend to build a thousand warships larger than triremes for his campaign against the Carthaginians, the Libyans, and the coastal region up to Sicily? To build a military road along the same coast up to the Pillars of Herakles? To erect six temples, each costing 1,500 talents, in Delos, Delphi, Dodona, Dium, Amphipolis, and Cyrnus? To establish cities and transplant populations from Asia to Europe and Europe to Asia? To build in Ilium (Troy) a temple to honor Athena that could never be surpassed by any other? To erect a pyramid in honor of his father, Philip, to match the greatest of the pyramids in Egypt?

But it is naïve to dismiss these projects on the grounds of their size and expense. Alexander never had done anything by half measures, and in 324 he had the financial and human resources to do whatever he wanted. He was the richest and most powerful man in the history of the world up to that point in time. Tens of thousands of men and women in Asia and Europe waited on his every word. He was already living on an unprecedented scale. Alexander's personal "tent" (really an enormous pavilion) contained a hundred couches and was supported by fifty golden uprights. The canopies that stretched out over the top of the pavilion were elaborately embroidered with gold. Inside, Alexander was guarded by 500 Persian "Apple Bearers" dressed in purple and quince yellow. A thousand bowmen wearing mantles in flame color, crimson, and dark blue stood next to them, and at the head of these stood 500 of the "Silver Shields," Macedon's elite infantry warriors. In the center of the tent stood a chair of pure gold on which Alexander sat holding court, with his bodyguard stationed close on all sides. Modern professional athletes and rock stars can only dream of living the way Alexander did during the last few years of his life.

Before Alexander conquered the Persian empire and marched to the Indus River, no one would have believed that a young Macedonian king and his army could overthrow history's largest empire within a few years. Yet they had done it. To dismiss Alexander's plans outright, however extravagant they seem, makes little sense. Nor do we even know that these plans were Alexander's "last," except in the sense that he died after making them.

Alexander had done what no one else had ever done, and he intended to continue his conquests until his empire extended over all the earth ruled by his father Zeus. He too was aware that "he was a man like no other man." Having survived against all the odds after repeatedly taking terrible risks in desperate battles, he could have had no doubt but that he was beloved of some god, or perhaps of all of them. His future projects were intended to exemplify his unprecedented and unique accomplishments and position in the histories of Europe and Asia. There is no reason to doubt that at his age—he was not yet thirty-three years old—and given all he already had accomplished, he had these and many other equally fantastic aims in mind.

EMBASSIES AND THE EXILES' DECREE

Whatever were his future plans, in the winter of 324–23, after the death of his dearest friend, Alexander returned to what he personally did better than any man in history: conquer. To lighten his sorrow, according to one hostile tradition, Alexander subdued the tribe of the Cossaeans, massacring the whole male population from the young men upward, as a sacrifice to the spirit of Hephaestion. More likely, he did what he did because he was unwilling to put up with the semi-independence of these tribes, who controlled the direct route between Ecbatana and Susa, a strategically important road within his empire. Whatever his motive, in action the king showed he had not altered his trademark procedures of striking rapidly, finishing the job quickly (within forty days), and then founding cities at strategic points within his newly conquered possessions.

Alexander and his court then began to make their way to Babylon. On his way he was greeted by embassies from Libya and from the Bruttians, Lucanians, and Etruscans in Italy. Carthage also sent a delegation. Others came from the Ethiopians, the European Scythians, the Celts, and the Iberians.

The peoples of the western Mediterranean had especially pressing reasons to seek Alexander's favor. This was true of the Carthaginians, in particular; the assistance they had promised Tyre during the siege of that city years earlier must have seemed in retrospect an embarrassing and potentially fatal mistake. The Indians had been annihilated, Alexander was back, and Carthage lay along the route of Alexander's planned conquest of the western Mediterranean. He never forgot anyone who crossed him. His forgiveness extended only to old friends and, like most gifts, could be redeemed just once. After that, Alexander's response invariably was lethal. The Carthaginians had every reason for concern.

Later, after Alexander entered the city of Babylon, Greek delegations came to him to offer him the victor's crowns and to congratulate him on his many victories, especially those in India. In fact, so many deputations appeared that Alexander had to make a list of them and arrange a schedule of audiences.

First, in order of the importance of their sanctuaries, the king heard those ambassadors who came on matters concerning religion—yet another indication of Alexander's priorities. Alexander dealt with the Eleians, then the Ammonians, next the Delphians, then the Corinthians, the Epidaurians, and the rest.

Second, he saw those who brought gifts. Third, he received those who had disputes with their neighbors. Fourth came those who had problems concerning themselves alone. Finally, we are told, he listened to those who wished to present arguments against receiving exiles back.

Only this last group of embassies presented serious political or potential military problems. From Diodorus, we know that Alexander, by a letter read at the Olympic Games in early August 324, had announced the restoration of exiles throughout the Greek world (except the Thebans) and the restoration of the exiles' confiscated property. His motive appears to have been a mixture of desire for glory, as he himself claimed, as well as political gain, for the returned exiles naturally would become his partisans in their cities. The only exceptions, besides the one for Thebes, applied to exiles judged guilty of sacrilege or, possibly, murder. Antipater had been ordered to enforce the decree.

Nevertheless, the beginning of the return of these exiles had caused unrest in many cities, and nearly war with the city of Athens, whose settlers on the island of Samos would be replaced by returning Samians if the decree were enforced.

The embassies that came to Alexander in Babylon about the Exiles' Decree were there, however, only to discuss how it affected their own cities or situations, not to debate the constitutionality of the decree itself. Alexander's publication of the decree clearly indicates that he no longer saw himself merely as the leader (*hegemon*) of a pan-Hellenic league (the League of Corinth) that was theoretically a body of autonomous equals, as his father, Philip, had intended the alliance to be seen. That idea had died long ago, after the murder of Darius. Alexander was now the king of all Asia—and of Hellas too, in effect, although this was not stated openly. The publication of the Exiles' Decree was really a taste of the power Alexander now felt confident enough to exercise throughout his empire.

To the envoys who approached him the king now paid honors. He also gave to them the statues, images, and other votive offerings that Xerxes had removed from Greece, including the bronze statues of the so-called Athenian tyrant slayers, Harmodius and Aristogeiton, and the Celcaean Artemis (which were returned to Athens). Harmodius and Aristogeiton, as we have seen, were wrongly believed by many Athenians to have slain the last of the Athenian tyrants during the late sixth century and thus to have laid the foundations for the development of the Athenian democracy. The irony of the return of these statues of two heroes of the Athenian democracy by a Macedonian king, who now was the ruler not only of Persia but of Greece as well, cannot have been lost upon the Athenians.

Aristus and Asclepiades declare that a certain small city in central Italy also sent envoys to Alexander at this time. When Alexander discerned the orderliness of the envoys and their diligence and freedom and learned about their constitutions, he prophesied something of their future greatness. Or, alternatively and somewhat more ominously, it was also reported that, as part of his future plans of conquest, Alexander intended to make for Sicily and the Iapygian coast, being rather distressed already at the extension of Rome's fame.

PROPHETS' BEST GUESSES

Before Alexander received all these embassies, however, there were suggestions that the king should look after his own well-being. After Alexander crossed the Tigris, but before he had even entered Babylon, priests of Bel came to him and advised him to halt his advance to Babylon. They had an oracle from their god, they claimed, that his approach to Babylon at the time would lead to disaster. Alexander replied to the priests with a line from a now lost play of Euripides: "Prophets are best who make the best guess."

Hearing this, the priests urged him at least not to look toward the west, nor to lead his army westward, but rather to wheel his force and lead it eastward.

Alexander, however, suspected that the priests were less concerned with his health than with their own self-interest. Xerxes, it was alleged, had razed the temple of Bel, and Alexander intended to rebuild it on a larger scale. But the Babylonian "contractors" had pursued the rebuilding languidly, and Alexander proposed to complete the work. The priests, Alexander perhaps believed, were worried that he would compel them to subsidize the reconstruction of the temple from their own surplus revenues.

Despite his suspicions concerning the priests' motives, Alexander nevertheless attempted to avoid entering the city from the west. But this proved to be too difficult for the army. Because of swampy land and pools around the other approaches, Alexander with the army finally entered the city from the west after all.

PREPARATIONS IN BABYLON

In Babylon the most important item on Alexander's agenda was the detailed preparation for the next campaign. Nearchus, with his fleet, already had been summoned up the Euphrates to Babylon. Two Phoenician quinqueremes (in which the upper and middle oars were rowed by two men, the lower by one man), three quadriremes, twelve triremes, and thirty thirty-oared galleys also had been disassembled on the Phoenician coast, brought overland to Thapsacus, and sailed down the Euphrates.

But Alexander was having a new flotilla built as well, using the cypresses of Babylonia. To accommodate this enormous fleet of 1,000 warships, the harbor of Babylon was being dredged. At the same time, Miccalus of the city of Clazomenae was sent to Phoenicia and Syria with 500 talents with which to hire or purchase men familiar with the sea.

These naval preparations were to be directed against the Arabs, ostensibly because they alone of the barbarians had sent no delegation or done anything complimentary to pay honor to Alexander. But the wealth of the country was also an incentive, particularly its cassia, its frankincense and myrrh, and its cinnamon and nard. Alexander also had heard that Arabia had harbors everywhere suitable for his fleet, which also might provide sites for prosperous new cities.

Finally, Alexander had heard that the Arabs worshipped only two gods, Uranus and Dionysos. Since he had achieved even more famous deeds than Dionysos, Alexander did not think it inappropriate to provide the

Arabs with a third god for their small pantheon: himself. But in truth, of course, as Arrian understood, Alexander simply was insatiate for further conquest.

In assessing Alexander's plan to conquer Arabia, some historians have supposed that, after the march across Gedrosia and the death of Hephaestion, Alexander really had no purpose left and that there was nothing left worth doing, as far as Alexander was concerned.

But planning the invasion of Arabia was not the activity of a man in the depths of despair. There is no evidence that Alexander had lost his mind, that his mental capacities had deteriorated in any way, or that he had lost his desire to go on by 324/3.

What is incredible and indisputable is rather that after all of the battles he already had fought; after all the miles he and the Macedonians had marched together; the drunken brawls; the wounds; the deaths of Philotas, Parmenio, Cleitus, Bucephalas; the mutinies; Gedrosia; and the loss of his best friend, Alexander's fundamental desire to conquer was undiminished and unchanged. But he had always conquered to live, and there was no end in sight.

If the plan were mad, it had ever been thus, and Alexander now approached the next phase of his grand plan with the same care that he had devoted to the conquest of the Persian empire and India.

FINAL TOUCHES

The gigantic fleet was put together and exploratory expeditions to the islands of Icarus (Falaika) and Tylos (Bahrain) were made by the famous pilots Archias and Androsthenes. Androsthenes in fact ended up sailing around a part of the Arabian Peninsula. A third shipmaster, Hieron of Soli, was instructed to go even farther, circling the entire peninsula as far as Heröopolis on the Red Sea; but he turned back, reporting that the peninsula was of tremendous size, nearly as big as India, and that a great headland ran far out into the ocean.

But even the conquest of Arabia was only stage one of the larger enterprise. Alexander also commissioned Herakleides of Argos to explore the shores of the Caspian in furtherance of Alexander's wider goal of linking his eastern conquests to his European empire.

While the great fleet was assembling, Alexander also busied himself and his men clearing the canals of the Euphrates and founding the last of his Alexandrias after sailing down the Pallacopas (a canal leading off from the Euphrates) to the Arabian lakes. This city lay in what is now Kuwait and was populated by Greek mercenaries, volunteers, and super-annuated or unfit veterans.

Back in Babylon, the fleet was exercising constantly, with frequent rowing races and trials of skill for the helmsmen. The land invasion force was also mustering. Peucestas had brought 20,000 troops from Persia, including the Cossaeans (conquered just the year before) and Tapurians. Philoxenus had brought an army from Caria. Menander led troops from Lydia, and Menidas came with his cavalry.

The Persians, with whom Alexander intended to rule over his empire in harmony and fellowship, now were enrolled in various Macedonian brigades, so that the Macedonian line of infantry soldiers consisted of a Macedonian leader and two of his countrymen, twelve Persians, and then another Macedonian. Thus the Macedonians lined up first, second, and last in a line, with twelve Persians in between. These infantry lines provided the momentum behind the three ranks of pikemen at the front of the phalanx. Alexander had successfully incorporated Persians into the traditional Macedonian infantry brigades.

All was in readiness. More delegations from Greece then presented themselves, wearing ceremonial crowns. These delegates solemnly ap-proached Alexander and adorned him with gold crowns, as if they had come as sacred ambassadors to honor a god. Whether they (or their cities) signified by the wearing of such crowns that they actually believed Alexander to be a god (as he clearly was conceived of in some Greek cities by 323) is a vexed, and perhaps unanswerable, question. In Sparta, apparently in response to Alexander's own order that the Greeks should vote on declaring him to be divine, the Spartans passed a decree saying, "Since Alexander wishes to be a god, let him be a god." More seriously, we know that in Athens the politician Demades certainly had proposed a decree declaring Alexander a god. Whatever the envoys or the Atheni-ans believed about Alexander, or whatever the king thought about him-self, however, the end was not far off.

CHAPTER 29

Death in Babylon

THE EVE OF DESTRUCTION

By late spring of 323, Alexander was back in Babylon, receiving delegates from the Libyans and the Carthaginians. A massive armada had been built for his Arabian campaign, and a formidable land army of mixed Macedonian and Persian infantry had been mustered.

After his planned conquest of Arabia, Alexander had his eye trained on the western Mediterranean. The shores of the Caspian and the Black Sea also had been designated for exploration. The purpose of these exploratory missions was to lay the foundation for further military campaigns, leading to the eventual unification of Alexander's Asian and European empires.

Although Alexander had been wounded in battle eight times, had lost his best friend, and was drinking heavily, his appetite for conquest had only been whetted by his already unprecedented victories. Lawrence of Arabia was shattered by the revelation that he enjoyed giving and receiving pain. The inner citadel of Alexander's self-esteem was never punctured by the wounds he either dealt out or received. Alexander was not a broken man in the spring of 323. The real question was whether he was only a man, either in his own eyes or in others'.

Then, only a few days before the conquest of the rest of the known world was to begin, the god died.

Alexander's death, just as some Greek cities were about to accord him divine honors, is every bit as controversial as his life. That was probably to be expected. Alexander never gave himself or anyone else any rest while he was alive. Why should we have expected him to have gone gentle into that good night—or to have left us with a clear understanding of what, or who, finally conquered a man who could not be killed on any field of battle? Of course, Alexander's death, like Mozart's, is steeped in mystery, and the ancient sources are in irrevocable disagreement about its causes. Moreover, it almost inevitably attracted to it the charge that Alexander had been poisoned, not by some jealous Macedonian Salieri, but by the greatest philosopher in Western history, none other than his old tutor, Aristotle. For many, the appeal of a murder mystery in which the West's greatest conqueror was done in by its greatest philosopher has proved to be irresistible. But does it have any support from the evidence?

THE STORY OF THE FEVER

One tradition about Alexander's death was based upon the so-called *Royal Diaries*, in which his royal secretary, Eumenes of Cardia, and Diodotus of Erythrae supposedly recorded Alexander's daily activities. After Alexander's death the *Royal Diaries* were made public to document the course of the fever that reportedly killed him.

The story of the fever began as follows. Alexander gave a splendid banquet in honor of his Cretan friend Nearchus, the admiral of his fleet. After the banquet Alexander took a bath with the intention of going to bed. But a man named Medius from Larissa invited the king to come to his house to join another party, and there was drinking all through the next day. Alexander began to feel feverish while he was still at Medius' party.

On the eighteenth of the Macedonian month of Daisios (late May), according to the diaries, Alexander slept in a bathing room because of his fever. After taking a bath the next day the king moved to his bedchamber, where he spent the day playing dice with Medius. When it was late, Alexander took another bath, performed sacrifices to the gods, and ate a little, but remained feverish through the night. On the twentieth he bathed again, made his customary sacrifice, and, lying down on the floor of the bathing room, listened to Nearchus tell the story of his voyage and the great sea.

On the twenty-first of Daisios, Alexander spent the day in the same way, but was more inflamed and at night was grievously ill. The following day his fever was also very high. By the side of the bath the king nevertheless conversed with his officers about vacant posts in the army, and how they might be filled by experienced men.

On the twenty-fourth Alexander's fever was violent and he had to be carried to perform his sacrifices. He ordered his greatest officers to wait in the court of the palace (probably the palace of Nebuchadnezzar) and the commanders of brigades and companies to spend the night outside. The next day he was carried to the palace on the other side of the river, where he slept a little, but his fever did not lessen. When the chief officers came to his bedside on the twenty-fifth and twenty-sixth, he was speechless.

Because it seemed to the Macedonians that he was dead, they came to the doors of the palace shouting, and insisted on seeing him. They threatened the Companions until all opposition was broken. When the doors were thrown open to them, one by one, without military cloaks or armor, the soldiers slowly filed by Alexander's couch. On this day, too, the officers Python and Seleucus were sent to the temple of Serapis to ask whether they should bring Alexander there. The god replied that they should leave Alexander where he was. Alexander then died on the twenty-eighth of Daisios (June 10), toward the evening.

Arrian based his account of Alexander's illness and demise on the *Royal Diaries*, but provides some significant additional details. The first is that a few days into his illness Alexander instructed his officers to prepare to march three days later and told the fleet to set out the day after that. The invasion of Arabia, in other words, was imminent.

From Arrian we also learn that when the Macedonians came to see Alexander, although the king could not speak, he raised his head, with difficulty, and signed to them with his eyes. So he was not completely unconscious at the time.

Finally, Arrian gives a fuller account of the episode of the temple of Serapis: seven of Alexander's officers kept an all-night vigil, asking the god whether it would be better for the king to be moved into the temple and, after prayer, to be healed by the god. An oracle was given by the god that he should not be brought into the sanctuary, but that it would be better for him to remain where he was. This oracle the companions announced (and apparently followed). Alexander breathed his last shortly thereafter. The "better" thing for Alexander (according to the story preserved in Arrian) thus turned out to be death. After recounting this anecdote, Arrian states that the histories of both Ptolemy and Aristobulus ended here, but also tells us what other writers claimed were Alexander's last words.

When Alexander was very near death, his companions asked him to whom he wished to leave his empire. Alexander replied in Greek, *"to kratisto."*

It was left to the living to figure out whether Alexander meant "to the best man," or "to the strongest man": the translation of the prepositional phrase in Greek was ambiguous.

Alexander added that he knew very well that all his leading friends would stage a great contest in honor of his funeral. Craterus, Perdiccas, and the other great marshals of his empire, in other words, would fight to succeed Alexander and to rule his empire. Perdiccas then asked when Alexander wished divine honors to be paid to him. Alexander replied that he wanted them when they were happy. These were Alexander's last words. Alexander then died.

Such is the story about the death of Alexander that Plutarch and Arrian relate, and claim they believe, on the basis of the daily diary of Alexander's activities during the last few weeks of his life. Essentially, Alexander died of a fever, to which he succumbed only gradually.

THE STORY OF THE MURDER

But Plutarch and Arrian also report another tradition about Alexander's death, by which Alexander was murdered by a group of his officers and former friends. Diodorus and Justin naturally follow the more sinister story. Given Justin's overall picture of Alexander, it is hardly surprising that he believed the murder story: how else could a tyrant like Alexander have died, except by assassination?

Be that as it may, in fact the murder story agrees with the narrative of the *Royal Diaries* up to a point. In this version, Alexander went along to the party at Medius' house. But then, and here is where the traditions about Alexander's death differ fundamentally, at Medius' party Alexander drank much unmixed wine in commemoration of the death of Herakles. Perhaps inspired by the wine, Alexander is said to have acted from memory a scene from the *Andromeda* of Euripides. He then drank to the health of all twenty guests at the dinner party and received the same number of toasts in return. Finally, raising a huge beaker of wine, Alexander downed it in a single gulp. Instantly, the king shrieked aloud as if an arrow had pierced his liver. His friends then took him back to the royal apartments.

Alexander cried out because he had been poisoned. According to this tradition, it was Aristotle himself who advised Antipater, Alexander's regent back in Macedon, to arrange the murder, and it was thanks to Aristotle that the poison itself was obtained. The obvious motive was Alexander's destruction of Aristotle's kinsman Callisthenes, not to mention the rest of Alexander's tyrannical acts. Antipater, of course, had been terrified by his order to appear before Alexander.

The poison was water, procured from a cliff near the town of Nonacris in northern Arcadia; it was so cold and pungent that it could be stored only in the hoof of an ass. Once it had been brought secretly to Babylon, it was administered to Alexander at Medius' party by the king's royal cupbearer, Iollas, one of Antipater's sons and Medius' lover.

Thereafter (according to a pamphlet that eventually found its way into the medieval Alexander Romance, but was based upon some kind of narrative written within ten years of Alexander's death) Alexander returned to his house and asked for a feather to tickle his throat so that he would vomit up the wine. Iollas smeared a feather with poison and gave it to Alexander. Alexander then endured a night of agony and the next day sent everyone out, hoping to get some rest.

When night fell, Alexander, knowing that he was doomed, tried to kill himself by throwing himself in the Euphrates but was stopped by his wife, Roxane. The next day the Macedonians rioted and insisted upon seeing Alexander, who was writing out his will. When he had finished that and a letter to Olympias, Alexander was comforted by a young man named Charmides.

Eventually the air was filled with mist and a great star was seen descending from the sky, accompanied by an eagle. The statue of Zeus in Babylon trembled. When the star ascended again, still accompanied by the eagle, and disappeared, Alexander fell into his eternal sleep.

MODERN THEORIES

While the story presented in the *Royal Diaries* appears convincing because of the details it provides about Alexander's activities over the course of the fatal illness, it unfortunately includes one glaring anachronism that calls into question whether the diaries really were a completely factual account of Alexander's death.

Specifically, the healing god Serapis apparently was largely a creation of the reign of Alexander's ex-bodyguard and officer Ptolemy I in Egypt after Alexander's death; therefore there cannot have been a temple of Serapis in Babylon in 323. Thus, the detail about the vigil in the temple was a later addition to the story, added by Eumenes and his coauthor Diodotus, to help remove suspicions of foul play. The point of the anecdote was to show that the healing god had been consulted and his counsel followed; the men who were sitting in vigil had obeyed the instruction of the god. If Alexander subsequently died, it was the better thing, as the god willed it. The men named were blameless.

Indeed, the very careful attention the diaries give to the progress of Alexander's illness has suggested to some historians that the real purpose of its publication was to establish that Alexander had died of a progressive fever—in other words, that he was not murdered. The diaries exculpated those who took care of him during his illness.

But neither can the poisoning story be accepted simply at face value. Most of the poisons in use in the eastern Mediterranean during Alexander's lifetime, such as hemlock, acted quickly, causing immediate or nearly immediate death. But Alexander did not die right away, as both traditions agree. The essential feature of the poisoning story, that Alexander was poisoned by a particularly strong poison, but died over almost a fortnight, is self-contradictory.

A second problem with the poisoning story is that it apparently only appeared publicly five years after Alexander's death. Thus, the story of Alexander's murder by poison emerged exactly in the context of the vast contest to succeed him that, on his deathbed, he had predicted. Just as those who were close to Alexander in his last few days in Babylon made sure that the fever story got out to remove any suspicion of foul play on their part, the story of the poisoning may have been spread by the surviving members of Alexander's immediate family (especially Olympias) to tarnish the reputations of her political rivals after his death: Aristotle, Antipater, Cassander, Iollas, and others. To fix the blame on someone for murdering Alexander would have been a very effective piece of political propaganda during the wars that followed Alexander's death.

Neither source tradition, then, can be credited without reservation. Each story was published and circulated to achieve a political goal. Knowing they would be suspected, Antipater and his family perhaps made sure that the story of the fever was publicized as soon as possible. The poisoning story, on the other hand, was promoted years later to implicate Aristotle, perhaps some of the men who attended the dinner party of Medius, and the family of Antipater.

What we do know, however, based upon what is common to both traditions, is that whatever Alexander died of, he did not die right away. Given the supporting facts, that is, that most of the poisons in Alexander's world killed people right away and that the story of the poisoning came out only five years after his death, the fever story, or at least the natural-cause-of-death story, seems more plausible.

AUTOPSY

Guessing what kind of fever or natural cause led to Alexander's death also has become something of a contest among historians.

Some have argued for malaria, given the location of the death scene, around the swamps of Babylon; malaria remains endemic there. Others have attributed Alexander's demise to acute alcohol poisoning, brought on by years of heavy drinking. Alexander and his friends certainly were binge drinkers, as we have seen, and according to the diaries he often needed to sleep for two days and nights after a drinking spree. Acute alcohol poisoning, however, does not fit very well with the story of a lingering illness. If Alexander died of acute alcohol poisoning, he should have succumbed to its effects almost immediately. But he did not. Dionysos did not kill his rival.

A theory also has been advanced linking Alexander's death to the chest wound he suffered in India and to his severe grief after the death of Hephaestion. The proponents of this theory argue that these twin wounds to Alexander's chest weakened Alexander's immune system to such an extent that he became susceptible to some kind of secondary infection. Alexander, in other words, died of a broken heart.

It is an attractive idea, but Alexander's enthusiastic preparations for the invasion of Arabia suggest that while his heart may have been broken, his mind and spirit were fully intact. Alexander loved warfare even more than he loved Hephaestion.

Scholars as well as enthusiastic amateurs have made great efforts to prove their cases by citing the details found in the sources about the trajectory of Alexander's illness and arguing from parallel cases. Recently, West Nile virus has been proposed as the cause of Alexander's death because one source tells us that when Alexander stood before the gates of Babylon ravens fell dead at his feet. Ravens, however, like human beings, can die from many kinds of diseases. Undoubtedly, the game of identifying what killed Alexander, Alexander's continuing funeral games, will go on as long as the fascination with Alexander persists.

Short of finding Alexander's remains, however, and conducting comprehensive forensic tests, there is simply no way of settling the question definitively. We are unlikely to have the opportunity: after Alexander's death, his body was taken to Egypt (first to Memphis, later to Alexandria), where it was embalmed and then placed in a mausoleum called the Sema, which has disappeared without a trace.

In the last century there were no fewer than 150 archaeological excavations launched in search of Alexander's final resting place; and since the early nineteenth century there have been seven highly publicized "discoveries" of his tomb: all have turned out to be fraudulent. Alexander has taken the secret of what killed him to his lost grave.

CHAPTER 30

Alexander: Mass Murderer
or Messiah?

STALIN, HITLER, CORTÉS?

Alexander the Great should be subject to the same exacting scrutiny that historians have brought to bear upon figures such as Stalin, Hitler, and Cortés. The comparisons that have been made implicitly or explicitly between those notorious figures and Alexander are interesting, but fundamentally misleading.

Alexander was not a precursor of Stalin or Hitler. There was no "reign of terror" after Alexander returned from India comparable to what Stalin carried out in the Soviet Union. Rather, incompetent governors were replaced by Alexander because they had performed poorly. Those accused of maladministration or insurrection were tried according to customary Macedonian procedures, and if found guilty were executed with the full cooperation of the Macedonian army. Nor did Alexander ever consign tens of millions of his own countrymen to a Macedonian gulag, analogous to Stalin's forced labor camps.

As leader of the pan-Hellenic campaign to punish the Persians for their alleged crimes and sacrilege, Alexander bears responsibility for the deaths of hundreds of thousands of Greeks, Macedonians, Persians, Bactrians, Indians, and others. The campaign in India, in particular, was waged with great brutality. Alexander personally killed many men in combat, and he murdered Cleitus, one of his best officers, in a drunken rage, although that murder was not premeditated.

Alexander also was responsible for the assassination of Parmenio, though there were mitigating circumstances. After the execution of Philotas for treason it was impossible for Alexander to leave Parmenio alone in Ecbatana. Nor were Parmenio's hands completely clean. If tables had been turned, Parmenio would have sent one of Alexander's friends to assassinate him. Macedonian politics were a blood sport.

Alexander and the Macedonians did massacre and enslave Greek and Asian civilians on several occasions, usually after the victims had been accused of betraying the Greek cause or committing some crime. Often the "crimes" were linked to religious sacrilege in the past. Such justifications are not very appealing or convincing to modern readers. But unlike Genghis Khan or his generals, to cite one example, Alexander never made it a *policy* to wipe out the civilian populations of the cities or territories he conquered, as the Mongols did in the case of Nishapur (and other cities), where they killed every sentient being, including all the dogs and cats. Nor did Alexander make huge piles of his victims' skulls, as Tamerlane did.

For more than a decade Alexander fought in the front ranks of the Macedonian army. He personally charged at least three times into the serried ranks of some of the best cavalrymen on earth. At the battle of the Granicus River he was specifically targeted by some of the very best cavalrymen in the Persian army—and survived. At Issos he led the cavalry charge into the stream that separated the Macedonians from the Persians. He was the first to scale the Rock of Aornos and he was the first man up the ladder in the final assault on the stronghold of the Mallians. Alexander was not a hypochondriac like Hitler, obsessed with his own mortality.

It is no surprise that he was wounded in battle eight times; rather, it is miraculous that he survived. Of course, Alexander fought surrounded by a personal bodyguard of seven or eight of the bravest and most competent soldiers in the world. Yet once the clash of weapons began, Alexander did his own fighting. Perhaps no one has ever fought better.

Alexander never contemplated any "Final Solution" with respect to any ethnic group he encountered. The object of Alexander's campaigns was not to gather defenseless civilians into concentration camps and then to starve, torture, or gas them to death. Alexander never attempted or committed genocide against any of his enemies, whether soldiers or civilians. Nor was Alexander an ethnic fundamentalist, let alone an ethnic cleanser. Rather, Alexander incorporated his former enemies into his high command and into his army.

There is also no persuasive analogy between the campaigns of Alexander and those of Cortés. Although the Aztecs themselves were an imperial people, who relied upon a highly effective professional army to conquer their neighbors and take captives (whose hearts were often cut out to pay a debt of gratitude to the Aztec gods), the Aztecs had never invaded Spain. They had never ruled over or enslaved Spaniards, and they never had burned any of Spain's religious sanctuaries to the ground. Cortés and the conquistadors attacked an empire on the other side of the world that never had done any harm or good to the Spanish or to Spain.

Alexander and his army attacked the Persians on the grounds that the Persians had invaded the Greek mainland twice and had burned the temples on the Athenian acropolis to the ground in 480. These were facts of history. Whether they justified the belated Greek and Macedonian response is not a question that can be answered objectively.

When Alexander and his army crossed the Hellespont in 334, they challenged the army of the largest and most successful empire in the long history of great empires of the ancient Near East. The great Persian kings (Cyrus, Cambyses, Darius, Xerxes) had acquired that empire by force; and their empire, like every other one in history, was maintained by the same means, at the expense of its subjects, including many Greeks. We can, and should, study and even admire the Persian political, administrative, and cultural achievement. But we should not romanticize that achievement out of a sense of guilt, or because we have not accorded enough attention to the Achaemenids in the past.

Alexander turned out to be far better at the application of force than the Persians of his day. If Alexander is going to be criticized for acquiring his empire by force, it is a double standard not to consider how the Persians themselves came into possession of their empire and then held on to it for 200 years. Ironically, the figure with whom Alexander can be compared most profitably in the ancient world is Cyrus the Great of Persia: each conquered a vast empire; each could play the Fox as well as the Lion; each became a legend. Perhaps that is one of the reasons why

Alexander took such care to restore Cyrus' tomb after it had been vandalized. Alexander knew greatness when he saw it, and he honored it.

In sum, Alexander was not a genocidal thug like Stalin or Hitler. Nor was he a kind of ancient conquistador. Even Justin, who is invariably hostile to Alexander, noted that Alexander had kept his soldiers from ravaging Asia as they marched forward, telling them that they ought to spare their property and not destroy the very things they had come to take possession of. Self-interest was the motive for sparing Asia, but it was a motive that also profited the civilians of Asia and their property.

A PRODIGY OF WARFARE

Rather, Alexander was a prodigy of warfare. A virtuoso of violence personally, in battle Alexander recklessly exposed himself to the gravest dangers with courage beyond reason but not beyond explanation. Alexander belonged to that very select group of warriors who enjoy combat itself in the same way that some of the greatest composers in history have found their greatest fulfillment in the performance of their own masterpieces.

Alexander also possessed the luck of those who are dear to the gods. He should have been killed at the battle of the Granicus River in 334, during his very first encounter with the Persian army; or he should have died inside the mud-brick walls of the Mallian town. But Alexander was not destined to die in combat, perhaps because he was the very embodiment of ancient warfare itself, the wrath of Achilles directed against his enemies. For once, the Delphic oracle was unambiguously clear and correct: at least in battle Alexander III of Macedon really was "invincible."

Alexander's terrifying rage in battle, moreover, was the razor-sharp tip of an awesomely well-trained, experienced, and deadly force: the incomparable Macedonian army. As long as Alexander led it, the Macedonian army never was defeated in a pitched battle, even when hugely outnumbered.

In charge of that finely tempered instrument of organized violence, Alexander also showed himself to be a master strategist, logistical planner, and tactician. Although some military strategists have questioned the wisdom of Alexander's overall strategy for the conquest of the Persian empire, there can be no serious doubt about the daring originality of its conception, leaving aside consideration of the brilliance of its execution. Until Alexander conquered the Persian empire, few believed that it could be done. For scholars to assert now that Alexander should have accomplished the impossible in a different way is a bit like arguing that Edmund Hillary and Tenzing Norgay should have reached the summit of Mount Everest by a different route.

Moreover, by focusing upon the one logistical failure of the campaign, the terrible passage through Gedrosia, many historians have glossed over the most obvious fact about Alexander's conquests: the *miraculous* logistical fact that in a world completely without motorized transport (let alone air travel), Alexander personally led a reasonably well-provisioned and invariably successful army of tens of thousands of soldiers, plus pack animals and camp followers, from Macedon to India and back to Babylon on a ten-thousand-mile expedition that lasted for more than a decade. Alexander's logistical achievement is the standard by which all others in pre-modern military history are measured.

Alexander's tactics in the case of individual battles and sieges were based upon an uncanny ability to understand immediately and clearly the strengths and weaknesses of both his own and his opponents' forces in relation to the topography of the fields of battle. Within twenty-four hours of his arrival at what became the battlefields of the Granicus River, Issos, and Gaugamela, Alexander had designed troop formations (the tactical square at Gaugamela) and tactics (the pawn sacrifice at Granicus, the pinning and turning operation at the Hydaspes) exactly suited to the topography and to what he had learned about the deployment of the forces facing him. It was as if Alexander could see the impending conflict before it happened and then make the battle at least begin exactly as he envisioned it. It was a gift from the gods, developed and honed to perfection through early and repeated application. From earliest youth Alexander had been able to see what others could not see and draw the correct inferences from it. His sheer intelligence has never been fully appreciated. If his opening gambit went awry, as it did at Gaugamela, Alexander quickly adjusted. Long before Napoleon taught the war ministries of early nineteenth-century Europe how to plan in "branches," Alexander had shown Darius and the Persian army that he had a whole

treeful of secondary tactics plotted out in advance of each major encounter.

Only Napoleon ever has rivaled Alexander's extraordinary ability to
read the topography of a battlefield and then to make the tactical adjust-
ments necessary to produce victory. But Alexander never met a Persian
Duke of Wellington and never suffered an Asian Waterloo. He remains
the greatest site-reader of topography in military history. Like Napoleon's nemesis Wellington, Alexander was always there on the spot;
always read the topography for himself; and did everything else, too,
including leading the Macedonians into battle.

To win the big, pitched battles, whatever the variations of force and
topography were, and however the forces of the opposing armies were
maneuvered into contact, Alexander finally used the same tactic to
achieve victory. In the great set-piece battles of the campaign (the
Granicus, Issos, Gaugamela, and the Hydaspes), unlike virtually all
modern military general staff officers, Alexander *personally* led devastating cavalry charges into the lines of his enemies at exactly the right time,
in exactly the right place. Alexander was a master of concentrating his
forces to devastating effect. He could execute carefully planned attacks
and he could improvise on the spot. His sieges became models for later
imitators. He was the first to use catapults as field artillery. As in other
spheres of action, he broke out of the boundaries of accepted military
practice, using combinations of differently armed troops in ways never
before imagined, much less executed.

Moreover, campaigns of conquest of *entire continents* were carefully
planned, far in advance of their execution, right down to the smallest logistical detail. Long before modern military strategists had elaborated a
theoretical science of year-round military campaigning based upon
strategic principles, Alexander had perfected the practical application in
his own world. Had von Clausewitz been around during the fourth century B.C.E. to enumerate his strategic principles, Alexander might very
well have taught the German theorist some useful lessons.

Finally, once he had the taste of victory, Alexander pursued his adversaries with the relentless speed and insatiable appetite of a natural
predator. That speed allowed Alexander to double his own operative
time in action and to halve that of his adversaries. Because of Alexander's

relentless mobility he often sprang upon his enemies before they were fully aware of his presence. Even in antiquity Alexander was famous for surprising, not to say shocking, his enemies by his sudden appearances.

To those who surrendered and recognized his sovereignty, Alexander was generous to a fault; but to those who insisted upon resistance he was implacable and unmerciful. We are horrified at the sight of Alexander pouncing upon his victims; at the same time, we cannot help but watch.

Alexander was a military genius, indeed a great creative artist of warfare, the greatest conqueror in the history of Western civilization and perhaps in that of the world. His tactics, logistics, strategic vision, and leadership are intrinsically interesting and will be relevant as long as human beings practice war. But was Alexander the Great anything more than just a marvel of violence and warfare?

A MACEDONIAN MESSIAH?

Some have believed that he was a kind of messiah or forerunner of Jesus. He certainly was not a messianic or redemptive figure for all of humanity in the mold of Jesus. He was no disciple of the sixth commandment. Rather, Alexander apparently received a very different set of commandments from his gods. These were to strike quickly; to strike first; to strike with maximum force; and to follow up his lightning strikes with alacrity. Although Alexander was not a Macedonian messiah, was he nevertheless some kind of philosopher-king, sent on a mission from god to harmonize men generally and to be the reconciler of the world?

THE EMPIRE OF THE BEST

Alexander apparently believed that Zeus was the father of all mankind, as Homer, his first and most influential teacher, taught him. Greeks, Macedonians, Persians, Bactrians, and Indians all were sons of Zeus, if not loving brothers. But Alexander also believed that Zeus made the best of mankind particularly his own. These were the truths that Alexander held to be self-evident. Indeed, throughout his life he strove to prove by great, even unprecedented deeds that he was one of Zeus' very own.

Before and after every important battle or undertaking, Alexander prayed or sacrificed to the gods and goddesses of Greece and Asia, either for their support or to give thanks, and the results, victory against all odds, victory over all, victory without end, confirmed that his quest and his actions were sanctioned by the gods. Each and every triumph confirmed that Alexander indeed was among Zeus' beloved.

It was to this core belief, that the greatest of the Olympians especially loved Alexander and the best of the rest, that Alexander wished to reconcile the world. Alexander did not intend to establish the universal brotherhood of mankind. Rather, Alexander's prayer at Opis was that those apparently dearest to Zeus, the Macedonians and the Persians, might rule together in harmony and fellowship.

We should not forget that Alexander himself came from an ethnically mixed background, as Attalus himself fatally implied at the wedding of Philip II to Kleopatra. Alexander's mother, Olympias, was a Molossian princess from Epirus. Moreover, Alexander had surrounded himself with people of different ethnic backgrounds since he was a young man. His first city foundation, Alexandria in Egypt, was not an ethnically Greek city alone. His first wife was Bactrian. Two more wives were Persian. Alexander's father also had married non-Greek and non-Macedonian women, for diplomatic reasons. But Alexander married his royal Persian wives according to the custom of their country. He also installed Ada as the governor of Caria, treated the Persian noblewomen captured after the battle of Issos with restraint and magnanimity, gave a sumptuous funeral to Darius' wife Stateira, executed his own generals for their abuse of women, and kept his word to Sisygambis to see to it that her daughters married well. His treatment of women in general was extraordinary by the awful standard of mankind's history. In a recent collection of essays on the topic of rape in antiquity, Alexander's name does not appear in the index: with good reason, for Alexander despised the crime.

None of this is to suggest that the foundation of Alexander's perspective was not essentially that of a Macedonian nobleman, deeply steeped in Greek literature (especially Homer and Euripides), culture, and religion. Throughout his campaigns Alexander made regular sacrifices to the gods and organized Greek musical and athletic festivals. By these acts he showed that he saw the world through rather traditional Greek eyes. Nevertheless, in contact with the peoples of the Near East,

Alexander certainly developed a more open mind about the so-called barbarians and their customs than many of his Greek or Macedonian companions, and he was willing to accommodate himself and his empire to the best of what he found in Persia, in keeping with his fundamental principle.

Indeed, in every area of activity, in pursuit of his goal to inscribe over the whole earth his belief that Zeus made the best his very own, Alexander became a transgressor of those boundaries by which many of his contemporaries organized and defined the kind of world they wished to construct: boundaries on maps between West and East; boundaries of dress and custom among old enemies; boundaries of erotic impulses directed toward his fellow human beings; and, the final frontier, the boundaries that separated men and gods.

As Alexander swiftly and fearlessly crossed those boundaries, he outpaced many of his Greek and Macedonian companions who either could not or did not wish to keep up with a man who would never stop marching until he reached the ends of the earth over which his father ruled, and fulfilled what he clearly believed was his destiny: to conquer and rule all of Asia and Europe as a god, in harmony and fellowship with the best.

The government of Alexander's world empire would not have been one of the people, by the people, for the people; what Alexander had in mind, rather, was a world government of the best, by the best, for the best. Alexander was not a supporter of the egalitarian ideal because he did not believe that all men were created equal or that they were endowed with inalienable rights. Alexander was not a Macedonian Montesquieu or Locke. But he was a kind of proto-multiculturalist in the very limited sense that he could imagine the possibility that some of those most beloved of Zeus were not members of his own country.

Such was the world that Alexander was striving to create when he died in Babylon in June 323. His death prevented him from achieving his goal of conquering the world and establishing a world empire of the best. Did it also wipe out what he had done?

CHAPTER 31

Alexander and the
Ambiguity of Greatness

A MERE COMET?

It has become positively fashionable for historians to deny that Alexander had any historical legacies at all. Like a fiery comet, Alexander blazed across the sky at the end of the fourth century B.C.E., exploded, and then disappeared in a cloud of mythic vapor.

Such a preposterous view is a classic example, perhaps *the* classic example, of how the study of the past is influenced by contemporary trends. As war and empire became increasingly unpopular over the course of the twentieth century, so too did those who had been good at them. Indeed, Alexander's conquests seem to have become a source of embarrassment or guilt among Western historians—as historians of non-European heritage have duly noted.

War is undoubtedly bad. But human beings have always waged war. Indeed, war preceded the invention of history itself by thousands of years, if, by "history," we mean the formal, written inquiry into the past. But in Alexander's world, war was considered by many philosophers to be the normal, even natural state of human affairs. Moreover, nobody doubted how profound its effects were. War, as the sixth-century B.C.E. Ionian philosopher Heraclitus insisted, was the father of all. Peace, alas, was the childless maiden.

Those who have denied that Alexander had any real historical effects reveal more about their own attitudes and values than about Alexander and his world. Writing history according to modern values may make historians feel less guilty about their own nations' histories or superior to subjects who loom larger than life. But such an approach is anachronistic and does a disservice to the study of the past. It is also a costly disservice, because it prevents us from understanding how Alexander and his conquests continue to influence our world.

SHORT-TERM EFFECTS

If we try to set aside our own values and tendency to judge everyone in the past according to our mores, it is easy to see that Alexander's conquests had both more and less obvious short-, medium-, and long-term effects upon his own world and upon later history.

Most immediately, Alexander brought about the replacement of the main political and military authority in the Middle and Near East, the Achaemenid Persian dynasty. After Alexander, Macedonians or Greeks ruled over lands from western Asia Minor to the Indus for the first and only time in history.

Second, although Alexander's system of administering his empire was based initially upon the Persian system of administration, Alexander's conquests brought about profound changes as well. In his wake came the extension and substitution of the Greek language in place of Aramaic as the language of imperial administration from Asia Minor to India. Of equal importance, there was the foundation and spread of fundamentally Greek city-states from Alexandria in Egypt to Alexandria Eschate in modern Tajikistan, and beyond. While some of these new foundations did not survive long beyond the death of their founder, others did. Alexander projected the essential political unit of Greek civilization, the polis, all the way from Egypt into Central Asia.

Before Alexander, the essential forms of Greek civic life (ethnos and polis) and the Greek language were not widespread south and east of the Halys River in Asia Minor, except perhaps within a few isolated trading posts such as Al Mina, at the mouth of the Orontes River in northern Syria, and Naucratis, in the Nile Delta of Egypt. After Alexander, Greek civic life, as embodied especially in the polis, dominated the ancient Middle and Near East, both militarily and politically, and Greek became the language of public life. In the short term, Alexander thus transformed the military, political, and cultural map of both Europe and Asia.

MEDIUM-TERM EFFECTS

In the medium term, Alexander's effects were no less significant. Alexander was right about the funeral games after his death. His generals did stage a vast contest in his honor: they fought for decades to succeed him. Although many of Alexander's friends and generals were brilliant soldiers and administrators in their own right, none was able to reconstitute Alexander's vast empire.

But there were glittering prizes for the best of the rest: Ptolemy I and his descendants ruled Egypt down to 30 B.C.E.; Seleucus and his successors ruled Syria and the Near Eastern provinces of Alexander's empire; and Antigonus and his descendants ruled in Macedon and Greece. Eventually all of these successor dynasties would be conquered, at times reluctantly and after a "long hesitation," but, in the end, ruthlessly and comprehensively by the Romans.

Only recently have we begun to appreciate just how vigorous the politics and cultures of these successor kingdoms were. The period after Alexander's death was not one of stagnation or depoliticization. On the contrary, the so-called Hellenistic age, c. 323 to 30 B.C.E., was one of great political, religious, and cultural energy and creativity. By contact with the cultures of Alexander's successor dynasties, Roman culture itself was fundamentally transformed, as the Romans themselves explicitly recognized. All of this Alexander set in motion. How much more he might have catalyzed had he lived for only a few more years, and conquered Arabia and the western Mediterranean, can only be guessed.

LONG-TERM EFFECTS

If we look at Alexander's long-term effects, the picture is more striking still, though almost never fully appreciated. As we have seen, Alexander laid out the physical foundations of Greco-Macedonian, and subsequently Roman, civilization in the Middle and Near East, often by his very own hand. That Greco-Roman civilization dominated the eastern Mediterranean until the Arabic invasions of the seventh century c.e., but the eastern Roman empire survived in the form of Byzantium until the mid-fifteenth century, when Constantinople finally was conquered by the Ottoman Turks.

Alexander therefore was the original architect of an amalgam Greco-Roman civilization in the Near East, which endured politically for more than 1,700 years. For a mere comet, he had a long historical tail.

But Alexander's legacies may be even more enduring and profound. For it was within or on the borders of the Greco-Roman civilization that Alexander helped to establish that the three great religions of the book, Rabbinic Judaism, early Christianity, and early Islam, evolved or were born. These religions of the book ultimately evolved out of Judaism in relation to Greco-Roman civilization and its religious practices and frequently in opposition to them. To take but one example of the historical significance of those contacts and conflicts, few people seem to have reflected upon the question of how and why all of the central texts of Christianity came to be written in Greek. Or to make the point in another way, we might ask what the consequences would have been for the history of Christianity if all of its canonical texts had been written in Hebrew or Aramaic, the everyday language of Jesus and his closest disciples.

It was largely as a long-term result of Alexander's conquests that Greek became the primary language through which Christianity was spread throughout the Mediterranean world. Moreover, it was on the island of Pharos, near Alexandria in Egypt, Alexander's first and greatest foundation, that the Torah was translated into Greek, supposedly by seventy-two learned Jews from Jerusalem during the reign of Ptolemy II Philadelphus (308–246 b.c.e.). It was thus within the city whose plan Alexander himself marked out with barley-meal crumbs in the shape of a Macedonian military cloak that the Hebrew Bible was made into a book, the Septuagint, that could be read by Greeks.

Alexander's conquests laid the physical, linguistic, and cultural foundations for the contacts and conflicts between Greco-Roman polytheists and the peoples of the book. To the extent that the religious beliefs of the peoples of the book were shaped by their contacts and conflicts with the polytheists, we might say that those religions, as they are practiced today by more than three billion believers worldwide, owe more than a little to the ambitions of a Macedonian king.

As Alexander conquered the Middle and Near East, he believed that he was laying the foundations for a world empire of the best; instead he was building the civic substructure for the world empire of a god who makes redemption possible for all. History is full of ironies and unintended consequences; how Alexander's empire of the best was transformed into the empire of the redeemed is among the larger and more significant ones.

And so the oracle of Zeus Ammon may have been fulfilled, but in a different way. If Zeus Ammon told Alexander that he would remain invincible until he reached the ends of the very earth, then the oracle did not lie. Alexander's name, story, and legacies have conquered the world. Ammon never guaranteed that Alexander would be alive to see the day he conquered the world, nor did the ram-headed god reveal how he would do it. But then again, oracles are notoriously difficult to interpret. Whether the fulfillment of Ammon's oracle in this way would have at last satisfied the passionate longing of the ambiguous genius whose deeds have been described in this book can never be known.

THE AMBIGUITY OF GREATNESS

What mere mortals can know is that Alexander laid the foundations of the Greco-Roman civilization from which Western civilization eventually arose. Perhaps this is why we care so much whether Alexander was a mass murderer or a messiah. As the embarrassed or proud heirs of the civilization he helped to create, we want Alexander to be either a villain or a savior. I hope to have shown that Alexander was an ambiguous figure who combined great and admirable deeds and qualities with terrible mistakes, sporadic crimes, and lapses of judgment. Like Mozart, Alexander also disturbs our rest and reminds us that individual greatness often comes at a high price, that life indeed is fragile and uncertain, and that the interpretation of the end of the drama can be viewed from many different perspectives. But this has often been the case in history.

When he was First Lord of the Admiralty in 1915, Winston Churchill was responsible for strategic mistakes that led to the deaths of thousands of British and Anzac soldiers at Gallipoli. Between World War I and World War II, Churchill did everything possible to block self-rule by India, thereby helping to deprive hundreds of millions of Indians of political freedom. His plan to interdict the German supply of iron ore from Scandinavia in 1940 also led to disaster.

On the other hand, Churchill simply did not know how to give in to Hitler, and thereby, arguably, saved Western civilization at a time when men "considered its redemption worth any price." At the end of a recent biography of Churchill written by a former English Labour politician and historian of great distinction, Churchill was judged to be not only the greatest British prime minister of the twentieth century, but also the greatest human being ever to occupy 10 Downing Street.

On Tuesday, July 31, 1945, at 7:48 A.M., by one eleven-word message written with a lead pencil, Harry S. Truman signed the death certificates of about 130,000 Japanese civilians, who died instantly or within a few months after the first atomic bomb exploded over Hiroshima on August 5. And yet, the author of an enormous, prize-winning biography of Truman concluded that Truman "was the kind of president the founding fathers had in mind for the country. He came directly from the people. He *was* America."

The point of citing such cases is not to denigrate two great leaders of the twentieth century or to impugn the historical judgment of their biographers. It is to suggest, rather, that historical "greatness" itself is often a far more ambiguous and subjective concept than is usually appreciated, and that many great historical figures have made mistakes and caused great suffering without thereby becoming monsters. Men and women with great abilities often have possessed correspondingly great flaws and they have made terrible mistakes because, in the end, the great, just like the rest of us, finally are human beings. We must learn to live with the ambiguity of the great. If we are able to live with the ambiguity of the great, perhaps we may live better with our own. In the meantime, it may be wise to keep an eye out for eagles.

Epilogue

As we contemplate the ambiguity of greatness nearly two millennia later, Arrian's balanced judgment of Alexander is still well worth considering.

Alexander died in the hundred and fourteenth Olympiad, in the archonship at Athens of Hegesias. He lived thirty-two years and eight months, as Aristobulus says; he reigned twelve years and the aforesaid eight months. In body he was very handsome, a great lover of hardships; of much shrewdness, most courageous, most zealous for honor and danger, and most careful of religion; most temperate in bodily pleasure, but as for pleasures of the mind, insatiable of glory alone; most brilliant to seize on the right course of action, even where all was obscure; and where all was clear, most happy in his conjectures of likelihood; most masterly in marshaling an army, arming and equipping it; and in uplifting his soldiers' spirits and filling them with good hopes, and brushing away anything fearful in dangers by his own want of fear—in all this most noble. And all that had to be done in uncertainty he did with the utmost daring; he was most skilled in swift anticipation and gripping of his enemy before anyone had time to fear the event; he was most reliable in keeping promises or agreement; most guarded in not being trapped by the fraudulent; very sparing of money for his own pleasure, but most generous in benefits of others.

If, however, Alexander committed any error through haste or in anger, or if he went some distance in the direction of eastern arrogance, this I do not regard as important; if readers will consider in a spirit of charity Alexander's youth, his unbroken success, and those courtiers who associate with kings to flatter but not to improve them, and who always will so associate with kings to their harm. But I do know that Alexander alone of the kings of old did repentance for his faults, by reason of his noble nature; while most people, if they have admitted any error, by defending their misdeed, as if it were a good deed, think that they will conceal their error; and this is a great mistake. For I at least feel that the only cure for sin is a confession of sin and evidence of repentance, since the offended party will not feel the offenses so grievous if the offender agrees that he did not well; and for the man himself this good hope is left behind for the future, that he will not so offend again if he appear grieved at the errors of the past. But that he referred his birth to a god, even this I do not altogether think to be a grave fault, if it was not perhaps a mere device to impress his subjects, and to appear more dignified. In point of fact I hold him no less famous a king than Minos, Aeacus, or Radamanthus; they traced their origin back to Zeus, and yet this was not associated by men of old with any arrogance; nor yet Theseus' descent from Poseidon, nor Ion's from Apollo. Moreover, I feel that the adoption of Persian equipage was a device, both toward the Persians, so that their king might not appear wholly removed from them, and toward the Macedonians, to mark some reversion from Macedonian abruptness and arrogance; for the same reason, I suspect, he drafted into their ranks the Persian troops who carried the "golden apples" and the Persian nobles into their cavalry squadrons. And his carousings, as Aristobulus says, were prolonged not for the wine, for Alexander was no wine-bibber, but from a spirit of comradeship.

Whosoever speaks evil of Alexander, let him speak such evil, not merely by producing what deserves evil-speaking, but gathering all that Alexander did into a single whole; let such a one consider first himself, his own personality, his own fortunes, and then on the other hand Alexander, what he became, and the height of human prosperity which he reached, having made himself king, beyond all contradiction, of both continents, and having spread his fame over the widest possible span; let such a one, I say, consider of whom he speaks evil; himself being more puny, and busied about puny things, and not even bringing these to success. For I myself believe that there was at that time no race of mankind, no city, no single individual, whither the name of Alexander had not reached. And so not even I can suppose that a man quite beyond all other men was born without some divine influence. Moreover, oracles are said to have prophesied Alexander's death, and visions coming to different persons, and dreams, dreamed by different persons; there was also the general regard of mankind leading to this same conclusion, and the memory of one more than human; and even now there are other oracles, after this great gap of time, which have been delivered to the Macedonian race, and all tending to the highest estimation of him. True it is that I myself have quarreled with certain acts in my history of Alexander's deeds, but I am bold to admire Alexander himself; and those acts I blamed, both for the sake of my veracity, and also for the general benefit of mankind; and that is why I myself too took up this history, not without the help of God.

Appendix

Sources: Flacks, Hacks, and Historians

THE LOST ALEXANDER LIBRARY

Before there was a library of Alexandria, there was a library of books about Alexander. The original collection was made up of works written during and just after Alexander's lifetime. Unfortunately, all of the original volumes in the library of Alexander have disappeared; or they were taken out and never returned by writers of the Roman era, who cut and pasted quotations and information from the originals into their own books about Alexander, leaving us to figure out what the earliest works really said. The task is difficult but crucial.

To understand why the oracle of Zeus Ammon at Siwah revealed that a twenty-five-year-old Macedonian king would reach the ends of the world, we have to identify the major ancient sources for Alexander's life. We need to know who those sources are; when they lived; what they wrote; for whom they wrote or created objects; and why they wrote or made what they did. Only when we have understood the viewpoint of our sources can we assess the value of the information they have provided.

This is true whether our information comes from literary accounts or from material evidence such as inscriptions, coins, or archaeological artifacts. We can only infer who the real Alexander the Great was from what our sources have chosen to record about him and his deeds. With-out our sources, there simply is no Alexander, real or otherwise.

The ancient sources for Alexander's life can be divided up broadly into three groups: a handful of literary compositions and material evidence produced during his lifetime; about a dozen literary works belonging to the period from around 323 into the late second century B.C.E.; and, finally, about half a dozen narrative accounts written between the middle of the first century B.C.E. and the fourth century C.E.

CONTEMPORARY SOURCES

The most important contemporary literary source for Alexander's deeds is Callisthenes. Callisthenes was probably a nephew of the great philosopher Aristotle. He was selected to accompany Alexander on his campaign against the Persians and to write an account of it, which was entitled *The Deeds of Alexander.* Although the work has not survived, from the parts used by later writers we know that Callisthenes' book was eulogistic, glorifying Alexander's military achievements and his claims to divine parentage. When later authors quote from Callisthenes' work, it is important to remember that Callisthenes did not give us "just the facts," but rather what Alexander himself wanted to be known or believed about what had happened. Callisthenes was Alexander's official mouthpiece during the campaigns. For that very reason his perspective is invaluable.

Other works composed during Alexander's conquest of the Persian empire are nearly impossible to evaluate. A certain Anaximenes wrote two books titled "On Alexander" dealing with events down to the battle of the Issos (333), but only a few fragments survive. Somewhat more substantial are the fragments of Alexander's land surveyors, who went along on the expedition to measure the "stages" (distances) the Macedonians traveled.

The historical value of another contemporary document, the so-called *Ephemerides*, or *Royal Diaries*, is difficult to assess. It is purportedly a diary of Alexander's reign kept by his royal secretary, Eumenes of Cardia, and Diodotus of Erythrae; what has survived and is quoted by later authors largely focuses upon Alexander's last days and appears to confirm that he died of a fever. The evidence of the *Royal Diaries*, however, must be used with caution.

We also possess contemporary inscriptions, papyri, coins, sculpture, and archaeological artifacts that help cast light on Alexander's reign and personality. These material artifacts, however, cannot be taken at face value. "Object" does not mean "objective." Objects such as inscriptions need to be analyzed carefully with respect to their form and content before we can use them as evidence for what happened.

NEAR-CONTEMPORARY SOURCES

After Alexander's death a number of participants in the campaign wrote accounts of aspects of the expedition or histories of Alexander's reign. Included among these was Onesicritus of Astypalaea, the helmsman of the royal galley. The title of Onesicritus' lost work remains uncertain: in some sources it is called *The Education of Alexander*; in others, a history of Alexander. In antiquity Onesicritus was known as a spinner of tall tales, but he nevertheless provides intriguing evidence about the Macedonians' encounters with the so-called Gymnosophists, and for Alexander's conquests in India.

Nearchus, the son of Androtimus from the island of Crete, was one of Alexander's friends banished from Macedon by Philip II after the Pixodarus affair. Recalled after Philip's death, Nearchus commanded Alexander's fleet when it sailed down the Indus River and from the mouth of the Indus River along the coast to the mouth of the Euphrates.

Nearchus' memoirs of the campaign have not survived. From the fragments that appear in later accounts, though, we know that he emphasized the difficulties of the fleet's voyage along the sea, perhaps to enhance his own reputation at the expense of his rival Onesicritus.

Another vital source of information from the near-contemporary period is Ptolemy I, the son of Lagos (c. 367/66–283 B.C.E.). Ptolemy was made one of Alexander's personal bodyguards in the fall of 330, and subsequently was given many important commands. After Alexander's death he hijacked Alexander's body to Egypt, and established himself as satrap there. He later took on the titles of king and pharaoh and founded the Ptolemaic dynasty, which ruled Egypt until the death of Kleopatra VII, in 30 B.C.E.

Ptolemy wrote a history of Alexander's reign, although it has not survived. Among other later authors, Arrian used it extensively. We know that Ptolemy's history or memoir covered the period from at least 335 until Alexander's death. His narrative perhaps focused upon military matters.

But Ptolemy too did not simply present the "facts." Rather, he had his own agenda. He emphasized his own contributions to Alexander's success and denigrated or ignored the achievements of his rivals. In this way he justified his own political position after Alexander's death.

Another near-contemporary source of great importance is Aristobulus of Cassandreia, who took part in Alexander's expedition, perhaps in some minor capacity. Aristobulus wrote a history of Alexander's reign sometime after 301, begun when its author was eighty-four years old. Only fragments remain.

In antiquity Aristobulus was considered a flatterer, who claimed (for instance) that Alexander only drank heavily to be sociable. Nevertheless, Aristobulus' history is a vital source of information for Alexander's campaigns in India and for the details he provides about geography, botany, and local customs.

Alexander's court chamberlain, Chares of Mytilene, also wrote a (lost) *Histories of Alexander.* His work is a vital source of information about Alexander's attempted introduction of prostration at his court and about the mass marriage of his officers to Persian noblewomen at Susa in 324.

Cleitarchus of Alexandria, who did not accompany Alexander into Asia, wrote a history of his reign in at least twelve books, dated as early as 310. Cleitarchus' lost work was used extensively by authors of the late Roman republican and imperial periods. It probably formed the core of the so-called Vulgate tradition, from which Justin's epitome of Pompeius Trogus and the so-called *Metz Epitome* (a compilation dated to the late antique period that followed the same tradition as Curtius) were derived.

Cleitarchus was criticized in antiquity for inaccuracy and overembellishment. At the same time, because he did not go along on the expedition, his history was not subject to the influences of the Macedonian court, and the information he provides should be seen as an important independent perspective.

At one time there also existed various pamphlets written by contemporaries of Alexander such as Ephippus of Olynthus and Nicobule. What we know about Ephippus' pamphlet "On the Death [or "Funeral"] of Alexander and Hephaestion" is based upon five passages found in the *Deipnosophistae* ("Learned Banqueteers") of Athenaeus. Even taking into account the likelihood that Athenaeus' selection of passages from Ephippus concerns his own literary interests, we can surmise that Ephippus represented Alexander as bibulous, devoted to luxurious living, violent, and solicitous of flattery. Ephippus clearly was hostile to Alexander.

The theme of Alexander's excessive drinking, right up to his very last banquet, was taken up in a pamphlet by another writer, a woman named Nicobule, if the name, which means "the Victorious in Council" or "the Counselor of Victory," is not a pseudonym.

Alexander's drinking habits also were discussed in the *Histories* of Polycleitus, a Thessalian from the city of Larissa. Polycleitus, who probably accompanied Alexander's expedition, provided important geographical details about Alexander's campaigns, especially the rivers of Asia. From one of the fragments cited by Strabo, it is clear that Polycleitus played a role in the creation of the myth that Alexander reached the boundary of Asia.

Grouped among the flatterers of Alexander by some ancient writers was Medius of Larissa. Medius accompanied Alexander on the expedition to Asia and served as one of the *trierarchs* of Alexander's fleet on the Indus River. Most importantly, however, Medius was famous for hosting the drinking party at which Alexander either came down with the fever that killed him or was poisoned.

Hieronymos of Cardia did not take part in Alexander's expedition to Asia, and his now lost history began at Alexander's death and continued to at least the death of King Pyrrhus of Epirus (272). But his work was a particularly important source for Diodorus Siculus, who apparently duplicated Hieronymus' verbatim citation of the so-called Exiles' Decree, which Alexander issued in 324, and also gives us some invaluable information about its reception.

Finally, two writers of the third or second century B.C.E., Hegesias of Magnesia and Aristus of Salamis, should be mentioned. Hegesias was roundly criticized by writers such as Dionysius of Halicarnassus and Cicero for his bad taste in the use of rhymes, as well as for his "matter," which Cicero thought was just as absurd as his manner of speech. His work was also included among those books that were filled with "fables, things unheard of, incredible."

Aristus perhaps came from the city of Salamis on Cyprus and dates to the mid-second century B.C.E. Aristus also was interested in the drinking parties of the Macedonians and in Alexander's habit of dressing up like the god Hermes.

LATER NARRATIVE ACCOUNTS

Books 17 and 18 of Diodorus Siculus' *Bibliotheke*, or *Library*, a universal history from mythological times to 60 B.C.E., was composed closest in time to the contemporary or near-contemporary sources. The *Bibliotheke* was perhaps completed around 30 B.C.E. Cleitarchus was certainly one of Diodorus' most important sources for his information about Alexander.

Diodorus was especially interested in issues of individual and collective morality; throughout his vast work he judges individuals and nations by how benevolently they acted while enjoying good fortune. Diodorus' picture of Alexander must be understood within the framework of his history's program for moral living.

Diodorus' closest chronological contemporary, Strabo of Amaseia (Pontus) (born c. 64 B.C.E., survived until after 21 C.E.), wrote a *Geographia* in seventeen books, using Aristobulus and Nearchus as his sources from among the contemporary historians of Alexander. Book 15 of Strabo's work relies on the accounts of those Alexander historians who visited the northern parts of India.

The way Strabo interpreted Alexander's deeds reveals some Stoic overtones; Strabo also "strongly criticized historians of Alexander who distorted facts for the sake of flattery and betrayed the truth for propaganda purposes by 'moving' whole regions, such as the Caucasus, to the end of the world in order to create the impression that Alexander had reached the boundaries of the *oikoumene*."

Quintus Curtius Rufus wrote during the first or early second century C.E. (probably during the reign of the Roman emperor Claudius, 41–54). The first two books of his ten-book history of Alexander (*Historiae Alexandri Magni*), which apparently covered events down to the distribution of satrapies after Alexander's death, are lost. Curtius Rufus made extensive use of Cleitarchus and of Ptolemy. His history, while accurate in many respects, is filled with highly rhetorical speeches he could not possibly have heard and unverifiable attributions of motive.

Next we have L. Mestrius Plutarchos, known today as Plutarch, from Chaeronea in Greece, born probably before 50 C.E. and died after 120. Among other works, Plutarch wrote twenty-three parallel lives of famous Greeks and Romans. At the beginning of his life of Alexander (paired with Julius Caesar), Plutarch tells us that his object was not to create continuous political history but to exemplify virtue or vice in the careers of great men. Plutarch's life of Alexander should be read not as a factual account but as a kind of moral biography, written from the point of view of a well-read, sophisticated, and cosmopolitan inhabitant of the Roman empire who was influenced by Stoic ideals. Plutarch's moral biography of Alexander is filled with gossip and salacious anecdotes, and is particularly valuable for its chapters on his childhood.

Lucius Flavius Arrianus, Arrian for short, from Nicomedia in Bithynia, lived from about 86 to 160 C.E. and became a Roman consul (about 129) and governor (legate) of Cappadocia (131–137). The author of many important lost historical works, his *Anabasis* ("Journey Up-Country") of Alexander, in seven books, begins with Alexander's accession and ends with his death in Babylon in 323. A shorter companion work, the *Indike*, recounts Nearchus' voyage from the mouth of the Indus River to Susa, and is based upon Eratosthenes, Megasthenes, and Nearchus. For the *Anabasis*, Arrian's primary sources were Ptolemy and Aristobulus, contemporaries and friends of Alexander who had a mostly favorable view of the king. As a result, Arrian's account of Alexander's "journey up-country" focuses on military affairs and is largely sympathetic to Alexander.

Finally, of the main later narrative accounts we have Marcus Iunianus Iustinus, or Justin, the third- or fourth-century C.E. author of a Latin *epitome* (abridgment or summary) of the otherwise lost "Philippic Histories" (*Historiae Philippicae*) of Pompeius Trogus, a late-first-century B.C.E.

Vocontian from Gallia Narbonensis (Vasio or Vaison-la-Romaine) who covered Macedon in books 7–12 of his histories. Justin occasionally adds factual details about Alexander's life that no other sources report, and he presents some of those details in a way that suggests that while Alexander got his taste for strong, unmixed wine from his father, it was to his Molossian mother, Olympias, that he owed his thirst for blood.

Important evidence is also to be found in the *Deipnosophistae*, or "Learned Banqueteers," of Athenaeus from Naucratis in Egypt. This colorful work was completed in the years immediately following the death of the Roman emperor Commodus (c. 192 C.E.) and supposedly reports on discussions among guests about philosophy, literature, law, medicine, and many other topics at a banquet over a number of days during which some important events and incidents related to Alexander's life were discussed. Athenaeus provides some valuable information about the ceremonial practices and luxury of the Macedonian royal court.

FLACKS, HACKS, AND HISTORIANS

Such are the main ancient literary and material sources for Alexander's life and deeds. Among the writers who composed works while Alexander was alive or in the century after his death, there were perhaps no outright knaves. There were, however, various flacks, hacks, and party operatives, spinners of tall tales, flatterers and scandalmongers, self-aggrandizing Colonel Blimps and puritanical pamphleteers, along with one or two scientists and independent historians. In a modern bookstore the works of these writers would be shelved across many departments, from "Biography" to the magazine rack.

As a general rule, the closer the literary sources were composed in time and space to Alexander's lifetime, the more sympathetic they appear to be to him, as far as we can judge. But none of the earliest works have survived in their original forms. Virtually everything we think we know about the substance of these lost works, whether sympathetic or hostile to Alexander, derives from quotes or citations embedded in later accounts. Nor do we know *for certain* how or why those later writers selected these passages from the truly contemporary sources to quote or reference in their own works.

From the surviving volumes of what was once a larger collection of works about the life and accomplishments of Alexander, we now are left to craft an accurate, balanced, and convincing biography of the great king. Our modern biography inevitably has been created out of scattered references from lost contemporary or near-contemporary accounts of Alexander's deeds, written by authors who had their own agendas; from the fragments of material objects that have randomly survived from the great rubbish heap of Alexander's material world; and from later continuous narratives, composed by authors of the Roman imperial period, who often saw in Alexander reflections of their own complex, and, at times, savage emperors. Alexander's Roman-era historians or biographers clearly were influenced by their own backgrounds, educations, contemporary literary traditions, and historical circumstances.

The art of creating an objective and persuasive representation of Alexander out of such a jumble of sources is not a task for the faint of heart. Indeed, reconstructing what Alexander did (or did not do) can be done plausibly only after a careful sifting and weighing of the value of all the pieces of evidence provided by the sources for any given action of Alexander's.

Abbreviations of Frequently
Cited Texts in Notes

ANCIENT

Arrian	*Anabasis* or *Indike* (when latter, title provided)
Athenaeus	*Deipnosophistae*
Curtius	*Historiae*
Diodorus	*Bibliotheke*
Herodotus	*Histories*
Justin	*Epitome*
Plutarch	*Life of Alexander*
Strabo	*Geographia*
Xenophon	*Hellenica*

MODERN

Anglim et al. (2002)	S. Anglim, P. Jestice, R. Price, S. Rusch, and J. Serrati, *Fighting Techniques of the Ancient World, 3000 BC–AD 500* (New York, 2002).
Bosworth (1988)	A. Bosworth, *Conquest and Empire: The Reign of Alexander the Great* (Cambridge, 1988).
Brunt (1976)	P. Brunt, *Arrian*, volume 1 (Cambridge, 1976).
Fuller (1960)	J. Fuller, *The Generalship of Alexander the Great* (New Brunswick, 1960).
Greer (1969)	R. Greer, *Diodorus of Sicily*, volume 9 (Cambridge, 1969).

Hammond (1997)	N. Hammond, *The Genius of Alexander the Great* (Chapel Hill, 1997).
Hornblower (1983)	S. Hornblower, *The Greek World 479–323 BC* (London, 1983).
Jacoby (1961)	F. Jacoby, *Die Fragmente der griechischen Historiker*, second series, volume A (Leiden, 1961).
Jacoby (1962)	F. Jacoby, *Die Fragmente der griechischen Historiker*, second series, volume B (Leiden, 1962).
Kuhrt (1995)	A. Kuhrt, *The Ancient Near East c. 3000– 330 BC*, volumes 1 and 2 (London, 1995).
Lane Fox (1973)	R. Lane Fox, *Alexander the Great* (London, 1973).
Oldfather (1961)	C. Oldfather, *Diodorus Siculus*, volume 4 (Cambridge, 1961).
Pearson (1960)	L. Pearson, *The Lost Histories of Alexander the Great* (New York, 1960).
Perrin (1958)	B. Perrin, *Plutarch's Lives*, volume 7 (Cambridge, 1958).
Pomeroy et al. (1999)	S. Pomeroy, S. Burstein, W. Donlan, J. T. Roberts, *Ancient Greece* (Oxford, 1999).
Robson (1978)	E. Robson, *Arrian*, volume 2 (Cambridge, 1978).
Scott-Kilvert (1973)	I. Scott-Kilvert, *The Age of Alexander* (London, 1973).
Sélincourt (1971)	A. de Sélincourt, *The Campaigns of Alexander* (London, 1971).
Sherman (1963)	C. Sherman, *Diodorus Siculus*, volume 7 (Cambridge, 1963).
Stoneman (1991)	R. Stoneman, *The Greek Alexander Romance* (London, 1991).
Van de Mieroop (2004)	M. Van de Mieroop, *A History of the Ancient Near East ca. 3000–323 BC* (Oxford, 2004).
Welles (1963)	C. Welles, *Diodorus of Sicily*, volume 8 (Cambridge, 1963).
Yardley (1984)	J. Yardley, *Quintus Curtius Rufus: The History of Alexander* (London, 1984).
Yardley (1997)	J. Yardley, *Justin: Epitome of the Philippic History of Pompeius Trogus*, volume 1, books 11–12, *Alexander the Great* (Oxford, 1997).

Notes

These "blind notes" are organized sequentially by chapter. The left column gives the page numbers in the book to which the notes refer. To the right of the page numbers are cue phrases from the text or (usually) the first few words of quoted sources. These cue phrases and quotes are in the order that they appear on the pages of the book. After the cue phrases or quoted words, there are references to the ancient sources or scholarly works from which the information is derived. Unless otherwise noted, translations or summaries of sources are mine, based upon editions cited in the bibliography.

INTRODUCTION The Real Alexander

xv   *"mission from the deity"*   Tarn, W., "Alexander the Great and the Unity of Mankind," *Proceedings of the British Academy* 19 (1933), p. 127.

xv   *rages and violence*   O'Brien, J., *Alexander the Great: The Invisible Enemy* (London, 1992).

xv   *political terrorist Stalin*   As is certainly implied in at least some of the essays of E. Badian, one of the most brilliant scholars of Alexander; e.g., in his article "Harpalus," *JHS* 81 (1961), pp. 16–43 (in which Badian refers frequently to Alexander's "reign of terror" against the governors of his empire after his return from the East); and also in his seminal "Alexander the Great and the Loneliness of Power," *Studies in Greek and Roman History* (1968), pp. 192–205, in which (p. 200) Badian compares the death in action of one of Alexander's officers (Coenus), after he had played an important role in a mutiny against Alexander at the Hyphasis River in 327 B.C.E., to the fate of the World War II German general Erwin Rommel, who was given the choice of facing a firing squad or committing suicide in 1944 after Hitler's discovery that he had condoned a plot against the Führer's life. Elsewhere, e.g., "The Death of Parmenio," *TAPA* 91 (1960), p. 324, Badian represents Alexander more neutrally, as an autocrat, whose autocracy can and should be compared to the reigns of other autocrats, such as Augustus or Napoleon. I am in complete agreement with the latter point of view.

xv   *the ancient world*   Burn, A., *Alexander the Great and the Hellenistic World*, 2nd ed. (New York, 1962), pp. 203–210.

xv   *between 1519 and 1522*   Bosworth, A., "A Tale of Two Empires: Hernán Cortés and Alexander the Great," in Bosworth, A., and E. Baynham, eds., *Alexander the Great in Fact and Fiction* (Oxford, 2002), pp. 23–49.

xvi   *who he was*   For a sketch of the main ancient sources for Alexander's life, see Appendix : Sources: Flacks, Hacks, and Historians.

xvi   *conquest, and empire*   This is perhaps clearest in the work of Bosworth, possibly the most widely influential scholar of Alexander over the last fifty years.

xvii   *re-foundations of cities*   And those of his successors.

xvii   *the seventh century c.e.*   c.e. is the Common Era, or after the birth of Jesus Christ.

xviii   aniketos–*invincible*   Plutarch, 14.4, reports that before Alexander set off on his expedition against Asia, he went to Delphi to consult the god concerning the endeavor, but he arrived on one of the inauspicious days, when it was not lawful for the prophetess to deliver oracles. Alexander himself tried to drag the prophetess to the temple (where she could give him an oracular response to his question), at which point she proclaimed, "You are invincible, my son."

CHAPTER 1   The Blood of Heroes

3   *"I will when"*   Anecdote quoted in Thayer, A., *Life of Beethoven* (London, 2001), p. 22, revised by E. Forbes.

4   *and a god*   Hamilton, J., "Alexander's Early Life," *GaR* 12 (1965), pp. 117–124.

4   *Andromache and Neoptolemus*   Hammond (1997), pp. 64–65, for the family tree. Neoptolemus subsequently had selected Andromache, the granddaughter of Priam, as his prize, as recounted in the lost *Iliu Persis*, attributed to Arctinus or Lesches, which formed part of the so-called Epic Cycle; see Hammond (1997), p. 64.

4   *island of Samothrace*   Plutarch, 2.1.

4   *the male spectators*   Plutarch, 2.6.

5   *it disappeared*   Plutarch, 2.2.

5   *bold and lion-like*   Plutarch, 2.3.

5   *burned to the ground*   Plutarch, 3.3.

5   *attending the birth*   Plutarch, 3.3.

5   *would be invincible*   Plutarch, 3.5.

5   *his parentage*   Plutarch, 3.2.

5   *his ambitious nature*   Plutarch, 5.3.

5   *"if I have kings"*   Plutarch, 4.5, translation from Scott-Kilvert (1973), p. 256.

5   *nation's military strength*   Plutarch, 5.1.

6   *"Boys, my father"*   Plutarch, 5.2, translation from Scott-Kilvert (1973), p. 256.

6   *thirteen talents*   Technically, a talent designated a weight of metal from which weight coins could be minted. According to the Attic-Euboic standard, one talent equaled 60 minas or 25.86 kg of metal.

6   *be led away*   Plutarch, 6.1.

6   *"My boy, you"*   Plutarch, 6.5, translation from Scott-Kilvert (1973), p. 258.

7   *Achilles' old tutor*   Plutarch, 5.5.

7   *with his incense*   Plutarch, 25.5.

8   *parsimoniously with the gods*   Plutarch, 25.5.

8   *formal disputation*   Plutarch, 7.3.

8   *for Alexander*   Plutarch, 8.2.

8   *along with a dagger*   Plutarch, 8.2.

8   *spring of 334*   Plutarch, 15.4.

8   *of his fame*   Plutarch, 15.4.

8   *his own death*   Iliad, 18.97–126.

8   *would be near*   Iliad, 18.94–99.

9   *"a handbook of"*   Plutarch, 8.2.

9   *what he did*   For the individual style of fighting that dominates the narrative of the *Iliad*, see the fascinating article by H. van Wees, "Homeric Warfare," in *A New Companion to Homer*, ed. I. Morris and B. Powell (Leiden, 1997), pp. 668–693.

9   *plants or animals*   Plutarch, *Moralia*, 329 b–d. For an important discussion of the controversy over whether Aristotle actually gave this advice to Alexander, see Isaac, B., *The Invention of Racism in Classical Antiquity* (Princeton, 2004), pp. 298–302.

9   *to their conquerors*   Isaac, B., *The Invention of Racism in Classical Antiquity* (Princeton, 2004), pp. 175–181.

CHAPTER 2 Ahuramazda's Plan

10   *without a fight*   Herodotus, 7.132.1.

10   *tokens of submission*   Herodotus, 7.132.1. Among the Boeotians, the Plataeans and Thespians alone had refused to submit—and their cities were razed.

10   *the pass at Thermopylae*   Herodotus, 7.224.1.

10   *neared Athens*   5,283,320 men, according to Herodotus, 7.186.2.

10   *abandoned their city*   Herodotus, 8.41.1.

10   *of Athena Polias*   Herodotus, 8.51.2.

10   *"the wooden wall"*   Herodotus, 8.51.2.

10   *Kekrops' daughter Aglauros*   Herodotus, 8.53.1.

10   *to the ground*   Herodotus, 8.53.2.

11   *impiety in history*   Diodorus, 11.29.3.

11   *of the "barbarians"*   Diodorus, 11.29.3.

11   *half a century*   The fighting did not end officially until c. 450 and the controversial Peace of Kallias; see Diodorus, 12.4.4.

11   *first the Medes*   Centered around Ecbatana (modern Hamadan), in the north. In book 1, chapters 95–109, of his *Histories*, Herodotus tells the story of the development of the Median empire into Asia Minor (including the encounter between the Median King Cyaxares and King Croesus of Lydia). While historians are uncertain whether Herodotus' tale corresponds to any historical reality, what is clear is that the Medes were close neighbors of the Persians, spoke a similar language, and shared some cultural similarities.

11   *under Persian rule*   Kuhrt (1995), pp. 656–661. These conquests today would comprise the larger parts of Afghanistan, Turkmenistan, Uzbekistan, and Tajikistan.

11   *in central Fars*   Located c. 75 km northwest of Anshan and named after Cyrus' tribe; see Kuhrt (1995), p. 661.

11   *to the Persian empire*   Kuhrt (1995), pp. 661–664.

11   *the empire's frontiers*   Kuhrt (1995), pp. 664–670.

11   *their great god*   The theme of Ahuramazda's favor is sounded in royal inscriptions from the reign of Darius I onward, including in the famous Behistun inscription that accompanied the relief of Darius triumphing over the rebels against his rule. See Kuhrt (1995), p. 666.

11   *protection of Ahuramazda*   In the Behistun inscription of Darius, translated and quoted by Van de Mieroop (2004), p. 272.

12   *"put down"*   Kuhrt (1995), pp. 676–678.

12   *native goddess Cybele*   Herodotus, 5.97.1–102.3.

12   *coast of Asia*   Herodotus, 6.32.1.

12   *plundered and burned*   Herodotus, 6.19.1–3.

12   *to the Ionians*   Herodotus, 6.43.4.

12   *September 490*   Herodotus, 6.108ff.

12   *Athenian Acropolis was burned*   Kuhrt (1995), p. 671.

12   *Straits of Salamis*   Herodotus, 8.84.1–96.2.

12   *army on land*   Herodotus, 8.115.1.

12   *Plataea in 479*   Herodotus, 9.49.1–86.2.

13   *out of Asia Minor*   The events from the departure of the "Medes" from Europe after Salamis, Plataea, and Mycale to the beginnings of the Peloponnesian War are described by Thucydides, 1.89.1–117.3.

13   *Persian king Darius II*   Xenophon, 1.5.1; rightly emphasized by Pomeroy et al. (1999), p. 317.

13   *Artaxerxes II (405–359)*   Xenophon, 5.1.31.

13   *against Sparta*   Xenophon, 5.4.34.

13   *satisfy the Thebans*   Xenophon, 5.3.19–20.

13   *hoplite infantry*   For the equipment, training, and tactics of hoplites, see chapter 3, p 18ff.

13   *at Leuctra*   Xenophon, 6.4.6–15; Hornblower (1983), p. 219.

13   *depth of fifty shields*   Xenophon, 6.4.12.

13   *oblique angle of attack*   So that the more heavily weighted left side of the Theban line met the enemy first, before their center and right flank closed quarters with the enemy.

13   *point of death*   Plutarch, *Life of Pelopidas*, 18.1–19.5; Hornblower (1983), p. 219.

13   *the officer class*   Xenophon, 6.4.15.

14   *sought their freedom*   Diodorus, 15.66.1–6; Pausanias, *Description of Greece* 9.14.5.

14   *killed in the battle*   Xenophon, 7.5.18–27; Hornblower (1983), pp. 235–236.

14   *Chios revolted in 357*   Pomeroy et al. (1999), p. 342.

14   *the alliance as well*   Hornblower (1983), p. 241ff.

14   *Greek cities of Asia Minor*   Kuhrt (1995), pp. 674–675; Bosworth (1988), p. 17.

CHAPTER 3 The Emergence of a Superpower

15   *slumbering superpower*   For general accounts, see Hammond, N., *A History of Macedonia*, volume 1 (Oxford, 1972); Hammond, N., and G. Griffith,

A History of Macedonia, volume 2 (Oxford, 1979); and Hammond, N., and
F. Walbank, *A History of Macedonia*, volume 3 (Oxford, 1988), which are fun-
damental for matters topographical and historical; also Ginouves, R., ed.,
Macedonia from Philip II to the Roman Conquest (Princeton, 1994).

15   *distinct geographical regions*   Herodotus, 7.173.1, 7.128.1, 8.137.1. Both
Strabo, 7.11ff, and Justin, 7.1.1–6, claim that Macedon formerly had been
called Emathia (after a certain king Emathion) and provide (not completely
reliable) historical accounts of how the territory of Macedon came under the
rule of the Macedonian kings.

15   *Illyria and Epirus*   Pomeroy et al. (1999), pp. 372–373.

15   *enthusiastic wine drinkers*   As we shall see, during the campaigns in
the east, Alexander and his companions held a series of ritualized drinking parties, some of which ended in brawls and worse. This was not simply the result
of the hard fighting the Macedonians did in Asia; the Macedonian royal court
always had drunk heavily.

16   *large population*   There are no census figures, but to judge by the size
of the army that Alexander was able to muster for his crossing into Asia (as
well as the supply of fresh recruits who were sent out periodically while Alexander was in Asia), the population of Macedonia was far larger than that of any
Greek city-state. In 336, for instance, the number of Companion infantrymen
has been estimated as 36,000 by Hammond (1997), p. 15. In 338 the troops of
Boeotia, Athens, Megara, Corinth, and Achaea who fought at the battle of
Chaeronea numbered 35,000 *combined*.

16   *fourth-century capital*   Xenophon, 5.2.13.

16   *royal house of Macedonia*   Hammond (1997), p. 201.

16   *Mount Pangaion*   Borza, E., *In the Shadow of Olympus: The Emergence
of Macedon* (Princeton, 1992), pp. 53–54. For the natural resources of Macedon in general, see Borza, E., "The natural resources of early Macedonia," in
Philip II, Alexander the Great and the Macedonian Heritage, ed. W. Adams and
E. Borza (Washington, D.C., 1982), pp. 1–20.

16   *Argead kings of Lower Macedon*   According to Strabo, 7.11ff., the
Argeadae were the tribe who were able to make themselves supreme in early
Emathia, later Macedon. Justin, 7.2.2ff., gives a different account of how the
"Argead" name of the dynasty came into existence: on his deathbed, the king
Perdiccas indicated where he wanted to be buried and ordered that not only
his bones but those of his successors were to be interred there (in Aegae), de-
claring that the throne would stay in the family as long as the remains of their
descendants were buried there.

17   *the Greek city-states*   For a general analysis, see Errington, R., "The
Nature of the Macedonian State Under the Monarchy," *Chiron* 8 (1978),
pp. 77–133.

17   *Greek or not*   Pomeroy et al. (1999), p. 373.

17   *all petitions*   Pomeroy et al. (1999), p. 375.

17   *arbitrary or despotic*   In general, see the still-useful Lock, R., "The Macedonian Army Assembly in the Time of Alexander the Great," *CP* 72 (1977), pp. 91–107.

17   *parties were famous*   See chapter 25, p. 239, for one fourth-century historian's observations about the sexual practices of some of Philip's companions at his court.

18   *against the Greeks*   Herodotus, 9.44.1.

18   *the Axius and Strymon Rivers*   For the details of Macedonian history during the period, see Hornblower (1983), p. 74ff.

18   *the late fifth century*   Hornblower (1983), p. 79.

18   *many Macedonian nobles*   Diodorus, 16.2.4; Hornblower (1983), p. 239.

18   *given the situation*   Hornblower (1983), p. 239.

18   *Philip II of Macedon*   Hammond, N., *Philip of Macedon* (Baltimore, 1994).

19   *in Greek history*   Lloyd, A., "Philip II and Alexander the Great: The Moulding of Macedon's Army," in *Battle in Antiquity*, ed. A. Lloyd (London, 1996), pp. 169–198.

19   *torsion catapults*   Marsden, E., "Macedonian Military Machinery and Its Designers Under Philip and Alexander," in *Ancient Macedonia*, volume 2 (Thessaloniki, 1977), pp. 211–223, arguing that it was really under Philip's direction and subsidization that the major advances in the construction of torsion stone-throwers were made. Philip's engineers developed artillery that could project ten-pound stones more than fifteen hundred feet.

19   *Argive-style* (hoplon)   Anglim et al. (2002), p. 18.

19   *constituted a phalanx*   For general issues, see Adcock, F., *The Greek and Macedonian Art of War* (Berkeley, 1957); Anderson, J., *Military Theory and Practice in the Age of Xenophon* (Berkeley, 1970); Anglim et al. (2002), pp. 17–28.

19   *Foot Companions*   Bosworth (1988), p. 259.

19   *called the Companions*   Devine, A., "Alexander the Great," in *Warfare in the Ancient World*, ed. J. Hackett (New York, 1989), p. 105.

19   *was affirmed*   Lloyd, A., "Philip II and Alexander the Great: The Moulding of Macedon's Army," in *Battle in Antiquity*, ed. A. Lloyd (London, 1996), pp. 169–198.

20   *made of straw*   Anglim et al. (2002), p. 36.

20   *abdomen and groin*   Anglim et al. (2002), p. 19.

20   *close combat*   Anglim et al. (2002), p. 36.

20   *slung over the left shoulder*   Anglim et al. (2002), p. 36.

20   *the* sarissa   Hammond (1997), p. 13.

20   *held with one hand*   Hammond (1997), p. 13.

20   *around fourteen pounds*   Devine, A., "Alexander the Great," in *Warfare in the Ancient World*, ed. J. Hackett (New York, 1989), p. 106.

20   *Polybius observed*   Polybius, *Histories*, 18.29.5.

20   *men in front*   Polybius, *Histories*, 18.29.3.

20   *as a unit*   Bosworth (1988), p. 259.

20   *called a* taxis   Bosworth (1988), p. 259.

21   *basis within Macedonia*   Bosworth (1988), p. 259.

21   *Greek infantry*   Around 7,000 crossed over to Asia with Alexander in 334.

21   *Thracians, Triballians, and Illyrians*   Bosworth (1988), pp. 264–265; 7,000 of these infantrymen served in the army Alexander brought to Asia.

21   *consisted of Macedonians*   Arrian, 3.12.3.

21   *javelin men, as well*   Arrian, 1.28.4, 6.8.7.

21   *"rapid movement"*   Bosworth (1988), p. 263.

21   *archers from Macedon*   Arrian, 3.12.2.

21   *organized into chiliarchies*   Arrian, 2.9.3, 4.24.10.

21   *lines of its enemies*   Anglim et al. (2002), p. 33.

21   *decisive offensive thrust*   Anglim et al. (2002), p. 33.

22   *modern mounts*   Anglim et al. (2002), pp. 93–94. For a detailed discussion of Greek horses, see the interesting work of Gaebel, R., *Cavalry Operations in the Ancient Greek World* (Norman, 2002), pp. 19–43.

22   *the Middle Ages*   Anglim et al. (2002), pp. 92–93; Gaebel, R., *Cavalry Operations in the Ancient Greek World* (Norman, 2002), pp. 11–12.

22   *mounts in combat*   Anglim et al. (2002), p. 93. Gaebel, R., *Cavalry Operations in the Ancient Greek World* (Norman, 2002), pp. 10–15 on ancient horsemanship.

22   *Companions, mentioned above*   Brunt, P., "Alexander's Macedonian Cavalry," *JHS* 83 (1963), pp. 27–46; Hammond, N., "Cavalry Recruited in Macedonia Down to 322 B.C.," *Historia* 47 (1998), pp. 404–425; Anglim et al. (2002), p. 99.

22   *fought on horseback*   Bosworth (1988), p. 261.

23   *recruited regionally*   Bosworth (1988), p. 261.

23   *larger blade at its back end*   Confusingly, this weapon is also sometimes identified in the sources as a *sarissa*. But the primary offensive weapon of the Macedonian Companion cavalryman cannot have been the same as the longer, heavier pike of the Companion infantry. No rider on earth could have wielded a sixteen-foot-long pike with one hand effectively, while riding on horseback, without a saddle or stirrups. The weapon of the Companion cavalryman was essentially a shorter lance-type weapon, which could be held with one hand.

For the controversies surrounding the terminology, see Manti, P., "The Macedonian Sarissa, Again," *AncW* 25, no. 1 (1994), pp. 77–91.

23   *central, balance point*   Anglim et al. (2002), p. 99.

23   *the* kausia   Bosworth (1988), p. 262.

23   *cover a retreat*   Anglim et al. (2002), p. 99.

23   *into the enemy's weak points*   Anglim et al. (2002), p. 99.

23   *during pitched battle*   Bosworth (1988), p. 262.

24   *lightly armed cavalry units*   Arrian, 4.4.6; Bosworth (1988), p. 262.

24   *deployed alongside them*   Arrian, 3.8.1; Bosworth (1988), p. 265.

24   *left wing of the Macedonian line*   Bosworth (1988), p. 264.

24   *defensive combat*   Anglim et al. (2002), p. 99.

24   *to pay them*   Arrian, 3.25.4; Bosworth (1988), pp. 265–266.

25   *little choice but to fight*   Bosworth (1988), p. 16.

25   *broke through the allies' line*   Diodorus, 16.86.3.

25   *"Sacred Band" of Thebes*   Diodorus, 16.86.1–6. For the destruction of the Sacred Band, see Rahe, P., "The Annihilation of the Sacred Band at Chaeronea," *AJA* 85 (1981), pp. 84–87. Surveying the corpses of all 300 members of the unit heaped up together along with their armor on the battlefield of Chaeronea, Philip is said by Plutarch, *Life of Pelopidas*, 18.7, to have wept and exclaimed, "Let those who think these men did or suffered anything disgraceful die miserably."

25   *alliance with Macedon*   Diodorus, 16.87.3.

26   *oligarchy was imposed on them*   Diodorus, 16.87.3.

26   *other strategic locations*   Bosworth (1988), pp. 16–17.

26   *but for implementation*   Hammond (1997), p. 20.

26   *declare war on Persia*   Hammond (1997), p. 20.

26   *the invasion of 480*   Diodorus, 16.89.2–3.

26   *became regent*   Heckel, W., *The Marshals of Alexander's Empire* (London, 1992), pp. 13–23.

26   *Parmenio*   Plutarch, *Moralia*, 177c.

26   *autumn of the same year*   Hammond (1997), p. 20.

CHAPTER 4   The Assassination of Philip II

28   *a tawdry affair*   Diodorus, 16.91.1–95.5; Badian, E., "The Death of Philip II," *Phoenix* 17 (1963), pp. 244–250; also Hammond, N., "The End of

Philip," in *Philip of Macedon*, ed. M. Hatzopoulos and L. Loukopoulos (Athens, 1980), pp. 166–175; Develin, R., "The Murder of Philip II," *Antichthon* 15 (1981), pp. 86–99; and Ellis, J., "The Assassination of Philip II," in *Ancient Macedonian Studies in Honor of Charles Edson*, ed. H. Dell (Thessaloniki, 1981), pp. 99–137.

28 *wife number eight* Hammond (1997), pp. 21–22.

28 *niece of Attalus* Plutarch, 9.4–5.

28 *the Macedonian army* For Attalus' biography, see Heckel, W., *The Marshals of Alexander's Empire* (London, 1992), no. 1.1, pp. 4–5.

28 *"that the union"* Plutarch, 9.4, translation from Scott-Kilvert (1973), p. 261.

29 *biographies of Alexander* In a world in which ethnic differences were seen as contributing to inherited characteristics, such issues were extremely important.

29 *"Wretch, do you"* Plutarch, 9.4.

29 *at Attalus* Plutarch, 9.4.

29 *"Look, men, here"* Plutarch, 9.5.

29 *irreconcilably alienated* For the events, see Hammond (1997), p. 23.

29 *left for Illyria* Plutarch, 9.5.

29 *the satrap's eldest daughter* Plutarch, 10.1. For an in-depth interpretation, see Hatzopoulos, M., "A Reconsideration of the Pixodarus Affair," in *Macedonia and Greece in Late Classical and Early Hellenistic Times* (Washington, D.C., 1982), pp. 59–66. Hammond (1997), p. 24, dismisses the entire episode as false, but confirmation of its effects is certainly accepted by Arrian, 3.6.5, in a passage connected to Asia Minor.

29 *replace him as heir* Plutarch, 10.1.

29 *the bridegroom instead* Plutarch, 10.2.

29 *(the King of Persia)* Plutarch, 10.3.

29 *and Ptolemy* After Philip's assassination in 336, Alexander recalled these men and eventually elevated them all to the highest honors; see Plutarch, 10.3.

30 *liberate the Greek cities of Asia Minor* Diodorus, 16.91.2.

30 *"Wreathed in the bull"* Diodorus, 16.91.2, translation from Welles (1963), p. 89.

30 *(Olympias' brother)* Diodorus, 16.91.4.

31 *war against Persia* Diodorus, 16.91.6.

31 *up for trial* Diodorus, 16.92.1–2.

31 Your thoughts reach Diodorus, 16.92.3, translation from Welles (1963), p. 93. The ode Neoptolemus sang perhaps came from a lost tragedy

of Aeschylus. After the assassination, the meaning and significance of the ode was reinterpreted.

32   *along with a thirteenth—of himself*   Diodorus, 16.92.5. For the scholarly debates about whether Philip already had been awarded divine honors, see Fredricksmeyer, E., "Divine Honours for Philip II," *TAPA* 109 (1979), pp. 39–61.

32   *guard of spearmen*   Diodorus, 16.93.1.

32   *Alexander of Epirus*   Justin, 9.6.3–4.

32   *a certain Pausanias*   Fears, J., "Pausanias, the Assassin of Philip II," *Athenaeum* 53 (1975), pp. 111–135.

32   *from Orestis*   A region in western Macedonia, bordering on Illyria.

32   *Celtic dagger*   Diodorus, 16.94.3.

32   *on the spot*   According to Justin, 9.8.1, Philip was forty-seven years old at his death.

32   *pursued the assassin*   Not Attalus, the uncle of the Kleopatra Philip had married, but another Attalus, the son of a certain Andromenes.

32   *with their javelins*   Diodorus, 16.94.4.

33   *canton of Lyncestis*   Arrian, 1.25.1–2.

33   *"to accept the"*   Diodorus, 16.93.3–4, translation from Welles (1963), p. 97.

33   *meant for him*   Diodorus, 16.93.5–6.

33   *to abuse*   Diodorus, 16.93.7.

33   *among the guards*   Diodorus, 16.93.8–9.

33   *avenged him*   Diodorus, 16.94.1.

33   *insolence, violence, or rape*   Aristotle, *Politics*, 5.1311.b.2.

34   *after the assassination*   Arrian, 1.25.2; Justin, 11.2.2.

34   *"both of whom"*   Arrian, 1.25.1.

34   *at the tumulus of Philip*   Justin, 11.2.1.

34   *escaped his brothers' fate*   In addition to his immediate indications of loyalty to Alexander, Alexander of Lyncestis perhaps did not share the fate of his brothers because of his marriage to a daughter of Antipater, one of Alexander's chief supporters: see Curtius, 7.1.7; Justin, 11.7.1, 12.14.1.

34   *following the assassination*   Grenfell, B., and A. Hunt, *The Oxyrhynchus Papyri*, volume 15 (London, 1927), no. 1798, pp. 122–135. The papyrus plant grew mainly on the swamplands of lower Egypt and especially the Nile Delta. It was used by the Egyptians and the Greeks in Egypt as a writing material. Its later Greek name, *pápuros*, means "of the pharaoh," which suggests that its manufacture and marketing were a royal monopoly. The Greeks used rolls of papyrus sheets made from cut and glued sections of the plant for both

documentary and literary texts. For the interpretation of the *P. Oxy.* 1798, see Hammond, N., "Philip's Tomb in Historical Context," *GRBS* 19 (1978), esp. pp. 343–349; and for a more conservative edition of the text, see Parsons, P., "The Burial of Philip II," *AJAH* 4 (1979), pp. 97–101.

34   *"was murdered by assassins"*   Arrian, 2.14.5, translation from Sélincourt (1971), p. 127; cf. Curtius, 4.1.12.

35   *to his revenge*   Plutarch, 10.4.

35   *"the giver of the bride"*   Plutarch, 10.4.

35   *Medea's example*   Plutarch, 10.4.

36   *the king had been stabbed*   According to Valerius Maximus 1.8.9 (whose work, *Memorable Deeds and Sayings in Nine Books,* composed during the reign of Tiberius, 14–37 c.e., drew upon Pompeius Trogus), there was an engraving of a four-horse chariot on the weapon with which Pausanias killed Philip.

36   *being proven innocent*   Justin, 9.7.1–14.

36   *a single toast cost him his life*   Diodorus, 17.5.1–2.

37   *most experienced soldiers*   Heckel, W., *The Marshals of Alexander's Empire* (London, 1992), pp. 38–49.

37   *"moved to recover"*   Diodorus, 17.3.1–5, translation adapted from Welles (1963), p. 125.

37   *and with flattery*   Diodorus, 17.4.1–3.

37   *"tardy recognition"*   Diodorus, 17.4.6, translation from Welles (1963), p. 127.

38   *expedition against Persia*   Diodorus, 17.4.9.

38   *that his father had planned*   None of the contemporary sources for Alexander's campaigns seems to have questioned or even reflected seriously upon the professed justification for the war. There are perhaps two reasons for this.

First, wars in the Greek world often were justified by writers in terms of the requital of harm done by enemies in the past. That tradition, in fact, went right back to Homer and the very origins of Greek literary culture. By Alexander's day the idea of a war of revenge certainly was a literary cliché, if not an accepted fact of interstate relations.

Moreover, war waged for the sake of revenge did not exclude other motives for imperialism, such as the desire for material gain. In fact, ancient Greek and Roman writers usually took it for granted that war was waged for the sake of gain, whatever those who waged it said about their reasons for going to war. The benefits of warfare, like those of slavery, were taken for granted. Revenge and gain were not mutually exclusive motives for Alexander and his Greek allies. For the main points, see Austin, M., "Alexander and the Macedonian Invasion of Asia," in *War and Society in the Greek World*, ed. J. Rich and G. Shipley (London, 1993), pp. 197–223.

38   *Diogenes of Sinope*   Plutarch, 14.1–3, for the encounter.

38   *"If I were not Alexander"*   Plutarch, 14.3.

38   *Triballi and the Illyrians*   Arrian, 1.1.4.

39   *died in Illyria*   Arrian, 1.7.2.

39   *Alexander was dead*   Arrian, 1.7.6.

39   *arrived in Boeotia*   Arrian, 1.7.6.

39   *pardon in return*   Plutarch, 11.4.

39   *Philotas and Antipater*   Plutarch, 11.4.

39   *30,000 were captured*   Diodorus, 17.14.1.

39   *public slavery*   Plutarch, 11.6.

39   *were spared*   Plutarch, 11.6.

40   *to leave Thebes*   Plutarch, 12.1–3.

40   *the house of Pindar*   Diodorus, 17.14.4; Arrian, 1.9.10.

CHAPTER 5   The Spear-Won Prize of Asia

41   *and the Muses*   Diodorus, 17.16.4.

41   *among the Greeks*   Diodorus, 17 17 5.

41   *to the city of Sestos in twenty days*   Arrian, 1.11.5.

41   *approximately 5,100 cavalry*   Diodorus, 17.17.3–4.

41   *crack* hypaspistai   Devine, A., "Alexander the Great," in *Warfare in the Ancient World*, ed. J. Hackett (New York, 1989), p. 105.

41   *the advance force*   Diodorus, 17.7.10.

42   *"plunging ahead from"*   *Iliad*, 2.698–702.

42   *we are told*   Arrian, 1.11.5.

42   *soon followed*   The shock of Alexander's departure from the campaign's symbolic script of a Greek war of revenge after the death of Darius must have been considerable to those who had helped Alexander plan and act out the scenes of the script (such as the visit to Troy).

42   *of the flagship*   Arrian, 1.11.6.

42   *propitiate the Nereids*   Arrian, 1.11.6.

42   *a pair of fetters*   Herodotus, 7.35.1; the fetters were meant to bind the uncooperative body of water.

43   *in the ground*   Diodorus, 17.17.2.

43   *by the gods*   Diodorus, 17.17.2.

43   *by divine will*   For a similar argument, see Hammond, N., "The Kingdom of Asia and the Persian Throne," *Antichthon* 20 (1986), pp. 73–85.

43 *landed in Asia* Arrian, 1.11.7.

43 *"put pains thousandfold"* *Iliad*, 1.1–4.

43 *to the heroes* Plutarch, 15.4.

43 *grave of Achilles* Plutarch, 15.4.

43 *grave with garlands* Plutarch, 15.4.

43 *tomb of Patroklos* Arrian, 1.12.1.

43 *brought up with Alexander* Curtius, 3.12.16.

43 *Philip's royal pages* For a very complete summary of what is known about Hephaestion, see Heckel, W., *The Marshals of Alexander's Empire* (London, 1992), pp. 65–90.

43 *"without Alexander's favor"* Plutarch, 47.6.

43 *all Alexander's friends* Curtius, 3.12.16.

43 *loved Alexander* Plutarch, 47.5.

44 *before the king* Arrian, 1.11.8.

44 *from the temple* Arrian, 6.10.2, 6.11.1.

44 *(that is, Alexander himself)* Hammond (1997), p. 64.

44 *the Aesepus River* Arrian, 1.12.8.

44 *(Hellespontine) Phrygia* Arrian, 1.12.8.

45 *also native levies* Arrian, 1.14.4.

45 *avoid military engagement* Arrian, 1.12.9.

45 *military confrontation* Arrian, 1.12.9.

45 *for thirty days* Plutarch, 15.1, quoting Duris.

45 *town of Dimetoka* For an in-depth scholarly analysis of the battle, see Devine, A., "A Pawn-Sacrifice at the Battle of The Granicus: The Origins of a Favorite Stratagem of Alexander the Great," *AncW* 18 (1988), pp. 3–20; and also Devine, A., "Alexander the Great," in *Warfare in the Ancient World*, ed. J. Hackett (New York, 1989), pp. 104–129.

45 *the eastern banks* Arrian, 1.14.4–5. Arrian claims that the Persian cavalry were drawn up in an extended phalanx on the bank parallel to the river; but if the Persian cavalrymen were stationed at the very edge of the riverbank, their tactical advantage as cavalrymen would have been wasted.

45 *Greek mercenary infantry* Devine, A., "Alexander the Great," in *Warfare in the Ancient World*, ed. J. Hackett (New York, 1989), p. 109.

45 *to meet them* Arrian, 1.13.3. According to Diodorus, 17.19.2–3, Alexander followed Parmenio's advice, waiting until dawn before he brought his army across the river, before the Persians could stop him. Diodorus does not explain, however, how the Persians managed to miss tens of thousands of Macedonians crossing the river at dawn, thus giving away their carefully pre-

pared positional advantage. If the Persian commanders allowed this to happen, they really were incompetent.

45   *crossing the Hellespont* Arrian, 1.13.6.

45   *numbers were superior* Devine, A., "Alexander the Great," in *Warfare in the Ancient World*, ed. J. Hackett (New York, 1989), p. 109.

46   *several infantry battalions* Arrian, 1.14.1–3.

46   *his helmet's crest* Plutarch, 16.4.

46   *opposite it* Arrian, 1.14.4.

46   *precipitate the combat* Arrian, 1.14.5.

46   *into the water* Arrian, 1.14.6. For other interpretations of the battle, see Badian, E., "The Battle of the Granicus: A New Look," *Ancient Macedonia* 2 (1977), pp. 271–293; Foss, C., "The Battle of the Granicus," *Ancient Macedonia* 2 (1977), pp. 495–502; Hammond, N., "The Battle of the Granicus River," *JHS* 100 (1980), pp. 73–88.

46   *around three feet* The time of year when the battle was fought. See Plutarch, 16.2, and Hammond, N., "The Battle of the Granicus River," *JHS* 100 (1980), pp. 73–88.

46   *mentioned by Arrian* Arrian, 1.14.4, also cited in the article by Foss, C., "The Battle of the Granicus: A New Look," *Ancient Macedonia* 2 (1977), pp. 495–502.

47   *it could be attacked effectively* Devine, A., "A Pawn-Sacrifice at the Battle of The Granicus: The Origins of a Favorite Stratagem of Alexander the Great," *AncW* 18 (1988), p. 12.

47   *the Thessalian cavalry* Diodorus, 17.19.6.

47   *slightly wounding him* Diodorus, 17.20.6.

47   *had been a bit shorter* Pascal, *Pensées*, 2.162.

47   *commanders fell fighting* Arrian, 1.16.3

49   *asked for quarter* Arrian, 1.16.2; Plutarch, 16.6, alone reports the request for quarter. Devine, A., "A Pawn-Sacrifice at the Battle of The Granicus: The Origins of a Favorite Stratagem of Alexander the Great," *AncW* 18 (1988), pp. 9–10, argues that the figures for the number of Greek mercenaries have been highly inflated.

49   *on his behalf* Griffith, G., *The Mercenaries of the Hellenistic World* (Cambridge, 1935); and more recently, Thompson, M., "Paying the Mercenaries," in *Festschrift für Leo Mildenberg: Numismatik, Kunstgeschichte, Archäologie*, ed. A. Houghton (Wetteren, 1984), pp. 241–247.

50   *expect no mercy* One indication that the fate of the Greek mercenaries at Granicus did not deter other mercenaries is the fact that Darius gathered together an even larger number of Greek mercenaries to fight at the subsequent battle of Issos.

50   *Dium in Macedonia* Arrian, 1.16.4.

50   *"granted immunity from"*   Arrian, 1.16.5, translation from Sélincourt (1971), p. 75.

50   *who had died*   Arrian, 1.16.6.

51   *city of Miletos*   Diodorus, 17.22.1.

51   *"against their countrymen"*   Arrian, 1.16.6, translation from Sélincourt (1971), p. 76.

51   *"Alexander, son of Philip"*   Arrian, 1.16.7.

51   *with the Greeks*   Diodorus, 16.89.2.

52   *Risky Visions of Genius*   See Solomon, M., *Mozart: A Life* (New York, 1995), pp. 363–382, for Mozart's risky juxtaposition of the beautiful and the disturbing in his mature instrumental music.

CHAPTER 6 The Greek Cities of Asia Minor

54   *of his empire*   For the details, see the important article of Badian, E., "Alexander the Great and the Greeks of Asia," in *Ancient Society and Institutions* (studies presented to V. Ehrenberg) (Oxford, 1966), pp. 37–69.

55   *rather than conviction*   Arrian, 1.17.2.

55   *satrapal capital*   Arrian, 1.17.2.

55   *Hermos Valley*   For the story of the ruling dynasty of Lydia, see Herodotus, 1.6–94.

55   *Achaemenid Persian province*   For its incorporation into the Persian empire, see Kuhrt (1995), pp. 567–572.

55   *"in charge of"*   Arrian, 1.17.7, translation from Sélincourt (1971), p. 77.

55   *garrison the fortress*   Arrian, 1.17.8.

55   *admitting the Macedonians*   The popular party in this context refers to the supporters of "democratic" government; that is, government by the many poorer citizens rather than government by the fewer, wealthy Ephesians. For the political history of Ephesos during these years, see Karwiese, S., *Groß ist die Artemis von Ephesos* (Wien, 1995), pp. 60–62.

55   *in her temple*   Arrian, 1.17.11.

56   *the mercenaries fled*   Arrian, 1.17.9.

56   *halted further bloodshed*   Arrian, 1.17.12.

56   *offerings to gods*   Strabo, 14.1.22.

56   *accept the offer*   Arrian, 1.18.1.

56   *paid the Persians*   Arrian, 1.18.1–2. Wirth, G., "Die σύνταξις" von Kleinasien 334 v. Chr.," *Chiron* 2 (1972), pp. 91–98.

58   *city's Persian garrison*   Arrian, 1.18.4–5.

58   *the city wall*   Arrian, 1.19.2.

58   *at the Granicus*   Arrian, 1.19.6.

58   *imposed upon Miletos*   Bosworth (1988), p. 46.

58   *used for transport*   Arrian, 1.20.1.

58   *disaster at sea*   Arrian, 1.20.1.

59   *characteristic of him*   Hammond (1997), p. 75.

60   *the Mausoleum*   Hornblower, S., *Mausolus* (Oxford, 1982).

60   *of the Granicus*   Arrian, 1.20.3.

60   *(described in great detail)*   Diodorus, 17.24.1–27.6.

60   *defenders in check*   Arrian, 1.23.6.

60   *Alexander appointed Ada*   Arrian, 1.23.8.

60   *under her control*   Arrian, 1.23.8.

60   *brought to Alexander*   Arrian, 1.25.4.

60   *in assassinating Alexander*   Arrian, 1.25.3.

61   *him as king*   Arrian, 1.25.1–2; Justin, 11.2.2.

61   *the Macedonian army*   Arrian, 1.25.2.

61   *arrest the Lyncestian*   Arrian, 1.25.10.

61   *before the conqueror*   Jacoby (1962), 124 F31, pp. 427–428.

61   *holding on to force*   Arrian, 1.27.4.

61   *of the Termessians*   Arrian, 1.28.1.

61   *assault or surrendered*   Arrian, 1.28.2–8.

62   *within sixty days*   Arrian, 1.29.1–3.

62   *(who had been)*   Arrian, 1.24.3–5.

62   *men from Elis*   Arrian, 1.29.4.

62   *to the sea*   Kuhrt (1995), pp. 562–566.

62   *for the "barbarians"*   Arrian, 1.29.5.

62   *the northern Aegean*   Arrian, 2.1.1–2; Diodorus, 17.29.2.

62   *"a change in"*   Diodorus, 17.29.3, translation from Welles (1963), p. 199.

62   *a Persian attack*   Arrian, 2.2.3–4.

63   *large, pitched battle*   Diodorus, 17.30.7.

63   *together in Babylon*   Diodorus, 17.31.2; Arrian, 2.8.8, gives the Persian total as 600,000.

63   *of the war*   Arrian, 2.1.3.

63   *tied its yoke*   Arrian, 2.3.1. For the episode, see Schmidt, L., "Der gordische Knoten und seine Lösung," *Antaios* 1 (1959), pp. 305–318; and Fredricksmeyer, E., "Alexander, Midas and the Oracle at Gordium," *CP* 56 (1961), pp. 160–168.

63   *civil strife*   Arrian, 2.3.5.

63   *would rule Asia*   Arrian, 2.3.6.

63   *"I have untied it"*   Arrian, 2.3.7. Callisthenes, the official historian of the campaign, who (we can be sure) reflected how Alexander wanted this episode to be remembered, possibly is behind this version of the story. The story of Alexander cutting the knot with a sword perhaps was meant to symbolize how Alexander would become lord of Asia.

63   *pulling the yoke free*   Arrian, 2.3.7.

63   *undo the knot*   Arrian, 2.3.8.

64   *pillars and caves*   Arrian, 2.4.1–2.

64   *out of the pass*   Arrian, 2.4.4.

64   *at Alexander's advance*   Arrian, 2.4.6.

CHAPTER 7 The Battle of Issos

65   *and sleeplessness*   Arrian, 2.4.7–8.

65   *"Beware of Philip"*   Arrian, 2.4.9.

65   *he would recover*   Arrian, 2.4.10.

65   *category of friends*   Diodorus, 17.31.6.

66   *as Sardanapalus*   Sardanapalus was the Greek name for the real Assyrian king Assurbanipal of the neo-Assyrian period (c. 668–631). Later Greek writers such as Ktesias attributed his downfall to his luxurious lifestyle. For the history of Assyria during the period, see Kuhrt (1995), pp. 473–546.

66   *"Sardanapalus, son of Anakyndaraxes"*   Arrian, 2.5.4.

66   *Harpalus, fled*   For the episode, see Badian, E., "The First Flight of Harpalus," *Historia* 9 (1960), pp. 245–246; Heckel, W., "The Flight of Harpalus and Tauriskos," *CP* 72 (1977), pp. 133–135; Bosworth (1988), p. 57; and Worthington, I. "The First Flight of Harpalus Reconsidered," *GaR* 31 (1984), pp. 161–169.

66   *spring of 331*   Arrian, 3.6.4.

66   *welcomed back*   For that reason, some historians have speculated that Harpalus' "first flight" from Alexander was a cover for what was in fact a secret mission of some kind. It must be said that if Harpalus embarked upon a secret mission, the evidence for what that mission was has been very effectively hidden.

66   *600,000 fighting men*   Arrian, 2.8.8.

66   *Plutarch concurs*   Plutarch, 18.4.

67   *number as 400,000*   Diodorus, 17.31.2; Justin, 11.6.11.

67   *alone as 30,000*   Curtius, 3.2.1–9.

67   *(the so-called Kardakes)*   Arrian, 2.8.5–6; Bosworth (1988), p. 57.

67   *the smaller force*   For Charidemus, see Arrian, 1.10.4–6. It is fascinating that both Alexander and Darius are represented in the Greek and Roman sources as ignoring the advice of their advisers; but in Darius' case, ignoring the advice of sage Greeks always leads to disaster.

67   *for his empire*   Bosworth (1988), p. 34.

67   *to Darius I*   Herodotus, 5.18.1, 6.44.1.

67   *and the Macedonians*   Arrian, 2.6.1.

67   *south to Damascus*   Diodorus, 17.32.3; Arrian, 2.11.9–10.

67   *(where he learned)*   Arrian, 2.6.1.

67   *finally to Issos*   Arrian, 2.7.1; on Alexander's (disputed) route, see Devine, A., "The Location of Castabulum and Alexander's Route from Mallus to Myriandrus," *Acta Classica 27* (1984), pp. 127–129.

67   *to Myriandrus*   Arrian, 2.6.2.

67   *for protection*   Curtius, 3.7.8–10.

68   *his vast infantry*   Arrian, 2.6.3.

68   *north of Issos*   Arrian, 2.7.1.

68   *had left there*   Arrian, 2.7.1.

68   *haunt the perpetrators*   For instance, on the island of Iwo Jima, where in the early weeks of 1945, the Japanese torture and execution of American prisoners helped to motivate the U.S. Marines to take the island, after one of the bloodiest battles of World War II. For the story, see the incredibly powerful account written by the son of one of the Marines who fought there, Bradley, J., *Flags of Our Fathers* (New York, 2000).

68   *behind the Macedonians*   Arrian, 2.7.2.

68   *embarrassment of choice*   Vauvenargues, *Reflections and Maxims*, 1746.

68   *cut off by land*   He certainly could not be resupplied by sea indefinitely.

69   *Pillar of Jonah*   Arrian, 2.8.1–2; Bosworth (1988), p. 60.

69   *South of the Pinarus River*   The exact location of this river has been debated by scholars for most of this past century. Given the changes in the courses of the rivers running down from the Amanus mountains in this area, it is probable that the exact site of the battle never will be identified certainly, although strong arguments have been put forth for the Kuru Çay, a stream about fifteen km north of the Pillar of Jonah, where the coastal plain is about

four km wide. See Bosworth (1988), p. 60. Devine, A., "Grand Tactics at the Battle of Issus," *AncW* 12 (1985), pp. 42–46, has argued for an identification of the Pinarus with the Payas, but in my view that identification causes insuperable difficulties with some of the reported details of the action of the battle, above all, the cavalry charge of Alexander. The effect of that charge upon Darius may have been exaggerated (as will be argued), but to claim that it really could not or did not take place because of the topographical features of the Payas (steep banks of the river, etc.) is problematic.

69   *into formation safely*   Arrian, 2.8.5.

69   *the Amanus Range*   Quoted in Polybius, *Histories,* 12.17.4.

69   *army into position*   Arrian, 2.8.5.

69   *from the rear*   Arrian, 2.8.8.

69   *the numbers involved*   Arrian, 2.8.8.

70   *fighting for Greece*   Arrian, 2.7.3–9.

70   *on the rocky ground*   Arrian, 2.8.2.

70   *to a depth of eight men*   Arrian, 2.8.2.

70   *the seaward side*   Arrian, 2.8.3–4.

70   *Parmenio on the left*   Arrian, 2.8.9.

70   *kings in battle*   Arrian, 2.8.10–11.

70   *that high ground*   Arrian, 2.9.1–2.

71   *concealing the movement*   Arrian, 2.9.3.

71   *main attacking force*   Arrian, 2.9.4.

71   *elsewhere with stockades*   Arrian, 2.10.1.

71   *relatively quickly*   The exact date is uncertain; the battle probably was fought in November 333 B.C.E. For in-depth scholarly studies of the battle, see Devine, A., "The Strategies of Alexander the Great and Darius III in the Issus Campaign (333 BC)," *AncW* 12 (1985), pp. 25–38; and Devine, A., "Grand Tactics at the Battle of Issus," *AncW* 12 (1985), pp. 39–59. Devine bases his reconstruction of the battle on Arrian (whose source must have been Ptolemy, who in turn used Callisthenes as a framework) and Curtius (based also upon Callisthenes), but does so without ignoring Parmenio's contribution to the Macedonians' success or denigrating Darius. A similar reconstruction is given in Devine, A., "Alexander the Great," in *Warfare in the Ancient World*, ed. J. Hackett (New York, 1989), pp. 113–116.

71   *Alexander was upon them*   Arrian, 2.10.4.

71   *and unbroken line*   Arrian, 2.10.5.

73   *lost their lives*   Arrian, 2.10.7.

73   *cutting them to pieces*   Arrian, 2.11.1.

73   *in headlong flight*   Arrian, 2.11.2.

73   *under Alexander's attack*   Arrian, 2.11.4.

73   *Persian king himself*   Diodorus, 17.33.5.

73   *battle raged indecisively*   Diodorus, 17.33.6.

73   *in the front of their bodies*   Curtius, 3.11.9.

73   *dagger wound in the thigh*   Diodorus, 17.34.5–6.

73   *distracted with pain*   Curtius, 3.11.11. According to Aelian, *On the Nature of Animals*, 6.48., the horse was a mare who had just recently given birth.

74   *the Persian left collapsed*   This aspect of Arrian's presentation perhaps is based upon Callisthenes' propaganda.

74   *Philoxenos of Eretria*   Bosworth (1988), pp. 61–62.

74   *during the engagement*   Rumpf, A., "Zum Alexander Mosaik," *MdI(A)* 77 (1962), pp. 229–241; Cohen, A., *The Alexander Mosaic: Stories of Victory and Defeat* (Cambridge, 1997); see also Badian, E., "A Note on the 'Alexander Mosaic,'" in *The Eye Expanded: Life and the Arts in Greco-Roman Antiquity*, ed. F. Titchener and R. Moorton, Jr. (Berkeley, 1999), pp. 75–92.

74   *personal bravery*   Diodorus, 17.6.1–2.

74   *not be unbroken*   Nylander, C., "Darius III—the Coward King: Point and Counterpoint," in *Alexander the Great: Reality and Myth*, ed. J. Carlsen et al. (Rome, 1993), pp. 145–159.

74   *covered with bodies*   Diodorus, 17.34.9.

74   *the Persian dead*   Arrian, 2.11.8.

75   *than 10,000 cavalry*   Arrian, 2.11.8; Diodorus, 17.36.6; Curtius, 3.11.27; Plutarch, 20.5; although Justin, 11.9.10, reports 61,000 infantry, 10,000 cavalry, and 40,000 captured.

75   *appears in Curtius*   Curtius, 3.11.27.

75   *allied cavalry casualties*   Diodorus, 17.36.6.

75   *to the Euphrates*   Arrian, 2.13.1.

75   *the Persian cause*   Curtius, 4.1.34–35.

75   *8,000 mercenaries*   Arrian, 2.13.2–3. They eventually reached Tripolis in Phoenicia and from there sailed first to Cyprus and then over to Egypt, where Amyntas attempted (unsuccessfully) to make himself governor.

75   *their allies there*   For Agis and his war against the Macedonians, see Badian, E., "Agis III," *Hermes* 95 (1967), pp. 170–192; Bosworth, A., "The Mission of Amphoterus and the Outbreak of Agis' War," *Phoenix* 29 (1975), pp. 27–43; Bosworth (1988), p. 63; and again Badian, E., "Agis III: Revisions and Reflections," in *Ventures into Greek History: Essays in Honour of N. G. L. Hammond*, ed. I. Worthington (Oxford, 1994), pp. 258–292.

75   *fleet around Chios*   Arrian, 2.13.5.

76   *with great enthusiasm*   Arrian, 2.11.9–10.

76   *the whole army*   Arrian, 2.12.1.

76   *by their courage*   Diodorus, 17.40.1.

76   *the victory followed*   Diodorus, 17.40.1.

76   *during the battle*   Arrian, 2.12.2.

76   *"This, so it seems"*   Plutarch, 20.8.

76   *marks, ceremonies*   Arrian, 2.12.3–5, translation from Sélincourt (1971), p. 123.

77   *protector of men*   Arrian, 2.12.6–7. A play on Alexander's name in Greek, which could be translated as "Protector of men."

77   *"If it really happened"*   Arrian, 2.12.8.

CHAPTER 8   Master of Sieges

78   *surrendered it*   Arrian, 2.13.7–8.

78   *letter from Darius*   Arrian, 2.14.1.

78   *friendship and alliance*   Arrian, 2.14.2–3; Curtius, 4.1.7–10.

79   *seek him out*   Arrian, 2.14.4–9.

81   *on two fronts*   Keegan, J., *The Mask of Command* (New York, 1987), pp. 27–28. Keegan characteristically has understood with great acuity the problems facing Alexander at the time.

81   *Byblos and Sidon*   Arrian, 2.15.6.

81   *in his place*   Curtius, 4.1.16–26.

81   *might give them*   Arrian, 2.15.6–7.

81   *sacrifice to Herakles*   Arrian, 2.15.7.

81   *Alexander's sovereignty*   Arrian, 2.16.7.

81   *the Persians alike*   Arrian, 2.16.7.

82   *military preparations*   Diodorus, 17.40.3.

82   *the Persian fleet*   Arrian, 2.17.1–4.

82   *must be captured*   Presumably as opposed to invested and left behind, just as the Macedonians had done at Halicarnassos.

82   *had achieved*   Arrian, 2.18.1.

82   *lofty walls*   Arrian, 2.18.2.

82   *to the island city*   Diodorus, 17.40.4–5.

82   *on the mole*   Arrian, 2.18.6.

82   *the siege engines*   Arrian, 2.19.1–5.

83   *new siege engines*   Arrian, 2.19.6.

83   *lost momentum*   Arrian, 2.20.1–3.

83   *without further peril*   Plutarch, 24.6–8, based upon Chares.

83   *to reinforce the army*   Arrian, 2.20.5.

83   *the Tyrian fleet*   Arrian, 2.20.10.

83   *length of the wall*   Arrian, 2.22.7.

84   *toward the royal quarters*   Arrian, 2.23.4–6.

84   *undefended northern harbor*   Arrian, 2.24.1–2.

84   *were pursued*   Arrian, 2.24.2.

84   *deserting the city*   Diodorus, 17.41.7–8.

84   *8,000 Tyrians were killed*   Arrian, 2.24.4.

84   *descendant of Herakles*   Diodorus, 17.46.4.

84   *women and children*   Diodorus, 17.46.4.

84   *some ancient custom*   Arrian, 2.24.5.

84   *war against Syracuse*   Curtius, 4.2.10–11, 4.3.19–20.

84   *formal declaration of war*   Curtius, 4.4.18.

84   *wall to the temple*   Arrian, 2.24.6.

84   *friend of Alexander*   Diodorus, 17.46.6.

85   *bodies into the sea*   Arrian, 2.24.3.

85   *rage of the Macedonians*   Arrian, 2.24.3.

85   *the historian intended*   Arrian, 2.24.2.

85   *"the siege bravely"*   Diodorus, 17.46.5, translation from Welles (1963), p. 81.

85   *protracted siege*   Arrian, 2.25.4.

85   *to November 332*   Arrian, 2.26.1. For a good, brief account of the siege, see Romane, P., "Alexander's Siege of Gaza—332 B.C.," *AncW* 18 (1988), pp. 21–30.

86   *could not dodge*   Curtius, 4.6.7–20.

86   *sold into slavery*   Arrian, 2.27.1–7.

86   *with the gods*   Plutarch, 25.4–5; Hammond (1997), p. 5.

86   *around the walls of Troy*   Curtius, 4.6.29

CHAPTER 9 The Gift of the River

87   *"gift of the river"*   Herodotus, 2.5.1.

88   *as Plutarch claimed*   Plutarch, *Moralia*, 328.e.

88   *at Wejh in April 1917*   Lawrence, T., *Seven Pillars of Wisdom*, with an introduction by M. Asher (London, 2000), pp. 174–179.

88   *before Alexander's arrival*   Kuhrt (1995), p. 123.

88   *king Cambyses II*   Kuhrt (1995), pp. 661–664.

88   *Alexander arrived*   Kuhrt (1995), p. 646.

89   *entry into Egypt*   Arrian, 3.1.1–2.

89   *Napoleon in 1798*   Chandler, D., *The Campaigns of Napoleon* (London, 2002), pp. 222–232.

89   *as a liberator*   Diodorus, 17.49.2.

89   *performers in Greece*   Arrian, 3.1.3–4.

89   *Egyptian god Ptah*   Arrian, 3.1.4.

89   *the Apis bull*   Herodotus, 3.27.1–29.3.

89   *(alleged) Persian sacrilege*   Kuhrt (1995), p. 664.

89   *pharaoh in Memphis*   Stoneman (1991), 1.34, p. 68.

89   *a libation to the god*   Bosworth (1988), pp. 70–71.

90   *after sailing upstream*   Curtius, 4.7.5.

90   *the god there*   Arrian, 3.3.1.

90   *their own Zeus*   For the historical background, see Classen, D., "The Libyan God Ammon in Greece Before 331 B.C.," *Historia* 8 (1959), pp. 349–355. Lane Fox (1973), pp. 190–205, supplies an evocative narrative.

90   *and in Olympia*   Pausanias, *Description of Greece*, 3.18.3, 5.15.11.

90   *and its god*   *Pythian Ode* 4.5.9; Pausanias, *Description of Greece*, 3.18.3.

90   *Athens' Port*   *Inscriptiones Graecae*, 2 ² 1496, line 95; Lane Fox (1973), p. 193.

90   *consulted Zeus Ammon*   Arrian, 3.3.1.

90   *Antaeus and Busiris*   Arrian, 3.3.1.

90   *that he had*   Arrian, 3.3.2.

91   *visit Libya*   Curtius, 4.7.9.

91   *facing civil unrest*   Bosworth (1988), p. 72.

91   *200 miles from the coast*   Arrian, 3.3.3.

91   *outright inventions*   Such as birds calling back those who had straggled away from the main party in the night, as cited by Plutarch, 27.3. For the criticisms, see Jacoby (1962), 124 F14, pp. 421–422. Timaeus, in Polybius, *Histories*, 12.12b.2.

91   *out of water*   Diodorus, 17.49.3.

91   *quantities of rain*   Diodorus, 17.49.4.

91   *Zeus Ammon himself*   Arrian, 3.3.4.

91   *back again from it*   Arrian, 3.3.5.

91   *acting as guides*   Arrian, 3.3.6; Plutarch, 27.3.

91   *in the Libyan desert*   Having traveled through the desert in the area recently, I can attest to the continuing presence of all three phenomena.

92   *protect the king*   Kuhrt (1995), p. 148.

92   *in eight days*   Diodorus, 17.49.3–5.

92   *its copious trees*   Arrian, 3.4.1. For a modern description of the oasis and the excavation of the ancient site there, see Fakhry, A., *Siwa Oasis, Its Customs, History and Monuments* (Cairo, 1950).

92   *olive and palm trees*   Arrian, 3.4.1.

92   *the Spring of the Sun*   Diodorus, 17.50.4.

92   *coldest at noon*   Arrian, 3.4.2.

92   *now called Aghurmi*   Bosworth (1988), p. 73.

92   *for a while*   Probably the egg-shaped stone representation of the god described on page 89.

92   *"Greetings, O son"*   Diodorus, 17.51.1, translation slightly adapted from Welles (1963), p. 265.

92   *"I accept, O father"*   Diodorus, 17.51.2, translation slightly adapted from Welles (1963), p. 265.

93   *"O son of Zeus"*   Plutarch, 27.5.

93   *(or mankind)*   Diodorus, 17.51.2; Curtius, 4.7.26; Plutarch, 27.4.

93   *his father's murder*   Diodorus, 17.51.2; Curtius, 4.7.27; Plutarch, 27.3.

93   *the god directed them*   Perhaps as a result of the weight of the stone and the boat.

93   *asked of the god*   Curtius, 4.7.24; Bosworth (1988), p. 73.

93   *granted Alexander his request*   Diodorus, 17.51.2.

93   *had been avenged*   Plutarch, 27.4.

94   *his heart desired*   Arrian, 3.4.5.

94   *to other gods*   Arrian, 6.19.4.

94   *the Outer Ocean*   For more on Alexander, Ammon, and the significance of Alexander's visit to the oracle, see Fredericksmeyer, E., "Alexander, Zeus Ammon, and the Conquest of Asia," *TAPA* 121 (1991), pp. 199–214.

95   *off for Egypt*   Diodorus, 17.51.4.

95   *visit to the oracle*   Diodorus, 17.52.1–7; Curtius, 4.8.1–3.

95   *by the same route*   According to Aristobulus, cited in Arrian, 3.4.5.
Ptolemy, however, reports that Alexander took a different route and went directly to Memphis. The conflict between these contemporary sources, whose
reports are found in Arrian, perhaps can be explained by Arrian's methodology, as Bosworth (1988), p. 74, has argued. If Ptolemy skipped over the inter-
mediate stages of the journey back to Memphis, then Arrian perhaps inferred
that Alexander took the direct route back to Memphis across the eastern
desert. If not, the sources are in irresolvable contradiction. Such contradic-
tions among primary sources are frustrating reminders that there are times
when we simply no longer can know with certainty what happened in the past.

95   *later, Roman tradition*   Bosworth (1988), p. 74.

95   *April 7, 331* B.C.E.   For the development of the city, see Fraser, P.,
Ptolemaic Alexandria, volumes 1–2 (Oxford, 1972); and for the scholarly debates over the dating of the foundation, Jouguet, P., "La date Alexandrine
de la fondation d'Alexandrie," *RÉA* 42 (1940), pp. 192–197; and Bagnall, R.,
"The Date of the Foundation of Alexandria," *AJAH* 4 (1979), pp. 46–49.

95   *city in Egypt*   Diodorus, 17.52.1; Plutarch, 26.2; Arrian, 3.1.5; Curtius,
4.8.1–2.

95   *its general layout*   Arrian, 3.1.5.

95   *stood by his side*   Plutarch, 26.3.

95   *"Out of the tossing sea"*   *Odyssey*, 4. 354–355, quoted in Scott-Kilvert
(1973), p. 281.

95   *military cloak, the* chlamys   Plutarch, 26.5.

95   *every nation*   Plutarch, 26.5–6.

96   *with a large population*   Curtius, 4.8.5.

96   *its circuit wall*   Arrian, 3.1.5.

96   *increasingly have disclosed*   E.g., Goddio, F., *Alexandria: The Submerged
Royal Quarters* (London, 1998).

96   *Middle and Near East*   Meineke, A., *Stepahnos Byzantinii EΘNIKΩN
(A Geographical Lexicon on Ancient Cities, Peoples, Tribes and Toponyms)* (Chicago,
1992), pp. 70–72, s.v. "Alexandrias." For an astute critique of Stephanus' list,
essentially concluding that most of Alexander's foundations that can be documented were part of a policy of commercial and strategic consolidation in the
interests of imperial rule, see Fraser, P., *Cities of Alexander the Great* (Oxford,
1996), esp. pp. 188–190.

97   *and musical contests*   Arrian, 3.5.2.

97   *rules is divine*   Plutarch, 27.6. Plutarch places the anecdote after his
account of Alexander's visit to Siwah.

97   *especially his own*   Plutarch, 27.6.

97   *time or not*   Because the name Psammon appears to be unique (that is,
it appears only here in classical literature), some scholars have argued that
Psammon never existed and his exchange with Alexander never took place.

By the same logic, because we have no other examples of individuals who could trace their ancestry to the tribe of Benjamin but also were citizens of a Greek city (Tarsus) and were citizens of Rome as well, a certain Saul of Tarsos never existed.

97   *both men and gods*   *Iliad*, 1.503, 533; Burkert, W., *Greek Religion* (Cambridge, 1985), p. 129.

97   *theme of the* Iliad   Nagy, G., *The Best of the Achaeans* (Baltimore, 1999), pp. 26–41.

97   *blue eyes and red hair*   Lesher, J. *Xenophones of Colophon: Fragments* (Toronto, 1992), fragment 16, p. 25.

98   *also were made*   Arrian, 3.5.2–6.

99   equites, *or knights*   Arrian, 3.5.7. For the Roman practices, see Tacitus, *Annals*, 2.5.9; *Histories*, 1.11; Dio Cassius, *Roman History*, 51.17.

CHAPTER 10   The Battle of Gaugamela

100   *in charge of Syria*   Curtius, 4.8.9–11.

100   *anticipated great labors*   Arrian, 3.6.1.

100   *the money*   Plutarch, 29.3.

100   *Diophantus and Achilles, arrived*   Envoys with names of heroes to whom Alexander supposedly was related obviously were chosen to take part in the embassy to flatter Alexander.

100   *battle of the Granicus*   Arrian, 3.6.2.

100   *two years before*   Arrian, 1.29.5–6.

101   *prisoners of war*   Arrian, 3.6.3.

101   *to the Spartans*   Arrian, 3.6.3.

101   *in the Peloponnese*   Arrian, 3.6.3.

101   *rule of the whole empire*   Diodorus, 17.54.2.

101   *"If I were Alexander"*   Diodorus, 17.54.3–5.

101   *by Alexander's generosity*   Diodorus, 17.54.5–6.

102   *died, in childbirth*   Plutarch, 30.1.

102   *sumptuous funeral*   Diodorus, 17.54.7.

102   *his wife's misfortune*   Plutarch, 30.4–7.

103   *had taken up arms*   For the complete list, see Arrian, 3.8.3–6.

103   *book 2 of the* Iliad   *Iliad*, 2.494–759.

103   *according to Arrian*   Arrian, 3.8.6.

103   *carried into battle*   Diodorus, 17.53.1.

103   *from the sides*   Diodorus, 17.53.2.

103   *Macedonian cavalry charge*   Arrian, 3.8.6.

104   *at his disposal*   Diodorus, 17.53.4.

104   *crossing of the Euphrates*   Arrian, 3.7.1.

104   *the Zagros Mountains*   Bosworth (1988), p. 78.

104   *the movement of cavalry*   Arrian, 3.8.7.

104   *spoken by his soldiers*   Diodorus, 17.53.4.

104   *cross the river*   Arrian, 3.7.1–2. For a monograph on the campaign, see Marsden, E., *The Campaign of Gaugamela* (Liverpool, 1964).

105   *(the Assyrian city in northwestern Mesopotamia)*   Destroyed along with its famous temple of the moon-god Sin, but rebuilt by the Babylonian Nabonidus; see Kuhrt (1995), p. 600.

105   *the Tigris River*   Arrian, 3.7.3–4; Bosworth (1988), p. 79.

105   *the swift current*   Arrian, 3.7.5; Stein, A., "Notes on Alexander's Crossing of the Tigris and the Battle of Arbela," *Geographical Journal* 100 (1942), pp. 155–164.

105   *eclipse of the moon*   Arrian, 3.7.6.

105   *September 20, 331*   Bosworth (1988), p. 79.

105   *sacrifices portended victory*   Arrian, 3.7.6.

105   *accurately assessed*   Arrian, 3.7.7.

105   *with a powerful force*   Arrian, 3.8.1–2.

105   *for four days*   Arrian, 3.9.1.

105   *unfit for duty*   Arrian, 3.9.1.

105   *the enormous enemy host*   Arrian, 3.9.3.

107   *inspect the terrain*   Arrian, 3.9.3–5; for the battle and Alexander's tactics see Devine, A., "Grand Tactics at Gaugamela," *Phoenix* 29 (1975), pp. 374–385.

107   *the common success*   Arrian, 3.9.5–8.

107   *face imminent combat*   For such "pep" talks, see Lloyd, A., "Philip II and Alexander the Great: The Moulding of Macedon's Army," in *Battle in Antiquity*, ed. A. Lloyd (London, 1996), pp. 180–181.

107   *eat and rest*   Arrian, 3.10.1.

107   *and without stratagem*   Arrian, 3.10.2.

107   *contrary to expectation*   Surely, the *locus classicus* for the vicissitudes of warfare at night, and especially the dangers it often brought to those who initiated it, is Thucydides' description of the attempted seizure of the small city-state of Plataea by some three hundred Thebans at the beginning of the Peloponnesian War (*The Peloponnesian War*, book 2, pp. 2–6).

108   *in a hostile country*   Arrian, 3.10.3–4.

108   *first and only time*   Plutarch, 31.4.

108   *review of them by torchlight*   Plutarch, 31.4.

108   *more than anything else*   Arrian, 3.11.2.

108   *while Alexander overslept*   Plutarch, 32.1.

109   *two or three times*   Plutarch, 32.1.

109   *fled the fight*   Plutarch, 32.2.

109   *hands afterward*   Arrian, 3.11.3.

109   *Cadusian contingents*   Arrian, 3.11.3.

109   *Albanians and Sacesinians*   Arrian, 3.11.4.

109   *deep formation behind them*   Arrian, 3.11.5.

109   *king's cavalry*   Arrian, 3.11.6.

109   *his Persian guard*   Arrian, 3.11.7.

112   *used thus far*   Devine, A., "The Macedonian Army at Gaugamela," *AncW* 19 (1989), pp. 77–80.

112   *Polyperchon, and Simmias*   Arrian, 3.11.8–9.

112   *Thessalian cavalry*   Arrian, 3.11.10.

112   *coming from the rear*   Arrian, 3.12.1.

112   *mercenaries under Cleander*   Arrian, 3.12.2.

112   *cavalry under Menidas*   Arrian, 3.12.3.

112   *Persian scythed chariots*   Arrian, 3.12.3.

113   *about 40,000 infantry*   Arrian, 3.12.4–5.

113   *against the barbarians*   Plutarch, 33.1.

113   *his sword in battle*   Plutarch, 32.5–6.

113   *anyone else nearby*   Curtius, 4.13.38.

113   *now mounted on Bucephalas*   Plutarch, 32.7. It was Alexander's practice to use another horse as long as he was riding up and down his lines before battle but to mount Bucephalas for the attack itself.

113   *strengthen the Greeks*   Plutarch, 33.1, quoting Callisthenes, and thus, what Alexander wanted to be reported about his actions at the beginning of the battle. This prayer probably should be seen as confirmation that Alexander had been told something by the oracle of Zeus Ammon about his divine parentage.

114   *with great courage*   Plutarch, 33.2.

114   *most dear to Zeus*   Burkert, W., *Greek Religion* (Cambridge, 1985), pp. 127–128.

114   *farther to that side*   Arrian, 3.13.1.

114   *out to their left*   Arrian, 3.13.2.

114   *soldier of his day*   Keegan, J., *The Mask of Command* (New York, 1987), p. 86.

114   *the Companion cavalry*   For the importance of force economizing here and in other battles, see Fuller (1960), pp. 298–299.

115   *devastating counterattack*   Devine, A., "The Battle of Gaugamela: A Tactical and Source-Critical Study," *AncW* 13 (1986), pp. 108–109.

115   *not into disorder*   Devine, A., "The Battle of Gaugamela: A Tactical and Source-Critical Study," *AncW* 13 (1986), p. 109.

115   *broke the enemy formation*   Arrian, 3.13.3–4.

115   *Alexander's grooms*   Arrian, 3.13.5–6. The role of the royal guards in dealing with this attack as reported by Arrian is hard to square with their placement (by Arrian, at 3.11.9) in the front line.

115   *the first onslaught*   Diodorus, 17.59.5.

115   *we are told*   Diodorus, 17.59.7.

115   *gave ground*   Diodorus, 17.59.8.

116   *direction of Darius himself*   Arrian, 3.14.2.

116   *victory to one side*   "Correspondence de Napoléon I[ier], 'Précis des guerres de J. César,'" volume 32, p. 27, quoted by Fuller, J., *The Generalship of Alexander the Great* (New Brunswick, 1960), p. 298.

116   *rode for safety*   Arrian, 3.14.3.

116   *was having difficulties*   Arrian, 3.14.4.

116   *these Indians and Persians*   Arrian, 3.14.5–6.

116   *dispatch rider*   Arrian, 3.15.1. The dispatch rider, identified subsequently as a certain Polydamas, later was to play a crucial role in the assassination of Parmenio; see Curtius, 4.15.6.

116   *or riders*   Diodorus, 17.60.7.

117   *reaching him*   Diodorus, 17.60.7.

117   *by Darius' flight*   Diodorus, 17.60.8.

117   *elephants, and camels*   Arrian, 3.15.4.

117   *the Persian king himself*   Arrian, 3.15.5.

117   *alternative tradition*   Arrian, 3.15.1; and Plutarch, 33.6, citing Callisthenes, and thus the official version of what happened.

117   *once again victorious*   Arrian, 3.15.2.

117   *Darius was fleeing*   Diodorus, 17.60.4.

118   *had won it*   Arrian, 3.15.7.

118   *cavalry and infantry killed*   Diodorus, 17.61.3.

CHAPTER 11 The Sack of Persepolis

119   *the Khorasan road*   Kuhrt (1995), p. 652; Van de Mieroop (2004), p. 255.

119   *the foreign mercenaries*   Arrian, 3.15.5, 16.1–2.

119   *to capture him*   Arrian, 3.15.5.

119   *was still alive*   Plutarch, 34.1.

120   *were autonomous*   Plutarch, 34.1.

120   *(against the Persians in 479)*   Plutarch, 34.1.

120   *the common danger*   Plutarch, 34.2.

120   *after the battle*   Curtius, 5.1.17.

120   *and the city*   Curtius, 5.1.17.

120   *frankincense and perfumes*   Curtius, 5.1.20.

120   *Babylonian cavalry*   Curtius, 5.1.21–23.

120   *storm god, Baal*   Arrian, 3.16.4. The story of Xerxes' (486–465 B.C.E.) destruction of Babylon's temples is discounted by scholars of the ancient Near East, including Kuhrt (1995), p. 671. It is possible that the state of the temples in Babylon in which Alexander found them was the result of neglect by the Babylonians rather than active destruction by Xerxes.

120   *instructions of the Chaldaeans*   Arrian, 3.16.5. The Chaldaeans were a tribal people who periodically had seized the throne of Babylon since c. 850 B.C.E.

120   *and tax collector*   Arrian, 3.16.4.

120   *friendly to strangers*   Diodorus, 17.64.4.

121   *was paid for*   Curtius, 5.1.36–37.

121   *shared common interests*   Curtius, 5.1.36–38.

121   *two months' pay*   Diodorus, 17.64.6; a mina consisted of one hundred drachmae, and was one-sixtieth of a talent. The average pay for a cavalryman must have been at least two drachmae per day.

121   *and 380 cavalry*   Diodorus, 17.65.1; Curtius 5.1.39–41.

121   *of proven courage*   Arrian, 3.16.11.

121   *while he slept*   Curtius, 5.1.42.

121   *in twenty days*   Arrian, 3.16.7.

121   *of his empire*   Van de Mieroop (2004), p. 275.

121   *surrendered the city*   Curtius, 5.2.9–10.

122   *the royal footstool*   Diodorus, 17.66.3–7.

122   *dangling legs*   Diodorus, 17.66.3.

122   *form of Persian Darics*   Diodorus, 17.66.1–2; the Daric was the standard Persian gold coin, minted by the Persian kings with an image of the king as archer on one side.

122   *the Lacedaemonian war*   Arrian, 3.16.10.

122   *Athens in 480*   Arrian, 3.16.7–8.

122   *called the Kerameikos*   Arrian, 3.16.8. Originally, a potter's quarter in the northwestern district of Athens, which was also later used as an extramural cemetery. There were many elaborate funerary statues and inscriptions in the district.

122   *an athletic contest*   Arrian, 3.16.9.

122   *made general there*   Arrian, 3.16.9.

122   *with Greek tutors*   Diodorus, 17.67.1.

123   *his own mother*   Curtius, 5.2.18–22.

123   *including Persian kings*   Arrian, 3.17.1.

123   *their usual payment*   The exact location of the pass is uncertain; see Bosworth (1988), p. 89.

123   *they had demanded*   Arrian, 3.17.2.

123   *wiped out by Craterus*   Arrian, 3.17.4–5.

123   *30,000 sheep*   Arrian, 3.17.6.

123   *the baggage train*   For Parmenio's route, see Bosworth (1988), p. 90.

123   *and advanced scouts*   Arrian, 3.18.1–2.

123   *(perhaps the gorge known as Tang-i Mohammed Reza)*   Bosworth (1988), p. 90.

124   *Ariobarzanes' men survived*   Arrian, 3.18.3–9.

124   *the city to Alexander*   Diodoros, 17.69.1.

124   *ears and noses*   Diodorus, 17.69.2–4.

124   *the Persian alphabet*   Curtius, 5.5.6.

124   *moved to tears*   Diodorus, 17.69.4.

125   *no one harmed them*   Diodorus, 17.69.8.

125   *his natural kindness*   Diodorus, 17.69.9.

125   *blot Persepolis out*   Curtius, 5.6.1. For Alexander and Persepolis generally, see Borza, E., "Fire from Heaven: Alexander at Persepolis," *CP* 67 (1972), pp. 233–245.

125   *plunder and murder*   Diodorus, 17.70.1–6; Curtius, 5.6.1–8.

125   *hands off the women*   Curtius, 5.6.8.

125   *"an act of outrage"*   Bosworth (1988), p. 92.

125 *throughout its history* As is indeed implied by Diodorus, 17.70.2.

125 *6,000 talents was confiscated* Curtius, 5.6.10. Herzfeld, E., "Pasargadae," *Klio* 8 (1908), pp. 20–25; and more recently, Stronach, D., *Pasargadae* (Oxford, 1978).

125 *120,000 talents* Curtius, 5.6.9.

126 *kept with the army* Curtius, 5.6.9; it took 10,000 pairs of mules and 5,000 camels to carry off the wealth of Persepolis, according to Plutarch, 37.2.

126 *April of 330* Curtius, 5.6.12–20.

126 *Persian kings* Arrian, 3.18.11; for a recent reevaluation, see Hammond, N., "The Archaeological and Literary Evidence for the Burning of the Persepolis Palace," *CQ* 42 (1992), pp. 358–364.

126 *pan-Hellenic campaign itself* Arrian, 3.18.12.

126 *more scandalous tale* Plutarch, 38.1–4; Curtius Rufus, 5.7.3–10; Diodorus, 17.72.1–6.

126 *of the Persians* Diodorus, 17.72.2.

126 *into the palaces* Diodorus, 17.72.6.

126 *and in sport* Diodorus, 17.72.6.

127 *to extinguish it* Plutarch, 38.4; Curtius, 5.7.11.

127 *his next objective* Arrian 3.18.11, 19.1.

CHAPTER 12 The Death of Darius

131 *claws its hunter* Kuhrt (1995), pp. 683, 679.

131 *of the kingdom* For the connections between the ethos of the hunt and warfare in Macedon, see Lloyd, A., "Philip II and Alexander the Great: The Moulding of Macedon's Army," in *Battle in Antiquity*, ed. A. Lloyd (London, 1996), pp. 173–174.

132 *the Median satrapy* Kuhrt (1995), p. 657.

132 *made of silver* Polybius, *Histories*, 10.27.5–10.

132 *Media and Parthyene* Arrian, 3.19.1–2.

132 *satrap over them* Arrian, 3.19.2.

132 *and 6,000 infantry* Arrian, 3.19.4–5; Diodorus, 17.73.2, puts the number of Persians and Greek mercenaries with Darius at 30,000.

132 *and the archers* Arrian, 3.20.1.

132 *a few light troops* Arrian, 3.19.7.

134 *the Caspian Gates* Arrian, 3.20.2.

134 *Arachotia and Drangiana* Arrian, 3.21.1.

134   *the day before*   Arrian, 3.21.1.

134   *(Shahr-i Qumis)*   Arrian, 3.21.6–9; Bosworth (1988), p. 96.

134   *died of his wounds*   July 330 B.C.E.

134   *had seen him*   Arrian, 3.21.10; Diodorus, 17.73.3; according to Curtius, 5.13.25, the Macedonians found Darius half-alive, run through many times by spears. Plutarch, 43.1–2, also recounts a dramatic death scene, with Darius receiving a last sip of cold water from a Macedonian soldier named Polystratus.

134   *full, royal funeral*   Diodorus, 17.73.3.

134   *divinely selected ancestors*   Arrian, 3.22.1.

134   *moderate and decent*   Arrian, 3.22.2–6.

135   *some god willed it*   For a balanced assessment, see Nylander, C., "Darius III—the Coward King: Point and Counterpoint," in *Alexander the Great: Reality and Myth*, ed. J. Carlsen et al. (Rome, 1993), pp. 145–159.

135   *in association with him*   Arrian, 3.22.1

135   *the wives and children*   Justin, 12.3.2; Diodorus, 17.74.1; Curtius, 6.2.18–21.

135   *the Persian race*   Curtius, 6.3.1–18.

136   *he wished to go*   Curtius, 6.4.1.

136   *ten minas*   Diodorus, 17.74.3.

136   *in Alexander's eyes*   For the congress held at Corinth establishing the alliance in 337, see Diodorus, 16.89.1–3, and reconfirmed at Corinth after Philip's death in 335–33 B.C.E., 17.4.9.

136   *three talents each*   Diodorus, 17.74.4.

136   *she had conceived*   Justin, 12.3.1–7.

136   *The story has been*   Diodorus, 17.77.1–3; Curtius, 6.5.24–32; Justin, 12.3.5–7; Plutarch, 46.1–2; Arrian, 4.15.2–4. The core of the Amazon story perhaps goes back to Cleitarchus, who was known to embellish the truth, but he may have got the basic story from Onesicritus, who was there. The story cannot be dismissed out of hand.

137   *(probably modern Sari)*   Arrian, 3.23.1–2.

137   *gave themselves up*   Arrian, 3.23.4.

137   *to his post*   Arrian, 3.23.7.

137   *respect and honor*   Arrian, 3.23.7.

137   *of their options*   Arrian, 3.23.8–9.

137   *mountain strongholds*   Diodorus, 17.76.3–4.

137   *satrap of Tapuria*   Arrian, 3.24.3.

138   *beg for forgiveness*   Diodorus, 17.76.5–8.

138   *rate of pay*   Arrian, 3.24.5.

139   *was still raging*   Arrian, 3.24.4

139   *their own king*   Arrian, 3.24.4.

139   *mounted javelin troops*   Arrian, 3.25.1–2.

139   *from Scythia*   Arrian, 3.25.3.

139   *and allied troops*   Arrian, 3.25.4.

139   *arrogance and dissipation*   Diodorus, 17.77.4–7; Curtius, 6.6.1–8; Plutarch, 45.1–2; Justin, 12.3.8–12.

139   *upper garment*   Athenaeus, 12.535f.

140   *he added concubines*   Diodorus, 17.77.6–7, translation from Welles (1963), p. 343.

140   *barbaric and effeminate*   E.g., Alexander's speech before the battle of the Issos as reported by Curtius, 3.10.1–10.

140   *suddenly died*   Curtius, 6.6.18.

141   *after Bessus*   Curtius, 6.6.19.

141   *opportunity should arise*   Arrian, 3.25.5.

141   *new governor of Areia*   Arrian, 3.25.7.

141   *treachery to Darius*   Arrian, 3.25.8.

CHAPTER 13 Anticipation

142   *his father, Philip*   Badian, E., "The Death of Parmenio," *TAPA* 91 (1960), p. 324; Heckel, W., "The Conspiracy Against Philotas," *Phoenix* 31 (1977), pp. 9–21.

142   *report the episode*   Plutarch, 48.1–49.7; Justin, 12.5.1–8; Arrian, 3.26.1–27.5; Diodorus, 17.79.1–80.4.

142   *commander of the phalanx*   Curtius, 6.7.1–7.2.38.

143   *distinguished men*   Curtius, 6.7.2–6.

143   *(not the phalanx commander)*   Curtius, 6.7.15.

143   *without delay*   Curtius, 6.7.18.

143   *during his arrest*   Curtius, 6.7.19–30.

143   *an object of ridicule*   Curtius, 6.7.31–33.

144   *in the crime*   Curtius, 6.8.1–15.

144   *"Your majesty"*   Curtius, 6.8.19–22, translation from Yardley (1984), p. 135.

144   *6,000 soldiers*   Curtius, 6.8.23; the presence of only 6,000 soldiers shows that Philotas was not tried, at least initially, before the entire army.

144   *in the case*   But he was not the judge, let alone a member of the jury. The Macedonian army acted as the jury.

144   *he alleged*   Curtius, 6.9.1–12.

144   *twice a day*   Arrian, 3.26.2.

144   *dangerous plot*   Curtius, 6.9.13–15.

144   *and army*   Curtius, 6.9.28–31.

144   *a lover's quarrel*   Curtius, 6.10.1–37.

145   *divine parentage*   Curtius, 6.11.1–7.

145   *certain Hegelochus*   Hegelochus perhaps had died in battle at Gaugamela; see Heckel, W., "Who Was Hegelochus," *RhM* 125 (1982), pp. 78–87. Heckel argues persuasively in this article and elsewhere that Hegelochus indeed had reason to plot against Alexander (being a relation of one of Alexander's former enemies). If that was the case, then Parmenio's involvement in a conspiracy hatched in Egypt (but not carried out at the time because Darius was still alive) becomes a real possibility.

145   *as his father*   Curtius, 6.11.13–33.

145   *customary practice*   Curtius, 6.11.34–38.

145   *"lacking words"*   Diodorus, 17.80.2, translation from Welles (1963), p. 351; cf. Curtius, 7.1.5–9.

145   *closeness to Philotas*   Arrian, 3.27.1–3.

145   *good name intact*   Arrian, 3.27.3.

146   *battle of Gaugamela*   Curtius, 4.15.6.

146   *and Menidas*   Arrian, 3.26.3.

146   *to Parmenio*   Curtius, 7.2.23.

146   *stabbed him to death*   Curtius, 7.2.24–27.

146   *"Disciplinary Company"*   Diodorus, 17.80.4.

146   *the two divisions*   Arrian, 3.27.4.

146   *the executed Demetrius*   Arrian, 3.27.5, who probably mistakenly places the arrest of Demetrius and the appointment of Ptolemy later, when Alexander had moved into the country of the Ariaspians. Curtius, 6.11.35–38, is probably correct that Demetrius was executed at the same time as Philotas.

146   *Prophthasia, "Anticipation"*   Meineke, A., *Stephanos Byzantinii EΘNIKΩN* (*A Geographical Lexicon on Ancient Cities, Peoples, Tribes and Toponyms*) (Chicago, 1992), p. 670, s.v. προφΘασία; Plutarch, *Moralia*, 328f.

146   *varied reactions*   See the seminal article of Badian, E., "The Death of Parmenio," *TAPA* 91 (1960), pp. 324–338.

146   *Philotas' implication*   Hammond (1997), pp. 132–135.

147   *Persian customs*   Especially, Badian, E., "The Death of Parmenio," *TAPA* 91 (1960), p. 324.

147   *his brother Nicomachus*   Curtius, 6.7.18.

147   *"passive disloyalty"*   Bosworth (1988), p. 102.

148   *under torture*   In the ancient view, such a confession was not suspect, as it is in our eyes. Torture was routinely used on suspects to uncover the "truth."

148   *faraway Phrada*   Hammond (1997), pp. 132–133.

149   *and his own*   After the assassination of Philip, when agents of Alexander were sent to Asia Minor to get rid of Attalus, who had insulted Alexander at the fateful wedding feast of Kleopatra and Philip. Parmenio could have resisted the assassination of Attalus, but he chose to be on the winning side—Alexander's.

CHAPTER 14   The Massacre of the Branchidae

150   *Cyrus the Great*   Curtius, 7.3.1–3. The Ariaspians were given the title of the Benefactors by Cyrus after they had brought 30,000 wagons with provisions to his army when it was campaigning in the desert nearby and had nearly run out of food according to Arrian, 3.27.5, and Diodorus, 17.81.1.

150   *lands of their neighbors*   Arrian, 3.27.5.

150   *to the south*   Curtius, 7.3.4; Diodorus, 17.81.2.

150   *revolt in Areia*   Diodorus, 17.81.3.

150   *Caranus*   The leaders according to Arrian, 3.28.2.

150   *Andronicus*   Curtius, 7.3.2.

150   *suppress the rebellion*   Arrian, 3.28.2.

150   *put down the revolt*   Arrian, 3.28.2.

150   *his overall objective*   For the wisdom of the strategy, see Fuller (1960), p. 289.

151   *with a spear*   Arrian, 3.28.3.

151   *turn and flee*   Arrian, 3.28.3.

151   *to the king*   Curtius, 7.4.40.

151   *some 5,600 Greeks*   Curtius, 7.3.4.

151   *and 600 cavalry*   Curtius, 7.3.5.

151   *by March 329*   Bosworth (1988), p. 105.

151   *wild temperature swings*   Curtius, 7.3.12; Diodorus, 17.82.2, says that the land was snow-covered and not easily approached by other tribes because of the extreme cold.

151   *are not unknown*   Gritzner, J., *Afghanistan* (Philadelphia, 2002), p. 19.

151   *supply of provisions*   Curtius, 7.3.18.

151   (*perhaps located near modern Begram*)   Bosworth (1988), p. 107.

151   *Alexandria-in-the-Caucasus*   Curtius, 7.3.22–23; Arrian, 3.28.4; Diodorus, 17.83.1.

151   *spring of 329*   Curtius, 7.3.21; Arrian, 3.28.4.

151   *pursued him*   Curtius, 7.4.1.

153   *ravaging the countryside*   Arrian, 3.28.8.

153   *in Bactria*   Arrian, 3.29.1.

153   *raise an army*   Diodorus, 17.83.3.

153   *or 8,000*   Arrian, 3.28.8; Curtius, 7.4.20.

153   (*Amu Darya*)   Which flows along the border of Afghanistan with modern Tajikistan, Uzbekistan, and Turkmenistan for 680 miles before turning northwestward toward the Aral Sea; see Gritzner, J., *Afghanistan* (Philadelphia, 2002), p. 20.

153   *planning to flee*   Arrian, 3.28.9–10.

153   *governor of the region*   Arrian, 3.29.1

153   *across the river*   Arrian, 3.29.2–4.

153   *the Persian empire*   Curtius, 7.5.28–29.

154   *into slavery*   Curtius, 7.5.30–35.

154   *face of the earth*   For a similar analysis of what led Alexander to commit this atrocity, see Hammond (1997), pp. 141–143.

154   *hand him over*   Arrian, 3.29.6–7.

154   *his men had left*   Arrian, 3.29.7–30.2.

154   *Macedonians would pass*   Arrian, 3.30.3.

155   *save their lives*   Arrian, 3.30.4.

155   *for execution*   Arrian, 3.30.5.

155   *arrows shot into him*   Curtius, 7.5.38–40.

CHAPTER 15 The Wrath of Dionysos

157   *royal city of Maracanda*   Arrian, 3.30.6.

157   *out of the 30,000 survived*   Arrian, 3.30.10–11.

157   (*the modern Syr Dar'ya*)   Arrian, 3.30.7.

157   *the European Tanais*   *Metaphysics*, 1.13.350a24–25; Bosworth (1988), p. 109.

157   *Asia and Europe*   Arrian, 3.30.9.

158   *with the latter*   Arrian, 4.1.2, 15.5.

158   *across the river*   Arrian, 4.1.3–4. For a detailed analysis of the foundation, see Fraser, P., *Cities of Alexander the Great* (Oxford, 1996), pp. 66–67,
151–153.

158   *in Tajikistan*   Bosworth (1988), pp. 110, 248.

158   *time-expired Macedonians*   Arrian, 4.4.1; Holt, F., "Alexander's Settlements in Central Asia," *Ancient Macedonia* 4 (1986), pp. 315–323; Fraser, P.,
Cities of Alexander the Great (Oxford, 1996), p. 152.

158   *Bactrians as well*   Arrian, 4.1.4–5.

158   *sinister purpose*   Arrian, 4.1.5.

158   *Cyrus the Great*   Arrian, 4.2.2–3.5.

158   *at Cyropolis alone*   Arrian, 4.3.4.

158   *behind at Maracanda*   Arrian, 4.3.6.

159   *the local peoples*   Arrian, 4.3.7. For Alexander's ultimately successful
pursuit of Spitamenes, see Holt, F., "Spitamenes Against Alexander," *Historikogeographika* 4 (1994), pp. 51–58.

159   *securing his rear*   Fuller (1960), p. 289, once again, here identifies Alexander's strategic practice of securing his rear before proceeding with offensive
operations

159   *across the Jaxartes*   Arrian, 4.4.2–3.

159   *history of warfare*   Fuller (1960), p. 296.

159   *in serious danger*   Arrian, 4.4.4–9.

159   *Alexander might give*   Arrian, 4.5.1.

159   *left alone*   In the longer term, however, as Holt, F., "Alexander's Settlements in Central Asia," *Ancient Macedonia* 4 (1986), pp. 315–323, has pointed
out, this foundation and Alexander's other settlements in Bactria-Sogdiana,
while established without too much opposition as long as Alexander was in the
neighborhood, after he left, became magnets of local resistance. There was
also dissent within the foundations. That said, it is equally clear from archaeological excavation of sites such as Ai Khanoum in southeastern Sogdiana that
Greek culture did have its effects. For excavations at Ai Khanoum, see the
Select Modern Bibliography.

159   *relief force*   Arrian, 4.5.3.

159   *Sacae nomads*   Curtius, 7.7.32–33; Bosworth (1988), p. 111.

159   *up to him*   Arrian, 4.5.4.

160   *Polytimetus (Zeravshan)*   Arrian, 4.5.5–6.

160   *put to death, too*   Arrian, 4.5.7–9.

160   *300 infantry survived*   Arrian, 4.6.1–2.

160   *Maracanda once again*   Arrian, 4.6.3.

160   *were butchered*   Arrian, 4.6.4–5.

160   *and Stasanor*   Arrian, 4.7.1.

160   *sent by Antipater*   Curtius, 7.10.10–12.

160   *into Sogdiana*   Curtius, 7.10.13–15.

160   *and Artabazus*   Reported out of time sequence by Arrian, 4.16.2.

161   *in Sogdiana*   Bosworth (1988), pp. 112–113.

161   *18,000 feet*   Curtius, 7.11.1–29; Arrian, 4.18.4–19.6, who places the episode a year later during the spring of 327.

161   *Darius' wife*   Arrian, 4.19.5.

161   *indeed could fly*   Curtius, 7.11.5–6.

161   *first man up*   Arrian, 4.18.7.

161   *did have wings*   Curtius, 7.11.24.

161   *gave up*   For Alexander's use of surprises in warfare, see Fuller (1960), pp. 300–301.

161   *in marriage*   Arrian, 4.19.5.

162   *the Chorasmians*   Arrian, 4.15.1–4.

162   *his offer*   Arrian, 4.15.5–6.

162   *a single stroke*   Bazaira, in Curtius, 8.1.10–19; Basista, in the summary of Diodorus' book 17.

162   *since 330*   Hammond (1997), p. 150.

162   *advanced age*   Curtius, 8.1.19.

162   *the Dioscuri*   Arrian, 4.8.1–2.

162   *early-starting banquets*   Curtius, 8.1.22.

162   *to Tyndareus*   Arrian, 4.8.2.

162   *they suggested*   Arrian, 4.8.3.

163   *as a whole*   Arrian, 4.8.4–5.

163   *nor marvelous*   Arrian, 4.8.6.

163   *"This very hand"*   Arrian, 4.8.7.

163   *by the barbarians*   Plutarch, 50.4.

163   *named Andronicus*   Carney, E., "The Death of Clitus," *GRBS* 22 (1981), pp. 149–160.

163   *his sister's husband*   Carney, E., "The Death of Clitus," *GRBS* 22 (1981), pp. 149–160.

163   *laughing at them*   Plutarch, 50.5.

163   *his own case*   Plutarch, 50.6.

164   *"Indeed, this cowardice"*   Plutarch, 50.6.

164   *"Wretched fellow"*   Plutarch, 51.1.

164   *"But we"*   Plutarch, 51.1.

164   *"Do not"*   Plutarch, 51.2.

164   *his Persian girdle*   Plutarch, 51.3.

164   *to turn out*   Arrian, 4.8.8.

165   *"he had come"*   Arrian, 4.8.8, translation from Brunt (1976), p. 367.

165   *with his fist*   Plutarch, 51.4.

165   *another door*   Plutarch, 51.5.

165   *"Alas, in Hellas"*   Euripides, *Andromache*, line 693, as reported by Plutarch, 51.5, translation from Perrin (1958), p. 373.

165   *as Cleitus did*   In fact, in addition to knowing Euripides well, Alexander may also have been a dramatist in his own right. He possibly composed a Satyr-play titled *Agên*, which may have been performed later at the Hydaspes River during the celebration of the Dionysia. For the play, see Athenaeus, 2.50.f and 13.595.c.

165   *ran him through*   Plutarch, 51.5.

165   *"it was not"*   Arrian, 4.9.2, translation from Brunt (1976), p. 367.

165   *all bodily needs*   Arrian, 4.9.3–4.

165   *paid no attention*   Plutarch, 52.1.

165   *decreed by fate*   Plutarch, 52.1.

166   *all were dead*   Plutarch, 50.2–3.

166   *conquer his shame*   Plutarch, 52.2.

166   *Alexander's feelings*   Plutarch, 52.2.

166   *lawful and just*   Arrian, 4.9.7.

166   *lawless than before*   Plutarch, 52.4.

166   *had done wrong*   Arrian, 4.9.5–6.

CHAPTER 16   The End of the Revolts

168   *to be done*   Curtius, 8.2.12.

168   *governor of Bactria*   Curtius, 8.2.14.

169   *Zariaspa (Balkh)*   Arrian, 4.16.4–5.

169   *"with more courage"*   Arrian, 4.16.7, translation from Brunt (1976), p. 395.

169   *fled into the desert*   Arrian, 4.17.1–2.

169   *surrendered to Coenus*   Arrian, 4.17.3–6.

169   *winter of 328/27*   Arrian, 4.18.1–2.

169   *rule of the area*   Curtius, 8.2.19–33.

170   *magnificent funerals*   Curtius, 8.2.33–40.

170   *drinking and eating*   Curtius, 8.3.1–8.

170   *ex-husband's head*   Curtius, 8.3.9.

170   *identification was not possible*   Curtius, 8.3.11–13.

170   *away from them*   Arrian, 4.17.7.

170   *to Alexander*   Curtius, 8.3.16.

170   *in Parthia and Areia*   Arrian, 4.18.1.

171   *a new force*   Arrian, 4.18.2–3.

171   *keep the peace*   Arrian, 4.22.3.

171   *native phalanx*   Plutarch, 47.3; Bosworth (1988), pp. 117, 272.

171   *nobleman Oxyartes*   For an older interpretation, see Renard, M., and J. Servais, "À propos du mariage d'Alexandre et de Roxane," *ACl* 24 (1955), pp. 29–50.

172   *Macedonian style*   Curtius, 8.4.27.

172   *same loaf*   Curtius, 8.4.27.

172   *of his empire*   Hammond (1997), p. 154.

172   *a son, Herakles*   Hammond (1997), p. 154.

172   *(though possessed with)*   Curtius, 8.4.25.

172   *a captive, Briseis*   Curtius, 8.4.26.

173   *at a banquet*   Plutarch, 47.4.

CHAPTER 17 One Kiss the Poorer

174   *called Gazaba*   Curtius, 8.4.1.

174   *camp followers*   Curtius, 8.4.2–13.

174   *saving the army*   Curtius, 8.4.19–20.

174   *toward Bactra*   Arrian, 4.22.1–2.

174   *for Bactra*   Arrian, 4.22.2.

175   *before the king*   Lane Fox (1973), p. 314.

175   *to the king*   For the Persian background, see Frye, R., "Gestures of Deference to Royalty in Ancient Iran," *IrAnt* 9 (1972), pp. 102–107; and Lane Fox (1973), p. 315. My discussion is deeply indebted to Lane Fox's excellent presentation.

175   *(or their images)*   Lane Fox (1973), pp. 314–315.

Notes 353

175   *act of worship*   Aeschylus, *Persai*, lines 588–589.

175   *among Greeks*   Euripides, *Orestes*, 1508.

175   *barbarian act*   Aristotle, *Rhetoric*, 1361.a.36.

175   *any human*   Herodotus, 7.136.1.

175   *freedom of a citizen*   Xenophon, 4.1.35; Bosworth (1988), pp. 284–287.

175   *private drinking party*   Plutarch, 54.3–4; Arrian, 4.12.3–5.

176   *"after he [Alexander] had drunk"*   Plutarch, 54.3–4, translation from Scott-Kilvert (1973), p. 312.

176   *ahead of the party*   Arrian, 4.12.3.

176   *at the party*   Plutarch, 55.1.

176   *another drinking party*   Arrian, 4.10.5.

176   *Anaxarchus*   Cleon, in Curtius, 8.5.10.

176   *"Alexander had a better claim"*   Arrian, 4.10.6–7, translation from Sélincourt (1971), p. 219.

177   *kept quiet*   Arrian, 4.11.1.

177   *"For my part"*   Arrian, 4.11.2–3, translation from Sélincourt (1971), pp. 219–220.

177   *"Not even Herakles"*   Arrian, 4.11.6–9, translation from Sélincourt (1971), pp. 221–222.

178   *prostration further*   Arrian, 4.12.1.

178   *before Alexander*   Arrian, 4.12.2.

178   *(with his chin)*   Curtius, 8.5.22.

178   *"You see"*   Curtius, 8.5.24.

178   *came to an end*   Curtius, 8.5.24.

180   *visit to Siwah*   After careful and full consideration of the episode, Bosworth (1988), p. 287, has reached the same conclusion.

180   *away from him*   Arrian, 4.13.2.

180   *consented to help*   Arrian, 4.13.3–4.

180   *in his sleep*   Arrian, 4.13.4.

180   *opportunity to arise*   Curtius, 8.6.11.

181   *and lived*   Arrian, 4.13.5–6.

181   *Alexander right away*   Arrian, 4.13.7.

181   *commit the crime*   Arrian, 4.13.7–14.1.

181   *close to the sophist*   Arrian, 4.14.1.

181   *Alexander's hubris*   Arrian, 4.14.2.

181   *and the Macedonians*   Arrian, 4.14.2; Curtius, 8.7.1–15.

181   *on the spot*   Arrian, 4.14.3.

181   *tortured to death*   Curtius, 8.8.20.

181   *denounced him*   Plutarch, 55.3.

181   *kill the king*   Curtius, 8.8.21.

181   *"By killing the most famous"*   Plutarch, 55.2.

182   *like anybody else*   Plutarch, 55.2.

182   *and then hanged*   Arrian, 4.14.3.

182   *from sickness*   Arrian, 4.14.3.

182   *kill the king*   Curtius, 8.8.21.

182   *disease of lice*   Plutarch, 55.5.

183   *winter of 328/27*   Arrian, 4.18.3.

183   *governorship of Syria*   Arrian, 3.6.8; Curtius, 7.10.12.

183   *and sea forces*   Arrian, 4.15.6.

183   *before his campaign*   Arrian, 3.8.3.

183   *(or Omphis)*   Curtius, 8.12.5.

183   *against his enemies*   Diodorus, 17.86.4.

184   *conquered Bactria*   Kuhrt (1995), pp. 491, 528, 609.

184   *visited India*   Curtius, 8.10.1.

184   *(modern Begram)*   Arrian, 4.22.3.–4.

184   *in the city*   Arrian, 4.22.5.

184   *the Indus River*   Arrian, 4.22.6.

CHAPTER 18   In the Footsteps of Dionysos

185   *British India*   Hammond (1997), p. 162.

185   *European enemies*   For these characters and their missions, see the superb account of Hopkirk, P., *The Great Game: The Struggle for Empire in Central Asia* (New York, 1992).

185   *Indus River*   Arrian, 4.22.7. See also Ferrill, A., "Alexander in India," *Military History Quarterly* 1 (1988), pp. 76–84; and Hahn, J., *Alexander in Indien, 327–325 v. Chr.* (Stuttgart, 2000).

185   *and Pakistan*   Gritzner, J., *Afghanistan* (Philadelphia, 2002), p. 19.

186   *(in modern Pakistan)*   Arrian, 4.23.1.

186   *Alexander's wound*   Arrian, 4.23.2–5.

186   *did not surrender*   Arrian, 4.23.5.

186   *again prevailed*   Arrian, 4.24.5.

186   *and his colleagues*   Arrian, 4.24.6.

186   *unfit for duty*   Arrian, 4.24.7.

186   *site* synoikismos   Fraser, P., *Cities of Alexander the Great* (Oxford, 1996), pp. 69, 159, 187.

186   *back to Macedon*   Arrian, 4.24.8–25.4.

186   *to their god*   Arrian, 5.1.3.

187   *after his nurse*   Arrian, 5.1.5.

187   *accompany him*   Arrian, 5.2.1–4; Acuphis also gave his son and his daughter's son as hostages.

187   *the territory*   Arrian, 5.2.2.

187   *Bacchic revel*   Arrian, 5.2.5–7.

187   *had done*   Euripides, *The Bacchae*, line 142.

187   *less friendly*   Arrian, 4.25.5.

187   *30 elephants*   Arrian, 4.25.5.

187   *or abandoned*   Arrian, 4.26.1–28.1.

187   *join his army*   Arrian, 4.27.2–4. Narain, A., "Alexander and India," *GaR* 12 (1965), pp. 155–165, claims, "At Massaga Alexander massacred 7,000 mercenaries because they refused to join him against their own countrymen," but does not cite the evidence that the mercenaries had reneged on their agreement with Alexander.

187   *Attock City*   Arrian, 4.28.1; Bosworth (1988), p. 123.

187   *arable land*   Arrian, 4.28.1–3.

187   *had failed*   Arrian, 4.28.4.

187   *because of an earthquake*   Curtius, 8.11.2.

188   *of the region*   Arrian, 4.28.6. The satrap, Nicanor, had responsibility for the region between the borders of Parapamisadae and the Indus River.

188   *at Embolima*   Arrian, 4.28.6–7. Ecbolima, in Bosworth (1988), p. 123.

188   *of the army*   Arrian, 4.29.1–6.

188   *as they worked*   Arrian, 4.30.1.

188   *every commander since*   See Fuller (1960), p. 296.

188   *cliffs of the Rock*   Arrian, 4.30.4.

188   *set up*   Curtius, 8.11.24.

188   *then collapsed*   Arrian, 4.30.5.

188   *near the Indus*   Arrian, 4.30.7.

188   *Alexander's army*   Arrian, 4.30.8.

188   *after thirty days*   Arrian, 4.22.8.

189   *Ohind (Udabhandapura)*   Arrian, 4.30.9, 5.3.5; Bosworth (1988), p. 125.

189   *prepared as well*   Arrian, 5.3.5.

189   *30 elephants*   Arrian, 5.3.5.

189   *Hydaspes Rivers*   Arrian, 5.3.6.

189   *the crossing*   Arrian, 5.3.6.

189   *of the river*   Arrian, 5.7.1–8.2.

189   *large army*   Hammond (1997), p. 164.

189   *to Taxila*   Arrian, 5.8.2.

189   *son Mophis*   Diodorus, 17.86.4; Omphis, in Curtius, 8.12.5.

189   *140 cubits*   Arrian, 5.8.2–3; Strabo, 15.1.28; nominally, a cubit is a forearm in length.

189   *3,000 bulls*   Curtius, 8.12.11.

191   *under Hephaestion*   Not mentioned by Arrian at 5.3.5.

191   *coined silver*   Curtius, 8.12.15.

191   *their trappings*   Curtius, 8.12.16.

191   *worth 1,000 talents*   Curtius, 8.12.17.

191   *"envious men"*   Curtius, 8.12.18, translation from Yardley (1984), p. 204.

191   *governors of the district*   Arrian, 5.8.5.

191   *(the modern Jhelum)*   Arrian, 5.8.3.

191   *(modern Chenab) Rivers*   For the region, see Bosworth (1988), p. 126.

191   *Porus' realm*   Strabo, 15.1.29.

191   *under arms*   Curtius, 8.13.2.

191   *war elephants*   Arrian, 5.15.4, gives 4,000 cavalry, 300 chariots, 200 elephants, and 30,000 infantry; Curtius, 8.13.6, 85 elephants, 300 chariots, 30,000 infantry; Plutarch, 62.1, 20,000 infantry, 2,000 cavalry. Devine, A., "The Battle of Hydaspes: A Tactical and Source-Critical Study," *AncW* 16 (1987), pp. 91–95, argues persuasively for the lower figures given by Plutarch.

191   *75,000 combatants*   Although only including c. 15,000 Macedonians. See Hammond (1997), p. 164.

191   *defensive position*   Arrian, 5.9.1.

191   *opposite Haranpur*   Stein, A., "The Site of Alexander's Passage of the Hydaspes and the Battle with Poros," *Geographical Journal* 80 (1932), pp. 31–46; Stein, A., *Archaeological Reconnaissances in North-West India and*

South-East Iran (London, 1937), pp. 1–36; cited by Devine, A., "The Battle of Hydaspes: A Tactical and Source-Critical Study," *AncW* 16 (1987), p. 96.

191 *posted guards* Arrian, 5.9.1.

192 *the Danube* Devine, A., "The Battle of Hydaspes: A Tactical and Source-Critical Study," *AncW* 16 (1987), p. 96.

CHAPTER 19 The Battle of the Hydaspes

193 *Taxiles/Mophis* Arrian, 5.9.3.

193 *number of places* Arrian, 5.9.3–4.

193 *September 326* Bosworth (1988), p. 127.

194 *when to deceive* Crick, B., "Introduction," in *Machiavelli: The Discourses* (London, 1978), pp. 29–30.

194 *shadowing his movements* Arrian, 5.10.3–4.

194 *modern Haranpur* Arrian, 5.11.2.

194 *(Adana)* Arrian, 5.11.1; Devine, A., "The Battle of Hydaspes: A Tactical and Source-Critical Study," *AncW* 16 (1987), p. 96.

194 *5,000 Indians* Arrian, 5.11.3.

194 *the river immediately* Arrian, 5.11.4.

194 *"pinning force"* Devine, A., "The Battle of Hydaspes: A Tactical and Source-Critical Study," *AncW* 16 (1987), p. 97.

194 *Indians engaged* Arrian, 5.12.1.

196 *5,000 cavalry troops* Arrian, 5.12.2, 5.14.1.

196 *final preparations* Arrian, 5.12.2–3.

196 *was initiated* Devine, A., "The Battle of Hydaspes: A Tactical and Source-Critical Study," *AncW* 16 (1987), pp. 91–113, basing his reconstruction on Arrian's account, which is by far the most tactically coherent (p. 97), although it is also not without its problems (as Arrian on the Granicus also is).

196 *Seleucus* The future founder of the Seleucid dynasty, which would rule Alexander's Asian empire after his death in 323 B.C.E.

196 *the hypaspists* Arrian, 5.12.4–13.1. See Stein, A., "The Site of Alexander's Passage of the Hydaspes and the Battle with Poros," *Geographical Journal* 80 (1932), pp. 31–46.

196 *of their approach* Arrian, 5.13.1.

196 *by a stream* Arrian, 5.13.2.

196 *to the necks of the horses* Arrian, 5.13.2–3.

197 *infantry phalanx* Arrian, 5.13.4.

197 *for his infantry* Arrian, 5.14.1

197   *the mounted archers*   Arrian, 5.14.3.

197   *killed Bucephalas*   Arrian, 5.14.4.

197   *because of the mud*   Arrian, 5.14.5–15.2.

197   *20,000 infantry*   These figures take into account the losses suffered by the Indians as a result of the destruction of the force sent out with Porus' son at the beginning of the battle. See Devine, A., "Alexander the Great," in *Warfare in the Ancient World,* ed. J. Hackett (New York, 1989), p. 125.

198   *on the flanks*   Arrian, 5.15.5–7.

198   *(opposite Porus' left)*   Arrian, 5.16.1.

198   *stay behind them*   Arrian, 5.16.2–3.

198   *Macedonian cavalry charge*   Arrian, 5.16.3.

198   *could mass*   Arrian, 5.16.4.

198   *and Coenus*   Arrian, 5.17.1.

198   *screen of elephants*   Arrian, 5.17.2.

199   *Alexander and his men*   Arrian, 5.17.3–18.1.

199   *taken prisoner*   Diodorus, 17.89.1–2.

199   *captured alive*   Diodorus, 17.89.2.

199   *were destroyed*   Arrian, 5.18.2.

199   *lost their lives*   Diodorus, 17.89.3.

200   *and execution*   Devine, A., "The Battle of Hydaspes: A Tactical and Source-Critical Study," *AncW* 16 (1987), p. 109.

200   *largest elephant*   Diodorus, 17.88.4. Goukowsky, P., "Le roi Poros et son éléphant," *BCH* 96 (1972), pp. 473–502.

200   *seven feet tall himself*   Arrian, 5.19.1; Diodorus, 17.88.4. Plutarch, 60.6, gives Porus' height as four cubits and a span, or about six feet and three inches.

200   *without riders*   Arrian, 5.18.4–5, translation adapted from Sélincourt (1971), p. 280.

200   *"What do you"*   Arrian, 5.19.2.

200   *"Treat me, O Alexander"*   Arrian, 5.19.2.

200   *enlarged his realm*   Arrian, 5.19.3.

200   *exhaustion and age*   Arrian, 5.19.4. For the foundations, see Fraser, P., *Cities of Alexander the Great* (Oxford, 1996), pp. 161–162. Neither site has been excavated.

201   *"In former days"*   Arrian, 5.19.5–6, translation from Sélincourt (1971), pp. 282–283. On the founding of the city named after Bucephalas, see Miller, M., "The 'Porus' Decadrachm and the Founding of Bucephala," *AncW* 25 (1994), pp. 109–120.

CHAPTER 20 The Mutiny at the Hyphasis River

202   *for the victory*   Arrian, 5.20.1.

202   *many of their friends*   For the point, see Lloyd, A., "Philip II and Alexander the Great: The Moulding of Macedon's Army," in *Battle in Antiquity*, ed. A. Lloyd (London, 1996), pp. 173–174.

202   *riding an elephant*   A so-called *decadrachma*. See Holt, F., *Alexander the Great and the Mystery of the Elephant Medallions* (Berkeley, 2003).

202   *(in what is now Kashmir)*   Arrian, 5.20.1–2; Hammond (1997), p. 169.

203   *alliance with Alexander*   Arrian, 5.19.2–4.

203   *sent home*   Arrian, 5.20.4.

203   *conquest of India*   Diodorus, 17.89.4–5.

203   *slung from trees*   Diodorus, 17.90.7.

203   *variety of monkeys*   Diodorus, 17.90.1.

203   *easier to catch*   Diodorus, 17.90.1–3.

204   *forty elephants*   Arrian, 5.20.5.

204   *an unpleasant sight*   Arrian, 5.20.6.

204   *named Porus*   Arrian, 5.20.6.

204   *with his army*   Bosworth (1988), p. 131.

204   *from the monsoons*   Bosworth (1988), p. 131.

204   *were wrecked*   Arrian, 5.20.8–9.

204   *to Alexander*   Arrian, 5.21.1–2.

204   *thunder and lightning*   Diodorus, 17.94.2–3.

205   *search for provisions*   Arrian, 5.21.4.

205   *and Amritsar*   Arrian, 5.21.5–22.2; Bosworth (1988), p. 132.

205   *triple defensive ring*   Arrian, 5.22.4.

205   *outer ring of wagons*   Arrian, 5.23.1–2.

205   *denser formation*   Arrian, 5.23.2.

205   *under his command*   Arrian, 5.24.1–3.

205   *personal bodyguards*   Arrian, 5.24.4–5.

205   *Sangala's capture*   Arrian, 5.24.6–7.

205   *viewed as rebels*   Arrian, 5.24.7.

205   *in those cities*   Arrian, 5.24.8.

205   *the Indians there*   A few miles within the union of modern India; see Narain, A., "Alexander and India," *GaR* 12 (1965), pp. 155–165.

205   *to the war*   Arrian, 5.24.8.

206   *to the west*   According to the measurement of Baeton, one of Alexander's land-surveyors. See Jacoby (1962), 119F 2a, p. 623.

206   *of the river*   Diodorus, 17.93.2.

206   *to the Ganges*   The actual distance was c. 205 miles; see Bosworth (1988), p. 133.

206   *fighting elephants*   Plutarch, 62.2.

206   *barber's son*   Diodorus, 17.93.3.

206   *whole earth*   Diodorus, 17.93.4.

206   *without respite*   Diodorus, 17.94.1–2.

207   *military records*   Diodorus, 17.94.3–4.

207   *should lead them*   Arrian, 5.25.2. For the mutiny, see Holt, F., "The Hyphasis 'Mutiny': A Source Study," *AncW* 5 (1982), pp. 33–59.

207   *the whole world*   Arrian, 5.25.3–26.2.

207   *when to stop*   Arrian, 5.27.2–9.

207   *"I shall have others"*   Arrian, 5.28.2, translation adapted from Sélincourt (1971), p. 298.

208   *presumably deafening*   Arrian, 5.28.4.

208   *fortuitously proved*   Arrian, 5.28.4.

208   *Alexander ever suffered*   Arrian, 5.29.1.

208   *low birth*   Plutarch, 62.4.

209   *"To Father Ammon"*   Philostratus, *Life of Apollonius*, 2.43.

209   *cavalry exercises*   Arrian, 5.29.1–2.

209   *huge stature*   Diodorus, 17.95.1–2.

209   *abandoning the area*   Arrian, 5.29.4–5.

209   *by an illness*   Arrian, 6.2.1; and Curtius, 9.3.20, who also reports that Coenus died of a disease, but mistakenly claims that Coenus died at the Acesines (on the way back to the Hydaspes). But Curtius' mistake about where Coenus died in no way alters the fact that he died of a disease.

209   *in Coenus' death*   Badian, E., "Harpalus," *JHS* 81 (1961), p. 20, where Alexander's involvement is only possibly intimated, without pushing the clear evidence; see also Worthington, I., "How 'Great' Was Alexander?" *Ancient History Bulletin* 13, no. 2 (1999), pp. 39–55; and again in Worthington, I., "Alexander and 'the Interests of Historical Accuracy': A Reply," *Ancient History Bulletin* 13, no. 4 (1999), pp. 136–140.

210   *evidence for that*   For a refutation of the implication that Alexander somehow was involved in the death of Coenus, see Holt, F., "The Hyphasis 'Mutiny': A Source Study," *AncW* 5 (1982), pp. 49–55.

210   *"it was merely"*   Curtius, 9.3.20, translation from Yardley (1984), p. 219.

210   *at least some gods*   Badian, E., "Harpalus," *JHS* 81 (1961), p. 20.

CHAPTER 21 The Meed of Great Deeds

213   *120,000 men*   Arrian, *Indike* 19.5.

213   *front-line infantrymen*   Hammond (1997), p. 171.

213   *short of 2,000*   Arrian, 6.1.1, 6.2.4. Nearchus, Alexander's chief naval commander, alternatively gives a figure of 1,800, including warships, merchantmen, and horse transports, Arrian, *Indike*, 19.7.

213   *ever assembled*   Ambrose, S., *D-Day, June 6, 1944: The Climactic Battle of World War II* (New York, 1994), pp. 24–25.

213   *the expedition*   Arrian, *Indike*, 18.1.

213   *nautical expertise*   Arrian, *Indike*, 18.2.

214   *and friends*   Arrian, *Indike*, 18.3–9.

214   *from Crete*   Arrian, *Indike*, 18.10.

214   *royal flagship*   Arrian, *Indike*, 18.9.

214   *set out*   Arrian, *Indike*, 18.12.

214   *Indus, too*   Arrian, 6.3.1.

214   *he usually honored*   Arrian, 6.3.2.

214   *Companion cavalry*   Arrian, 6.2.2.

214   *200 elephants*   Arrian, 6.2.2.

214   *Alexander, and Hephaestion*   Arrian, 6.2.2–3.

214   *and Acesines*   Arrian, 6.4.4; Curtius, 9.4.1.

214   *with their troops*   Arrian, 6.5.5.

215   *human history*   Narain, A., "Alexander and India," *GaR* 12 (1965), pp. 155–165.

215   *of the river*   Arrian, 6.5.6.

215   *intercept stragglers*   Arrian, 6.5.6; and thus eight days after Alexander himself set out.

215   *against the Mallians*   Arrian, 6.6.1.

215   *waged thus far*   Rightly emphasized by Narain, A., "Alexander and India," *GaR* 12 (1965), pp. 155–165.

215   *stormed their towns*   Arrian, 6.6.2–5.

215   *in local marshes*   Arrian, 6.6.6.

215   *many of them*   Arrian, 6.7.1–2.

215   *were enslaved*   Arrian, 6.7.3.

215   *ascetic religious sect*   Hammond (1997), p. 172.

215   *successfully undermined*   Arrian, 6.7.5–6.

215   *survivors captured alive*   Arrian, 6.7.6.

216   *cities nearby*   Arrian, 6.8.4–8.

216   *had been captured*   Arrian, 6.9.1–2.

216   *of the city*   Arrian, 6.9.2.

216   *his shield*   Arrian, 6.9.3.

216   *another ladder*   Arrian, 6.9.3.

216   *virtually alone*   Arrian, 6.9.4.

217   *into the citadel itself*   Arrian, 6.9.5.

217   *on his right*   Diodorus, 17.99.2.

217   *commander of the Indians*   Arrian, 6.9.6; Diodorus, 17.99.2.

217   *well-aimed stones*   Arrian, 6.9.6.

217   *missile at Alexander*   Arrian, 6.9.6.

217   *in his defense*   Arrian, 6.10.1.

217   *his loss of blood*   Arrian, 6.10.2, translation adapted from Sélincourt (1971), p. 314.

217   *protecting Alexander*   Arrian, 6.10.3–4.

218   *shield over Alexander*   Arrian, 6.10.4.

218   *No one was spared*   Arrian, 6.11.1.

218   *its barbed head*   Curtius, 9.5.25–28.

218   *pulled out the arrow*   Arrian, 6.11.1.

218   *three inches thick*   Plutarch, *On the Fortune or Virtue of Alexander,* 341c.

218   *were removed*   Arrian, 6.12.2.

218   *and officers*   Arrian, 6.12.3.

219   *at the time*   Arrian, 6.13.3.

219   *out of dangers*   Arrian, 6.13.4.

219   *a great deed*   Arrian, 6.13.5; the iambic lines apparently come from a lost tragedy of Aeschylus, fragment 282.

220   *and the Mallians*   Arrian, 6.14.1–3.

220   *with the Indus*   Arrian, 6.14.4–5.

220   *juncture of the rivers*   Arrian, 6.15.2.

220   *conduit for trade*   Arrian, 6.15.2; Hammond (1997), p. 173.

220   *his office ineffectively*   Arrian, 6.15.3.

221   *damaged boats*   Arrian, 6.15.4.

221   *region of India*   Arrian, 6.15.4.

221   *realm in India*   Arrian, 6.15.5.

221   *installed in it*   Arrian, 6.15.6–7; Bosworth (1988), p. 137.

221   *a certain Oxycanus*   Arrian, 6.16.2.

221   *Indian hill tribes*   Arrian, 6.16.3.

221   *his enemy Musicanus*   Arrian, 6.16.4.

221   *enslaved the inhabitants*   Diodorus, 17.102.6.

221   *encouraging the revolt*   Diodorus, 17.102.7; Arrian, 6.16.5.

221   *in this campaign*   Diodorus, 17.102.6–7; Curtius, 9.8.15, citing Cleitarchus.

221   *the revolt executed*   Arrian, 6.17.2; Curtius, 9.8.16.

221   *venom of snakes*   Diodorus, 17.103.4.

222   *and gangrene*   Diodorus, 17.103.5.

222   *in its mouth*   Diodorus, 17.103.7.

222   *spared them*   Diodorus, 17.103.8.

222   *"For what reason"*   Plutarch, 65.3.

222   *Indian word* Cale   Plutarch, 65.3.

222   *on the borders*   Plutarch, 65.3.

CHAPTER 22   Fulfillment of an Oracle

223   *over to Alexander*   Arrian, 6.17.2.

223   *Alexander at Pattala*   Arrian, 6.17.2–4; Bosworth (1988), p. 138.

224   *virtually deserted*   Arrian, 6.17.5.

224   *did return*   Arrian, 6.17.6.

224   *were also built*   Arrian, 6.18.1–2.

224   *westerly stream*   Arrian, 6.18.2–3.

224   *build new ones*   Arrian, 6.18.4.

224   *by the receding tide*   Arrian, 6.18.5–19.2.

224   *island of Cilluta*   Arrian, 6.19.3.

225   *so honor*   Arrian, 6.19.3–4.

225   *oracle of Ammon*   Arrian, 6.19.4.

225   *under Nearchus' command*   Arrian, 6.19.5.

225   *(but slower)*   Arrian, 6.20.4.

225   *fleet with water*   Arrian, 6.20.4, 6.19.5.

226   *the coastal voyage*   Arrian, 6.20.5.

226   *"peace and with it"*   Hammond (1997), p. 175.

226   *was a failure*   For the claim, see Bosworth, A., "The Indian Satrapies Under Alexander the Great," *Antichthon* 17 (1983), pp. 37–46.

227   *to the Indian Ocean*   As Bosworth, A., "The Indian Satrapies Under Alexander the Great," *Antichthon* 17 (1983), pp. 37–46, himself admits.

227   *Russian campaign*   Brunt, P., "The Aims of Alexander," *GaR* 12 (1965), pp. 205–215.

CHAPTER 23   Death in the Desert

228   *August 325*   Arrian, 6.21.3.

228   *rest of the army*   Arrian, 6.21.3.

228   *(wives, concubines, children)*   Bosworth (1988), p. 142.

228   *early November*   Arrian 6.21.1; Bosworth (1988), p. 140.

228   *branch of the river*   Arrian, *Indike*, 21.1ff.

228   *"by the foothills"*   Bosworth (1988), p. 142.

229   *called the Oreitai*   Arrian, 6.21.3.

229   *many surrendered*   Arrian, 6.21.5.

229   *territory of the Gedrosians*   Arrian, 6.22.3.

229   *Cyrus and Semiramis*   Arrian, 6.24.1–3.

231   *market or anchorage*   Arrian, 6.23.1.

231   *without a plan*   Badian, E., "Harpalus," *JHS* 81 (1961), pp. 20–21.

231   *inhospitable coast*   Arrian, 6.23.2, who says that the coastline was entirely desert.

231   *the Coastal Range*   See Stein, A., "On Alexander's Route into Gedrosia: An Archaeological Tour in Las Bela," *Geographical Journal* 102 (1943), pp. 193–227; and Bosworth (1988), p. 144.

231   *no water*   Arrian, 6.23.1.

231   *down to the coast*   Arrian, 6.23.1.

231   *not exactly sweet*   Arrian, 6.23.2–3.

232   *by the receding tide*   Arrian, *Indike*, 29.9.

232 *animal skins* Diodorus, 17.105.3–5.

232 *(perhaps the oasis of Turbat in southwestern Pakistan)* Bosworth (1988), p. 144.

232 *into the provisions* Arrian, 6.23.4–5.

232 *the baggage animals* Arrian, 6.24.4–26.5.

232 *in sandy graves* Arrian, 6.25.3.

232 *had poured away* Arrian, 6.26.1–3. An incident that some writers claimed took place earlier in Parapamisadae, but suits the context of Gedrosia far better.

233 *the royal tent* Arrian, 6.25.4–6.

233 *sixty days* Arrian, 6.24.1, 27.1.

233 *satrap of Drangiana* Diodorus, 17.105.6–7; Curtius, 9.10.17.

233 *and elsewhere* Arrian, 6.27.6.

233 *such a disaster* Curtius, 9.10.17.

233 *"to expiate its contumacy"* Badian, E., "Harpalus," *JHS* 81 (1961), p. 21.

233 *"his prior knowledge"* Bosworth (1988), p. 146.

233 *an anchorage* Arrian, 6.23.1.

233 *the baggage train* Arrian, 6.23.4.

233 *they had done* Arrian, 6.23.4–5.

234 *were better* Arrian, 6.23.2.

234 *at face value* Plutarch, 66.2. We know that at least 18,000 Macedonians made it back to Opis; see Bosworth (1988), p. 145.

234 *Alexander's ambition* It is worth noting that we have no idea how many of those who accompanied Alexander through Gedrosia died from the heat or lack of food or water, as opposed to the flood.

CHAPTER 24 The Reign of Terror?

235 *replaced him with Thoas* Arrian, 6.27.1.

235 *rebellious Oreitae* Arrian, *Indike*, 23.5.

235 *and the Gedrosians* Arrian, 6.27.1.

235 *Philip's satrapy* Arrian, 6.27.2.

236 *the reports about him* Curtius, 9.10.21.

236 *after he revolted* Arrian, 6.27.3.

236 *also arrived* Curtius, 9.10.22.

236 *by the Carmanians* Arrian, 6.28.1; Curtius, 9.10.25.

236   *honor of Dionysos*   Arrian, 6.28.2.

236   *in decorated wagons*   Curtius, 9.10.26.

236   *"seven days on"*   Curtius, 9.10.27, translation from Yardley (1984), p. 237.

236   *did not happen*   Arrian, 6.28.1–2.

236   *governors and officers*   For the events interpreted along with the flight of Harpalus, see Badian, E., "Harpalus," *JHS* 81 (1961), pp. 16–43.

236   *governor of Carmania*   Curtius, 9.10.21.

236   *was executed*   Curtius, 9.10.29.

236   *"luxurious living"*   Curtius, 9.10.29, translation from Yardley (1984), p. 237.

236   *perhaps Agathon*   Curtius, 10.1.1.

237   *in Ecbatana*   Arrian, 6.27.3.

237   *of the province*   Arrian, 6.27.4.

237   *as a concubine*   Curtius, 10.1.3–5.

237   *surrendered to Alexander*   Arrian, 6.27.4–5.

237   *commanders' orders*   Curtius, 10.1.8.

237   *he was executed*   Arrian, 6.27.5.

237   *called Ordanes*   Arrian, 6.27.3.

237   *put to death*   Curtius, 10.1.9.

238   *mercenaries at once*   Diodorus, 17.106.3; Bosworth (1988), p. 148.

238   *from Alexander*   Badian, E., "Harpalus," *JHS* 81 (1961), pp. 26–28.

238   *in Alexander's army*   Bosworth (1988), p. 148.

238   *acceptable level*   Bosworth (1988), p. 148.

238   *early in 324*   Arrian, 7.23.1, 24.1.

238   *hiring of mercenaries*   Bosworth (1988), p. 149.

239   *and fled*   Diodorus, 17.106.2.

239   *and 6,000 mercenaries*   Diodorus, 17.108.4–6.

239   *and expensive tastes*   Badian, E., "Harpalus," *JHS* 81 (1961), pp. 16–43.

239   *from the Red Sea*   Diodorus, 17.108.4.

239   *of the Attic type*   Diodorus, 17.108.5.

239   *a rainy day*   Diodorus, 17.108.6.

239   *(where he perhaps hoped to incite a revolt)*   Athenaeus, 13.594.e.

240   *in his wake*   Diodorus, 17.108.7–8. After Harpalus' death, there was an inquiry into funds that Harpalus had left in Athens, and Demosthenes and

other Athenian politicians were convicted of accepting bribes. Despite his consistent opposition to Macedon and Alexander, the Athenian orator Demosthenes wisely had had Harpalus arrested when he entered Athens in mid-June of 324 B.C.E., and an embassy was sent to Alexander to ask him what to do with his treasurer. Before the Athenians received a reply, Harpalus fortuitously escaped from Athens—less half of the 700 talents he had brought with him. Demosthenes was later accused of helping Harpalus to flee. For the events, see Worthington, I., "The Harpalus Affair and the Greek Response to the Macedonian Hegemony," in *Ventures into Greek History: Essays in Honour of N.G.L. Hammond*, ed. I. Worthington (Oxford, 1994), pp. 307–330.

CHAPTER 25   Nabarzanes' Gift

241   *capital of Carmania*   Diodorus, 17.106.4; Bosworth (1988), p. 150.

241   *athletic competitions*   Arrian, 6.28.3.

241   *satrap of Persia*   Arrian, 6.28.3–4.

241   *won the prize*   Plutarch, 67.4.

241   *kind of gift*   Curtius, 6.5.23.

241   *murder of Darius*   Curtius, 6.5.23.

241   *and kissed him*   Plutarch, 67.4.

242   *even took place*   Tarn, W., *Alexander the Great*, volume 2 (Cambridge, 1948), pp. 320–323.

242   *question its historicity*   For the episode, see Badian, E., "The Eunuch Bagoas: A Study in Method," *CQ* 8 (1958), pp. 144–157.

242   *an older man* (erastes)   Plutarch, 67.4.

242   *and Hellenistic periods*   For an excellent introduction to the topics of sexual preference and same-gender attractions in ancient Greece and Rome, see Hubbard, T., "Introduction," in *Homosexuality in Greece and Rome: A Sourcebook of Basic Documents* (Berkeley, 2003), pp. 1–20.

242   *the two men*   Curtius, 6.5.23.

242   *men in Athens*   It is very likely that the *eromenos/erastes* relationship was far more flexible than most scholars have credited, not only with respect to the time parameters of the relationship but far more crucially (at least for us, with our modern focus) with respect to sexual acts. The older idea that the younger *eromenos* was the passive sexual actor and the *erastes* the dominant, active partner is not supported by the full range of literary and especially artistic evidence. For a good discussion of the controversies, see Davidson, J., "Dover, Foucault and Greek Homosexuality," *Past and Present* 170 (2001), pp. 3–51.

243   *or three companions*   Jacoby (1962), 225a, p. 583, quoting Theopompus of Chios.

243   *was a homosexual*   Potts, M., and R. Short, *Ever Since Adam and Eve: The Evolution of Human Sexuality* (Cambridge, 1999), p. 76.

243   *was a heterosexual*   Tarn, W., *Alexander the Great*, volume 2 (Cambridge, 1948), pp. 320–323.

243   *was not effeminate*   Athenaeus, 10.435.a, quoting Hieronymous in his *Letters* citing Theophrastus.

244   *had sexual relations*   Aelian, *Varia Historia*, 12.34.

244   *son named Herakles*   Justin, 11.10.2–3.

244   *their provinces diminished*   Stewart, S., *In the Empire of Ghengis Khan* (Guilford, 2002), p. 17.

244   *for the eyes*   Plutarch, 21.5.

244   *to the Indus River*   Plutarch, 22.3.

244   *main port of Carmania*   Arrian, *Indike*, 34–36. Harmozeia was located southeast of modern Bandar-e-Abbas.

245   *of the voyage*   For the fragments quoted by Arrian and others, see Jacoby (1962), 133, pp. 677–722; and also Pearson (1960), pp. 131–139.

245   *eastern stream of the Indus*   Bosworth (1988), p. 140.

245   *in early November*   Strabo, 15.2.5; Arrian, *Indike*, 21.1.

245   *died down*   Arrian, *Indike*, 21.5–6.

245   *the satrap's part*   Arrian, 7.5.5; Arrian, *Indike*, 23.5. Thus, when Alexander replaced Apollophanes by Thoas at Pura, he was replacing a dead governor.

245   *at the earliest*   Bosworth (1988), p. 151.

246   *terrifying the Macedonians*   Arrian, *Indike*, 30.1–7.

246   *with their oars*   Arrian, *Indike*, 30.5–6.

246   *the south coast*   Arrian, *Indike*, 31.1–9.

246   *with the army*   Arrian, 6.28.6.

246   *road to Pasargadae*   Arrian, 6.29.1.

246   *usurped by Orxines*   Arrian, 6.29.2.

246   *as a satrap*   Curtius, 10.1.22–23.

247   *of silver coins*   Curtius, 10.1.24.

247   *put to death*   Arrian, 6.29.3.

247   *on the throne*   Curtius, 10.1.39.

247   *"O man!"*   Arrian, 6.29.8.

247   *the body of Cyrus*   Arrian, 6.29.9.

248   *every stolen object*   Arrian, 6.29.10.

248   *the guilty party*   Curtius, 10.1.33–35.

248 *"that women once"* Curtius, 10.1.37, translation from Yardley (1984), p. 240.

248 *to death illegally* Arrian, 6.30.1–2.

248 *learned Persian* Arrian, 6.30.3.

248 *to his own* Arrian, 6.30.3.

CHAPTER 26 Marriage: Persian Style

249 *Persia and Susiana* Strabo, 15.1.68; Diodorus, 17.107.1.

249 *his own life* Plutarch, 69.3; Arrian, 7.3.1.

249 *in his honor* Arrian, 7.3.1–6; Plutarch, 69.3–4; Diodorus, 17.107.1–6.

250 *from the flames* Arrian, 7.3.5.

250 *contempt for death* Diodorus, 17.107.5.

250 *the debauchery ended* Plutarch, 70.1.

250 *March 324* Diodorus, 17.107.6.

250 *from Harmozeia* Arrian, *Indike*, 42.7–8.

250 *were celebrated* Arrian, *Indike*, 42.8.

251 *of the bodyguard* Arrian, 7.5.4–6; Arrian, *Indike*, 42.9.

251 *promised to do* Diodorus, 17.38.1.

251 *Companions and friends* Arrian, 7.4.4–8.

251 *Artaxerxes III Ochus* Arrian, 7.4.4.

251 *the Bactrian Spitamenes* Arrian, 7.4.5–6.

251 *noblewomen as brides* Arrian, 7.4.6; Athenaeus, 12.538.b–539.a.

251 *the ceremony first* Arrian, 7.4.7–8.

252 *gift from Alexander* Arrian, 7.4.8.

252 *of a royal marriage* Bosworth (1988), p. 156.

253 *pleased about it* Arrian, 7.6.2.

253 *spendthrifts among them* Arrian, 7.5.1.

253 *9,870 talents* Plutarch, 70.2; Curtius, 10.2.9–11.

253 *the highest 20,000* Arrian, 7.5.3.

253 *to Asian traders* Hammond (1997), p. 188.

254 *Macedonian battle dress* Arrian, 7.6.1; Curtius, 8.5.1; Plutarch, 47.3 (selection in Hyrcania); Diodorus, 17.108.1, wrongly after Hyphasis.

254 *serve in it* Arrian, 7.6.2–4.

254   *their native javelins*   Arrian, 7.6.5.

254   *the Macedonians themselves*   Arrian, 7.6.5.

CHAPTER 27 The Mutiny at Opis

255   *the Companion cavalry*   Arrian, 7.7.1.

255   *(into the Tigris)*   Arrian, 7.7.2.

255   *with the army*   Arrian, 7.7.6.

255   *Spasinou Charax*   Pliny, *Natural History*, 6.31.138. For questions about the identification of the site of Alexander's foundation with Spasinouu Charax, rebuilt by the Arab ruler Spasines, now Karkh Maisan, see Fraser, P., *Cities of Alexander the Great* (Oxford, 1996), pp. 168–169.

255   *capital of Pella*   Bosworth (1988), p. 159.

255   *to invading fleets*   Arrian, 7.7.6–7.

256   *Nabonidus' immense empire*   Kuhrt (1995), p. 659.

256   *dangers and toils*   Arrian, 7.8.1; Curtius, 10.2.8; Diodorus, 17.109.2; Plutarch, 71.2; Justin, 12.11.4.

256   *conquer the world*   Plutarch, 71.2. For the mutiny, see Wüst, F., "Die Meuterei von Opis," *Historia* 2 (1953–1954b), pp. 418–431.

256   *respect his soldiers*   Justin, 12.11.5–6.

257   *with his own hands*   Curtius, 10.2.30; Diodorus, 17.109.2.

257   *executed without delay*   Arrian, 7.8.3.

257   *wherever they wanted*   Arrian, 7.9.1–10.7; Curtius, 10.2.15–29.

258   *out of his sight*   Arrian, 7.10.7.

258   *enter his quarters*   Arrian, 7.11.1.

258   *the customary kiss*   Arrian, 7.11.1.

259   *pity on them*   Arrian, 7.11.4.

259   *"O king"*   Arrian, 7.11.6.

259   *"But all of you"*   Arrian, 7.12.7.

259   *the victory paean*   Arrian, 7.11.7.

259   *all the Macedonians*   Arrian, 7.11.8.

259   *"any of the other"*   Arrian, 7.11.8–9, translation from Robson (1978), p. 241.

260   *paean of victory*   Arrian, 7.11.8–9.

260   *unity of mankind*   Tarn, W., "Alexander the Great and the Unity of Mankind," *ProcBritAc* 19 (1933), pp. 123–166.

260 *of the sort* See especially Badian, E., "Alexander the Great and the Unity of Mankind," *Historia* 7 (1958), pp. 425–444.

261 *of one talent* Arrian, 7.12.1.

261 *to their fathers* Arrian, 7.12.2.

261 *men sent home* Arrian, 7.12.3–4.

261 *regent in Macedon* Arrian, 7.12.5.

261 *constant interference* Arrian, 7.12.6.

261 *in her womb* Arrian, 7.12.6. On the other hand, according to Plutarch, 39.7, Alexander, after reading a long letter from Antipater criticizing Olympias, is reported to have remarked that Antipater did not realize that a single tear from a mother wiped out ten thousand letters.

262 *other Macedonians and Greeks* Arrian, 7.12.7.

262 *in Alexander's estimation* Arrian, 7.12.7.

262 *and his mother* Arrian, 7.12.6.

262 *of the shakes* Plutarch, 74.1–4.

262 *the Persian kings* Strabo, 11.13.1; Bosworth (1988), p. 163.

CHAPTER 28 Future Plans

263 *with his companions* Arrian, 7.14.1.

263 *arrived from Greece* Plutarch, 72.1.

263 *and royal sponsors* For background, see Roueché, C., *Performers and Partisans at Aphrodisias in the Roman and Late Roman Periods* (London, 1993), pp. 50–52.

263 *then rose quickly* Plutarch, 72.1.

263 *of his illness* Arrian, 7.14.1.

263 *already was dead* Arrian, 7.14.1.

263 *was Alexander-loving* Diodorus, 17.114.2.

264 *closest male friend* Arrian, 7.14.3, who uses the word *philtato*, or "most dear," to describe Alexander's relationship to Hephaestion.

264 *Alexander's own words* To Sisygambis after the battle at the Issos River; Diodorus, 17.114.2.

264 *neighboring cities demolished* Plutarch, 72.2.

264 *kept on drinking heavily* Arrian, 7.14.4.

264 *as a hero* Plutarch, 72.2.

264 *gestures of mourning* Arrian, 7.14.9.

264 *throughout the East* Arrian, 7.14.8–9.

264   *five successive friezes*   Diodorus, 17.115.1–5.

264   *carry them out*   Diodorus, 18.4.2–3, says that Perdiccas found orders
for the completion of Hephaestion's pyre as well as other plans in the so-called
Hypomnemata of the king after he died.

265   *pyramids in Egypt*   Diodorus, 18.4.4–5.

265   *and quince yellow*   "Apple Bearers" because on the butts of the spears
of these élite guards of the Persian kings were golden apples; see Athenaeus,
12.514.b.

265   *on all sides*   Athenaeus, 12.539.d–e.

265   *"he was a man"*   Bosworth (1988), p. 165.

266   *in history: conquer*   The empire of Ghengis Khan, of course, was four
times larger than Alexander's, but Ghengis Khan did not personally lead or
fight at the front of his victorious armies.

266   *spirit of Hephaestion*   Plutarch, 72.3.

266   *within his empire*   Diodorus, 17.111.5–6.

266   *and the Iberians*   Arrian, 7.15.4

267   *those in India*   Arrian, 7.19.1.

267   *schedule of audiences*   Diodorus, 17.113.3.

267   *and the rest*   Diodorus, 17.113.3–4.

267   *receiving exiles back*   Diodorus, 17.113.3.

267   *exiles' confiscated property*   The announcement (*diagramma*) was
probably made first to the army at Susa and later by letter to the Greeks at the
Olympic games. See Diodorus, 18.8.2–3; Hyperides, *Against Demosthenes*, 18;
Dinarchus, *Against Demosthenes*, 81ff; Plutarch, *Moralia*, 221A; Justin, 13.5.2;
Curtius, 10.2.4ff.

267   *as political gain*   Diodorus, 18.8.2.

267   *or, possibly, murder*   Diodorus, 17.109.1.

267   *enforce the decree*   Diodorus, 18.8.4.

267   *decree were enforced*   Diodorus, 18.8.6–7; for the effects with respect
to the island of Samos, see Dittenberger, W., *Sylloge Inscriptionum Graecorum*
(Leipzig, 1915–1924), no. 312; and generally, Bosworth (1988), pp. 220–228.
Ashton, N., "The Lamian War: A False Start," *Antichthon* 17 (1983), pp. 47–83,
has argued that the Athenians had decided to revolt from Macedonian control
in reaction to the Exiles' Decree before Harpalus fled to Athens in (perhaps)
mid-June 324 B.C.E. For compelling arguments against this interpretation, see,
Worthington, I., "The Harpalus Affair and the Greek Response to the Macedonian Hegemony," in *Ventures into Greek History: Essays in Honour of N.G.L.
Hammond*, ed. I. Worthington (Oxford, 1994), pp. 307–330.

267   *to be seen*   Bosworth (1988), pp. 221, 227–228.

267   *not stated openly*   Because of Alexander's death ten months after the proclamation of the decree, the Exiles' Decree never was enacted, at least in the way that Alexander intended it to be.

268   *returned to Athens*   Arrian, 7.19.2.

268   *at this time*   Arrian, 7.15.5.

268   *their future greatness*   Arrian, 7.15.5.

268   *of Rome's fame*   Arrian, 7.1.3.

268   *"Prophets are best"*   Arrian, 7.16.5–6.

268   *lead it eastward*   Arrian, 7.16.6.

269   *own surplus revenues*   Arrian, 7.17.1–4.

269   *the west after all*   Arrian, 7.17.6–7.

269   *(in which the upper)*   Hammond (1997), p. 179.

269   *down the Euphrates*   Arrian, 7.19.3.

269   *familiar with the sea*   Arrian, 7.19.5.

269   *honor to Alexander*   Arrian, 7.19.6.

269   *prosperous new cities*   Arrian, 7.20.2.

270   *pantheon: himself*   Arrian, 7.20.1.

270   *for further conquest*   Arrian, 7.19.6.

270   *Alexander was concerned*   Badian, E., "Alexander the Great and the Loneliness of Power," in *Studies in Greek and Roman History*, Oxford, 1968, pp. 192–205—a brilliant article, but I cannot agree with its conclusions about Alexander's state of mind in the spring of 323 B.C.E.

270   *Archias and Androsthenes*   Arrian, 7.20.3–7.

270   *into the ocean*   Arrian, 7.20.7–8.

270   *shores of the Caspian*   Arrian, 7.16.1–2.

271   *the Arabian lakes*   Arrian, 7.21.1.

271   *or unfit veterans*   Arrian, 7.21.7; Hammond (1997), p. 179.

271   *for the helmsmen*   Arrian, 7.23.5.

271   *with his cavalry*   Arrian, 7.23.1.

271   *then another Macedonian*   Arrian, 7.23.3–4. A ten-stater man received around forty drachmae per month for pay. The double-pay soldier got sixty drachmae per month; the ordinary infantryman was paid one drachma per day.

271   *honor a god*   Arrian, 7.23.2.

271   *unanswerable, question*   Hyperides, *Funeral Oration*, 21, implies that sacrifices to Alexander indeed had taken place. In Ephesos Alexander also was written of as a god, according to Strabo, 14.1.22.

271 *"Since Alexander wishes"* Wilson, N., *Aelian, Historical Miscellany* (Cambridge, 1997), 2.19, p. 91.

271 *Alexander a god* Athenaeus, 6.251.b.

271 *not far off* Arrian, 7.24.1. On the controversies related to Alexander's deification, see Balsdon, J., "The 'Divinity' of Alexander," *Historia* 1 (1950), pp. 363–388; Fredricksmeyer, E., "Three Notes on Alexander's Deification," *AJAH* 4 (1979), pp. 1–9; and Badian, E., "The Deification of Alexander the Great," in *Ancient Macedonian Studies in Honor of Charles F. Edson*, ed. H. Dell (Thessaloniki, 1981), pp. 27–71.

CHAPTER 29 Death in Babylon

273 *his old tutor* For a good introduction to the source traditions, see Bosworth, A., "The Death of Alexander the Great: Rumour and Propaganda," CQ 21 (1971), pp. 112–136.

273 *so-called* Royal Diaries Plutarch, 76.1–4; Arrian, 7.24.4–26.3, in Greek the *Ephemerides.*

273 *admiral of his fleet* Plutarch, 75.3.

273 *at Medius' party* Plutarch, 75.3; Arrian, 7.25.1. According to Arrian's version of the story, the fever came on Alexander after he had dined with Medius, drank until late at night, bathed, ate a little, and slept where he was—the fever already having come over him.

274 *toward the evening* Plutarch, 76.1–4.

274 *the* Royal Diaries Arrian, 7.25.1–6.

274 *day after that* Arrian, 7.25.2.

274 *with his eyes* Arrian, 7.26.1.

275 *by the god* Arrian, 7.26.2.

275 *where he was* Arrian, 7.26.2.

275 *to be death* Arrian, 7.26.3.

275 *ended here* Arrian, 7.26.3.

275 "to kratisto" Arrian, 7.26.3.

275 *was ambiguous* Diodorus, 17.117.4, also reports this exchange between Alexander and his friends.

275 *of his funeral* Diodorus, 17.117.4.

275 *they were happy* Curtius, 10.5.6.

275 *and former friends* Plutarch, 77.1–3; Arrian, 7.27.1–3.

275 *more sinister story* Diodorus, 17.117.5–118.2; Justin, 12.13.7–15.13.

276 Andromeda *of Euripides* Athenaeus, 12.537.d, quoting Ephippus. If the anecdote is true, it is another indication that while Alexander may

have lost his mind by the spring of 323 he most certainly had not lost his memory.

276 *toasts in return* Athenaeus, 10.434.c, quoting Nicobule.

276 *the royal apartments* Diodorus, 17.117.1–2.

276 *hoof of an ass* Plutarch, 77.2.

276 *and Medius' lover* Arrian, 7.27.1–2. Medius was the host of the fatal dinner party.

276 *vomit up the wine* Stoneman (1991), book 3, chapter 32. For the Alexander Romance generally, see Baynham, E., "Who Put the 'Romance' in the Alexander Romance? The Alexander Romance within Alexander Historiography," *Ancient History Bulletin* 9, no. 1 (1995), pp. 1–13.

277 *his eternal sleep* Stoneman (1991), book 3, chapter 32.

277 *Babylon in 323* See Fraser, P., "Current Problems Concerning the Early History of the Cult of Sarapis," *OpAth* 7 (1967), pp. 23–45; and Bosworth (1988), p. 172.

277 *of foul play* Bosworth (1988), p. 172.

277 *was not murdered* Bosworth (1988), p. 172.

277 *nearly immediate death* Lane Fox (1973), p. 471.

278 *after Alexander's death* Plutarch, 77.1. Although there may have been private rumors circulating earlier—as was to be expected in the case of the sudden death of a great public figure such as Alexander.

278 *as soon as possible* Lane Fox (1973), p. 470.

278 *seems more plausible* For a judicious weighing of the evidence and skepticism about the story of foul play, see Bosworth (1988), p. 173; Hammond also disbelieves the murder story (1997), p. 198.

278 *remains endemic there* See Engels, D., "A Note on Alexander's Death," *CP* 73 (1978), pp. 224–228; and Hammond (1997), p. 198.

278 *acute alcohol poisoning* See generally, O'Brien, J., *Alexander the Great: The Invisible Enemy* (London, 1992).

278 *a drinking spree* Athenaeus, 10.434.b.

279 *of secondary infection* Borza, E., and J. Reames-Zimmerman, "Some New Thoughts on the Death of Alexander the Great," *AncW* 31 (2000), pp. 22–30.

279 *dead at his feet* Plutarch, 73.1. The theory of John Marr, the chief epidemiologist of the Virginia Health Department of Health, cited in "Analysis: Alexander the Great May Have Been West Nile Victim," *Cedar Rapids Gazette*, December 13, 2003.

279 *with Alexander persists* For some recent theories, see Oldach, D., et al., "A Mysterious Death," *New England Journal of Medicine* 338 (1998), pp. 1764–1768.

279   *without a trace*   Bosworth (1988), p. 180.

279   *to be fraudulent*   Holt, F., "Dead Kings Are Hard to Find," *Saudi Aramco World* 52, no. 3 (2001), pp. 10–11.

279   *his lost grave*   Adriani, A., *La tomba di Alessandro: Realita, ipotesi e fantasie* (Rome, 2000); Holt, F., "Dead Kings Are Hard to Find," *Saudi Aramco World* 52, no. 3 (2001), pp. 10–11.

CHAPTER 30   Alexander: Mass Murderer or Messiah?

280   *forced labor camps*   For a vivid description, see Conquest, R., *Reflections on a Ravaged Century* (New York, 2000), esp. pp. 97–101. Reading Conquest's book, it becomes impossible to overestimate the differences between Stalinist Russia and Alexander's empire. As Conquest points out (with characteristic irony), the fact that we are not certain of the human cost of the terror within a few million is itself remarkable testimony to the extent of the Stalinist terror.

281   *his own mortality*   For which qualities of Hitler, see Kershaw, I., *Hitler, 1936–45: Nemesis* (London, 2000), pp. 411, 612, 727–727, 777, 36–37, 84, 92, 228.

282   *(whose hearts were)*   Hassig, R., *War and Society in Ancient Mesoamerica* (Berkeley, 1992), pp. 135–164; Smith, M., *The Aztecs* (Oxford, 1996), pp. 221–227.

282   *became a legend*   For a nice appreciation of Cyrus' accomplishments, see Kuhrt (1995), p. 661.

283   *come to take possession of*   Justin, 11.6.1.

284   *brilliance of its execution*   Especially, as we shall see, his defeat of the superior Persian navy through the capture of the port cities on the coast of Asia Minor (roughly modern western Turkey). For the strategy, see Keegan, J., *The Mask of Command* (New York, 1987), pp. 27–28.

284   *more than a decade*   As rightly emphasized by Engels, D., *Alexander the Great and the Logistics of the Macedonian Army* (Berkeley, 1978).

285   *to devastating effect*   Stressed by von Clausewitz as the second of his strategic principles of effective warfare, and discussed by Fuller (1960), p. 299.

285   *for later imitators*   Including especially some of his very own generals.

285   *some useful lessons*   For the phrase, see the underestimated work of Fuller (1960), p. 286. Because Fuller did not take fully into account source criticism, classicists often have dismissed his analyses. But his work is full of insights into Alexander's leadership, which perhaps only an experienced military officer could have offered.

285   *of his adversaries*   Fuller (1960), p. 297.

286   *reconciler of the world*   For similar conclusions, see Brunt, P., "The Aims of Alexander," *GaR* 12 (1965), p. 215.

287   *despised the crime*   Deacy, S., and K. Pierce, eds., *Rape in Antiquity* (London, 2002).

288   *for the people*   For exegesis of the phrase, see Wills, G., *Lincoln at Gettysburg* (New York, 1992), pp. 145–146.

288   *Montesquieu or Locke*   For the intellectual background, see Wills, G., *Inventing America: Jefferson's Declaration of Independence* (New York, 1978), p. 207ff.

CHAPTER 31 Alexander and the Ambiguity of Greatness

289   *have duly noted*   Narain, A., "Alexander and India," *GaR* 12 (1965), pp. 155–165.

289   *father of all*   Heraclitus, fragment 53.

290   *system of administration*   As was the system of administration of Alexander's Seleucid successors. See Kuhrt (1995), p. 701.

290   *Tajikistan, and beyond*   Fraser, P., *Cities of Alexander the Great* (Oxford, 1996), pp. 191–201.

290   *northern Syria*   Settled by Greeks from the island of Euboea and the Cycladic islands by 800 B.C.E.

290   *Nile Delta of Egypt*   As established by Psammetichus I (664–610 B.C.E.), by 625 at the latest. See Herodotus, 2.178.1; and Kuhrt (1995), p. 641.

291   *Macedon and Greece*   On the very complicated sequence of events following Alexander's death in Babylon to the carving-up of Alexander's empire into its three major sections, see Errington, R., "From Babylon to Triparadeisos: 323–320 B.C.," *JHS* 90 (1970), pp. 49–77; and then generally Walbank, F., *The Hellenistic World* (Cambridge, 1993); and now in more detail Bosworth, A., *The Legacy of Alexander* (Oxford, 2002).

291   *by the Romans*   For the best comprehensive work on the subject, see Gruen, E., *The Hellenistic World and the Coming of Rome* (Berkeley, 1984).

291   *successor kingdoms were*   For the vitality of the Greek city during the reign of Antiochos III, see the brilliant study of Ma, J., *Antiochos III and the Cities of Western Asia Minor* (Oxford, 1999).

291   *themselves explicitly recognized*   Millar, F., *The Roman Near East, 31 B.C.–A.D. 337* (Cambridge, 1993).

292   *very own hand*   As we have seen in the case of Alexandria and other city foundations. See Fraser, P., *Cities of Alexander the Great* (Oxford, 1996), p. 201.

292   *the Ottoman Turks*   Cameron, A., *The Mediterranean World in Late Antiquity, AD 395–600* (London, 1993).

292   *opposition to them*   Millar, F., *The Roman Near East, 31 B.C.–A.D. 337* (Cambridge, 1993).

293   *of a Macedonian king*   Including 2 billion Christians, 1.3 billion Muslims, and 13 million Jews, out of a world population of 6 billion. For the numbers of Christians, see Sengupta, S., and L. Rohter, "The Changing Church," *The International Herald Tribune*, October 15, 2003, pp. 1, 4.

293   *many different perspectives*   For an interpretation of Mozart's art framed in these terms (from which I have here humbly borrowed), see the astonishingly beautiful and moving biography of Mozart by Solomon, M., *Mozart: A Life* (New York, 1995), p. 509.

294   *soldiers at Gallipoli*   Jenkins, R., *Churchill: A Biography* (New York, 2001), pp. 255, 264, 266, 269, 280, 283.

294   *of political freedom*   Jenkins, R., *Churchill: A Biography* (New York, 2001), pp. 455–456.

294   *led to disaster*   Jenkins, R., *Churchill: A Biography* (New York, 2001), pp. 565, 573–575.

294   *give in to Hitler*   Manchester, W., *The Last Lion: Winston Spencer Churchill, Alone, 1932–1940* (Boston, 1988), p. 6.

294   *"considered its redemption"*   Manchester, W., *The Last Lion: Winston Spencer Churchill, Visions of Glory, 1874–1932* (New York, 1983), p. 6.

294   *10 Downing Street*   Jenkins, R., *Churchill: A Biography* (New York, 2001), p. 912.

294   *on August 5*   McCullough, D., *Truman* (New York, 1992), pp. 448, 456–457.

294   *"was the kind"*   McCullough, D., *Truman* (New York, 1992), p. 991.

CHAPTER 32   Epilogue: Arrian's Eulogy

295   *"Alexander died"*   Translation from Robson (1978), pp. 297–303.

APPENDIX   Sources: Flacks, Hacks, and Historians

300   Deeds of Alexander   For the fragments of Callisthenes' lost work, quoted by other writers, see Jacoby (1962), no. 124, pp. 631–657.

300   *to divine parentage*   For Callisthenes in general, see Brown, T., "Callisthenes and Alexander," *AJP* 70 (1949), pp. 225–248; Pearson (1960), pp. 22–49; and Prandi, L., *Callistene: Uno storico tra Aristotele e i re Macedoni* (Milan, 1985).

300   *few fragments survive*   For the collected fragments, see Jacoby (1961), 72F, 15–17, 29, pp. 122–123, 124–125; and in general Bosworth (1988), p. 296.

300   *the Macedonians traveled*   Men named Baeton, Diognetus, and Amyntas, whose work is used by Pliny, *Natural History*, 6.21.44–45, 61–63.

300   *difficult to assess*   For the fragments, see Jacoby (1962), 117, pp. 618–622.

300   *Eumenes of Cardia*   Arrian, 7.4.6.

300   *Diodotus of Erythrae*   Athenaeus, 10.434.b.

301   *died of a fever*   Plutarch, 76.1; Arrian, 7.25.1–26.3.

301   *used with caution*   Samuel, A., "Alexander's Royal Journals," *Historia* 14 (1965), pp. 1–12; Badian, E., "A King's Notebooks," *HSCP* 72 (1968), pp. 183–204.

301   *inscriptions*   Heisserer, A., *Alexander the Great and the Greeks of Asia Minor* (Norman, 1980).

301   *papyri*   The most important papyrus is *Oxyrhynchus Papyrus* 1798 (text in Jacoby [1962], 148, pp. 816–818), which probably was copied sometime during the second century B.C.E. The five preserved columns of this papyrus probably belonged to a lost history. The surviving fragments refer to the assassination of Philip, the destruction of Thebes, the story of Alexander's illness at Tarsus, the battle at the Issos, and the prelude to the battle at Gaugamela. In some instances the papyrus provides details about these events that cannot be found in any other sources. Scholars differ widely on the value of the details provided, as well as on the general skill and competence of the author. For a very negative assessment, see Pearson (1960), pp. 255–257.

301   *coins*   Price, M., *The Coinage in the Name of Alexander the Great and Philip Arrhidaeus*, 2 volumes (London, 1991); and most recently, see Holt, F., *Alexander the Great and the Mystery of the Elephant Medallions* (Berkeley, 2003) for a study of the victory medallions created after the battle of the Hydaspes.

301   *sculpture*   Ridgway, B., *Hellenistic Sculpture*, volume 1 (Madison, 1980), p. 108ff; Stewart, A., *Faces of Power: Alexander's Image and Hellenistic Politics* (Berkeley, 1993).

301   *the royal galley*   Diogenes Laertius, *Lives of Eminent Philosophers*, 6.84; Arrian, *Indike*, 18.9; Arrian, 7.5.6. For Onesicritus in general, see Brown, T., *Onesicritus: A Study in Hellenistic Historiography* (Berkeley, 1949); Pearson (1960), pp. 83–111; and Bosworth (1988), p. 296.

301   The Education of Alexander   Diogenes Laertius, *Lives of Eminent Philosophers*, 6.84.

301   *history of Alexander*   Lucian, *Octogenarians*, 14.

301   *Gymnosophists*   Strabo, 15.1.63–65.

301   *conquests in India*   E.g., in Pliny, *Natural History*, 6.26.96–100.

301   *the Pixodarus affair*   Arrian, 3.6.5–6. For Nearchus in general, see Pearson (1960), pp. 112–149.

301   *mouth of the Euphrates*   Arrian, *Indike*, 18.10, 20.1; Diodorus, 17.104.3.

301   *have not survived*   Although they were used both by Arrian and Strabo. For Strabo and Arrian as sources for Alexander's life and campaigns, see pp. 304–305.

301   *his rival Onesicritus*   E.g., as seen in Arrian, *Indike*, 32.9–13, or 7.20.9.

301   *(c. 367/66–283)*   For Ptolemy's dates and career, see Heckel, W., *The Marshals of Alexander's Empire* (London, 1992), pp. 222–227. For Ptolemy as a source, see Bosworth (1988), p. 297.

301   *fall of 330*   Arrian, 3.27.5.

301   *many important commands*   E.g., bringing in the regicide Bessus in 329 B.C.E., as described in Arrian, 3.29.7–30.5.

302   *Kleopatra VII, in 30 B.C.E.*   For Ptolemy and the period after the death of Alexander, see the useful summary of Bosworth (1988), pp. 174–181.

302   *has not survived*   For the collection of the fragments embedded in other authors, see Jacoby (1962), 138, pp. 752–769.

302   *upon military matters*   Bosworth (1988), p. 297.

302   *of his rivals*   E.g., in the case of Perdiccas. In his description of Alexander's assault on the city of Thebes in 335 B.C.E., Arrian, 1.8.1, quotes Ptolemy, who says that Perdiccas, who had been posted in the advance guard of the camp with his own brigade and was not far from the enemy's stockade, did not wait for Alexander's signal to commence the battle but of his own accord was the first to assault the stockade. On the general point, see Welles, C., "The Reliability of Ptolemy as an Historian," *Miscellanea di studi alessandri in memoria di A. Rostagni* (Turin, 1963), pp. 101–116; Errington, R., "Bias in Ptolemy's History of Alexander," *CQ* 19 (1969), pp. 233–242; and Roisman, J., "Ptolemy and His Rivals in His History of Alexander the Great," *CQ* 34 (1984), pp. 373–385.

302   *after Alexander's death*   Especially significant is Ptolemy's description of how Alexander was led to the oracle of Zeus Ammon at Siwah, as quoted by Arrian, 3.3.5.

302   *Aristobulus of Cassandreia*   Plutarch, *Life of Demosthenes*, 23.4.

302   *some minor capacity*   Arrian, preface, 1.2; Bosworth (1988), p. 297.

302   *eighty-four years old*   Lucian, *Octogenarians*, 22.

302   *to be sociable*   Arrian, 7.29.4.

302   *about geography*   E.g., as quoted by Strabo, 11.11.5, on the river Polytimetus in Sogdiana.

302   *botany*   Arrian, 6.22.4, on the myrrh trees Aristobulus saw in Gedrosia.

302   *and local customs*   E.g., Strabo, 15.1.62, on the marriage customs in Taxila described by Aristobulus.

302   *Chares of Mytilene*   Plutarch, 46.1.

302   *at his court*   As found in Plutarch, 54.3, and Athenaeus, 12.539.a.

302   *Alexander into Asia*   Diodorus, 2.7.3–4.

302   *as early as 310*   For Cleitarchus in general, see Pearson (1960), pp. 212–242. The fragments of his lost history of Alexander's reign can be

found in Jacoby (1962), 137, pp. 741–752; Hamilton, J., "Cleitarchus and Aristobulus," *Historia* 10 (1961), pp. 448–458; and Hamilton, J., "Cleitarchus and Diodorus 17," *Greece and the Ancient Mediterranean in History and Prehistory* (studies presented to Fritz Schachermeyr), ed. K. Kinzl (Berlin, 1977), pp. 126–146.

302   *were derived*   For the Vulgate tradition, see Bosworth, A., "Arrian and the Alexander Vulgate," *EntrHardt* 22 (1976), pp. 1–46; and Bosworth (1988), pp. 297–298.

302   *and overembellishment*   E.g., Quintilian, *Institutes*, 10.1.74; Cicero, *Brutus*, 42.

303   *important independent perspective*   For instance, his view that the Athenian courtesan Thais initiated the burning of the royal palaces of Persepolis, as reported in Athenaeus, 13.576.d–e.

303   *("Learned Banqueteers") of Athenaeus*   Athenaeus, 3.120.d–e, 4.146.c–d, 10.434.a–b, 12.537.d–e; 2.538.a–b.

303   *not a pseudonym*   For the fragments, see Jacoby (1962), 127, p. 667; and on what can be known about the writer, see Pearson (1960), pp. 67–68.

303   *city of Larissa*   For the fragments, see Jacoby (1962), 128, pp. 667–670; and Pearson (1960), pp. 70–77.

303   *rivers of Asia*   E.g., Strabo, 16.1.13, on the Euphrates River; and 15.3.4, on the Choaspes, Eulaeus, and the Tigris.

303   *boundary of Asia*   Strabo, 15.3.4; and Pearson (1960), p. 75.

303   *some ancient writers*   Especially Plutarch, in his essay "How to Know a Flatterer from a Friend," 24.CD, who calls Medius the leader and skilled master of the choir of flatterers that danced attendance on Alexander.

303   *Medius of Larissa*   For the fragments, see Jacoby (1962), 129, pp. 670–672; and Pearson (1960), pp. 68–70.

303   *on the Indus River*   Strabo, 11.14.12; Arrian, *Indike*, 18.7.

303   *or was poisoned*   Arrian, 7.25.1.

303   *of Epirus (272)*   For the fragments of his work, see Jacoby (1962), 154, pp. 829–835; Pearson (1960), p. 262; and generally, Hornblower, J., *Hieronymus of Cardia* (Oxford, 1981).

303   *about its reception*   Diodorus, 18.8.1–7; and see Bosworth (1988), p. 298.

304   *should be mentioned*   For the fragments of their works, see Jacoby (1962), 142 and 143, pp. 804–813; and Pearson (1960), pp. 246–248, 254–255.

304   *manner of speech*   Dionysios of Halicarnassos, *On Literary Composition*, 18, p. 120ff; Cicero, *Orator*, 226.

304   *"fables, things unheard of"*   Gellius, *Attic Nights*, 9.4.3.

304   *mid-second century B.C.E.*   For the fragments of his lost history, see Jacoby (1962), 143, pp. 812–813; and Pearson (1960), pp. 254–255.

304   *the god Hermes*   Athenaeus, 10.486.e; Clement of Alexandria, *Protrepticus ad Graecos*, 4.54.3.

304   *near-contemporary sources*   Goukowsky, P., *Diodore de Sicile XVII* (Paris, 1976); and Hamilton, J., "Cleitarchus and Diodorus 17," *Greece and the Ancient Mediterranean in History and Prehistory* (studies presented to Fritz Schachermeyr), ed. K. Kinzl (Berlin, 1977), pp. 126–146.

304   *enjoying good fortune*   For Diodorus and his methodology, see Sacks, K., *Diodorus and the First Century* (Princeton, 1990), esp. pp. 204–206.

304   *for moral living*   Sacks, K., *Diodorus and the First Century* (Princeton, 1990), p. 206.

304   *historians of Alexander*   Dueck, D., *Strabo of Amasia: A Greek Man of Letters in Augustan Rome* (London, 2000).

304   *northern parts of India*   For Strabo's contribution to our understanding of Alexander's campaigns, see Dueck, D., *Strabo of Amasia: A Greek Man of Letters in Augustan Rome* (London, 2000).

304   *some Stoic overtones*   Dueck, D., *Strabo of Amasia: A Greek Man of Letters in Augustan Rome* (London, 2000), p. 64.

304   *"strongly criticized historians"*   Dueck, D., *Strabo of Amasia: A Greek Man of Letters in Augustan Rome* (London, 2000), p. 73.

305   *(probably during the reign)*   For scholarly analyses, see Egge, R., *Untersuchungen zur Primärtradition bei Q. Curtius Rufus* (Freiburg, 1978); Atkinson, J., *A Commentary on Q. Curtius Rufus' Historiae Alexandri Magni, Books 3 & 4* (Amsterdam, 1980); Gunderson, L., "Quintus Curtius Rufus," in *Philip II, Alexander the Great and the Macedonian Heritage*, ed. W. Adams and E. Borza (Washington, D.C., 1982), pp. 177–196; and Baynham, E., *Alexander the Great: The Unique History of Quintus Curtius* (Ann Arbor, 1998), pp. 7–8, 201–219.

305   *and of Ptolemy*   Baynham, E., *Alexander the Great: The Unique History of Quintus Curtius* (Ann Arbor, 1998), pp. 58, 74–81, 139, 74–76, 82, 84–85.

305   *attributions of motive*   Baynham, E., *Alexander the Great: The Unique History of Quintus Curtius* (Ann Arbor, 1998), pp. 46–56.

305   *died after 120*   In general, see Jones, C., *Plutarch and Rome* (Oxford, 1971).

305   *Greeks and Romans*   Duff, T., *Plutarch's Lives: Exploring Virtue and Vice* (Oxford, 1999), esp. pp. 14–22.

305   *of great men*   Plutarch, 1.2.

305   *by Stoic ideals*   For an historical commentary on Plutarch's life of Alexander, see Hamilton, J., *Plutarch Alexander: A Commentary* (Oxford, 1969); Hammond, N., *Sources for Alexander the Great: An Analysis of Plutarch's "Life" and Arrian's "Anabasis Alexandrou"* (Cambridge, 1993); see also Mossman, J., ed., *Plutarch and His Intellectual World* (London, 1997).

305   *on his childhood*   For which we have surprisingly little information from other sources.

305   *Cappadocia (131–137)*   For Arrian's life and career, see Bosworth, A., *From Arrian to Alexander: Studies in Historical Interpretation* (Oxford, 1988), pp. 16–37.

305   *view of the king*   Arrian also draws from the works of Nearchus and Eratosthenes as sources in his book 6 of the *Anabasis*.

305   *sympathetic to Alexander*   For Arrian and his works, see Bosworth, A., "Errors in Arrian," *CQ* 26 (1976), pp. 117–139; Stadter, P., *Arrian of Nicomedia* (Chapel Hill, 1980); Bosworth, A., *From Arrian to Alexander: Studies in Historical Interpretation* (Oxford, 1988), which is far and away the most sophisticated study of Arrian's methodology; and Hammond, N., *Sources for Alexander the Great: An Analysis of Plutarch's "Life" and Arrian's "Anabasis Alexandrou"* (Cambridge, 1993).

306   *7–12 of his histories*   Yardley (1997), esp. commentary by W. Heckel, pp. 1–41.

306   *life were discussed*   For a rich collection of essays on different aspects of Athenaeus' works and world, see Braund, D., and J. Wilkins, *Athenaeus and His World* (Exeter, 2000).

306   *Macedonian royal court*   Athenaeus, see esp. 12.537.dff.

Select Modern Bibliography

Abbreviations for periodicals, series, and standard books are the same as those to be found in the list from the *American Journal of Archaeology*, volume 104, number 1 (January 2000), pp. 10–24. If a periodical, series listing, or book is not to be found in the *AJA* list, it has been spelled out.

Adcock, F. *The Greek and Macedonian Art of War.* Berkeley, 1957.

Adriani, A. *La tomba di Alessandro: Realita, ipotesi e fantasie.* Rome, 2000.

Ambrose, S. *D-Day, June 6, 1944: The Climactic Battle of World War II.* New York, 1994.

Anderson, A. "Bucephalus and His Legend."*AJP* 51 (1930), pp. 1–21.

Anderson, J. *Military Theory and Practice in the Age of Xenophon.* Berkeley, 1970.

Andronikos, M. "Sarissa." *BCH* 94 (1970), pp. 91–107.

———. "The Royal Tomb of Philip II." *Archaeology* 31, no. 4 (1978), pp. 33–41.

———. "The Finds from the Royal Tombs at Vergina." *PBA* 65 (1979), pp. 355–367.

———. "The Royal Tomb at Vergina and the Problem of the Dead." *AAA* 13 (1980), pp. 168–178.

Anglim, S., P. Jestice, R. Price, S. Rusch, and J. Serrati. *Fighting Techniques of the Ancient World, 3000 BC–AD 500.* New York, 2002.

Anson, E. "Alexander's Hypaspists and the Argyraspids." *Historia* 30 (1981), pp. 117–120.

Anspach, A. *De Alexandria Magni expeditione Indica.* Leipzig, 1903.

Ashton, N. "How Many *Pentereis?*" *GRBS* 20 (1979), pp. 327–342.

———. "The Lamian War: A False Start." *Antichthon* 17 (1983), pp. 47–61.

Atkinson, J. *A Commentary on Q. Curtius Rufus' Historiae Alexandri Magni, Books 3 & 4.* Amsterdam, 1980.

Atkinson, K. "Demosthenes, Alexander and Asebeia." *Athenaeum* 51 (1973), pp. 310–335.

Austin, M. *The Hellenistic World from Alexander to the Roman Conquest.* Cambridge, 1981.

———. "Hellenistic Kings, War and the Economy." *CQ* 36 (1986), pp. 450–466.

———. "Alexander and the Macedonian Invasion of Asia." In *War and Society in the Greek World.* Edited by J. Rich and G. Shipley. London, 1993, pp. 197–223.

Badian, E. "Alexander the Great and the Unity of Mankind." *Historia* 7 (1958), pp. 425–444.

———. "The Eunuch Bagoas: A Study in Method." *CQ* 8 (1958), pp. 144–157.

———. "The Death of Parmenio." *TAPA* 91 (1960), pp. 324–338.

———. "The First Flight of Harpalus." *Historia* 9 (1960), pp. 245–246.

———. "Harpalus." *JHS* 81 (1961), pp. 16–43.

———. "The Death of Philip II." *Phoenix* 17 (1963), pp. 244–250.

———. "The Administration of the Empire." *GaR* 12 (1965), pp. 166–182.

———. "The Date of Clitarchus." *PACA* 8 (1965), pp. 5–11.

———. "Orientals in Alexander's Army." *JHS* 85 (1965), pp. 160–161.

———. "Alexander the Great and the Greeks of Asia." In *Ancient Society and Institutions.* Studies presented to V. Ehrenberg. Oxford, 1966, pp. 37–69.

———. "Agis III." *Hermes* 95 (1967), pp. 170–192.

———. "Alexander the Great and the Loneliness of Power." In *Studies in Greek and Roman History.* Oxford, 1968, pp. 192–205.

———. "A King's Notebooks." *HSCP* 72 (1968), pp. 183–204.

———. "Alexander the Great, 1948–67." *CW* 65 (1971), pp. 37–56, 77–83.

———. "Nearchus the Cretan." *YCS* 24 (1975), pp. 147–170.

———. "A Comma in the History of Samos." *ZPE* 23 (1976), pp. 289–294.

———. "Some Recent Interpretations of Alexander." *EntrHardt* 22 (1976), pp. 279–311.

———. "The Battle of the Granicus: A New Look." *Ancient Macedonia* 2 (1977), pp. 271–293.

———. "A Document of Artaxerxes IV?" In *Greece and the Eastern Mediterranean in History and Prehistory.* Studies presented to F. Schachermeyr. Edited by K. Kinzl. Berlin, 1977, pp. 40–50.

———. "The Deification of Alexander the Great." In *Ancient Macedonian Studies in Honor of Charles F. Edson.* Edited by H. Dell. Thessaloniki, 1981, pp. 27–71.

———. "Greeks and Macedonians." In *Macedonia and Greece in Late Classical and Early Hellenistic Times.* Washington, D.C., 1982, pp. 33–51.

———. "Alexander in Iran." *Cambridge History of Iran* II. Cambridge, 1985, pp. 420–501.

———. "Alexander at Peucelaotis," *CQ* 37 (1987), pp. 117–128.

———. "Agis III: Revisions and Reflections." In *Ventures into Greek History: Essays in Honour of N.G.L. Hammond.* Edited by I. Worthington. Oxford, 1994, pp. 258–292.

———. "Alexander the Great Between Two Thrones and Heaven: Variations on an Old Theme." In *Subject and Ruler: The Cult of the Ruling Power in Classical Antiquity.* Edited by A. Small. Ann Arbor, 1996, pp. 11–26.

———. "Two Numismatic Phantoms: The False Priest and the Spurious Son." *Arctos* 32 (1998), pp. 45–60.

———. "A Note on the 'Alexander Mosaic.'" In *The Eye Expanded: Life and the Arts in Greco-Roman Antiquity.* Edited by F. Titchener and R. Moorton, Jr. Berkeley, 1999, pp. 75–92.

Bagnall, R. "The Date of the Foundation of Alexandria." *AJAH* 4 (1979), pp. 46–49.

Balsdon, J. "The 'Divinity' of Alexander." *Historia* 1 (1950), pp. 363–388.

Baynham, E. "Who Put the 'Romance' in the Alexander Romance? The Alexander Romance Within Alexander Historiography." *Ancient History Bulletin* 9, no. 1 (1995), pp. 1–13.

———. *Alexander the Great: The Unique History of Quintus Curtius.* Ann Arbor, 1998.

Bellinger, A. *Essays on the Coinage of Alexander the Great.* New York, 1963.

Bellinger, A., and M. Barlincourt. *Victory as a Coin Type.* Rockville Center, 2001.

Berchem, D. van. "Alexandre et la restauration de Priène." *MH* 27 (1970), pp. 198–205.

Bernard, P. "Fouilles d'Aï Khanoum. Campagnes de 1972 et 1973." *CRAI* (1970), 280–308.

———. *Fouilles d'Aï Khanoum* I. Mémoires de la délégation archéologique française en Afghanistan. No. 21. Paris, 1973.

———. "Campagne de fouilles 1974 à Aï Khanoum." *CRAI* (1975), pp. 167–197.

———. "Campagne de fouilles 1978 à Aï Khanoum." *CRAI* (1980), pp. 435–459.

————. "Le philosophe Anaxarque et le roi Nicocréon de Salamine." *JSav* (1984), pp. 3–49.

————. "Le temple du dieu Oxus à Takht-i Sangin en Bactriane: Temple du feu ou pas?" *StIr* 23 (1994), pp. 81–121.

————. "Greek Geography and Literary Fiction from Bactria to India: The Case of the Aornoi and Taxila." In *Coins, Art, and Chronology: Essays on the Pre-Islamic History of the Indo-Iranian Borderlands*, ed. M. Alram and D. Klimburg-Salter. Vienna, 1999, pp. 51–98.

Berve, H. *Das Alexanderreich auf prosopographischer Grundlage.* 2 vols. Munich, 1926.

————. "Die Verschmelzungspolitik Alexanders des Grossen." *Klio* 31 (1938), pp. 135–168.

Bieber, M. *Alexander the Great in Greek and Roman Art.* Chicago, 1964.

Borza, E. "Alexander and the Return from Siwah." *Historia* 16 (1967), p. 369.

————. "Fire from Heaven: Alexander at Persepolis." *CP* 67 (1972), pp. 233–245.

————. "Some Observations on Malaria and the Ecology of Central Macedonia in Antiquity." *AJAH* 4 (1979), pp. 102–124.

————. "The Macedonian Royal Tombs at Vergina: Some Cautionary Notes." *Archaeological News* 10 (1981), pp. 73–87; 11 (1982), pp. 8–10.

————. "The Natural Resources of Early Macedonia." In *Philip II, Alexander the Great and the Macedonian Heritage.* Edited by W. Adams and E. Borza. Washington, D.C., 1982, pp. 1–20.

————. "The Royal Macedonian Tombs and the Paraphernalia of Alexander the Great." *Phoenix* 41 (1987), pp. 105–121.

————. *In the Shadow of Olympus: The Emergence of Macedon.* Princeton, 1990.

————. and J. Reames-Zimmerman. "Some New Thoughts on the Death of Alexander the Great." *AncW* 31 (2000), pp. 22–30.

Bosworth, A. "Aristotle and Callisthenes." *Historia* 19 (1970), pp. 407–413.

————. "The Death of Alexander the Great: Rumour and Propaganda." *CQ* 21 (1971), pp. 112–136.

————. "Philip II and Upper Macedonia." *CQ* 21 (1971), pp. 93–105.

————. "ΑΣΘΕΤΑΙΡΟΙ." *CQ* 23 (1973), pp. 245–253.

————. "The Government of Syria Under Alexander the Great." *CQ* 24 (1974), pp. 46–64.

————. "The Mission of Amphoterus and the Outbreak of Agis' War." *Phoenix* 29 (1975), pp. 27–43.

————. "Arrian and the Alexander Vulgate." *EntrHardt* 22 (1976), pp. 1–46.

————. "Errors in Arrian." *CQ* 26 (1976), pp. 117–139.

———. "Alexander and Ammon." In *Greece and the Ancient Mediterranean in History and Prehistory*. Studies presented to Fritz Schachermeyr. Edited by K. Kinzl. Berlin, 1977, pp. 51–75.

———. "Early Relations Between Aetolia and Macedon." *AJAH* 1 (1977), pp. 164–181.

———. "Eumenes, Neoptolemus and *PSI* xii.1284." *GRBS* 19 (1978), pp. 227–237.

———. "Alexander and the Iranians." *JHS* 100 (1980), pp. 1–21.

———. *A Historical Commentary on Arrian's History of Alexander*. Vols. 1–2. Oxford, 1980, 1995.

———. "A Missing Year in the History of Alexander the Great." *JHS* 101 (1981), pp. 17–39.

———. "The Location of Alexander's Campaign Against the Illyrians in 335 B.C." In *Macedonia and Greece in Late Classical and Early Hellenistic Times*. Studies in the History of Art 10. Washington, D.C., 1982, pp. 175–184.

———. "The Indian Satrapies Under Alexander the Great." *Antichthon* 17 (1983), pp. 37–46.

———. "Alexander the Great and the Decline of Macedon." *JHS* 106 (1986), pp. 1–12.

———. "Nearchus in Susiana." *Zu Alexander dem Grossen*. Festschrift G. Wirth. Edited by W. Will. Amsterdam, 1987.

———. *Conquest and Empire: The Reign of Alexander the Great*. Cambridge, 1988.

———. *From Arrian to Alexander: Studies in Historical Interpretation*. Oxford, 1988.

———. *Alexander and the East: The Tragedy of Triumph*. Oxford, 1996.

———. "Calanus and the Brahman Opposition." In *Alexander der Grosse: Eine Welteroberung und ihr Hintergrund*. Bonn, 1998, pp. 173–203.

———. *The Legacy of Alexander*. Oxford, 2002.

———. "A Tale of Two Empires: Hernán Cortés and Alexander the Great." In *Alexander the Great in Fact and Fiction*. Edited by A. Bosworth and E. Baynham. Oxford, 2002, pp. 23–49.

Bothmer, D. von, et al. *Wealth of the Ancient World: The Nelson Bunker Hunt and William Herbert Hunt Collections*. Fort Worth, 1983.

Bradley, J. *Flags of Our Fathers*. New York, 2000.

Braund, D., and J. Wilkins. *Athenaeus and His World*. Exeter, 2000.

Braunert, H. "Staatstheorie und Staatsrecht in Hellenismus." *Saeculum* 19 (1968), pp. 47–66.

Briant, P. *Antigone le Borgne; les débuts de sa carrière et les problèmes de l'assemblée macédonienne*. Paris, 1973.

———. *État et pasteurs au Moyen-Orient ancient.* Paris, 1982.

———. *Rois, tributs et paysans.* Paris, 1982.

———. *Alexander the Great: Man of Action, Man of Spirit.* New York, 1996.

———. *Histoire de l'empire perse de Cyrus à Alexandre.* 2 vols. Leiden, 1996.

Brown, T. "Callisthenes and Alexander." *AJP* 70 (1949), pp. 225–248.

———. *Onesicritus: A Study in Hellenistic Historiography.* Berkeley, 1949.

———. "Alexander's Book Order (Plut. *Alex.* 8)." *Historia* 16 (1967), pp. 359–368.

Brundage, B. "Herakles the Levantine." *JNES* 17 (1958), pp. 225–236.

Brunt, P. "Alexander's Macedonian Cavalry." *JHS* 83 (1963), pp. 27–46.

———. "The Aims of Alexander." *GaR* (1965), pp. 205–215.

———. "Alexander, Barsine and Heracles." *RFIC* 103 (1975), pp. 22–34.

———. "Anaximenes and King Alexander I of Macedon." *JHS* 96 (1976), pp. 151–153.

———. *Arrian: History of Alexander and Indica.* Loeb Classical Library. Vols. 1–2. Cambridge, 1976–1983.

Burke, E. "*Contra Leocratem and de Corona*: Political Collaboration?" *Phoenix* 31 (1977), pp. 330–340.

Burkert, W. *Greek Religion.* Cambridge, 1985.

Burn, A. "Notes on Alexander's Campaigns 332–330 B.C." *JHS* 72 (1952), pp. 81–91.

———. *Alexander the Great and the Hellenistic World.* 2nd ed. New York, 1962.

———. "The Generalship of Alexander."*GaR* 12 (1965), pp. 140–154.

Burstein, S. *Graeco-Africana: Studies in the History of Greek Relations with Egypt and Nubia.* Athens, 1995.

Cameron, A. *The Mediterranean World in Late Antiquity, AD 395–600.* London, 1993.

Carlsen, J., et al., eds. *Alexander the Great: Reality and Myth.* Rome, 1993.

Carney, E. "The Death of Clitus." *GRBS* 22 (1981), pp. 149–160.

———. *Women and Monarchy in Macedonia.* Norman, 2000.

Cary, G. *The Medieval Alexander.* Cambridge, 1956.

Casson, L. *Ships and Seamanship in the Ancient World.* Princeton, 1971.

Cawkwell, G. "A Note on Ps.-Demosthenes 17.20." *Phoenix* 15 (1961), pp. 74–78.

———. "Eubulus." *JHS* 83 (1963), pp. 47–67.

———. "The Crowning of Demosthenes." *CQ* 19 (1969), pp. 161–180.

————. *Philip of Macedon.* London, 1978.

Chandler, D. *The Campaigns of Napoleon.* London, 2002.

Chugg, A. "The Sarcophagus of Alexander the Great?" *GaR* 49, no. 1 (2002), pp. 18–26.

Classen, D. "The Libyan God Ammon in Greece Before 331 B.C." *Historia* 8 (1959), pp. 349–355.

Cohen, A. *The Alexander Mosaic: Stories of Victory and Defeat.* Cambridge, 1997.

Cohen, G. *The Seleucid Colonies.* Wiesbaden, 1978.

Conquest, R. *Reflections on a Ravaged Century.* New York, 2000.

Conybeare, F. *Philostratus: The Life of Apollonius of Tyana.* Vol. 1. Cambridge, 1989.

Cook, J. *The Persian Empire.* London, 1983.

Crick, B. "Introduction." In *Machiavelli: The Discourses.* London, 1978.

Cross, F. "The Discovery of the Samaria Papyri." *BA* 26 (1963), pp. 110–121.

————. "Aspects of Samaritan and Jewish History in Late Persian and Hellenistic Times." *HTR* 52 (1966), pp. 201–211.

Davidson, J. "Dover, Foucault and Greek Homosexuality." *Past and Present* 170 (2001), pp. 3–51.

Davis, E. "The Persian Battle Plan at the Granicus." *James Sprunt Studies in History and Political Sciences* 46 (1964), pp. 34–44.

Davis, N., and C. Kraay. *The Hellenistic Kingdoms: Portrait Coins and History.* London, 1973.

Deacy, S., and K. Pierce, eds. *Rape in Antiquity.* London, 2002.

Demandt, A. "Politische Aspekte in Alexanderbild der Neuzeit." *Archiv für Kulturgeschichte* 54 (1972), pp. 325–326.

Develin, R. "The Murder of Philip II." *Antichthon* 15 (1981), pp. 86–99.

————. "Anaximenes (*FGrHist* 72) F4." *Historia* 34 (1985), pp. 493–496.

Devine, A. "Grand Tactics at Gaugamela." *Phoenix* 29 (1975), pp. 374–385.

————. "Embolon: A Study in Tactical Terminology." *Phoenix* 37 (1983), pp. 201–217.

————. "The Location of Castabulum and Alexander's Route from Mallus to Myriandrus." *Acta Classica* 27 (1984), pp. 127–129.

————. "Grand Tactics at the Battle of Issus." *AncW* 12 (1985), pp. 39–59.

————. "The Strategies of Alexander the Great and Darius III in the Issus Campaign (333 BC)." *AncW* 12 (1985), pp. 25–38.

————. "The Battle of Gaugamela: A Tactical and Source-Critical Study." *AncW* 13 (1986), pp. 87–116.

———. "The Battle of Hydaspes: A Tactical and Source-Critical Study." *AncW* 16 (1987), pp. 91–113.

———. "A Pawn-Sacrifice at the Battle of The Granicus: The Origins of a Favorite Stratagem of Alexander the Great." *AncW* 18 (1988), pp. 3–20.

———. "Alexander the Great." In *Warfare in the Ancient World.* Edited by J. Hackett. New York, 1989, pp. 104–129.

———. "The Macedonian Army at Gaugamela." *AncW* 19 (1989), pp. 77–80.

Dittenberger, W. *Sylloge Inscriptionum Graecorum.* Leipzig, 1915–1924, no. 312.

Dueck, D. *Strabo of Amasia: A Greek Man of Letters in Augustan Rome.* London, 2000.

Duerr, N. "Ein 'Elephantenstater' fur Porus." In *Actes du 8ème Congrès international de numismatique, New York–Washington, Septembre 1973.* 2 vols. Edited by H. Cahn and G. Rider. Paris, 1976, vol. 1, p. 43.

———. "New Porus Commemoratives." Translated by A. Ilsch. *Numismatic Digest* 2 (1978), pp. 4–7.

Duff, T. *Plutarch's Lives: Exploring Virtue and Vice.* Oxford, 1999.

Dupree, L. "Einige Bemerkungen zur Schlacht am Jhelum (326 v. Chr.)." In *Aus dem Osten des Alexanderreiches: Völker und Kulturen zwischen Orient und Okzident: Iran, Afghanistian, Pakistan, Indien.* Edited by J. Ozols and V. Thewalt. Cologne, 1984, pp. 51–56.

Edmunds, L. "The Religiosity of Alexander." *GRBS* 12 (1971), pp. 363–391.

Egge, R. *Untersuchungen zur Primärtradition bei Q. Curtius Rufus.* Freiburg, 1978.

Eggermont, P. "Alexander's Campaign in Gandhara and Ptolemy's List of Indo-Scythian Towns." *Orientalia Lovaniensia Periodica* I (1970), pp. 63–123.

———. *Alexander's Campaigns in Sind and Baluchistan.* Leuven, 1975.

Ellis, J. "Amyntas Perdikka, Philip II and Alexander the Great." *JHS* 91 (1971), pp. 15–24.

———. "Alexander's Hypaspists Again." *Historia* 24 (1975), pp. 617–618.

———. *Philip II and Macedonian Imperialism.* Princeton, 1976.

———. "The Assassination of Philip II." In *Ancient Macedonian Studies in Honor of Charles Edson.* Edited by H. Dell. Thessaloniki, 1981, pp. 99–137.

Engels, D. *Alexander the Great and the Logistics of the Macedonian Army.* Berkeley, 1978.

———. "A Note on Alexander's Death." *CP* 73 (1978), pp. 224–228.

———. "Alexander's Intelligence System." *CQ* 30 (1980), pp. 327–340.

Errington, R. "Bias in Ptolemy's History of Alexander." *CQ* 19 (1969), pp. 233–242.

————. "From Babylon to Triparadeisos: 323–320 B.C." *JHS* 90 (1970), pp. 49–77.

————. "Macedonian 'Royal Style' and Its Historical Significance." *JHS* 94 (1974), pp. 20–37.

————. "Arybbas the Molossian." *GRBS* 16 (1975), pp. 41–50.

————. "Samos and the Lamian War." *Chiron* 5 (1975), pp. 50–57.

————. "Alexander in the Hellenistic World." *EntrHardt* 22 (1976), pp. 137–179.

————. "The Nature of the Macedonian State Under the Monarchy." *Chiron* 8 (1978), pp. 77–133.

————. *Geschichte Makedoniens.* Munich, 1986.

Étienne, R., and M. Piérart. "Un décret du koinon des Hellènes à Platées." *BCH* 99 (1975), pp. 51–75.

Fakhry, A. *Siwa Oasis: Its History and Antiquities.* Cairo, 1944.

Farber, J. "The Cyropaedia and Hellenistic Kingship." *AJP* 100 (1979), pp. 497–574.

Fears, J. "Pausanias, the Assassin of Philip II." *Athenaeum* 53 (1975), pp. 111–135.

Ferrill, A. "Alexander in India." *Military History Quarterly* 1 (1988), pp. 76–84.

Foss, C. "The Battle of the Granicus: A New Look." *Ancient Macedonia.* Vol. 2. Thessaloniki, 1977, pp. 495–502.

Fraser, P. "Current Problems Concerning the Early History of the Cult of Sarapis." *OpAth* 7 (1967), pp. 23–45.

————. *Ptolemaic Alexandria.* Vols. 1–2. Oxford, 1972.

————. "The Son of Aristonax at Kandahar." *Afghan Studies* 2 (1979–1980), pp. 9–21.

————. *Cities of Alexander the Great.* Oxford, 1996.

Fredricksmeyer, E. "Alexander, Midas and the Oracle at Gordium." *CP* 56 (1961), pp. 160–168.

————. "Divine Honours for Philip II." *TAPA* 109 (1979), pp. 39–61.

————. "Three Notes on Alexander's Deification." *AJAH* 4 (1979), pp. 1–9.

————. "On the Background of the Ruler Cult." In *Ancient Macedonian Studies in Honor of Charles F. Edson.* Edited by H. Dell. Thessaloniki, 1981, pp. 145–156.

————. "Alexander, Zeus Ammon, and the Conquest of Asia." *TAPA* 121 (1991), pp. 199–214.

————. "Alexander and the Kingship of Asia." In *Alexander the Great in Fact and Fiction.* Edited by A. Bosworth and E. Baynham. Oxford, 2000, pp. 136–166.

Frye, R. "Gestures of deference to royalty in Ancient Iran." *IrAnt* 9 (1972), pp. 102–107.

Fuller, J. *The Generalship of Alexander the Great*. New Brunswick, 1960.

Gaebel, R. *Cavalry Operations in the Ancient Greek World*. Norman, 2002.

Gardin, J. "L'archéologie du paysage bactrien." *CRAI* (1980), pp. 480–501.

Gehrke, H. "Die Griechen und die Rache: ein Versuch in historischer Pyschologie." *Saeculum* 38 (1987), pp. 121–149.

Ginouves, R., ed. *Macedonia from Philip II to the Roman Conquest*. Princeton, 1994.

Goddio, F. *Alexandria: The Submerged Royal Quarters*. London, 1998.

Goukowsky, P. "Le roi Poros et son éléphant." *BCH* 96 (1972), pp. 473–502.

———. *Diodore de Sicile XVII*. Paris, 1976.

———. *Essai sur les origines du mythe d'Alexandre*. Vols. 1–2. Nancy, 1978–1981.

Green, P. *Alexander of Macedon*. London, 1974.

———. "Caesar and Alexander: *Aemulatio, imitatio, comparatio*." *AJAH* 3 (1978), pp. 1–26.

———. "The Royal Tombs of Vergina: A Historical Analysis." In *Philip II, Alexander the Great and the Macedonian Heritage*. Edited by W. Adams and E. Borza. Washington, D.C., 1982, pp. 129–151.

———. *Alexander of Macedon, 356–323 B.C.* Berkeley, 1991.

Greer, R. *Diodorus of Sicily*. Vol. 9. Cambridge, 1969.

Grenfell, B., and A. Hunt. *The Oxyrhynchus Papyri*. Vol. 15. London, 1922.

Griffith, G. *The Mercenaries of the Hellenistic World*. Cambridge, 1935.

———. "Alexander's Generalship at Gaugamela." *JHS* 67 (1947), pp. 77–89.

———. "Μακεδονικά: Notes on the Macedonians of Philip and Alexander." *PCPS* 4 (1956–1957), pp. 3–10.

———. "A Note on the Hipparchies of Alexander." *JHS* 83 (1963), pp. 68–74.

———. "Alexander the Great and an Experiment in Government." *PCPS* 10 (1964), pp. 23–39.

———. "The Letter of Darius at Arrian 2.14." *Proceedings of the Cambridge Philological Society* 14 (1968), pp. 33–48.

Gritzner, J. *Afghanistan*. Philadelphia, 2002.

Gruen, E. *The Hellenistic World and the Coming of Rome*. Berkeley, 1984.

Gullath, B. *Untersuchungen zur Geschichte Boiotiens in der Zeit Alexanders und der Diadochen*. Frankfurt am Main and Bern, 1982.

Gunderson, L. *Alexander's Letter to Aristotle About India*. Meisenheim am Glan, 1980.

————. "Quintus Curtius Rufus." In *Philip II, Alexander the Great and the Macedonian Heritage*. Edited by W. Adams and E. Borza. Washington, D.C., 1982, pp. 177–196.

Günther, W. *Das Orakel von Didyma in hellenistischer Zeit*. Tubingen, 1971.

Habicht, C. "Samische Volksbeschlusse der hellenistischen Zeit." *MdI(A)* 72 (1957), pp. 152–274.

————. *Gottmenschentum und griechische Städte*. Munich, 1970.

————. "Literarische und epigraphische Überlieferung zur Geschichte Alexanders und seiner ersten Nachfolger." In *Akten des VI Internationalen Kongresses für Gr. und Lat. Epigraphik*. Munich, 1973, pp. 367–377.

————. "Der Beitrag Spartas zur Restitution von Samos während des Lamischen Krieges." *Chiron* 5 (1975), pp. 45–50.

————. *Untersuchungen zur politischen Geschichte Athens im 3 Jahrhundert v. Chr.* Munich, 1979.

Hahn, J. *Alexander in Indien, 327–325 v. Chr.* Stuttgart, 2000.

Hall, E. *Inventing the Barbarian: Greek Self-Definition Through Tragedy*. Oxford, 1989.

Hamdy Bey, O., and T. Reinach. *Une nécropole royale à Sidon*. Paris, 1892.

Hamilton, J. "Alexander and His 'So-Called' Father." *CQ* 3 (1953), pp. 151–157.

————. "Three Passages in Arrian." *CQ* 5 (1955), pp. 217–221.

————. "The Cavalry Battle at the Hydaspes." *JHS* 76 (1956), pp. 26–31.

————. "Cleitarchus and Aristobulus." *Historia* 10 (1961), pp. 448–458.

————. "The Letters in Plutarch's *Alexander*." *Proceedings of the African Classical Association* 4 (1961), pp. 9–20.

————. "Alexander's Early Life." *GaR* 12 (1965), pp. 117–124.

————. *Plutarch Alexander: A Commentary*. Oxford, 1969.

————. "Alexander and the Aral." *CQ* 21 (1971), pp. 106–111.

————. "Alexander among the Oreitai." *Historia* 21 (1972), pp. 603–608.

————. *Alexander the Great*. London, 1973.

————. "Cleitarchus and Diodorus 17." *Greece and the Ancient Mediterranean in History and Prehistory*. Studies presented to Fritz Schachermeyr. Edited by K. Kinzl. Berlin, 1977, pp. 126–146.

————. "Alexander's Iranian Policy." In *Zu Alexander d. Gr. Festschrift G. Wirth*. Vol. 1. Edited by W. Will and J. Heinrichs. Amsterdam, 1988, pp. 467–486.

Hammond, N. *A History of Macedonia*. Vol. 1. Oxford, 1972.

————. "A Cavalry Unit in the Army of Antigonus Monophthalmus." *CQ* 28 (1978), pp. 128–135.

———. "'Philip's Tomb' in Historical Context." *GRBS* 19 (1978), pp. 331–350.

———. *Alexander the Great: King, Commander and Statesman*. Park Ridge, 1980.

———. "The Battle of the Granicus River." *JHS* 100 (1980), pp. 73–88.

———. "The End of Philip." In *Philip of Macedon*. Edited by M. Hatzopoulos and L. Loukopoulos. Athens, 1980, pp. 166–175.

———. "The March of Alexander the Great on Thebes in 335 B.C." In Μέγας Ἀλέξανδρος: 2300 χρόνια ᾿απὸ τὸν Θάνατον τοῦ. Thessaloniki, 1980, pp. 171–181.

———. "Some Passages in Arrian Concerning Alexander." *CQ* 30 (1980), pp. 455–476.

———. "The Evidence for the Identity of the Royal Tombs at Vergina." In *Philip II, Alexander the Great and the Macedonian Heritage*. Edited by W. Adams and E. Borza. Washington, D.C., 1982, pp. 111–127.

———. "The Text and the Meaning of Arrian VII 6.2–5." *JHS* 103 (1983), pp. 139–144.

———. *Three Historians of Alexander the Great*. Cambridge, 1983.

———. "The Kingdom of Asia and the Persian Throne." *Antichthon* 20 (1986), pp. 73–85.

———. "Arms and the King: The Insignia of Alexander the Great." *Phoenix* 43 (1989), pp. 217–224.

———. "The Archaeological and Literary Evidence for the Burning of the Persepolis Palace." *CQ* 42 (1992), pp. 358–364.

———. *Sources for Alexander the Great: An Analysis of Plutarch's "Life" and Arrian's "Anabasis Alexandrou."* Cambridge, 1993.

———. *Philip of Macedon*. Baltimore, 1994.

———. *The Genius of Alexander the Great*. Chapel Hill, 1997.

———. "Cavalry Recruited in Macedonia Down to 322 B.C." *Historia* 47 (1998), pp. 404–425.

Hammond, N., and G. Griffith. *A History of Macedonia*. Vol. 2. Oxford, 1979.

Hammond, N., and F. Walbank. *A History of Macedonia*. Vol. 3. Oxford, 1988.

Hampl, F. "Alexanders des Grossen Hypomnemata und letzte Pläne." In *Studies Presented to D.M. Robinson*. Vol. 2. St. Louis, 1953, pp. 816–829.

———. "Alexander der Grosse und die Beurteilung geschichtlichern Persönlichkeiten." *NouvClio* 6 (1954), pp. 115–124.

Hansman, J. "Charax and the Karkheh." *IrAnt* 7 (1967), pp. 21–58.

———. "Elamites, Achaemenians and Anshan." *Iran* 10 (1972), pp. 101–125.

Hansman, J., and D. Stronach. "Excavations at Shahr-i Qumis." *JRAS* (1970), pp. 29–62.

Hanson, V. *The Wars of the Ancient Greeks*. London, 1999.

Hassig, R. *War and Society in Ancient Mesoamerica*. Berkeley, 1992.

Hatzopoulos, M. "Dates of Philip II's Reign." In *Philip, Alexander the Great and the Macedonian Heritage*. Edited by W. Adams and E. Borza. Washington, D.C., 1982, pp. 32–42.

———. "A Reconsideration of the Pixodarus Affair." In *Macedonia and Greece in Late Classical and Early Hellenistic Times*. Washington, D.C., 1982, pp. 59–66.

Head, B. *Historia Numorum*. Oxford, 1887.

———. "The Earliest Graeco-Bactrian and Graeco-Indian Coins." *NC* 6 (1906), pp. 1–16.

Heckel, W. "Amyntas Son of Andromenes." *GRBS* 16 (1975), pp. 393–398.

———. "The Conspiracy Against Philotas." *Phoenix* 31 (1977), pp. 9–21.

———. "The Flight of Harpalus and Tauriskos." *CP* 72 (1977), pp. 133–135.

———. "Philip II, Kleopatra and Karanos." *RFIC* 107 (1979), pp. 384–393.

———. "Alexander at the Persian Gates." *Athenaeum* 58 (1980), pp. 168–174.

———. "Some Speculations on the Prosopography of the Alexanderreich." *LCM* 6 (1981), pp. 63–69.

———. "Who was Hegelochus?" *RhM* 125 (1982), pp. 78–87.

———. *The Marshals of Alexander's Empire*. London, 1992.

Heisserer, A. *Alexander the Great and the Greeks of Asia Minor*. Norman, 1980.

Hellenkemper, H. "Das wiedergefundene Issos." In *Aus dem Osten des Alexanderreiches*. Edited by J. Ozols and V. Thewalt. Cologne, 1984, pp. 43–50.

Herrmann, P. "Antiochos der Grosse und Teos." *Anadolu* 9 (1965), pp. 29–160.

Herzfeld, E. "Pasargadae." *Klio* 8 (1908), pp. 20–25.

———. *The Persian Empire*. Wiesbaden, 1968.

Higgins, W. "Aspects of Alexander's Imperial Administration: Some Modern Methods and Views Reviewed." *Athenaeum* 58 (1980), pp. 129–152.

Hill, G. *Ancient Greek and Roman Coins: A Handbook*. London, 1899.

———. *Catalogue of Greek Coins in the British Museum: Arabia, Mesopotamia, Persia*. London, 1922.

———. "Decadrachm Commemorating Alexander's Indian Campaign." *BMQ* I (1926–1927), pp. 36–37.

———. "Greek Coins Acquired by the British Museum." *NC* 5th ser., no. 7 (1927), pp. 204–206.

Högemann, P. *Alexander der Grosse und Arabien*. Munich, 1985.

Hollstein, W. "Taxiles' Prägung für Alexander den Grossen." *Schweizerische Numismatische Gesellschaft* 68 (1989), pp. 5–17.

Holt, F. "The Hyphasis 'Mutiny': A Source Study." *AncW* 5 (1982), pp. 33–59.

———. "The So-Called Pedigree Coins of the Bactrian Greeks." In *Ancient Coins of the Graeco-Roman World*. Edited by W. Heckel and R. Sullivan. Waterloo, 1984, pp. 69–91.

———. "Alexander's Settlements in Central Asia." *Ancient Macedonia* 4 (1986), pp. 315–323.

———. "The Missing Mummy of Alexander the Great." *Archaeology* 39 (January/February 1986), p. 80.

———. *Alexander the Great and Bactria: The Formation of a Greek Frontier in Central Asia*. Leiden, 1988.

———. "*Imperium Macedonicum* and the East: The Problem of Logistics." *Ancient Macedonia* 5 (1993), pp. 585–593.

———. "Spitamenes Against Alexander." *Historikogeographika* 4 (1994), pp. 51–58.

———. "Alexander the Great and the Spoils of War." *Ancient Macedonia* 6 (1999), pp. 499–506.

———. "Alexander the Great Today: In the Interests of Historical Accuracy?" *Ancient History Bulletin* 13, no. 3 (1999), pp. 111–117.

———. "Mimesis in Metal: The Fate of Greek Culture on Bactrian Coins." In *The Eye Expanded: Life and the Arts in Greco-Roman Antiquity*. Edited by F. Titchener and R. Moorton, Jr. Berkeley, 1999, pp. 93–104.

———. *Thundering Zeus: The Making of Hellenistic Bactria*. Berkeley, 1999.

———. "The Death of Coenus: Another Study in Method." *Ancient History Bulletin* 14, nos. 1–2 (2000), pp. 49–55.

———. "Dead Kings Are Hard to Find." *Saudi Aramco World* 52, no. 3 (2001), pp. 10–11.

———. *Alexander the Great and the Mystery of the Elephant Medallions*. Berkeley, 2003.

Hopkirk, P. *The Great Game: The Struggle for Empire in Central Asia*. New York, 1992.

Hornblower, J. *Hieronymus of Cardia*. Oxford, 1981.

Hornblower, S. *Mausolus*. Oxford, 1982.

———. *The Greek World 479–323 BC*. London, 1983.

Houghton, A., and A. Stewart. "The Equestrian Portrait of Alexander the Great on a New Tetradrachm of Seleucus I." *SNR* 78 (1999), pp. 27–35.

Hubbard, T., ed. *Homosexuality in Greece and Rome: A Sourcebook of Basic Documents*. Berkeley, 2003.

Instinsky, H. "Alexander, Pindar, Euripides." *Historia* 10 (1961), pp. 250–255.

Isaac, B. *The Invention of Racism in Classical Antiquity*. Princeton, 2004.

Jacoby, F. *Die Fragmente der griechischen Historiker.* Second series. Vols. A–B. Leiden, 1961–1962.

Jahne, A. "Die Ἀλεξανδρέων χώρα." *Klio* 63 (1981), pp. 63–103.

Jaschinski, S. *Alexander und Griechenland unter dem Eindruch der Flucht des Harpalos*. Bonn, 1981.

Jenkins, G. *Ancient Greek Coins*. London, 1990.

Jenkins, R. *Churchill: A Biography*. New York, 2001.

Jones, C. *Plutarch and Rome*. Oxford, 1971.

Jouguet, P. "La date Alexandrine de la fondation d'Alexandrie." *RÉA* 42 (1940), pp. 192–197.

Karwiese, S. *Groß ist die Artemis von Ephesos*. Vienna, 1995.

Keegan, J. *The Mask of Command*. New York, 1987.

Kershaw, I. *Hitler, 1936–45: Nemesis*. London, 2000.

Kingsley, B. "Harpalos in the Megarid and the Grain Shipments from Cyrene." *ZPE* 66 (1986), pp. 165–177.

Kuhrt, A. *The Ancient Near East c. 3000 330 BC*. Vols. 1 2. London, 1995.

Lane Fox, R. *Alexander the Great*. London, 1973.

———. "Text and Image: Alexander the Great, Coins and Elephants." *BICS* 41 (1996), pp. 87–108.

Lattimore, R. *The Iliad of Homer*. Chicago, 1951.

———. *The Odyssey of Homer*. New York, 1967.

Lawrence, T. *Seven Pillars of Wisdom*. Introduction by M. Asher. London, 2000.

Leo, Archipresbyter. *The History of Alexander's Battles: Historia de preliis, the J1 Version*. Translated with an introduction and notes by R. Pritchard. Toronto, 1992.

Lesher, J. *Xenophanes of Colophon: Fragments*. Toronto, 1992.

Levy, I. "Sérapis." *Revue de l'histoire des réligions* 67 (1913), pp. 308–317.

Lewis, D. *Sparta and Persia*. Leiden, 1977.

Lloyd, A. "Philip II and Alexander the Great: The Moulding of Macedon's Army." In *Battle in Antiquity*. Edited by A. Lloyd. London, 1996, pp. 169–198.

Lock, R. "The Macedonian Army Assembly in the Time of Alexander the Great." *CP* 72 (1977), pp. 91–107.

———. "The Origins of the Argyraspids." *Historia* 26 (1977), pp. 373–378.

Lunt, J. *Bokhara Burnes*. London, 1969.

Ma, J. *Antiochos III and the Cities of Western Asia Minor.* Oxford, 1999.

Machiavelli, N. *The Discourses.* Translated by L. Walker. London, 1978.

Manchester, W. *The Last Lion: Winston Spencer Churchill, Visions of Glory, 1874–1932.* New York, 1983.

————. *The Last Lion: Winston Spencer Churchill, Alone, 1932–1940.* Boston, 1988.

Manti, P. "The Macedonian Sarissa, Again." *AncW* 25, no. 1 (1994), pp. 77–91.

Markle, M. "The Macedonian Sarissa, Spear, and Related Armor." *AJA* 81 (1977), pp. 323–339.

————. "Use of the Macedonian Sarissa by Philip and Alexander of Macedon." *AJA* 82 (1978), pp. 483–497.

————. "Weapons from the Cemetery at Vergina and Alexander's Army." In Μέγας Ἀλέξανδρος: 2300 χρόνια ᾽ἀπὸ τὸν Θάνατον τοῦ. Thessaloniki, 1980, pp. 243–267.

————. "Macedonian Arms and Tactics Under Alexander the Great." In *Macedonia and Greece in Late Classical and Early Hellenistic Times.* Edited by W. Adams and E. Borza. Washington, D.C., 1982, pp. 87–111.

Marquart, J. "Untersuchungen zur Geschichte von Eran." *Philologus*, suppl. 10 (1908), pp. 1–258.

Marr, J. "Analysis: Alexander the Great May Have Been West Nile Victim." *Cedar Rapids Gazette*, December 13, 2003.

Marsden, E. *The Campaign of Gaugamela.* Liverpool, 1964.

————. *Greek and Roman Artillery.* Vol. 1. *Historical Development.* Vol. 2. *Technical Treatises.* Oxford, 1969–1971.

————. "Macedonian Military Machinery and Its Designers Under Philip and Alexander." *Ancient Macedonia.* Vol. 2. Thessaloniki, 1977, pp. 211–223.

Marshall, J. *Taxila.* Vols. 1–3. Cambridge, 1951.

Martin, T. "A Phantom Fragment of Theopompus and Philip II's First Campaign in Thessaly." *HSCP* 86 (1982), pp. 55–78.

————. *Sovereignty and Coinage in Classical Greece.* Princeton, 1985.

McCullough, D. *Truman.* New York, 1992.

McQueen, E. "Some Notes on the Anti-Macedonian Movement in the Peloponnese in 331 B.C." *Historia* 27 (1978), pp. 40–64.

Meinecke, A. *Stephanos Byzantinii ΕΘΝΙΚΩΝ (A Geographical Lexicon on Ancient Cities, Peoples, Tribes and Toponyms).* Chicago, 1992.

Mensching, E. "Peripatetiker über Alexander." *Historia* 12 (1963), pp. 274–282.

Merkelbach, R. *Die Quellen der griechischen Alexanderromans.* Munich, 1977.

Merlan, P. "Isocrates, Aristotle and Alexander the Great." *Historia* 3 (1954), pp. 60–81.

Metzger, H., E. Laroche, and A. Dupont-Sommer. "La stèle trilingue récemment découverte au Létôon de Xanthos." *CRAI* (1974), pp. 82–93, 115–125, 132–149.

Millar, F. *The Roman Near East, 31 B.C.–A.D. 337.* Cambridge, 1993.

Miller, M. "The 'Porus' Decadrachm and the Founding of Bucephala." *AncW* 25 (1994), pp. 109–120.

Milns, R. "Alexander's Macedonian Cavalry and Diodorus XVII. 17.4." *JHS* 86 (1966), pp. 167–168.

———. "Alexander's Seventh Phalanx Battalion." *GRBS* 7 (1966), pp. 159–166.

———. *Alexander the Great.* London, 1968.

———. "The Hypaspists of Alexander III: Some Problems." Historia 20 (1971), pp. 186–195.

———. "The Army of Alexander the Great." *EntrHardt* 22 (1976), pp. 87–136.

———. " 'ΑΣΘΙΠΠΟΙ' Again." *CQ* 31 (1981), pp. 347–354.

Mitchel, F. "Demades of Paeania and *IG* II2. 1413/4/5." *TAPA* 95 (1962), pp. 213–229.

———. "Athens in the Age of Alexander." *GaR* 12 (1965), pp. 189–201.

Morris, I., and B. Powell, eds. *A New Companion to Homer.* Leiden, 1997.

Morrisson, C. *La numismatique.* Paris, 1992.

Mossman, J., ed. *Plutarch and His Intellectual World.* London, 1997.

Mughal, M. "Excavations at Tulamba, West Pakistan." *Pakistan Archaeology* 4 (1967), pp. 1–152.

Murison, J. "Darius III and the Battle of Issus." *Historia* 21 (1972), pp. 399–423.

Nagy, G. *The Best of the Achaeans.* Baltimore, 1999, pp. 26–41.

Narain, A. "Alexander and India." *GaR* 12 (1965), pp. 155–165.

Nylander, C. "Darius III—the Coward King: Point and Counterpoint." In *Alexander the Great: Reality and Myth.* Edited by J. Carlsen et al. Rome, 1993, pp. 145–159.

O'Brien, J. *Alexander the Great: The Invisible Enemy.* London, 1992.

Oikonomides, A. "Decadrachm Aids in Identification of Alexander." *Coin World International,* Nov. 25, 1981, pp. 31–32.

———. "Scholarship, Research, and the Search for Alexander." *AncW* 4 (1981), pp. 67–89.

———. "The Real End of Alexander's Conquest of India." *AncW* 18 (1988), pp. 31–34.

Oldach, D., et al. "A Mysterious Death." *New England Journal of Medicine* 338 (1998), pp. 1764–1768.

Oldfather, C. *Diodorus Siculus*. Vol. 4. Cambridge, 1961.

Parke, H. *Greek Mercenary Soldiers*. Oxford, 1933.

―――. *The Oracles of Zeus*. Oxford, 1967.

―――. "The Massacre of the Branchidae." *JHS* 105 (1985), pp. 59–68.

Parsons, P. "The Burial of Philip II." *AJAH* 4 (1979), pp. 97–101.

Payne, M. "Alexander the Great: Myth, the Polis, and Afterward." In *Myth and the Polis*. Edited by D. Pozzi and J. Wickersham. Ithaca, 1991, pp. 164–181.

Pearson, L. "The Diary and the Letters of Alexander the Great." *Historia* 3 (1954–1955), pp. 429–439.

―――. *The Lost Histories of Alexander the Great*. New York, 1960.

Pédech, P. *Historiens compagnons d'Alexandre*. Paris, 1984.

Perrin, B. *Plutarch's Lives*. Vol. 7. Cambridge, 1958.

Picard, G., and C. "Hercule et Melqart." In *Hommages à J. Bayet*. Paris, 1964, pp. 569–578.

Pichikyan, I. "Rebirth of the Oxus Treasure: Second Part of the Oxus Treasure from the Miho Museum Collection." *Ancient Civilizations* 4 (1997), pp. 306–383.

Pomeroy, S., S. Burstein, W. Donlan, and J. Roberts. *Ancient Greece*. Oxford, 1999.

Potts, M., and R. Short. *Ever Since Adam and Eve: The Evolution of Human Sexuality*. Cambridge, 1999.

Prag, A., J. Musgrave, and R. Neave. "The skull from Tomb II at Vergina: King Philip II of Macedon." *JHS* 104 (1984), pp. 60–78.

Prandi, L. *Callistene: Uno storico tra Aristotele e i re Macedoni*. Milan, 1985.

Prestiannini Giallombardo, A. "Aspetti giuridici e problemi cronologici della reggenza di Filippo II di Macedonia." *Helikon* 13/14 (1973–1974), pp. 191–209.

Price, M. "The 'Porus' Coinage of Alexander the Great: A Symbol of Concord and Community." In *Studia Paulo Naster Oblata*. Vol. 1, *Numismatica Antiqua*. Edited by S. Scheers. Leuven, 1982, pp. 75–85.

―――. "Circulation at Babylon in 323 B.C." In *Mnemata: Papers in Memory of Nancy M. Waggoner*. Edited by W. Metcalf. New York, 1991, pp. 63–72.

―――. *The Coinage in the Name of Alexander the Great and Philip Arrhidaeus*. 2 vols. London, 1991.

Rahe, P. "The Annihilation of the Sacred Band at Chaeronea." *AJA* 85 (1981), pp. 84–87.

Renard, M., and J. Servais. "À propos du mariage d'Alexandre et de Roxane." *ACl* 24 (1955), pp. 29–50.

Rhodes, P. *A Commentary on the Aristotelian Athenaion Politeia*. Oxford, 1981.

Rice, E. "The Glorious Dead: Commemoration of the Fallen and Portrayal of Victory in the Late Classical and Hellenistic World." In *War and Society in the Greek World.* Edited by J. Rich and G. Shipley. London, 1993, pp. 224–257.

Rich, J., and G. Shipley, eds. *War and Society in the Greek World.* London, 1993.

Ridgway, B. *Hellenistic Sculpture.* Vol. 1. Madison, 1980.

Riginos, A. "The Wounding of Philip II of Macedon: Fact and Fabrication." *JHS* 114 (1994), pp. 103–119.

Ritter, H. *Diadem und Konigsherrschaft.* Munich, 1965.

Robert, J. "Une nouvelle inscription grecque de Sardes." *CRAI* (1975), pp. 306–330.

Robert, L. *Villes d'Asie Mineure.* Paris, 1962.

Robinson, C. *The History of Alexander the Great.* Vol. 1. Providence, 1953.

———. "The Extraordinary Ideas of Alexander the Great." *AHR* 62 (1957), pp. 326–344.

———. "The Two Worlds of Alexander." *Horizon* 1 (1959), pp. 28–59.

Robson, E. *Arrian.* Vol. 2. Cambridge, 1978.

Roisman, J. "Ptolemy and His Rivals in His History of Alexander the Great." *CQ* 34 (1984), pp. 373–385.

Rolfe, J. *Quintus Curtius with an English Translation.* Vols. 1–2. Cambridge, 1946.

Romane, P. "Alexander's Siege of Tyre." *AncW* 16 (1987), pp. 79–90.

———. "Alexander's Siege of Gaza." *AncW* 18 (1988), pp. 21–30.

Romm, J. "Aristotle's Elephant and the Myth of Alexander's Scientific Patronage." *AJP* 110 (1989), pp. 566–575.

Rosen, K. "Der 'gottliche' Alexander, Athen und Samos." *Historia* 27 (1978), pp. 20–39.

Roueché, C. *Performers and Partisans at Aphrodisias in the Roman and Late Roman Periods.* London, 1993.

Roueché, C., and S. Sherwin-White. "Some aspects of the Seleucid Empire: The Greek Inscriptions from Falaika, in the Arabian Gulf." *Chiron* 15 (1985), pp. 1–39.

Rubin, B. "Die Entstehung der Kataphraktenreiterei im Lichte der chorezmischen Ausgrabungen." *Historia* 4 (1955), pp. 264–283.

Rumpf, A. "Zum Alexander Mosaik." *MdI(A)* 77 (1962), pp. 229–241.

Rutz, W. "Zur Erzahlungskunst des Q. Curtius Rufus." *Hermes* 93 (1965), pp. 370–382.

Sacks, K. *Diodorus and the First Century.* Princeton, 1990.

Samuel, A. *Ptolemaic Chronology.* Munich, 1962.

————. "Alexander's Royal Journals." *Historia* 14 (1965), pp. 1–12.

Schachermeyr, F. "Die letzte Pläne Alexanders." *ÖJh* 41 (1954), pp. 118–140.

————. "Alexander und die Ganges-Länder." *Innsbrucker Beiträge zur Kulturgeschichte* 3 (1955), pp. 123–135.

————. *Alexander in Babylon und die Reichsordnung nach seinem Tode.* Vienna, 1970.

————. *Alexander der Grosse: das Problem seiner Persönlichkeit und seines Wirkens.* Vienna, 1973.

Schefold, K. *Der Alexander-Sarkophag.* Berlin, 1968.

Schmidt, E. *Persepolis.* Vols. 1–3. Chicago, 1953–1970.

Schmidt, L. "Der gordische Knoten und seine Lösung." *Antaios* 1 (1959), pp. 305–318.

Schmitthenner, W. "Über eine Formveränderung der Monarchie seit Alexander d. Grossen." *Saeculum* 19 (1968), pp. 31–46.

Schreider, H., and F. Schreider. "In the Footsteps of Alexander the Great." *National Geographic* 133 (January 1968), pp. 1–65.

Schwarzenberg, E. von. "Der Lysippische Alexander." *BJ* 167 (1967), pp. 58–118.

————. "The portraiture of Alexander." *EntrHardt* 22 (1976), pp. 223–278.

Scott-Kilvert, I. *The Age of Alexander.* London, 1973.

Sealey, R. "The Olympic Festival of 324 B.C." *CR* 10 (1960), pp. 185–186.

Seibert, J. *Alexander der Grosse.* Darmstadt, 1972.

————. *Die Erobenung des Perserreiches durch Alexander dem Grossen auf kartographischer Grundlage.* Wiesbaden, 1985.

Sélincourt, A. de. *Arrian: The Campaigns of Alexander.* London, 1971.

Sengupta, S., and L. Rohter. "The Changing Church." *The International Herald Tribune,* October 15, 2003, pp. 1, 4.

Shapiro, H. "Heros Theos: The Death and Apotheosis of Heracles." *CW* 77 (1983–1984), pp. 7–18.

Sherman, C. *Diodorus Siculus.* Vol. 7. Cambridge, 1963.

Sherwin-White, S. "Ancient Archives: The Alexander Edict." *JHS* 105 (1985), pp. 69–89.

Smith, F. *L'immagine di Alessandro il Grande sulle monete del regno (336–323 a.C.).* Milan, 2000.

Smith, M. *The Aztecs.* Oxford, 1996.

Solomon, M. *Mozart: A Life.* New York, 1995.

Stadter, P. *Arrian of Nicomedia.* Chapel Hill, 1980.

Standish, J. "The Caspian Gates." *GaR* 17 (1970), pp. 17–24.

Stein, A. *On Alexander's Track to the Indus.* London, 1929.

———. *An Archaeological Tour in Gedrosia.* Calcutta, 1931.

———. "The Site of Alexander's Passage of the Hydaspes and the Battle with Poros." *Geographical Journal* 80 (1932), pp. 31–46.

———. *Archaeological Reconnaissances in North-West India and South-East Iran.* London, 1937.

———. *Old Routes of Western Iran.* London, 1940.

———. "Notes on Alexander's Crossing of the Tigris and the Battle of Arbela." *Geographical Journal* 100 (1942), pp. 155–164.

———. "On Alexander's Route into Gedrosia: An Archaeological Tour in Las Bela." *Geographical Journal* 102 (1943), pp. 193–227.

Stewart, A. *Faces of Power: Alexander's Image and Hellenistic Politics.* Berkeley, 1993.

Stewart, S. *In the Empire of Ghengis Khan.* Guilford, 2002.

Stoneman, R. *The Greek Alexander Romance.* London, 1991.

———. *Legends of Alexander the Great.* London, 1994.

———. "Naked Philosophers. The Brahmans in the Alexander Historians and the Alexander Romance." *JHS* 105 (1995), pp. 99–114.

Straten, F. von. "Did the Greeks Kneel Before Their Gods?" *BABesch* 40 (1974), pp. 159–189.

Stronach, D. *Pasargadae.* Oxford, 1978.

Taeger, F. *Charisma. Studien zur Geschichte des antiken Herrscherkultes.* Vol. 1. Stuttgart, 1957.

Tarn, W. "Alexander the Great and the Unity of Mankind." *ProcBritAc* 19 (1933), pp. 123–166.

———. *Alexander the Great.* 2 vols. Cambridge, 1948.

Thayer, A. *Life of Beethoven.* Rev. ed. Edited by E. Forbes. London, 2001.

Thompson, M. "Paying the Mercenaries." In *Festschrift für Leo Mildenberg: Numismatik, Kunstgeschichte, Archäologie.* Edited by A. Houghton. Wetteren, 1984, pp. 241–247.

Tibiletti, G. "Alessandro e la liberazione delle città d'Asia Minore." *Athenaeum* 32 (1954), pp. 3–22.

Tronson, A. "Satyrus the Peripatetic and the Marriages of Philip II." *JHS* 104 (1984), pp. 116–126.

Troxell, H. *Studies in the Macedonian Coinage of Alexander the Great.* New York, 1997.

Unz, R. "Alexander's Brothers?" *JHS* 105 (1985), pp. 171–174.

Van de Mieroop, M. *A History of the Ancient Near East ca. 3000–323 BC.* Oxford, 2004.

Walbank, F. *The Hellenistic World*. Cambridge, 1993.

Wees, H. van. "Introduction: Homer and Early Greece." In *Homer: Critical Assessments*. Vol. 2. London, 1999, pp. 1–32.

Welles, C. *Royal Correspondence in the Hellenistic Period*. London, 1930.

———. "The Discovery of Sarapis and the Foundation of Alexandria." *Historia* II (1962), pp. 271–298.

———. *Diodorus of Sicily*. Vol. 8. Cambridge, 1963.

———. "The Reliability of Ptolemy as an Historian." *Miscellanea di studi alessandri in memoria di A. Rostagni*. Turin, 1963, pp. 101–116.

Welwei, K. "Der Kampf um das makedonische Lager bei Gaugamela." *RhM* 122 (1979), pp. 222–228.

Wheeler, M. *Charsadda: A Metropolis of the North-west Frontier*. Oxford, 1962.

———. *Flames over Persepolis*. New York, 1968.

Whitehead, R. "The Eastern Satrap Sophytes." *NC* 6th ser., vol. 3 (1943), pp. 60–72.

Wilcken, U. *Alexander the Great*. New York, 1967.

Wills, G. *Inventing America: Jefferson's Declaration of Independence*. New York, 1978.

———. *Lincoln at Gettysburg*. New York, 1992.

Wilson, N. *Aelian, Historical Miscellany*. Cambridge, 1997.

Wirth, G. "Dareios und Alexander." *Chiron* 1 (1971), pp. 133–152.

———. "Die σύνταξις" von Kleinasien 334 v. Chr." *Chiron* 2 (1972), pp. 91–98.

———. "Alexander und Rom." In *Alexandre le Grand: Image et réalité*. Edited by E. Badian. Geneva, 1976, pp. 181–221.

———. "Erwägungen zur Chronologie des Jahres 333 v. Chr." *Helikon* 17 (1977), pp. 23–55.

———. "Zwei Lager bei Gaugamela." *Quaderni Catanesi di Studi Classici e Medievali* 2 (1980), pp. 51–100; 3 (1981), pp. 5–61.

———. *Studien zur Alexandergeschichte*. Darmstadt, 1985.

———. "Zu einer Schweigenden Mehrheit. Alexander und die griechischen Söldner." In *Aus dem Osten des Alexanderreiches*. Edited by J. Ozols and V. Thewalt. Köln, 1985, pp. 9–31.

Wolohojian, A., ed. *The Romance of Alexander the Great by Pseudo-Callisthenes*. New York, 1969.

Wood, M. *In the Footsteps of Alexander the Great*. Berkeley, 1997.

Woodward, A. "Athens and the Oracle of Ammon." *Annual of the British School in Athens* 57 (1962), pp. 5–13.

Worthington, I. "The First Flight of Harpalus Reconsidered." *GaR* 31 (1984), pp. 161–169.

———. "The Harpalus Affair and the Greek Response to the Macedonian Hegemony." In *Ventures into Greek History: Essays in Honour of N.G.L. Hammond.* Edited by I. Worthington. Oxford, 1994, pp. 307–330.

———. "Alexander and 'the Interests of Historical Accuracy': A Reply." *Ancient History Bulletin* 13, no. 4 (1999), pp. 136–140.

———. "How 'Great' Was Alexander?" *Ancient History Bulletin* 13, no. 2 (1999), pp. 39–55.

Wüst, F. "Die Rede Alexanders des Grossen in Opis." *Historia* 2 (1953–1954a), pp. 177–188.

———. "Die Meuterei von Opis." *Historia* 2 (1953–1954b), pp. 418–431.

———. "Zu den Hypomnematen Alexanders: das Grabmal Hephaistions." *ÖJh* 44 (1959), pp. 147–157.

Yardley, J. *Quintus Curtius Rufus: The History of Alexander.* London, 1984.

———. *Justin: Epitome of the Philippic History of Pompeius Trogus.* Vol. 1, books 11–12, *Alexander the Great.* Oxford, 1997.

Permission Acknowledgments

Grateful acknowledgment is made to the following for permission to reprint previously published material:

LOEB CLASSICAL LIBRARY®, HARVARD UNIVERSITY PRESS: Excerpts from *Arrian: Volume I*, Loeb Classical Library Volume 236, translated by P. A. Brunt, Cambridge, Mass.: Harvard University Press, 1976, copyright © 1976 by The President and Fellows of Harvard College; excerpts from *Arrian: Volume II*, Loeb Classical Library Volume 269, translated by E. Iliff Robson, B. D., Cambridge, Mass.: Harvard University Press, 1933; excerpts from *Diodorus of Sicily, Volume VIII*, Loeb Classical Library Volume 422, translated by C. Bradford Welles, Cambridge, Mass.: Harvard University Press, 1963, copyright © 1963 by The President and Fellows of Harvard College; excerpts from *Plutarch's Lives, Volume VII*, Loeb Classical Library Volume 99, translated by Bernadotte Perrin, Cambridge, Mass.: Harvard University Press, 1919. The Loeb Classical Library® is a registered trademark of The President and Fellows of Harvard College. Reprinted by the publishers and the Trustees of the Loeb Classical Library.

PENGUIN GROUP (UK): Excerpts from *The Age of Alexander: Nine Greek Lives* by Plutarch, translated and annotated by Ian Scott-Kilvert (Penguin Classics, 1973), copyright © 1973 by Ian Scott-Kilvert; excerpts from *The Campaigns of Alexander* by Arrian, translated by Aubrey de Sélincourt, revised with an Introduction and Notes by J. R. Hamilton (Penguin Classics, 1958, revised edition 1971), copyright © 1958 by the Estate of Aubrey de Sélincourt; excerpts from *The History of Alexander* by Quintus Curtius Rufus, translated by John Yardley (Penguin Classics, 1984), copyright © 1984 by John Yardley. Reprinted by permission of Penguin Group (UK).

Index

About the Author

GUY MACLEAN ROGERS holds a Ph.D. in classics from Princeton University. He has received grants and fellowships from, among other institutions, the National Endowment for the Humanities, the American Philosophical Society, and All Souls College Oxford. His first book, *The Sacred Identity of Ephesos: Foundation Myths of a Roman City*, won the Routledge Ancient History Prize. Chairman of the Department of History of Wellesley College from 1997 to 2001, he grew up and still lives in Litchfield County, Connecticut.

About the Type

The text of this book was set in Janson, a misnamed typeface designed in about 1690 by Nicholas Kis, a Hungarian in Amsterdam. In 1919 the matrices became the property of the Stempel Foundry in Frankfurt. It is an old-style book face of excellent clarity and sharpness. Janson serifs are concave and splayed; the contrast between thick and thin strokes is marked.